# Missouri Genealogical Gleanings

## 1840 and Beyond
## Volume 1

Sherida K. Eddlemon

HERITAGE BOOKS
2007

# HERITAGE BOOKS
## AN IMPRINT OF HERITAGE BOOKS, INC.

**Books, CDs, and more—Worldwide**

For our listing of thousands of titles see our website at
www.HeritageBooks.com

Published 2007 by
HERITAGE BOOKS, INC.
Publishing Division
65 East Main Street
Westminster, Maryland 21157-5026

Copyright © 1994 Sherida K. Eddlemon

All rights reserved. No part of this book may be reproduced or transmitted in any form or by any means, electronic or mechanical, including photocopying, recording or by any information storage and retrieval system without written permission from the author, except for the inclusion of brief quotations in a review.

International Standard Book Number: 978-0-7884-0001-8

## DEDICATION

William H. Chatham, delinquent tax list, 1840, Jackson County, Missouri, page 85, where are your descendants and who was your father? Are you related to the Crabtree family?

## ACKNOWLEDGEMENTS

I want to thank my parents, Nelson and Amelia Eddlemon, for their continued support and encouragement; the staff of the Missouri States Archives; and Susan Gore, director, Historical Foundation of the Cumberland Presbyterian Church.

# PREFACE

Missouri was a gateway to the west. Both the Santa Fe trail to the southwest and the Oregon trail to the northwest began at Independence, Missouri. Settlers and new immigrants from Germany, Switzerland, Ireland, England, Poland, Bohemia and Italy flooded into Missouri when statehood was granted in 1821.

Kansas was part of the Missouri territory until 1821, but it was not until 1854 that the territory of Kansas was created luring new immigrants and settlers from Illinois, Ohio, Indiana and Missouri. So many Missourians relocated to Kansas that in 1855 Kansas was voted into the Union as a slave state.

Missouri was plagued with outlaws and raiders that had their beginning even before the Civil War. The 1857 Dred Scott Decision helped to inflame the anti-slavery feelings in Missouri. During the the Civil War, raiders such as Wm. Clarke Quantrill, Frank and Jesse James and the Cole Younger gangs terrorized Missouri. In the eyes of some these outlaws were heroes, but the law prevailed in the end.

Each new Gold Rush lured more people to Missouri on their way to make their fortune. There was a California Gold Rush in 1848; the Colorado Gold Rush in 1858 and the Klondike Gold Rush in the Yukon in 1896 - 1897. Many lost sons went to look for gold as well as whole families with only a child born in Missouri to show their passing through the state.

St. Joseph, Missouri was the starting point for the Pony Express. It promised delivery of the mail to Sacramento, California in 8 to 10 days. Although it was only in operation for eighteen months, these riders gained a glamorous spot in Missouri history.

Although there are extant census records for Missouri starting in 1830 many travelers and permanent settlers were missed in the census or only lived in the state between the census years. The purpose of this collection is to help the researcher pinpoint his ancestor between the census years.

All names appear as written on the records including the abbreviations of given names. No attempt has been made to make corrections in spelling. Cemetery listings and mortality schedules only include persons born in 1840 or later.

In some instances it was necessary to use abbreviations. They are as follows:

m - Month  
d - Day/Died  
OC - Original Claimant  
b - Born  

y - Year  
RD - Recorded date  
CLK - Clerk  
Twp - Township

P - Page            MD - Marriage Date
MG - Minister/Preacher

There was a Capitol fire in 1911 which destroyed many of the records of the State Auditor's office. The documents which survived the fire were microfilmed and are simply known as the "Capitol Fire Documents." The collection is available at the Missouri Archives. In some cases the records preserved here are not available on the county level. A general finding aid has been developed, but an indepth index has not been done.

The records for the Cumberland Presbyterian Church are held at the Historical Foundation of the Cumberland Presbyterian Church in Memphis, Tennessee. This organization does not do any genealogical research of any kind. The records are filed by the name of the church and are shown by appointment only. The Foundation is primarily concerned with preserving church history for church historians. An independent researcher would have to be hired to search these records.

Good luck to finding your ancestors within these pages.

# DATES TO REMEMBER

| | |
|---|---|
| 1821 | Missouri became the 24th state. |
| 1835 | Samuel K. Clemens or Mark Twain was born. |
| 1837 | Missouri gained six northwestern counties with the Platte Purchase. |
| 1846 | Mexican War |
| 1848 | California Gold Rush |
| 1854 | Kansas Territory was created. |
| 1855 | So many Missourians moved to Kansas that it was voted in as a slave state. |
| 1857 | Dred Scott Decision |
| 1858 | Colorado Gold Rush |
| 1858 | Butterfield Stage Line ran from St. Louis, Missouri to San Franciso, California |
| 1860 - 1861 | Pony Express mailrun from St. Joseph, Missouri to Sacremento, California. |
| 1861 - 1865 | Civil War |
| 1865 | New Missouri constitution was created with a "Test Oath" clause denying southern sympathizers the right the to vote. |
| 1865 | Wm. C. Quantrill, guerrilla raider, was killed. |
| 1870 | Great Mississippi steamboat race between the "Robert E. Lee" and the "Natchez" from St. Louis to New Orleans. |
| 1870 - 1872 | Missouri-Kansas-Texas railroad in operation. |
| 1875 | Sixty-eight men were elected to draft a new Missouri constitution. |
| 1882 | Jesse James was killed. |
| 1889 | Oklahoma Land Rush |
| 1893 | Oklahoma Land Rush |
| 1896 - 1897 | Gold Rush to the Klondike District of the Yukon |

# TABLE OF CONTENTS

### ANDREW COUNTY
(Founded 1841 from the Platte Purchase)

Rochester Cumberland Presbyterian Church Records . . .   194

### ATCHISON COUNTY
(Founded 1843 from Holt County)

County Home Cemetery . . . . . . . . . . . . . . . . .   96

### AUDRAIN COUNTY
(Founded 1843 from Monroe County)

1843 Tax List . . . . . . . . . . . . . . . . . . . .   43

### BENTON COUNTY
(Founded 1835 from Pettis and St. Clair Counties)

1863 Delinquent Tax List . . . . . . . . . . . . . .   123

### BUCHANAN COUNTY
(Founded 1838 from the Platte Purchase)

1840 Tax List . . . . . . . . . . . . . . . . . . . .   90

### CALLAWAY COUNTY
(Founded 1820 from Montgomery County)

1840 Poll List . . . . . . . . . . . . . . . . . . .   97
1843 Delinquent Tax List . . . . . . . . . . . . . .  187

### CARROLL COUNTY
(Founded 1833 from Ray County)

Grand Inquest, March, 1842 . . . . . . . . . . . . .  146

## CASS COUNTY
(Founded 1835 from Jackson County)

1848 Tax List . . . . . . . . . . . . . . . . . . . . 75

## CEDAR COUNTY
(Founded 1845 from Dade and St. Clair Counties)

Death Register, 1883 - 1886 . . . . . . . . . . . . 41

## CHARITON COUNTY
(Founded 1820 from Howard County)

Delinquent State and Advalorum Tax, October, 1842 . . 186

## CLARK COUNTY
(Founded 1836 from Lewis County)

Will of John M. Reed, Mason County, Kentucky . . . . . 116

## GRUNDY COUNTY
(Founded 1841 from Livingston)

Hatton Chapel Cemetery . . . . . . . . . . . . . . . 89

## HENRY COUNTY
(Founded 1834 Lafayette County)

Durnell Chapel Cemetery . . . . . . . . . . . . . . 66
Drake Chapel Cemetery . . . . . . . . . . . . . . . 95
Huntingdale Cemetery . . . . . . . . . . . . . . . . 122

## HICKORY COUNTY
(Founded 1845 from Benton and Polk Counties)

Nemo-Bethel Missionary Church Cemetery . . . . . . . 105

## JACKSON COUNTY
(Founded 1826 from Lafayette County)

Delinquent Tax List, 1840 . . . . . . . . . . . . . 85
Westport School Tax, 1869 . . . . . . . . . . . . . 108
Licenses, February, 1844 . . . . . . . . . . . . . 187

### JEFFERSON COUNTY
(Founded 1818 from Ste. Genevieve and St. Louis Counties)

Original Land Entries, 1840 - 1860 . . . . . . . . . . . 1
Runaway Slave Notice, December, 1844 . . . . . . . . . 189

### JOHNSON COUNTY
(Founded 1834 from Lafayette County)

Shawnee Mound Cumberland Presbyterian Church Records    117
Delinquent Tax List, 1843 . . . . . . . . . . . . . . 187
Aggregate Statement, 1843 . . . . . . . . . . . . . . 191

### LAFAYETTE COUNTY
(Founded 1820 from Cooper County)

Delinquent Tax List, 1844 . . . . . . . . . . . . . . 191

### LAWRENCE COUNTY
(Founded 1845 from Barry and Dade Counties)

Liberty Methodist Church Cemetery . . . . . . . . . . 38

### LEWIS COUNTY
(Founded 1833 from Marion County)

Index to Circuit Court Records, Vol. 2, 1841 - 1851 . 146
Delinquent Tax List, 1842 . . . . . . . . . . . . . . 191

### LINCOLN COUNTY
(Founded 1818 from St. Charles)

Poll Book, 1844 . . . . . . . . . . . . . . . . . . . 60
Delinquent Tax List, 1843 . . . . . . . . . . . . . . 183

### LINN COUNTY
(Founded 1837 from Chariton County)

Aggregate Tax Statement, 1842 . . . . . . . . . . . . 191

### MARIES COUNTY
(Founded 1855 from Osage and Pulaski Counties)

1880 Mortality Schedule . . . . . . . . . . . . . . . 110

### MONROE COUNTY
(Founded 1831 from Ralls County)

Poll Book, November, 1844 . . . . . . . . . . . . . . 68

### MONTGOMERY COUNTY
(Founded 1818 from St. Charles County)

Delinquent Tax List, 1840 . . . . . . . . . . . . . . 86

### PERRY COUNTY
(Founded 1820 from Ste. Genevieve County)

Licenses, February, 1840 . . . . . . . . . . . . . . . 75

### RALLS COUNTY
(Founded 1820 from Pike County)

Estate Settlements, 1840 - 1843 . . . . . . . . . . . 21

### RANDOLPH COUNTY
(Founded 1829 from Chariton County)

Warranty Deeds, January, 1896 - June, 1896 . . . . . . 140

### ST. CLAIR COUNTY
(Founded 1841 from Rives County, later named Henry County)

Grand Jury, May, 1856 . . . . . . . . . . . . . . . . 110
Aggregate Tax Statement, 1843 . . . . . . . . . . . . 194

### STE. GENEVIEVE COUNTY
(Founded 1812, Original District)

Aggregate Tax Statement, 1845 . . . . . . . . . . . . 191

## SALINE COUNTY
(Founded 1820 from Cooper and Howard Counties)

Licenses, September, 1845 . . . . . . . . . . . . . . .  190

## ST. LOUIS COUNTY
(Founded 1812, Original District)

Delinquent Tax List, 1840 . . . . . . . . . . . . . . .  86
Criminal Court, Bill of Costs, March, 1860 . . . . . .  146
Rejected House Bill, No. 19, Relief of Nathl. Childs . 194

## VERNON COUNTY
(Founded 1851 Bates County)

Qualified Voters List, 1866 . . . . . . . . . . . . . .  95

## WARREN COUNTY
(Founded 1833 from Montgomery County)

Poll Book, Hickory Grove Township, 1840 . . . . . . . .  58
Poll Book, Pinckney Township, 1840 . . . . . . . . . .  59

## MISSOURI MISCELLANEOUS

Mono County, California, Great Register . . . . . . . .  126
"History of Santa Clara County, California" . . . . .  127
Passenger Ship "Wieland", April 28, 1853 . . . . . . .  127
Passenger Ship "Hereme", September 27, 1852 . . . . .  128
Index of Election Returns, 1842 . . . . . . . . . . .  128
Correspondence to Michael K. McGrath, Sec. of State .  146
Land Patent Certification by Sam. B. Cook . . . . . .  146

Jefferson County, Missouri, Original Land Entries,(Note: Only Those Entries With Dates Of 1840 and After Are Included. Earlier Entries And Those With No Dates Are Listed In Volume Five of "Missouri Genealogical Records and Abstracts.")

| Name | Date | Residence |
|---|---|---|
| John Long | Oct. 22, 1851 | Cert. No. 102 |
| Elisha W. Rogers | Sep. 11, 1851 | Jefferson Co. |
| Samuel S. Gunn | Feb. 2, 1847 | St. Louis Co. |
| Daniel Eastwood | Aug. 28, 1840 | Jefferson Co. |
| Edmund H. McCabe | Dec. 2, 1844 | St. Louis Co. |
| John Lewis | Sep. 19, 1844 | Jefferson Co. |
| Edward Klein | Sep. 22, 1845 | St. Louis Co. |
| George Cragg | Aug. 15, 1844 | Jefferson Co. |
| Benjamin J. Vancourt | Aug. 1, 1844 | St. Louis Co. |
| Thomas F. Rick and James D. Houseman | Aug. 2, 1847 | St. Louis Co. |
| George W. Dent | Sep. 14, 1844 | St. Louis Co. |
| Henry G. Thewing | Aug. 2, 1847 | St. Louis Co. |
| Jesse Craig | Aug. 23, 1845 | Jefferson Co. |
| John Duncan | Jan. 20, 1846 | Jefferson Co. |
| Edward Waters | Jul. 2, 1851 | Franklin Co. |
| John Long | Oct. 29, 1846 | Cert. No. 105 |
| William A. Murphy | Jan. 8, 1852 | Jefferson Co. |
| George W. Davis | Apt. 10, 1845 | Franklin Co. |
| Henry W. Daniel | Oct. 6, 1851 | Franklin Co. |
| Edmund F. Frost | May 20, 1845 | Jefferson Co. |
| Robert Wilson | Apr. 13, 1850 | Jefferson Co. |
| Edmund Frost | Dec. 2, 1851 | Jefferson Co. |
| John Whitworth | Mar. 14, 1852 | War. No. 26716 |
| Francis K. Boyd | Apr. 12, 1852 | Franklin Co. |
| Abner Coble | Nov. 23, 1844 | Jefferson Co. |
| John G. Murphy | May 26, 1852 | Jefferson Co. |
| David A. Murphy | May 26, 1852 | Jefferson Co. |
| William A. Murphy | May 26, 1852 | Jefferson Co. |
| Sarah A. Murphy | May 26, 1852 | Jefferson Co. |
| Rebecca J. Murphy | May 26, 1852 | Jefferson Co. |
| Jonathan W. Murphy | May 26, 1852 | Jefferson Co. |
| Mary E. Murphy | May 26, 1852 | Jefferson Co. |
| Charlotte M. Murphy | May 26, 1852 | Jefferson Co. |
| Jacob L. Murphy | May 26, 1852 | Jefferson Co. |
| Elemuel Boyd | Dec. 27, 1851 | Franklin Co. |
| Etienne St. Pierre | Sep. 15, 1849 | Cert. No. 146 |
| James Mackay | Nov. 1, 1848 | Cert. No. 108 |
| George Frost | Dec. 19, 1851 | Jefferson Co. |
| James Wilhite | Jan. 8, 1852 | Jefferson Co. |
| Edmond F. Frost | Apr. 21, 1852 | Jefferson Co. |
| John F. Darby and Wm. W. Gett | Mar. 2, 1844 | St. Louis Co. |
| Levi Theel | Mar. 21, 1848 | Cert. No. 41 |

| Name | Date | Residence |
|---|---|---|
| John Long | Jun. 19, 1851 | Cert. No. 102 |
| Jeremiah Dugan | Sep. 22, 1851 | Jefferson Co. |
| Patrick Coyle | Apr. 14, 1841 | St. Louis Co. |
| Owen Casey | Mar. 23, 1843 | Jefferson Co. |
| Nathaniel H. Parker | Mar. 11, 1846 | Jefferson Co. |
| Lenerious B. Boatwright | Aug. 25, 1846 | Franklin Co. |
| James Cummiskey | Sep. 18, 1843 | Jefferson Co. |
| Oliver Pepper | Dec. 18, 1843 | Jefferson Co. |
| John W. Tooley | May 21, 1848 | Jefferson Co. |
| Isaiah S. Seal | Feb. 1, 1860 | --- |
| Martin Cagney | Feb. 1, 1860 | --- |
| Madison W. Daniel | Nov. 15, 1860 | Jefferson Co. |
| Priscilla Estep | Dec. 1, 1843 | --- |
| Richard Caulk | Sep. 30, 1847 | Cert. No. 35 |
| Isaac S. Clark | Jan. 22, 1844 | St. Louis Co. |
| James Higgins | Feb. 27, 1844 | Jefferson Co. |
| Michael Kelly | Sep. 14, 1844 | St. Louis Co. |
| Michael Kelly, jr. | Apr. 9, 1845 | St. Charles Co. |
| Isaac S. Clark | Jan. 22, 1844 | St. Louis Co. |
| Peggy Carter | Nov. 5, 1844 | --- |
| Forest Shepherd | Apr. 9, 1845 | New Haven, Ct. |
| Auguste P. Chouteau | Mar. 28, 1850 | Cert. No. 31 |
| Wm. P. Donnavan | Feb. 1, 1860 | --- |
| Allen Farrell | Jun. 21, 1841 | Jefferson Co. |
| James Hunt | Nov. 10, 1843 | Jefferson Co. |
| Louis Bolduc | Oct. 14, 1844 | Jefferson Co. |
| Mason Frizzell | Oct. 2, 1841 | Washington Co. |
| Elijah Manes, jr. | Apr. 9, 1845 | Jefferson Co. |
| Arnold C. Anton | Feb. 1, 1860 | --- |
| William Borge | Feb. 1, 1860 | --- |
| Robert Parker | Feb. 1, 1860 | --- |
| Calvin Johnson | Feb. 1, 1860 | --- |
| George W. Higginbotham | Sep. 2, 1844 | Washington Co. |
| John J. Anderson | Apr. 9, 1845 | --- |
| Edward Snider | Apr. 9, 1845 | --- |
| Elijah D. Turner | Apr. 9, 1845 | --- |
| Peter L. S. Virden | Apr. 9, 1845 | St. Louis Co, |
| Calvin Baker | Nov. 11, 1840 | St. Louis Co. |
| Julius Higgins | Aug. 24, 1843 | Jefferson Co. |
| Samuel C. White | Aug. 30, 1843 | Washington Co. |
| Louis Bolduc | Aug. 31, 1843 | Jefferson Co. |
| Thomas E. Mothershead | Jul. 30, 1853 | Jefferson Co. |
| John A. Alderson | Jul. 6, 1853 | Jefferson Co. |
| Francis M. Wilet | Jun. 30, 1848 | Jefferson Co. |
| Michael Rinhe | Feb. 1, 1860 | Jefferson Co. |
| Daniel Hipshear | Feb. 1, 1860 | --- |
| Samuel Block | Feb. 1, 1860 | |
| Elijah Thomas | Jun. 13, 1848 | Jefferson Co. |

| Name | Date | Residence |
|---|---|---|
| Orson Jamison | Feb. 1, 1860 | --- |
| Mary Kincaid | Sep. 27, 1848 | Jefferson Co. |
| Benjamin Talbott | Mar. 5, 1851 | Washington Co. |
| Starret P. McKeen, sr. | Apr. 21, 1852 | Jefferson Co. |
| Hiram H. McKeen | Apr. 21, 1852 | Jefferson Co. |
| Wilson Jones | Feb. 1, 1860 | --- |
| Silas Bolen | Feb. 1, 1860 | --- |
| Elijah McCreary | Jan. 3, 1848 | Jefferson Co. |
| George Waters | Jan. 22, 1844 | Jefferson Co. |
| Forest Shepherd | Apr. 9, 1845 | New Haven, Ct. |
| Joseph Couch | Jun. 9, 1845 | Jefferson Co. |
| Michael McAnulty and Bernard McAnulty | Apr. 10, 1845 | St. Louis Co. |
| Forrest Sheppard | Apr. 28, 1845 | New Haven, Ct |
| Charles W. Day | Apr. 28, 1845 | Suffolk, Ma. |
| Richard B. Lee | Jan. 21, 1841 | St. Louis Co. |
| John S. Mathews | Jun. 25, 1841 | Jefferson Co. |
| John A. Dougherty | Apr. 18, 1844 | St. Louis Co. |
| George Burnet | Oct. 22, 1844 | St. Louis Co. |
| Henry W. Newbrry | Nov. 26, 1844 | Jefferson Co. |
| William K. Burnet | Dec. 2, 1844 | St. Louis Co. |
| George B. Green | Nov. 20, 1845 | Jefferson Co. |
| Alden Harlow | Dec. 18, 1840 | Monroe Co., Il |
| Phildelio Williams | Apr. 8, 1844 | Jefferson Co. |
| James Baker | Jun. 14, 1844 | Jefferson Co. |
| Joseph Atkinson | Jul. 17, 1845 | Jefferson Co. |
| Jacob Lanius | May 16, 1844 | Washington Co. |
| Joseph W. Smith | May 21, 1844 | St. Louis Co. |
| James Baker | Aug. 2, 1845 | Jefferson Co. |
| John F. Darby | Aug. 2, 1845 | St. Louis Co. |
| Justis Gamble | Mar. 25, 1848 | Bty. War. #805 |
| Charles Wall | Jan. 26, 1842 | Jefferson Co. |
| Frances Johnson | Feb. 4, 1842 | Jefferson Co. |
| Justus Gamble | Aug. 9, 1847 | Jefferson Co. |
| Isaac B. Willey | Mar. 5, 1840 | Jefferson Co. |
| Robert Davis | Jun. 9, 1840 | Jefferson Co. |
| Thomas Wall | Jan. 6, 1842 | Jefferson Co. |
| Charles Wall | Jan. 26, 1842 | Jefferson Co. |
| Ruebin Pounds | Sep. 3, 1845 | Jefferson Co. |
| Felix A. Williams | Jun. 20, 1844 | Jefferson Co. |
| Aben H. Glasby | Feb. 27, 1850 | Jefferson Co. |
| Willard Frisell | Sep. 29, 1850 | War. No. 69497 |
| William Frisell | Mar. 28, 1850 | Jefferson Co. |
| Thompson Graham | Dec. 19, 1842 | Jefferson Co. |
| James Rogers | Apr. 8, 1844 | Jefferson Co. |
| William Gibson | Nov. 12, 1845 | Jefferson Co. |
| Elisha Maness, jr. | Nov. 15, 1845 | Jefferson Co. |
| Willard Frissell | Aug. 3, 1844 | Jefferson Co. |

| Name | Date | Residence |
|---|---|---|
| Harrison Hynson | Sep. 23, 1844 | Washington Co. |
| William K. Burnet | Nov. 28, 1844 | St. Louis Co. |
| Elijah Maness, jr. | Nov. 19, 1844 | Jefferson Co. |
| Sanders Burgess | Dec. 3, 1844 | Jefferson Co. |
| Louis C. Stootee | Dec. 3, 1844 | Jefferson Co. |
| James Hunt | Nov. 10, 1843 | Jefferson Co. |
| Johann Williams | Nov. 23, 1843 | Jefferson Co. |
| James W. Colloch and Nerre Valle | Dec. 7, 1843 | Jefferson Co. |
| Newton Mathews | Dec. 4, 1851 | Washington Co. |
| Samuel Herrington | Oct. 3, 1851 | Jefferson Co. |
| James S. Wideman | Apr. 10, 1845 | Jefferson Co. |
| John Mayfield | Apr. 28, 1845 | Jefferson Co. |
| Solomon B. Wheeler | Nov. 21, 1845 | Jefferson Co. |
| John Long | Jan. 27, 1852 | Cert. No. 102 |
| Johann D. Dierks | Oct. 9, 1845 | Jefferson Co. |
| John Mayfield | Feb. 11, 1846 | --- |
| John Long | Oct. 31, 1846 | --- |
| John Long | May 17, 1846 | --- |
| Mark Ware | Aug. 18, 1847 | Jefferson Co. |
| John Diedrick Rolhje | Apr. 9, 1845 | Jefferson Co. |
| Frederick Drier | Sep. 22, 1848 | Warr. No. 2841 |
| John D. Rolhje | Jan. 10, 1857 | Jefferson Co. |
| Frederick W. Springer | Jul. 10, 1857 | Jefferson Co. |
| Johann I. Kramme | Feb. 9, 1852 | Jefferson Co. |
| Pricilla Estep | Dec. 1, 1843 | --- |
| Richard Caulk | Sep. 3, 1847 | Cert. No. 35 |
| Antoine Gautier | Oct. 5, 1850 | Cert. No. 139 |
| Mary Duncan | Jan. 20, 1852 | Jefferson Co. |
| Richard G. Duncan | Jun. 5, 1852 | Jefferson Co. |
| Achilles Wade | Jan. 5, 1852 | Franklin Co. |
| Francis M. Wideman | Aug. 11, 1847 | Jefferson Co. |
| James S. Wideman | Dec. 19, 1851 | Jefferson Co. |
| Michael Cohan | Feb. 1, 1860 | Jefferson Co. |
| Adam Wilson | Dec. 19, 1851 | Jefferson Co. |
| John M. Wilson | Oct. 2, 1841 | Jefferson Co. |
| Ephraim Wilson | Dec. 7, 1844 | Jefferson Co. |
| Robert Wilson | Jan. 8, 1852 | Jefferson Co. |
| Michael McKay | Apr. 1, 1852 | Jefferson Co. |
| Milton Long | Feb. 27, 1851 | Jefferson Co. |
| John M. Wilson | Dec. 19, 1851 | Jefferson Co. |
| Christopher E. Frost | Feb. 9, 1852 | Jefferson Co. |
| William McKay | Nov. 13, 1841 | Jefferson Co. |
| Fred Folly | Feb. 1, 1860 | --- |
| Charles Wilson | Feb. 1, 1860 | --- |
| Andrew Barry | Feb. 1, 1860 | --- |
| John Manion | Nov. 13, 1851 | Jefferson Co. |
| William McKay | Nov. 13, 1851 | Jefferson Co. |

| Name | Date | Residence |
|---|---|---|
| Joseph Campbell | Jan. 17, 1852 | Jefferson Co. |
| Christopher E. Frost | Feb. 9, 1852 | Jefferson Co. |
| James O'Marra | Feb. 1, 1860 | --- |
| James Pound | Apr. 6, 1852 | Warr. No. 35733 |
| James Evans | Mar. 13, 1852 | Jefferson Co. |
| Miller Cadwalladen | Aug. 8, 1851 | Jefferson Co. |
| Philip Pipkin | Sep. 14, 1849 | Jefferson Co. |
| Pricilla Estepts | Dec. --, 1843 | --- |
| Thompson H. Whitworth | Nov. 15, 1860 | Jefferson Co. |
| Sanford Whitworth | Dec. 13, 1845 | Jefferson Co. |
| Samuel Perry | Mar. 7, 1846 | Jefferson Co. |
| Michael E. Dace | Apr. 16, 1847 | Jefferson Co. |
| David W. Wright | Sep. 21, 1841 | Jefferson Co. |
| Francis Beehler | May 28, 1848 | Jefferson Co. |
| John James | May 28, 1848 | Jefferson Co. |
| John Long | May 26, 1848 | Cert. No. 33 |
| Patrick Lynce | May 24, 1850 | Franklin Co. |
| Margaret Lynce | Jun. 2, 1852 | Franklin Co. |
| Michael Galvin | Jul. 20, 1840 | Franklin Co. |
| Owen Casey | Dec. 8, 1843 | Jefferson Co. |
| Curmac Smith | Oct. 1, 1846 | Jefferson Co. |
| John James | Jun. 24, 1848 | Warr. No. 10299 |
| John Galvin | Dec. 12, 1850 | St. Louis Co. |
| James M. Courtney | Dec. 15, 1840 | Jefferson Co. |
| Thomas Welsh | Feb. 23, 1843 | Franklin Co. |
| Thomas Madden | May 26, 1848 | Cert. No. 33 |
| Andrew Masterson | Dec. 27, 1851 | Jefferson Co. |
| Peter Murphy | Aug. 9, 1843 | Jefferson Co. |
| Luke Galalay | Aug. 9, 1843 | Jefferson Co. |
| John Ferley | Sep. 4, 1847 | Jefferson Co. |
| John Carty | Jun. 19, 1843 | Jefferson Co. |
| James Masterson | Oct. 2, 1843 | St. Louis Co. |
| Michael Masterson | Mar. 13, 1847 | New Orleans, La. |
| James Rogers | Apr. 16, 1845 | --- |
| Christopher Pyeatt | Feb. 7, 1842 | Jefferson Co. |
| Lawrence O'Brien | Feb. 9, 1852 | Warr. No. 15885 |
| Lawrence O'Brien | Feb. 9, 1852 | Warr. No. 5856 |
| Joseph Crawford | Jan. 17, 1840 | Jefferson Co. |
| Edmund Sale | Dec. 4, 1840 | St. Louis Co. |
| Arthur Traynor | Sep. 27, 1844 | Jefferson Co. |
| Patrick Cummisky | Dec. 24, 1842 | St. Louis Co. |
| James Hagan | Aug. 14, 1843 | Jefferson Co. |
| James Threayner | Jan. 19, 1846 | Jefferson Co. |
| Thomas Welsh | Jun. 25, 1841 | Jefferson Co. |
| James Craddick | Jul. 23, 1846 | Jefferson Co. |
| Lydia Hays | May 29, 1848 | St. Louis Co. |
| Margaret Wright | Jun. 1, 1850 | Jefferson Co. |
| Julius Emmons | May 5, 1845 | Jefferson Co. |

| Name | Date | Residence |
|---|---|---|
| Hiram Wright | Mar. 8, 1841 | Jefferson Co. |
| Jesse H. Isgrig | Sep. 14, 1841 | Jefferson Co. |
| Thomas M. Cole | Aug. 15, 1848 | Jefferson Co. |
| Samuel Peppers | Oct. 14, 1851 | Jefferson Co. |
| Alexander B. Henderson | Feb. 25, 1852 | Jefferson Co. |
| William M. McDaniel | Feb. 1, 1860 | --- |
| Alex Henderson | Feb. 1, 1860 | --- |
| Arthur Crewsbauer | Jan. 6, 1840 | St. Louis Co. |
| James Hagan | Aug. 27, 1849 | Jefferson Co. |
| Phillip Owens | Feb. 2, 1850 | Jefferson Co. |
| James Cole | Oct. 11, 1850 | Jefferson Co. |
| Terrance Cummisky | May 10, 1843 | St. Louis Co. |
| Arthur Cummisky | Jan. 6, 1840 | St. Louis Co. |
| John Farley | Jun. 25, 1844 | Jefferson Co. |
| Edward M. Lane | Mar. 9, 1846 | Jefferson Co. |
| Barnard Terfeler | Oct. 5, 1847 | Jefferson Co. |
| Louisa Richter | Mar. 9, 1840 | Jefferson Co. |
| Diederick Sanne | Jun. 19, 1840 | Jefferson Co. |
| Garhard Gelker | Jan. 28, 1841 | St. Louis Co. |
| Charles S. Megrann | Jul. 23, 1844 | Jefferson Co. |
| Patrick Cummisky | Mar. 24, 1846 | St. Louis Co. |
| Samuel Perry | Aug. 13, 1849 | Jefferson Co. |
| Thomas Hines | Jan. 12, 1852 | St. Louis Co. |
| Antoine Gotier | Sep. 4, 1849 | Cert. No. 139 |
| Daniel O'Brien | Feb. 1, 1860 | --- |
| John Long | Nov. 30, 1846 | Cert. No. 105 |
| John Long | Oct. 28, 1847 | Cert. No. 99 |
| John Long | Feb. 12, 1850 | Cert. No. 102 |
| David Pink | Jan. 7, 1850 | Warr. No. 63153 |
| Conrad Beeler | Apr. 9, 1845 | Jefferson Co. |
| Dulguid Pitzer | Apr. 22, 1845 | Jefferson Co. |
| Samuel Johnston | Mar. 2, 1848 | Jefferson Co. |
| James Macksey | Jan. 9, 1851 | Cert. No. 104 |
| Jacob Harness | Apr. 19, 1852 | Warr. No. 10613 |
| Conrad Beeler | Apr. 15, 1845 | Jefferson Co. |
| John Welbals | Jun. 19, 1845 | Franklin Co. |
| Wilhelm Richter | Feb. 2, 1846 | Jefferson Co. |
| John Henry | Oct. 10, 1848 | Cert. No. 138 |
| Herman Meuzebraff | Feb. 9, 1852 | Jefferson Co. |
| Frederick Crewbauer | Dec. 30, 1845 | Jefferson Co. |
| Eri Wells | Dec. 6, 1844 | Jefferson Co. |
| Frederick Crewbauer | Dec. 6, 1844 | Jefferson Co. |
| Henrich A. Gerken | Jan. 26, 1846 | Jefferson Co. |
| Oliver Wells | Feb. 17, 1846 | Jefferson Co. |
| John Henry | Oct. 10, 1848 | Cert. No. 138 |
| John Kerrigan | Oct. 17, 1851 | Hamilton Co., Ohio |
| Henry Gerkin | Jan. 27, 1852 | Jefferson Co. |

| Name | Date | Residence |
|---|---|---|
| John Dittmer | Feb. 3, 1852 | Jefferson Co. |
| Henrich Hayes | Feb. 6, 1852 | Jefferson Co. |
| James Rogers | Apr. 15, 1845 | --- |
| Edward Young | Nov. 1, 1848 | Cert. No. 107 |
| John McCool | Jun. 3, 1850 | Hamilton Co., Ohio |
| Edward Nonan | Mar. 8, 1850 | Warr. No. 65172 |
| Moses Thompson | Feb. 4, 1850 | Jefferson Co. |
| James Rogers | Apr. 16, 1845 | --- |
| Madison McDaniel | Apr. 1, 1850 | Jefferson Co. |
| Thomas M. Cole | Jan. 27, 1850 | Jefferson Co. |
| Jourdan Davidson | Jan. 22, 1842 | Franklin Co. |
| Priscilla Estep | Dec. 1, 1846 | --- |
| John Ficken | Jan. 30, 1851 | --- |
| John Hennesy | Feb. 1, 1860 | --- |
| Michael Null | Jan. 26, 1846 | Jefferson Co. |
| William Weber | Jan. 31, 1851 | Jefferson Co. |
| Henry Rotermund | Nov. 21, 1851 | Jefferson Co. |
| Joel McDaniel | Jan. 3, 1852 | Jefferson Co. |
| Johann D. Cordes | Apr. 27, 1846 | Jefferson Co. |
| James Macksey | May 30, 1850 | Cert. No. 100 |
| Edward Young | Sep. 30, 1850 | Cert. No. 142 |
| Joshua Davis | Jan. 13, 1851 | Jefferson Co. |
| Antoine Gautier | Mar. 18, 1851 | Cert. No. 139 |
| Joel McDaniel | Jan. 3, 1852 | Jefferson Co. |
| Henrich Heimseth | Jan. 31, 1852 | Jefferson Co. |
| Jonathan Wise | Feb. 19, 1846 | Jefferson Co. |
| Leonard Wilson | Aug. 6, 1845 | Jefferson Co. |
| James McKay | Jun. 13, 1850 | Cert. No. 100 |
| Jackson Hilderbrand | Jul. 3, 1848 | Jefferson Co. |
| William T. Christy | Apr. 10, 1851 | St. Louis Co. |
| Robert K. Wood | Apr. 10, 1851 | St. Louis Co. |
| Philip B. Hockaday | Jul. 8, 1851 | St. Louis Co. |
| Peter Coffery | Jul. 20, 1841 | St. Louis Co. |
| John W. Skinner | May 29, 1852 | St. Louis Co. |
| Nicolas Siferd | Apr. 23, 1840 | Jefferson Co. |
| Richard Walsh | Jul. 11, 1842 | St. Louis Co. |
| Lewis C. Wilson | May 8, 1845 | Jefferson Co. |
| Jubal Wilson | Jun. 26, 1846 | Jefferson Co. |
| John Long | Oct. 2, 1848 | Cert. No. 102 |
| *Lewis C. Wilson | Nov. 15, 1860 | Jefferson Co. |
| *(Homestead Entry No. 996) | | |
| James Mackay | Aug. 22, 1851 | Cert. No. 104 |
| Peter Dily | Dec. 29, 1841 | St. Louis Co. |
| Reuben Willard | Sep. 22, 1851 | Jefferson Co. |
| Peter Caffery (sic) | Jul. 20, 1841 | St. Louis Co. |
| Charles Coffery (sic) | Oct. 4, 1841 | St. Louis Co. |
| Anthony Coffery (sic) | Jul. 6, 1844 | St. Louis Co. |

| Name | Date | Residence |
|---|---|---|
| David C. Neely | Oct. 9, 1851 | Jefferson Co. |
| Aman Mich--- Melchur | Jun. 1, 1852 | Cert. No. 112 |
| William Brown | Jun. 15, 1842 | Jefferson Co. |
| Anthony Caffery | Jul. 6, 1844 | St. Louis Co. |
| Elias Jane Hardin | Mar. 20, 1846 | Jefferson Co. |
| John Long | Jun. 11, 1850 | Cert. No. 103 |
| Philip B. Hockaday | Jul. 10, 1852 | Warr. No. 5669 |
| Philip B. Hockaday | Jul. 10, 1852 | Warr. No. 14875 |
| Philip B. Hockaday | Jul. 10, 1852 | Warr. No. 3792 |
| Philip B. Hockaday | Jul. 10, 1852 | Warr. No. 5343 |
| David W. Wright | Jun. 8, 1840 | Jefferson Co. |
| Michael Donegan | Sep. 7, 1847 | Jefferson Co. |
| Samuel Green | Mar. 16, 1848 | Jefferson Co. |
| Michael Donegan | Feb. 23, 1848 | Jefferson Co. |
| Richard Caulk | Jul. 19, 1847 | Cert. No. 35 |
| Peter Farvally | Mar. 5, 1847 | St. Louis Co. |
| Benjamin F. Buster | Jun. 20, 1845 | Jefferson Co. |
| Isaiseh Roberts | Jun. 20, 1845 | Jefferson Co. |
| Eliza Hill | Nov. 13, 1847 | Jefferson Co. |
| Peter Price | Oct. 11, 1850 | St. Genevieve |
| David Horine | Aug. 7, 1846 | Cert. No. 13 |
| Jobes Greer | May 25, 1847 | Jefferson Co. |
| James Moore | Apr. 7, 1849 | Warr. No. 41105 |
| Godfried Reando | Sep. 18, 1851 | Warr. No. 53381 |
| David Wilson | Jan. 20, 1840 | Jefferson Co. |
| Peter Vinyard | Jan. 20, 1840 | Jefferson Co. |
| William A. Whiting and Samuel J. Smith | Jul. 8, 1853 | Warr. No. 21674 |
| Caleb W. Christopher | Apr. 9, 1845 | Washington Co. |
| John Jones | Jul. 7, 1845 | --- |
| Samuel Magaffin | Jul. 22, 1853 | St. Louis Co. |
| Thomas Long | May 19, 1845 | Jefferson Co. |
| Peter Paul Robert | May 17, 1845 | Jefferson Co. |
| *David Horine *(Warrant No. 60573) | Aug. 14, 1849 | Jefferson Co. |
| Samuel Higgerson | Oct. 20, 1843 | Jefferson Co. |
| Allen R. Moon | Jul. 5, 1845 | Jefferson Co. |
| Thomas Cooper | Mar. 21, 1846 | Jefferson Co. |
| Charles Kraus | Jul. 6, 1853 | Warr. No. 20879 |
| Charles Kraus | Jul. 6, 1853 | Warr. No. 10819 |
| George W. Larkin | Apr. 22, 1845 | Jefferson Co. |
| Joseph H. Moon | Feb. 23, 1841 | Jefferson Co. |
| Silas B. Larkin | Jul. 12, 1848 | St. Francois |
| Ebin Turley | Feb. 25, 1848 | --- |
| Thomas Brown | Jul. 11, 1853 | St. Louis Co. |
| Samuel Maguffin | Jul. 27, 1853 | Warr. No. 89195 |
| Samuel Maguffin | Jul. 27, 1853 | Warr. No. 89205 |
| Thomas Brown | Jul. 12, 1853 | St. Louis Co. |

| Name | Date | Residence |
|---|---|---|
| Edward Boyne | Apr. 26, 1852 | St. Louis Co. |
| Edwin Boyne | May 19, 1852 | Jefferson Co. |
| Charles Boyne | Jul. 6, 1853 | Jefferson Co. |
| James B. Bowlin | Jul. 7, 1853 | St. Louis Co. |
| William E. Wood | Nov. 13, 1851 | Washington Co. |
| John D. Hearst | Jul. 6, 1853 | Jefferson Co. |
| John Pence | Jul. 6, 1853 | Jefferson Co. |
| Richard Keef | Aug. 5, 1851 | Warr. No. 22328 |
| William E. Wood | Jul. 14, 1853 | Washington Co. |
| Augustus F. Shapleigh | Jul. 27, 1853 | Warr. No. 66411 |
| Augustus F. Shapleigh | Jul. 27, 1853 | Warr. No. 78372 |
| Augustus F. Shapleigh | Jul. 27, 1853 | Warr. No. 78378 |
| Augustus F. Shapleigh | Jul. 27, 1853 | Warr. No. 45899 |
| Augustus F. Shapleigh | Jul. 27, 1863 | Warr. No. 40622 |
| Calvin Baker | Nov. 11, 1840 | Jefferson Co. |
| Michael Kelly | Sep. 16, 1844 | St. Louis Co. |
| Zebulon Pritchett | Sep. 6, 1847 | Jefferson Co. |
| Thomas Wiley | Sep. 6, 1847 | Jefferson Co. |
| Edward Cotter | May 10, 1852 | Warr. No. 8528 |
| Julius Higgins | Apr. 9, 1845 | Jefferson Co. |
| Archibald Gamble | May 14, 1845 | St. Louis Co. |
| Ephraim Price | May 15, 1850 | Warr. No. 56639 |
| Richard Keef | Aug. 5, 1851 | Grant No. 22328 |
| Isaac Moon | Jul. 6, 1853 | Jefferson Co. |
| Augustus F. Shapleigh | Jul. 23, 1853 | Warr. No. 62478 |
| Augustus F. Shapleigh | Jul. 23, 1853 | Warr. No. 88454 |
| Augustus F. Shapleigh | Jul. 23, 1853 | Warr. No. 74743 |
| Augustus F. Shapleigh | Jul. 23, 1853 | Warr. No. 49390 |
| Augustus F. Shapleigh | Jul. 23, 1853 | Warr. No. 35200 |
| Augustus F. Shapleigh | Jul. 23, 1853 | Warr. No. 21917 |
| Augustus F. Shapleigh | Jul. 23, 1853 | Warr. No. 77978 |
| Julius Higgins | Apr. 9, 1845 | Jefferson Co. |
| Archibald Gamble | May 14, 1845 | St. Louis Co. |
| Ephraim Price | May 15, 1850 | Warr. No. 56639 |
| Samuel Magoffin | Jul. 12, 1853 | Warr. No. 77978 |
| John S. Gooch | Jun. 15, 1848 | Jefferson Co. |
| Alexander Vancourt and and Benjamin J. Vancourt | Jul. 5, 1848 | St. Louis Co. |
| John D. Hearst | Jul. 6, 1853 | Warr. No. 43355 |
| John Pence | Jul. 6, 1853 | Jefferson Co. |
| Hamilton S. Reppy | Jul. 12, 1853 | Jefferson Co. |
| Samuel Magoffin | Jul. 11, 1853 | St. Louis Co. |
| Samuel Magoffin | Jul. 12, 1853 | Warr. No. 77979 |
| William Robertson | Apr. 27, 1848 | Jefferson Co. |
| Charles Staples | Jul. 11, 1848 | Jefferson Co. |
| George W. Higginbotham | May 30. 1851 | Washington Co. |
| James B. Bowlin | Jul. 7, 1853 | St. Louis Co. |
| James S. Williams | Jul. 6, 1853 | Jefferson Co. |

| Name | Date | Residence |
|---|---|---|
| Leander W. Pinson | Jul. 6, 1853 | Jefferson Co. |
| Samuel Magoffin | Jul. 11, 1853 | St. Louis Co. |
| George W. Harrison | Jul. 6, 1843 | Jefferson Co. |
| George M. Edwards | Jul. 12, 1853 | Jefferson Co. |
| *Willis J. Williams | Jul. 6, 1853 | Jefferson Co. |
| *(Warrant 54131) | | |
| Wm. H. Moon | Jul. 5, 1845 | Jefferson Co. |
| Eliel Donnell | Mar. 18, 1847 | Jefferson Co. |
| James C. Cape | Jul. 6, 1853 | Jefferson Co. |
| William H. Moon | Jul. 27, 1853 | Jefferson Co. |
| Willis J. Williams | Feb. 1, 1860 | ---- |
| George W. Higginbotham | Feb. 27, 1847 | Washington Co. |
| George W. Higginbotham | May 30, 1857 | Washington Co. |
| Samuel Magoffin | Jul. 11, 1853 | St. Louis Co. |
| Thomas Brown | Jul. 11, 1853 | St. Louis Co. |
| Albert G. Cross | Aug. 21, 1844 | Jefferson Co. |
| Wm. R. Cross | Aug. 21, 1844 | Jefferson Co. |
| Lawson Cooley | May 14, 1846 | Jefferson Co. |
| Joseph Magean | May 14, 1846 | St. Louis Co. |
| James B. Bowlin | Jul. 7, 1853 | St. Louis Co. |
| Samuel Magoffin | Jul. 12, 1853 | St. Louis Co. |
| Elias Dobson | Oct. 13, 1850 | Warr. No. 31119 |
| George F. Perkins | Feb. 26, 1851 | Jefferson Co. |
| Albert G. Cross | Aug. 21, 1844 | Jefferson Co. |
| Archalaus Lee | Sep. 20, 1844 | Jefferson Co. |
| Albert G. Smith | Jul. 3, 1849 | Jefferson Co. |
| Felix Valle | Jul. 12, 1849 | Ste. Genevieve |
| William R. Cross | Aug. 21, 1844 | Jefferson Co. |
| Henry Dielle | Feb. 27, 1846 | Cert. No. 43 |
| *Bernard Pratte | Feb. 27, 1846 | St. Louis Co. |
| *(Cert. No. 43) | | |
| *Thomas Brown | Jul. 8, 1853 | Jefferson Co. |
| *(Warrant Nos. 856 and 24342) | | |
| Lindley T. McMullin | Aug. 11, 1848 | Jefferson Co. |
| James R. McDonald | Aug. 13, 1844 | Jefferson Co. |
| Charles L. Tucker | May 27, 1848 | Warr. No. 24920 |
| Charles L. Tucker | May 17, 1848 | Warr. No. 350 |
| Samuel Magaffin | Jul. 11, 1853 | St. Louis Co. |
| John Jones | Jul. 8, 1853 | Warr. No. 59374 |
| Vincent C. Pullin | Jul. 6, 1853 | Jefferson Co. |
| Louis Bolduc | Apr. 30, 1845 | Jefferson Co. |
| Harvey Blackwell | Jul. 6, 1853 | Washington Co. |
| Thomas Brown | Jul. 12, 1853 | St. Louis Co. |
| John C. Porter | Jul. 18, 1853 | St. Louis Co. |
| Rufus K. Porter | Jul. 27, 1853 | Warr. No. 83916 |
| *Samuel Magoffin | Jul. 12, 1853 | St. Louis Co. |
| *(Warr. No. 77985) | | |
| William Blackwell | Feb. 24, 1852 | Washington Co. |

| Name | Date | Residence |
|---|---|---|
| Andrew Richardson | Jan. 20, 1840 | Jefferson Co. |
| Edward Wyman | Jul. 26, 1853 | Warr. No. 5578 |
| Edward Wyman | Jul. 26, 1853 | Warr. No. 5774 |
| Edward Wyman | Jul. 26, 1853 | Warr. No. 6173 |
| Edward Wyman | Jul. 26, 1853 | Warr. No. 5540 |
| Edward Wyman | Jul. 26, 1853 | Warr. No. 5940 |
| Edward Wyman | Jul. 26, 1853 | Warr. No. 89018 |
| Richard Caulk | Mar. 10, 1848 | Cert. No. 35 |
| Charles S. Tucker | May 17, 1848 | Warr. No. 524 |
| Charles Manwarring | Jul. 26, 1853 | Jul. 26, 1853 |
| Horace A. Honey | May 17, 1847 | Jefferson Co. |
| Lucy Honey | Jun. 12, 1847 | Jefferson Co. |
| William Huskey | Jul. 11, 1853 | Jefferson Co. |
| Margaret E. Williams | Mar. 6, 1840 | Jefferson Co. |
| John S. Mathews | Dec. 9, 1841 | Jefferson Co. |
| Talmon C. Palmer and Clark S. Smith | Dec. 9, 1841 | Jefferson Co. |
| John Williams | Jul. 14, 1853 | Jefferson Co. |
| Delafayette Ogle | Jul. 26, 1853 | Jefferson Co. |
| Talmon C. Palmer | Mar. 2, 1842 | Jefferson Co. |
| Francis D. Sargant | Feb. 10, 1846 | Jefferson Co. |
| Peggy Carter | Nov. 5, 1844 | --- |
| Thomas C. Ogle | Dec. 17, 1846 | Jefferson Co. |
| Isham Williams | Feb. 28, 1848 | Jefferson Co. |
| Philip Pipkin | Jul. 6, 1853 | Jefferson Co. |
| John White | Aug. 1, 1845 | Jefferson Co. |
| George W. Lemons | Sep. 6, 1851 | Jefferson Co. |
| Joseph R. Gamble | Mar. 9, 1852 | Jefferson Co. |
| George M. Pierce | Jul. 14, 1853 | Jefferson Co. |
| Alexander Reynolds | Apr. 7, 1842 | Jefferson Co. |
| William Lemons | Apr. 29, 1845 | Jefferson Co. |
| Thomas C. Ogle | Mar. 2, 1847 | Jefferson Co. |
| Joshua I. Reynolds | Feb. 18, 1851 | Jefferson Co. |
| Robert W. Creery | Dec. 10, 1851 | Warr. No. 6268 |
| James O. Williams | Jul. 30, 1853 | Jefferson Co. |
| Thomas D. Sargant | Feb. 9, 1846 | Jefferson Co. |
| Thomas Williams | Jul. 12, 1853 | Jefferson Co. |
| Louis J. Rankin | Jul. 12, 1853 | Jefferson Co. |
| Rudolph Haverstick | Apr. 29, 1840 | Jefferson Co. |
| Peggy Carter | Nov. 5, 1844 | --- |
| William A. Gish | Oct. 13, 1845 | Jefferson Co. |
| William H. Moon | Jul. 6, 1853 | Jefferson Co. |
| Tolbot C. Clark | Oct. 10, 1844 | Jefferson Co. |
| Thomas W. Floyd | Jul. 20, 1853 | Warr. No. 89412 |
| Thomas W. Floyd | Jul. 20, 1853 | Warr. No. 49018 |
| James O. Williams | Jul. 30, 1853 | Jefferson Co. |
| Basil Hiney | Jul. 29, 1853 | Jefferson Co. |
| Isham Williams | Apr. 27, 1843 | Jefferson Co. |

| Name | Date | Residence |
|---|---|---|
| James Seabourn | Jan. 26, 1844 | Jefferson Co. |
| Solomon Webb | Jan. 27, 1841 | St. Louis Co. |
| Mary W. Webb | Oct. 7, 1845 | St. Louis Co. |
| Charles Vinyard | Mar. 23, 1850 | Jefferson Co. |
| John Vinyard | Jan. 26, 1844 | Jefferson Co. |
| Thomas Ogle | Sep. 28, 1841 | Jefferson Co. |
| Charles Vinyard | Mar. 23, 1840 | Jefferson Co. |
| James B. Bowlin | Jul. 7, 1853 | St. Louis Co. |
| William G. Reid | Nov. 15, 1860 | Jefferson Co. |
| Alexander T. Drisdale | Apr. 12, 1849 | Jefferson Co. |
| Louis T. Crosby | Jul. 6, 1853 | Warr. No. 77017 |
| Samuel Magoffin | Jul. 11, 1853 | St. Louis Co. |
| Paris Pipkin | Nov. 15, 1860 | St. Louis Co. |
| George Martin | Oct. 12, 1854 | Pat. No. 23312 |
| Michael Brindley | Nov. 13, 1849 | --- |
| Levi Brindley | Jul. 9, 1853 | Jefferson Co. |
| Francis Johnson | Mar. 28, 1842 | Jefferson Co. |
| Michael Brinley (sic) | Aug. 17, 1850 | Jefferson Co. |
| Newton Matthews | Sep. 16, 1847 | Jefferson Co. |
| Whitaker A. Mothershead | Apr. 28, 1845 | Jefferson Co. |
| John P. Riley | Feb. 10, 1842 | Jefferson Co. |
| James Robinson | Jan. 10, 1840 | Jefferson Co. |
| Elisha Manes | Jul. 6, 1853 | Warr. No. 33396 |
| James B. Bowlin | Jul. 7, 1853 | St. Louis Co. |
| James Bowlin | Jul. 7, 1853 | St. Louis Co. |
| John Carregane | Feb. 1, 1860 | --- |
| Jane Moss | Oct. 30, 1843 | Jefferson Co. |
| James Mackay | Oct. 7, 1850 | Cert. No. 101 |
| James Mackay | Feb. 4, 1851 | Cert. No. 139 |
| James Mackay | Feb. 17, 1851 | Cert. No. 107 |
| James Mackay | Aug. 15, 1850 | Cert. No. 100 |
| Stephen Smith | Feb. 17, 1852 | Warr. No. 14049 |
| Antoine Gautier | Dec. 3, 1849 | Cert. No. 139 |
| Lewis Riddle | Aug. 18, 1840 | Jefferson Co. |
| John Long | Sep. 21, 1846 | --- |
| Samuel S. Greer | Feb. 20, 1851 | --- |
| Eliza Jane Gully | Mar. 9, 1852 | Jefferson Co. |
| John Henry | Apr. 21, 1851 | Cert. No. 138 |
| David Johnson | Feb. 1, 1860 | --- |
| Albert B. Haile | Dec. 5, 1846 | Jefferson C. |
| John Long | Apr. 5, 1850 | Cert. No. 102 |
| Antoine Gautier | Sep. 9, 1850 | Cert. No. 139 |
| James McKay | May 29, 1851 | Cert. No. 104 |
| Augustus B. Blumenthal | Mar. 21, 1852 | Warr. No. 73935 |
| John Long | Nov. 9, 1846 | Cert. No. 105 |
| Louisa Chandler | Jan. 29, 1848 | Jefferson Co. |
| Mary Maupin | Mar. 22, 1848 | Jefferson Co. |
| Samuel Parker | Oct. 29, 1849 | Warr. No. 57488 |

| Name | Date | Residence |
|---|---|---|
| George Marsden | Apr. 17, 1851 | Jefferson Co. |
| Elias Huskey | Mar. 31, 1841 | Jefferson Co. |
| Thomas I. Chandler | Mar. 31, 1846 | Jefferson Co. |
| James Hensley | Oct. 4, 1844 | Jefferson Co. |
| John Huskey | Nov. 26, 1844 | Jefferson Co. |
| William Williams | Apr. 13, 1848 | Warr. No. 985 |
| *Willis P. Hamick | Nov. 19, 1849 | Jefferson Co. |
| *(Warrant No. 16916) | | |
| John R. Campbell | Jul. 12, 1840 | St. Louis Co. |
| Stephen Huskey | May 4, 1847 | Jefferson Co. |
| Samuel S. Blake | Feb. 17, 1851 | Jefferson Co. |
| Henry Rowe | Dec. 30, 1851 | Warr. No. 1948 |
| Elizabeth Shelton | Feb. 1, 1850 | Warr. No. 58428 |
| Joseph Frazier | Feb. 19, 1840 | Jefferson Co. |
| Alexander Boughton | Nov. 18, 1844 | Jefferson Co. |
| Manuel Metts | Apr. 2, 1846 | Jefferson Co. |
| John Evans | Apr. 2, 1846 | Jefferson Co. |
| Thomas Lanham | Feb. 24, 1848 | Jefferson Co. |
| William Breaddy | Nov. 27, 1841 | Jefferson Co. |
| David Padelford | Sep. 15, 1843 | Jefferson Co. |
| John Shelton | Nov. 22, 1849 | Jefferson Co. |
| Henry Edner | Nov. 27, 1849 | Jefferson Co. |
| Henry Edner | Nov. 15, 1849 | Warr. No. 4198 |
| Wm. Shelton | Jan. 18, 1842 | Jefferson Co. |
| Saunders Burgess | Jul. 21, 1842 | Jefferson Co. |
| Isham Williams | Sep. 25, 1849 | Jefferson Co. |
| William Shelton | Dec. 7, 1849 | Jefferson Co. |
| Israel F. Dodge | Aug. 13, 1850 | St. Louis Co. |
| Samuel S. Black | Feb. 7, 1851 | Jefferson Co. |
| John Kyle | Mar. 23, 1842 | Jefferson Co. |
| Daniel Swaney | Mar. 25, 1842 | Jefferson Co. |
| Nicholas Lewicki | Apr. 6, 1842 | St. Louis Co. |
| Joseph Strselecrki (sic) | Apr. 4, 1842 | St. Louis Co. |
| Michael Teodorski | Apr. 4, 1842 | St. Louis Co. |
| Willis P. Hamrick | Nov. 10, 1849 | Warr. No. 16916 |
| David Livingston | Feb. 8, 1842 | Jefferson Co. |
| Elias Huskey | Feb. 9, 1842 | Jefferson Co. |
| John S. Mathews | Dec. 9, 1841 | Jefferson Co. |
| Ferdenand Kennett | Mar. 22, 1841 | St. Louis Co. |
| Michael Teodorski | Apr. 4, 1842 | St. Louis Co. |
| Clark L. Smith | Dec. 9, 1841 | Jefferson Co. |
| Francis Meaneca | Dec. 14, 1841 | Jefferson Co. |
| Peter Meaneca | Jan. 19, 1842 | Jefferson Co. |
| Louis I. Rankin | Jan. 19, 1842 | Jefferson Co. |
| Henry Edner | Nov. 15, 1849 | Warr. No. 4198 |
| Pierre Vasques | Aug. 21, 1850 | Cert. No. 150 |
| Jonis Gates | Dec. 1, 1846 | Jefferson Co. |
| Richard Thomas | May 24, 1851 | Jefferson Co. |

| Name | Date | Residence |
|---|---|---|
| Antoine Gautier | May 2, 1849 | Cert. No. 139 |
| Edward Young | May 2, 1849 | Cert. No. 142 |
| Andrew Hurst | Mar. 8, 1844 | Jefferson Co. |
| Louis Keepers | Nov. 7, 1844 | Jefferson Co. |
| Israel F. Hale | Mar. 2, 1844 | Jefferson Co. |
| Joseph Stoker | Feb. 25, 1848 | Jefferson Co. |
| Cornelius H. DeMaree | Mar. 5, 1852 | Jefferson Co. |
| Wm. Warren | Feb. 1, 1860 | --- |
| Nathan Sullens | Dec. 29, 1845 | Jefferson Co. |
| David Lewis | Nov. 13, 1846 | Jefferson Co. |
| Richard Everingham | Dec. 22, 1851 | St. Louis Co. |
| Henry Pallett | Jan. 14, 1852 | St. Louis Co. |
| James Rogers | Apr. 16, 1845 | --- |
| Michall Boly | Apr. 1, 1847 | Jefferson Co. |
| David B. Null | Mar. 22, 1852 | Jefferson Co. |
| James Mackay | Oct. 21, 1850 | Cert. No. 101 |
| Samuel Byrns | Feb. 3, 1846 | --- |
| John Long | Jun. 2, 1846 | Cert No. 9 |
| David Ragan | Aug. 7, 1846 | Jefferson Co. |
| James Mackay | May 27, 1850 | Cert. No. 101 |
| Thomas Thomas | Aug. 18, 1850 | Grant No. 37972 |
| John Henry | Feb. 20, 1849 | Cert. No. 138 |
| Edward Young | Apr. 19, 1849 | Cert. No. 142 |
| Richard Caulk | Jun. 19, 1848 | Cert. No. 116 |
| Jane M. Miller | Apr. 12, 1852 | Jefferson Co. |
| Matthew M'Carty | Feb. 1, 1860 | --- |
| James Rogers | Mar. 27, 1841 | Jefferson Co. |
| John Henry | Aug. 31, 1849 | Cert. No. 138 |
| Amandus Crull | Nov. 12, 1849 | Jefferson Co. |
| John T. Whitham | Mar. 12, 1849 | Warr. No. 14976 |
| James McKay | Nov. 18, 1850 | Cert. No. 100 |
| James McKay | Apr. 9, 1851 | Cert. No. 104 |
| James Rogers | Nov. 28, 1851 | Warr. No. 10601 |
| Joseph Bailie | Aug. 22, 1842 | Jefferson Co. |
| William Alexander | Jan. 4, 1849 | Warr. No. 53677 |
| John T. Whitham | Mar. 12, 1849 | Warr. No. 14076 |
| William T. Dorrance | Apr. 29, 1852 | Warr. No. 13225 |
| William Alexander | Jul. 4, 1849 | Warr. No. 53677 |
| John Henry | Mar. 29, 1850 | Cert. No. 138 |
| Thomas Thomas | Aug. 18, 1850 | Warr. No. 37972 |
| Duiquid Pitzer | Aug. 7, 1847 | Jefferson Co. |
| John T. Whitham | Mar. 12, 1849 | Warr. No. 14076 |
| Hugh O'Bryan | Jul. 31, 1840 | St. Louis Co. |
| Lewis Richter | Feb. 10, 1852 | Warr. No. 8223 |
| George S. Smirl | Aug. 20, 1836 | Jefferson Co. |
| John Long | Sep. 21, 1846 | --- |
| Edward Young | Aug. 28, 1851 | Cert. No. 107 |
| Lewis Ritcher | Feb. 10, 1852 | Warr. No. 8223 |

| Name | Date | Residence |
|---|---|---|
| John Wilson, sr. | Feb. 6, 1840 | --- |
| Peter Cassidy | Feb. 1, 1860 | Madison Co., Il |
| John Bates | Sep. 23, 1843 | Jefferson Co. |
| Thornton Jarvis | Nov. 8, 1843 | Jefferson Co. |
| Stark Cockrill | Jun. 15, 1852 | Warr. No. 39852 |
| George McCune | Dec. 6, 1842 | Jefferson Co. |
| John Long | Mar. 22, 1850 | Cert. No. 102 |
| Mary Oberchon | Dec. 27, 1851 | St. Louis Co. |
| Antoine Gautier | Aug. 9, 1849 | Cert. No. 139 |
| James Mackay | Oct. 21, 1850 | Cert. No. 101 |
| Antoine Gautier | Oct. 25, 1849 | Cert. No. 1139 |
| James Scott | Aug. 6, 1849 | Jefferson Co. |
| Philip Dillon | Aug. 13, 1849 | Jefferson Co. |
| John Long | Jun. 23, 1850 | Cert. No. 102 |
| Levy Block | Jun. 6, 1852 | Warr. No. 3509 |
| Thomas H. Maddox | Feb. 9, 1841 | --- |
| John M. Peterson | Jan. 11, 1842 | --- |
| William Toy | May 12, 1852 | Jefferson Co. |
| Jesse Dowling | Jun. 4, 1840 | Jefferson Co. |
| Basil Colbert | Apr. 24, 1843 | Jefferson Co. |
| Walter Cummings | Jan. 2, 1852 | Jefferson Co. |
| Elvin W. Cooke | Feb. 1, 1860 | --- |
| John B. Mannen | Jun. 23, 1843 | St. Louis Co. |
| Willis H. Bittick | Aug. 28, 1843 | Jefferson Co. |
| John Long | Nov, 13, 1848 | Cert. No. 99 |
| James Mackay | Nov. 13, 1848 | Cert. No. 108 |
| James Kidd | Dec. 18, 1851 | Jefferson Co. |
| Robert Propst | Apr. 15, 1843 | St. Louis Co. |
| David Carter | Jul. 13, 1848 | Jefferson Co. |
| Adam Harness | Jul. 13, 1848 | Jefferson Co. |
| Charles Bohling | Apr. 15, 1843 | St. Louis Co. |
| Edward Young | Apr. 19, 1849 | Cert. No. 142 |
| Edward Young | Apr. 19, 1849 | Cert. No. 162 |
| James Mackay | May 27, 1850 | Cert. No. 101 |
| James Mackay | Jan. 9, 1851 | Cert. No. 104 |
| James Mackay | May 10, 1851 | Cert. No. 100 |
| John Long | Jul. 24, 1846 | Cert. No. 99 |
| John Long | Oct. 22, 1851 | Cert. No. 102 |
| Antoine Gautier | Oct. 15, 1849 | Cert. No. 139 |
| William Hill | May 26, 1845 | Jefferson Co. |
| Dawson Bones | Feb. 23, 1846 | Jefferson Co. |
| Joel W. Stow | Sep. 22, 1840 | Jefferson Co. |
| Adam Harness | Oct. 8, 1844 | Jefferson Co. |
| Henry Heils | Mar. 29, 1852 | Jefferson Co. |
| Thomas W. Servant | Sep. 29, 1851 | Warr. No. 5696 |
| David Null | May 2, 1846 | Jefferson Co. |
| James Mackay | Nov. 13, 1848 | Cert. No. 108 |
| Thomas Murphy | Feb. 1, 1860 | --- |

| Name | Date | Residence |
|---|---|---|
| Ralph Smedley | Apr. 26, 1841 | Jefferson Co. |
| Elihu Edwards | May 24, 1847 | Jefferson Co. |
| Rudolph Haverstick | Jul. 27, 1853 | Warr. No. 7583 |
| Augustus Penrod | May 12, 1840 | --- |
| William Roberts | Oct. 21, 1845 | --- |
| Margaret McCormack | Dec. 16, 1840 | Jefferson Co. |
| Carmil Tucker | Jul. 16, 1853 | Jefferson Co. |
| John T. McMullin | Jul. 16, 1853 | Jefferson Co. |
| Jeremiah McClain | Jul. 16, 1853 | Jefferson Co. |
| Thorton Jarvis | Jul. 30, 1853 | Jefferson Co. |
| Thomas O. Smith | Jul. 30, 1853 | Jefferson Co. |
| Thomas I. Barron and William Rothwell, jr. | Dec. 11, 1845 | St. Louis Co. |
| Lorenz Armbruster | Jul. 19, 1853 | Jefferson Co. |
| William G. Walker | Jul. 30, 1853 | Jefferson Co. |
| Benjamin W. Berry | Feb. 10, 1852 | Jefferson Co. |
| John Harder | May 8, 1845 | Jefferson Co. |
| Christian G. Knorpp | Jun. 11, 1845 | Jefferson Co. |
| John Helstab | Jun. 23, 1845 | Jefferson Co. |
| Jacob Smith | Oct. 20, 1847 | --- |
| John C. Knorpp | Jun. 18, 1847 | Jefferson Co. |
| William Butler | Jul. 27, 1853 | Jefferson Co. |
| George W. Harrison | Jul. 27, 1853 | Jefferson Co. |
| James Wise | Feb. 1, 1860 | --- |
| Christian G. Knorpp | Dec. 9, 1844 | Jefferson Co. |
| Aquila H. Cole | Mar. 19, 1844 | Jefferson Co. |
| Wilhelme Ritter | Jul. 18, 1846 | Jefferson Co. |
| John Pfnister | Dec. 1, 1849 | Jefferson Co. |
| Aquilla H. Cole | Apr. 10, 1845 | Jefferson Co. |
| Asa I. N. Bishop | Nov. 26, 1844 | Jefferson Co. |
| Reed Sweet | Jul. 18, 1853 | Jefferson Co. |
| John Pfinester | May 10, 1852 | Jefferson Co. |
| John H. Rhea | Dec. 20, 1851 | Jefferson Co. |
| Kemp P. Finney | Aug. 28, 1840 | Jefferson Co. |
| David L. Michard | Sep. 7, 1840 | Jefferson Co. |
| ---athiel Cole and John Cole | Dec. 11, 1851 | Jefferson Co. |
| John L. Renard | Aug. 31, 1840 | Jefferson Co. |
| Wade W. Gonza | Sep. 28, 1850 | Jefferson Co. |
| Henry Henried | Aug. 31, 1840 | Jefferson Co. |
| Emele Permaud | Dec. 27, 1847 | Jefferson Co. |
| Mitchell McCormack | Sep. 21, 1847 | Jefferson Co. |
| Rudolph Haverstick | Jul. 27, 1853 | Warr. No. 7583 |
| Wm. Bailey, jr. | Feb. 1, 1860 | --- |
| Mary Philips | Feb. 1, 1860 | --- |
| James B. Bowlin | Jul. 7, 1853 | St. Louis Co. |
| John Strap | May 6, 1845 | Jefferson Co. |
| Louis Frazier | Jun. 12, 1848 | Jefferson Co. |

| Name | Date | Residence |
|---|---|---|
| William Hull | Jul. 6, 1853 | Jefferson Co. |
| Stephen Osburne | Jul. 6, 1853 | Jefferson Co. |
| George Stroup | Jul. 12, 1853 | Jefferson Co. |
| Thomas Williams | Oct. 2, 1840 | Jefferson Co. |
| William Husk | Mar. 16, 1847 | Jefferson Co. |
| Flemming Dodson | Sep. 25, 1851 | Jefferson Co. |
| Flemming Dodson | Jul. 13, 1852 | Warr. No. 17563 |
| John Stroup | Jul. 11, 1853 | Jefferson Co. |
| Louis J. Rankin | Jul. 21, 1853 | Jefferson Co. |
| James B. Bowlin | Jul. 7, 1853 | St. Louis Co. |
| William Null | Jul. 27, 1853 | Jefferson Co. |
| George McNutt | Oct. 23, 1846 | Jefferson Co. |
| Catherine Henry | Nov. 25, 1848 | Jefferson Co. |
| Rueben I. Palmer | Feb. 1, 1850 | Jefferson Co. |
| Louis Frazier | Feb. 14, 1846 | Jefferson Co. |
| William Donnell | Jul. 5, 1853 | Jefferson Co. |
| James A. Bowlin | Jul. 7, 1853 | St. Louis Co. |
| William E. Bage | Oct. 27, 1845 | Jefferson Co. |
| Samuel A. Bage | Oct. 30, 1851 | Jefferson Co. |
| Stephen Osburne (sic) | Jul. 6, 1853 | Jefferson Co. |
| Thomas Ogle | Oct. 18, 1849 | Jefferson Co. |
| William Donnell | Jul. 6, 1853 | Jefferson Co. |
| Stephen Osbourn (sic) | Jul. 6, 1853 | Jefferson Co. |
| John W. Null | Jul. 6, 1853 | Warr. No. 47106 |
| Giles Lee | Jul. 6, 1853 | Jefferson Co. |
| William E. Bage | Jul. 6, 1853 | Jefferson Co. |
| Lewis T. Crosby | Jul. 5, 1853 | Warr. No. 77017 |
| Charles W. S. Vinyard | Jul. 6, 1853 | Jefferson Co. |
| William Haverstick | Oct. 3, 1845 | Jefferson Co. |
| Thomas J. Barrow | Oct. 7, 1845 | St. Louis Co. |
| Henry Ogle | Jul. 6, 1853 | Jefferson Co. |
| Sarah S. Skeel | Jul. 6, 1853 | Jefferson Co. |
| Francis A. Brickey | Jul. 6, 1853 | Jefferson Co. |
| Elizabeth Nash | Feb. 5, 1840 | Jefferson Co. |
| Amon N. Hunt | Aug. 3, 1848 | --- |
| John Weaver | Sep. 14, 1841 | St. Louis Co. |
| Norris Colburn | Oct. 13, 1841 | St. Louis Co. |
| William H. Hensley | Feb. 7, 1846 | Jefferson Co. |
| George M. Willing | Jan. 25, 1853 | Warr. No. 31207 |
| Frederick Sear | Apr. 8, 1853 | Warr. No. 23004 |
| John R. A. Campbell | Oct. 7, 1840 | Jefferson Co. |
| Jacques Landott | Jun. 2, 1849 | Warr. No. 56752 |
| Henry Helterbrand | Feb. 28, 1849 | Jefferson Co. |
| John Yeida | May 1, 1849 | Jefferson Co. |
| Ernest Kassebaume | Oct. 10, 1848 | St. Louis Co. |
| Benjamin I. Boughton | Apr. 6, 1840 | Jefferson Co. |
| Gen. Washington Johnston | Nov. 10, 1841 | Jefferson Co. |
| Joseph Adams | Jan. 21, 1848 | Jefferson Co. |

| Name | Date | Residence |
|---|---|---|
| Thornton Jarvis | Jan. 29, 1847 | Jefferson Co. |
| John Bell | Apr. 10, 1848 | St. Louis Co. |
| William Williams | Apr. 3, 1848 | Jefferson Co. |
| Henry Pattison | Jan. 12, 1842 | Jefferson Co. |
| Thornton Jarvis | Jun. 1, 1849 | Warr. No. 46804 |
| Casper H. Kirchoff | Mar. 1, 1850 | Jefferson Co. |
| Jackson Boughton | Mar. 13, 1848 | Jefferson Co. |
| Benjamin I. Boughton | Apr. 6, 1840 | Jefferson Co. |
| Joshua Craft | Jan. 5, 1848 | Jefferson Co. |
| Francis Beehler | Feb. 14, 1846 | St. Louis Co. |
| Benjamin Boughton | Mar. 1, 1850 | Warr. No. 53011 |
| Peggy Carter | Nov. 5, 1844 | --- |
| Louis Todd | Jan. 29, 1847 | Jefferson Co. |
| Harris R. Williams | Feb. 25, 1841 | Jefferson Co. |
| George M. Fightencam | Apr. 9, 1845 | Jefferson Co. |
| Thomas Burgess | Mar. 20, 1846 | Jefferson Co. |
| James Ogle | Mar. 25, 1847 | Jefferson Co. |
| Thomas Burgess | Feb. 25, 1848 | Jefferson Co. |
| Francis J. Smith | Oct. 24, 1849 | Jefferson Co. |
| Oliver S. Davis | Oct. 11, 1841 | St. Louis Co. |
| Henry Rounsberger | Aug. 20, 1844 | Jefferson Co. |
| Thornton Jarvis | Jun. 2, 1849 | Jefferson Co. |
| Amos N. Hunt | Jul. 7, 1846 | Jefferson Co. |
| Harris R. Williams | Mar. 20, 1851 | Jefferson Co. |
| Francis Beehler | Feb. 23, 1846 | St. Louis Co. |
| John Hammond | Jul. 25, 1846 | Jefferson Co. |
| Pierre Hempell | Dec. 19, 1840 | Jefferson Co. |
| Joseph Sterhli | Apr. 5, 1842 | St. Louis Co. |
| Peter Hemphell | Feb. 4, 1850 | Jefferson Co. |
| Christian Gillman | May 29, 1840 | St. Louis Co. |
| Joseph D. Koenig | Dec. 28, 1841 | Jefferson Co. |
| Louis Resch | Jan. 23, 1843 | St. Louis Co. |
| David Keller | Oct. 7, 1843 | St. Louis Co. |
| Jacob Edinger | Oct. 29, 1851 | Jefferson Co. |
| Christian Gilliam | May 29, 1840 | St. Louis Co. |
| James Murphy | Oct. 15, 1840 | St. Louis Co. |
| Lynchberg Wille | Jul. 16, 1850 | Jefferson Co. |
| Hugh Flood | Sep. 21, 1851 | Warr. No. 1970 |
| *Johannes Echarett | Apr. 9, 1849 | St. Louis Co. |
| *(Warrant No. 37546) | | |
| John Steinberg | Mar. 27, 1851 | Warr. No. 53285 |
| Thomas H. Maddox | Dec. 18, 1840 | St. Louis Co. |
| John Mausel | Apr. 28, 1851 | Warr. No. 54483 |
| Christian Gillman | Feb. 2, 1846 | Jefferson Co. |
| Herman Dorria | Dec. 29, 1849 | Warr. No. 4519 |
| Geo. Briester | Aug. 11, 1849 | Warr. No. 60929 |
| Lucas Rash | Feb. 14, 1850 | Jefferson Co. |
| John Adam Kipler | Aug. 23, 1850 | Jefferson Co. |

| Name | Date | Residence |
|---|---|---|
| Sarah Stover | Mar. 11, 1840 | Jefferson Co. |
| James Burgess, jr. | May 29, 1840 | Jefferson CO. |
| William C. Fine | Nov. 8, 1847 | Jefferson Co. |
| George Arnold | Feb. 25, 1850 | Jefferson Co. |
| John Arnold | May 6, 1845 | Jefferson Co. |
| Pierre Vasques | Feb. 2, 1850 | Cert. No. 15 |
| George Arnold | Feb. 26, 1850 | Jefferson Co. |
| Saunders Burgess | Mar. 9, 1848 | Jefferson Co. |
| John Wingles | Sep. 25, 1849 | Warr. No. 57818 |
| *Bernhard Thiet | Nov. 16, 1854 | Jefferson Co. |
| *(Warrant No. 23864) | | |
| Milton Baker | Feb. 29, 1848 | --- |
| Charles Valle | Feb. 17, 1848 | Cert. No. 20 |
| John M. Bowles | Feb. 25, 1852 | Jefferson Co. |
| Daniel Enright | Nov. 23, 1841 | Jefferson Co. |
| George W. Lamkin | Feb. 2, 1842 | St. Louis Co. |
| Selina Lamkin | Mar. 24, 1842 | St. Louis C. |
| Jane Brison | Dec. 21, 1847 | Jefferson Co. |
| John Everett | Dec. 21, 1847 | Jefferson Co. |
| Thomas Chapman | Apr. 12, 1843 | Jefferson Co. |
| Edward Young | May 9, 1850 | Cert. No. 142 |
| Antoine Gautier | Oct. 31, 1849 | Cert. No. 139 |
| John Henry | Oct. 8, 1849 | Cert. No. 138 |
| James W. Scott | Mar. 9, 1841 | St. Louis Co. |
| Ann Nichols | Sep. 29, 1849 | Jefferson Co. |
| James Mackay | Oct. 7, 1850 | Cert. No. 101 |
| Joseph Willjack | Nov. 25, 1850 | Jefferson Co. |
| Thomas W. Williams | Feb. 14, 1842 | Jefferson Co. |
| Joseph T. Bowles | Nov. 22, 1843 | Jefferson Co. |
| Sallas Keesar (?) | Jun. 30, 1849 | Warr. No. 30385 |
| Elizabeth Sipp | Sep. 17, 1849 | Jefferson Co. |
| James W. Doughty | Mar. 2, 1850 | Warr. No. 47430 |
| James W. Doughty | Mar. 2, 1850 | Warr. No. 36442 |
| James W. Doughty | Mar. 2, 1850 | Warr. No. 42011 |
| James G. Crow | Jan. 21, 1848 | Jefferson Co. |
| Bernard Thiet | Jan. 8, 1851 | Jefferson Co. |
| James Mackay | Mar. 25, 1852 | Cert. No. 100 |
| Antoine Gautier | Aug. 9, 1849 | Cert. No. 139 |
| Bernhart Thiet | Dec. 19, 1849 | Warr. No. 53462 |
| Bernhart Thiet | Dec. 19, 1849 | Warr. No. 37199 |
| Robert T. Baldwin | Aug. 27, 1849 | Warr. No. 57375 |
| James W. Doughty | Feb. 4, 1850 | St. Louis Co. |
| John Nolan | Jul. 27, 1850 | Jefferson Co. |
| Elisha Gorton | Jul. 27, 1850 | --- |
| Nelson Nolan | Feb. 26, 1851 | --- |
| Josiah Earp | Jan. 19, 1844 | Warr. No. 27172 |
| Peter Kriet | Jun. 9, 1851 | St. Louis Co. |
| Christine Klan | May 31, 1847 | Jefferson Co. |

| Name | Date | Residence |
|---|---|---|
| Florence Spetts | May 31, 1847 | Jefferson Co. |
| Joseph Spetts | May 11, 1848 | Jefferson Co. |
| Henry Blank | May 31, 1852 | Jefferson Co. |
| Alexander Burns | Sep. 11, 1847 | Jefferson Co. |
| William M. McDaniel | Nov. 9, 1847 | Jefferson Co. |
| Merrel Parke | Jun. 27, 1842 | Jefferson Co. |
| Francis Gregari | May 13, 1852 | Jefferson Co. |
| George Wissner | Dec. 13, 1841 | St. Louis Co. |
| Henrich C. Bonacker | Oct. 21, 1847 | Jefferson Co. |
| Porter Phillips | Dec. 6, 1847 | Jefferson Co. |
| Henry Porter | Dec. 1, 1851 | Jefferson Co. |
| Margaret Baker | Sep. 30, 1847 | Jefferson Co. |
| Daniel Doerrie | Oct. 14, 1851 | Jefferson Co. |
| Nicholas Baker | Dec. 1, 1851 | Jefferson Co. |
| Daniel Bonacker | Jan. 22, 1852 | Jefferson Co. |
| Sebastian Sceit | Mar. 19, 1841 | Jefferson Co. |
| Henry Erp | Sep. 29, 1851 | Warr. No. 1279 |
| Joseph Light | Mar. 9, 1852 | Jefferson Co. |
| Severin Puellin | Jul. 6, 1850 | Warr. No. 57602 |
| Valentine Recisar | Jun. 4, 1850 | Jefferson Co. |
| Lewis Rapp | Oct. 2, 1851 | Warr. No. 1268 |
| Wilhelm Holtman | Sep. 25, 1841 | St. Louis Co. |
| Robert Thomas | Aug. 20, 1851 | Jefferson Co. |
| Bartholomew Ucher | Aug. 25, 1851 | St. Louis Co. |
| Franz Wodieza | Aug. 25, 1851 | St. Louis Co. |
| Josephine Johnston | Sep. 6, 1851 | Jefferson Co. |
| Peggy Carter | Nov. 5, 1840 | --- |
| Elizabeth Gamache | May 18, 1846 | Jefferson Co. |
| Luneberg Wille | Mar. 12, 1850 | Jefferson Co. |
| Michael Kesler | Nov. 22, 1844 | Jefferson Co. |
| Jacob Becker | Dec. 13, 1844 | Jefferson Co. |
| Valentine Reiser | Sep. 4, 1845 | Jefferson Co, |
| Philip H. Kohner | Nov. 13, 1849 | Jefferson Co. |
| George Whitmier | Jun. 12, 1850 | Jefferson Co. |
| Henrich Ehlers | Mar. 12, 1850 | Jefferson Co. |
| Jacob Becker | Oct. 9, 1851 | Jefferson Co. |
| Richard Ransley | Dec. 2, 1851 | Warr. No. 1541 |
| Elijah D. Turner | Apr, 14, 1840 | St. Louis Co. |
| Nicholas Ems | Dec. 21, 1840 | Jefferson Co. |
| George Ems | Jul. 19, 1841 | Jefferson Co. |
| John Ulrich | Nov. 1, 1842 | Jefferson Co. |
| Adam Kesler | Nov. 22, 1844 | Jefferson Co. |
| Kalbamus (?) Resch | Nov. 29, 1844 | Jefferson Co. |
| George Ems | Apr. 15, 1845 | Jefferson Co. |
| Valentine Reiser | Sep. 1, 1845 | Jefferson Co. |
| John Frederecy | Jun. 27, 1842 | Jefferson Co. |
| William S. Taylor | May 15, 1848 | Ste. Genevieve |
| Thomas Havens | Mar. 19, 1850 | Warr. No. 14571 |

| Name | Date | Residence |
|---|---|---|
| Nathaniel Stanford | Feb. 1, 1850 | --- |

Ralls County, Missouri, Estate Settlements, 1840 to 1843.

107) Settlement of Joseph Fanning, adm. of the estate of Middleton Fanning, dec. February term, 1840.
Notes due August 4, 1839 and not yet collected: Margaret Hilton, John Rinny, Jacob Fudge, J. Calhourn.
Notes on Account: Sary Lee, James Fanning.
Credits: Wm. Leek.
Expenditures: John Lyle, - Rice, - Carstaphen, - Pierce. (RD) February 5, 1840, (CLK) John Ralls.

108) Settlement of James Inlow, adm. of the estate of Paton P. Wright. February term, 1840.
Monies received: I. Wright, Joel Ledford, H. Inlow, Wm. Inlow, Eaton Turner, W. Johnston (note due on December 25, 1840).
Monies Expended: John A. Wright, guard. of infant heirs of P. P. Wright; Lewis Tracy; Dr. McCay; Joseph Wright; H. Brown; D. Jones; Shields & Emerson; P. Pierce; Henry Inlow; Joseph and Sanford. (RD) February 3, 1840, (CLK) John Ralls.

109) Annual Settlement by John H. Lynch and Matthew Elliott, exrs., of the the estate of Bernard I. Lynch. February term, 1840.
Monies Received: Sale of personal property on November 23, 1838.
Monies Expended - Name/Date: Jas. T. I. McElroy, June 13, 1840; Hays & Gore (funeral expenses), August 14, 1839; Ortha Brashears (for crying), July 18, 1839; Hays & Gore, August 14, 1840; L. W. Watkins, June 13, 1840; Cornelius N. Lynch, February 1, 1840; J. J. Lyle, February 1, 1840; Luke W. Watkins (for counsel), February 5, 1840; C. Carstarphen, June 8, 1839; John M. Byars; Chars. M. Asher for William L. Lynch. (RD) February 3, 1840; (CLK) John Ralls.

110) Annual Settlement of Robert Moss, adm. of the estate of Joseph C. Epperson. February term, 1840.
Monies Received: Joseph Hardy (for rent of land); sale of negro man, Darrell, to Joseph Wright on January 1, 1840. (RD) February 4, 1840, (CLK) John Ralls.

111) William Rogers, adm. of the estate of Hamilton Rogers, dec. made an annual settlement. February term, 1840.
No names given. (RD) February 4, 1840, (CLK) John Ralls.

112) Dabney Jones, adm. of the estate of P. M. Glenn, dec. made an annual settlement. February term, 1840.
No names given. (RD) February 4, 1840, (CLK) John Ralls.

113) Annual settlement of the estate of John Dorshimer, dec., by William Sox, jr., adm. February term, 1840.
Monies Received: Acy Glascock, --- Culbertson, John Ely, William Jameson, J. Krigbaum.

Monies Expended: William Tracy. (RD) February 5, 1850, (CLK) John Ralls.
114) Annual settlement of Lewis S. Anderson, adm. of the estate of John H. Anderson, dec. February Adjourned term, 1840, on March 16, 1840.
Monies Received: Widow mentioned, but no name given.
Monies Expended: Hays & Gore, Widow, Mrs. Anderson, mentioned. (RD) March 16, 1840, (CLK) John Ralls.
115) Final settlement of the estate of Stephen Elliott, dec. by Matthew Elliott, exr. May term, 1840.
No names given. (RD) May 18, 1840, (CLK) John Ralls.
116) Final settlement of the estate of John Field, dec. by Phillip F. Field, adm. May term, 1840.
Monies Expended: H. Glascock, Jno. Ralls. (RD) May 18, 1840, (CLK) John Ralls.
117) Annual settlement of William W. Cartwill, adm. of the estate of John Crocket, dec. May term, 1840.
Monies Received: Hire of negro girl to Johnson Barnard; Hire of negro boy to Andrew McElroy; Rent of place for 1839 from G. Leney, Sale of negro girl to James Fagan. (RD) May 19, 1840, (CLK) John Ralls.
118) Annual settlement of Benjamin Ely, adm. of the estate of Thomas Ely, dec. August term, 1840.
Monies Expended: Margaret Ely, Joshua Ely, Benjn. Ely, S. and M. Boyd. (RD) August 5, 1840, (CLK) John Ralls.
119) First annual settlement of Joel Finks, adm. of the estate of Robert Jones, dec. August term, 1840.
Monies Expended: Joshua Wilson, C. T. Taylor, Matthew Elliott. (RD) August 3, 1840, (CLK) John Ralls.
120) Annual settlement of Elizabeth Wilson, adm. of the estate of Presly Wilson. August term, 1840.
Monies Received: Receipt on J. J. Slosson for a note on J. Fanning and Jonah Jackson, note on Levy N. Bolvar, note on George L. Hardy, note on Aron Blakeman. Sale bill was made on July 12, 1839.
Monies Expended: David Thomas, B. F. Haden, L. Andersin, J. J. Slosson, Jacob Fuque, J. F. Hawkins, John F. Austin, Hays & Gore, N. T. Pierce, W. P. Torrance, --- Haden, Benj. Ely, Joseph Fanning. (RD) August 5, 1840, (CLK) John Ralls.
121) Final settlement of Johnson Barnard, adm. of the estate of Peter Grant, dec. August term, 1840.
Monies Received: Joseph Biggers (sale of land); -- Buckhannon.
Monies Expended: Cissell & Roberts, Magruder & Handon, -- Chawming, Byant & Son, Bryant & Payne, Meredith & Thomas, Robert Hainer, Enoch Fruit, Robert Hanna, John Rlls, L. F. Hall, G. C. Hays, Mrs. Grant. (RD) September 14, 1840 (CLK) John Ralls.
122) Annual settlement of William W. Cartwill, adm. of

the estate of John Crocket, dec. August term, 1840.
Monies Received: Robert Crocket, John Crocket of Kentucky, --- Underwood, George Linney, William Martin.
Monies Expended: Elijah Crocket, James Crocket, Jackson Crocket, Eli Crocket, Carlile Crocket, Robert Crocket, William Linney, Julian Nucum, J. Barnard, M.J. Noyce, J. Ralls, Wm. Martin. (RD) September 16, 1840, (CLK) John Ralls.

123) Final settlement of Thomas Campbell, exr. of the estate of James Campbell, dec. November term, 1840.
Monies Expended: Apperson & Chile, James D. Caldwell, W. N. Penn, John Scobee, Johnathan Abbay, sr., Thomas M. Campbell, H. Glascock, J. Abbay, J. Ralls. (RD) November 2, 1840, (CLK) John Ralls.

124) Final settlement of John H. Lynch and Matthew Elliott, exrs. of the estate of Bernard I. Lynch. November term, 1840.
Monies Received: Daniel B. Kendrick, John Blue.
Monies Expended: John H. Lynch, Speed Ely, Isaac Ely, George C. Hays, A. H. Buckner, Andrew McElroy, B. W. Brown, George W. Patee, Cornelius N. Lynch, Chas. Glascock, Robt. Steward, John Ralls, Matthew Elliott, --- Noyes, William L. Lynch, Elisha Lynch, James Fagan. (RD) November 4, 1840, (CLK) John Ralls.

125) Settlement of Gabriel Penn, adm. of Horatio Penn. December term, 1840.
Monies Expended: S. W. Mayhall, --- Eastman, Joseph F. Abbington. (RD) December 14, 1840, (CLK) John Ralls.

126) First annual settlement of French Glascock, adm. of the estate of Charles Glascock, dec. November Adjourned term, 1840.
Monies Received: Note of Jas. Neal for 1445-1/2 gal. of whiskey that was sold to -- Shoteau in St. Louis, bill against the heirs of R. Brewer, 533-1/3 gal. of whiskey sold to B. Markle, 63-1/2 gal. sold to John Bates, 47-3/4 bush. of rye sold to B. Settle, John M. Johnson for rent, payment in full by Aaron Gernsay for his note, payment in full by W Moss for his note, Johnson Saunders account with the estate, Wm. Graham, Samuel Newland, Samuel Smith, Jos. Rice, Joseph Canaway, Harris Hopkins, William S. Sims, T. F. Offett. (RD) December 44, 1840, (CLK) John Ralls.

127) Final settlement of Elijah Hudson, adm. of the estate of William Hudson, dec. November term, 1840.
Monies Received: Land bought by David Brothers, Achilas McGinas.
Monies Expended: Heirs of Nimrod Triplitt, Daniel F. J. Brownsing, Pleasant Hudson, John P. Turner, Thomas Cleaver, James Hudson, David Shepard, Peter D. Moyer, Aaron Figgins, David Brothers, Achilles McGinnis, W. S. Lofland, H. Glascock. (RD) December 15, 1840, (CLK) John Ralls.

128) James D. Watson, exr. of the will of John Watson, dec.
Monies Expended: William L. Sergeant, Shilton Watson, William Watson, John Brockman, Joseph Polson, Shelton (sic) Watson. (RD) February 1, 1841, (CLK) John Ralls.

129) Annual settlement of Neal Camron, adm. of the estate of Joshua Ralls, dec. February term, 1841.
Monies Received: Note dated April 1, 1839 by Thomas H. Griffith. S. B. Pavilion paid wages on May 11, 1840. S. D. Philpas noted dated March 31, 1839. Cash received of Thomas H. Griffith for the one sixteenth part of S. D. Pavilion sold to him on February 25, 1840 and to be paid on December 17th. (RD) February 1, 1841, (CLK) John Ralls.

130) Final settlement by James Inlow, adm. of the estate of Peyton P. Wright, dec. February term, 1841.
John A. Wright was mentioned with a guardian receipt. (RD) February 2, 1841, (CLK) John Ralls.

131) First annual settlement of Rebecca Haines, adm. of the estate of Jesse Haines, dec. February term, 1841.
Monies Received: $763 on hand in July, 1835.
Monies Expended: Boarding of Mary Anders from July 4, 1835 to November 12, 1840. Boarding of Nancy and Martha Haines from July 4, 1835 to February 2, 1841. (RD) February 2, 1841, (CLK) John Haines.

132) Annual of Robert Moss, adm. of the estate of --- Epperson, dec. February term, 1841.
Monies Expended: J. S. Crosthwait, Abner Smith, Gilmore S. Morehead, --- Ely, William McCune (assignee of Posey N. Smith), Bernard Roce, Robert Moss, E. G. McGrea, Samuel D. Rice, Wm. H. Peake, Wm. McCune, Joseph Wright, Dabney Jones, Elizabeth Jefferies, John N. Daniel, P. N. Smith, Emerson & Shields, Robert Dillard, Isaac Lettr (sic), Hosey Northcutt, Campbell & Chiton, J. S. Crosthwait. (RD) February 2, 1841, (CLK) John Ralls.

133) Settlement of Philip Field, adm. of John Field, dec. February term, 1841.
Money Expended: J. Hornback, John D. Field, Mary Field, Silas Field. (RD) February 13, 1841, (CLK) John Ralls.

134) First annual settlement of James Culbertson and Wm. H. Vardeman, adms. of the estate of Richard Matson, dec. February term, 1841.
Monies Received: Uriel Wright's receipt for a note on P. A. Labeaume dated May 5, 1837. One note on James L. Fisher and C. Rice dated March 5, 1838 and due September 15, 1839. One note on James L. Fisher and C. Rice dated March 5, 1838 and due September 15, 1840. One note on Charles Rice dated February 19, 1833 and due seven years later. Monies received from Rueben D. H. Low, James L. Fisher, Joseph Hardy and A. S. Saul. One note on A. McGinnis assigned by J. A. Boar-

man dated November, 1829 and with a credit of $2.37 on October 25, 1850. Interest on Hosea Northcutt's note. One note on A. S. Saul and Simon Davis dated July 7, 1840 and due December 25, 1840. Money received from James L. Fisher for the hire of Washington (sic) from November 15, 1838 to September 15, 1839. Money received from a note on Thomas and Jessy Lear. One note on James L. Fisher and Simon Davis dated September 14, 1840 and due a year later. One note on Thomas and Jesse (sic) Lear dated January 22, 1841. Money received from James L. Fisher for the hire of Washington from September 15, 1839 to 1840. Monies received from Thomas and Jesse Lear, James Culbertson and James L. Fisher.

Monies Expended: January 1st - cash paid to --- Garick for a cap for Wash. January 1st - cash paid to --- Eastman for boots for Wash. December 30, 1839 to J. Lasey, February 4, 1840 to James L. Fisher, February 4, 1840 to J. B. Vardeman, August 5, 1850 to James L. Fisher, August 14, 1840 J. Sosey, September 14, 1840 to James L. Fisher, November 1, 1840 to N. Pierce and D. Wilcox, November 3, 1840 to George Fisher, money paid for taxes on land in Marion County, December 3, 1841 to A. S. Saul, January 27, 1841 to G.C. Hays and Joseph Hardy, January 22, 1841 to Thomas Lear, Jesse Lear and James Culbertson. (RD) February 13, 1841, (CLK) John Ralls.

135) Annaul settlement of James McGee, exr. of the estate of James Lee, dec. February term, 1841.

Monies Recieved: James T. McElroy, Thos. L. Anderson, William Muldron.

Monies Expended: --- Steward, --- Hardy, D. Rice, Hays & Gore, Dr. McElroy and to the Widow. (RD) March 22, 1841, (CLK) John Ralls.

136) First annual settlement of Daniel B. Kendrick and Guilford D. Hansborough, adms. of the estate of Harvey Wilson, dec. May term, 1841.

Monies Received: Sale Bill on July 25, 1841. (sic)

Monies Expended: Tax receipts paid for 1839 and 1840. Evan Antwerp for tuition, George L. Hardy, Narciccus Wilson's receipt for a note on James Donelson, Dallis & Able, Hays & Gore, the Widow. (RD) May 3, 1841. (CLK) John Ralls.

137) First annual settlement by James G. Wylie and Peasant Cox, adms. of the estate of William Wylie, dec. May term, 1841.

Monies Expended: February 25, 1841 to Isaac L. Holt, April 23, 1840 to T. B. Stevens, April 25, 1840 to I. S. Buchannon, March 1, 1841 to Russel King, May 3, 1841 to N. Pierce, April 7, 1840 to I. Paterson for clothing for a negro woman, and monies paid to Pleasant Cox, J. G. Wylie and J. C. Wilbern. (RD) May 3, 1841, (CLK) John Ralls.

138) Annual settlement of John and George Billings, exr.

of the estate of Abraham Billings, dec. May term, 1841.
Monies Received: One note on Harvey Wellman due January, 1840. One note on Harvey Wellman due January 1, 1841. One note on J. A. Francis and due on December 25, 1838, and notes on E. N. Hicall and S. C. Haldebeck.
Monies Expended: January 25, 1840 to John Akin, January, 1841 to James Hampton, January, 1841 to Margaret Carson, February, 1840 to John Akin, October, 1840 to Joh Akin, February, 1840 to E. N. Hiscal and F. Hiscal. (RD) May 3, 1841, (CLK) John Ralls.

139) Final settlement of William Rodgers, adm. of the estate of Hamilton Rogers, dec. May term, 1841.
Monies Received: Money on had as of February, 1838.
Monies Expended: May 3, 1841 to Joseph Rogers, May 3, 1841 to Lorinda R. Rogers, H. Glascock, J. Ralls. (RD) May 4, 1841, (CLK) John Ralls.

140) First annual settlement of Richard Bolware, adm. of the estate of Logan Bolware, dec. May term, 1841.
Money Expended: Widow mentioned. John Blue, John Straer. (RD) May 4, 1841, (CLK) John Ralls.

141) First annual settlement of C. Carstarphen, adm. of the estate of Wm. R. Brown, dec. May adjourned term, 1841.
Monies Expended: January 5th to James D. Caldwell, A. B. Combs. (RD) June 4, 1841, (CLK) John Ralls.

142) Annual settlement of Rapheal Leake, adm. of the estate of John Gillespie, dec. June term, 1841.
Monies Expended: June 7, 1841 to J. Piereall. (RD) June 7, 1841, (CLK) John Ralls.

143) Settlement of Peggy Davis, extrix. of the will of Robert Davis, dec. June term, 1841.
Heirs: Malinda Davis now named Malinda Hyde, Robert Montgomery Davis, Catharine Davis, Adaline Davis.
Extrx. Signature: Margaret M. Davis. (RD) June 8, 1841, (CLK) John Ralls.

144) Final Settlement of Lewis S. Anderson, adm. of the estate of John H. Anderson, dec. May term, 1841.
Monies Expended: Dr. Lyle, Lewis Anderson, Elizabeth Anderson, Martha Anderson, Nancy Anderson, James Anderson, John H. Anderson. (RD) June 8, 1841, (CLK) John Ralls.

145) Annual settlement by Benjamin Ely, adm. of the estate Thomas Ely, dec. August term, 1841.
Monies Received: Monies due on August 5, 1840 to the guardian of Benjamin Ely, James Ely and Thomas Ely.
Monies Expended: Tax collector's receipt for 1839 and 1840, Sarah Lee and John Ralls. (RD) August 3, 1841, (CLK) John Ralls.

146) James D. Watson, exr. for the estate of John Watson, dec. August term, 1841.
Monies Expended: Trips by the executor to Virginia and

Tennessee. (RD) August 3, 1841, (CLK) John Ralls.
147) Annual settlement of Elizabeth Wilson, adm. of the estate of Presley Wilson, dec. September term, 1841.
Monies Expended: J. Culbert, Joseph M. Hampton, Hays & Gore, Extr. of the estate of Harvey Wilson, dec., William Wilson as one of the heirs, Elizabeth Wilson. (RD) September 13, 1841, (CLK) John Ralls.
148) First annual settlement by Abraham Buford, jr., adm. of the estate of John Buford, dec. September term, 1841.
Monies Received: October 5, 1840 sale bill.
Monies Expended: August, 1840 to J. D. Buchanon, August 30, 1840 to --- McMurty for shoes, August, 21, 1840 to --- Tracy for coffin, John Ralls. (RD) September 13, 1840, (CLK) John Ralls.
149) Settlement of Eliza Offut (sic), adm. of the estate of Thornton F. Offutt, dec. September term, 1841.
Monies Received: Inventory of estate September, 1841.
Monies Expended: September, 1841 to Stephen Smith for funeral expenses, M. Floweree, V. P. Demmitt, Mrs. Parker, D. Bowling. (RD) September 13, 1841, (CLK) John Ralls.
150) First annual settlement of James Epperson, adm. of the estate of Joel Taylor, dec. September term, 1841.
Monies Received: Judgement against John V. Mills on October 24, 1840. (RD) September 13, 1840, (CLK) John Ralls.
151) First annual settlement of Stephen E. Elliott, adm. of the estate of John Elliott, dec. August term, 1841.
Monies Expended: John M. Colhourne for coffin, J. B. Gore for funeral, J. L. Lyle, physician. (RD) September 13, 1841, (CLK) John Ralls.
152) First annual settlement by Stephen McPherson, adm. of the estate of Eli C. Galleher, dec. September term, 1841.
Monies Received: Hire of Isaac, a black man. Sale bill dated August 12, 1840. Sale of land mentioned. Monies received from Stephen McPherson and Thomas F. Offutt.
Monies Expended: Floweree & Menifee, Stephen Smith, Wm. O. Lofland, Samuel Ely, Samuel Smith, S. W. Mayhall, A. W. McMurty, Uirel Wright, N. T. Pierce, --- Buckhannon, John Glascock, Stephen Cleaver, Stephen McPherson, Mrs. Bahanan. (RD) September 14, 1841, (CLK) John Ralls.
153) First annual settlement of Abraham Selly, adm. of the estate of Nelly Johnston, dec. November term, 1841.
Monies Received: Cash from the estate of John N. Seely, dec. for the use said Nelly Johnston, dec. (RD) November 1, 1841, (CLK) John Ralls.
154) First annual settlement of Otho Brashears and Charles Rice, exrs. of the estate of Thomas Hicklin, dec. November, 1841.
Monies Received: Sale Bill dated November 1, 1841.

Monies Expended: --- Eastman. (RD) November 1, 1841, (CLK) John Ralls.

155) First annual settlement of James Culbertson, adm. of the estate of Catharine Bast, dec. November term, 1841.

Monies Received: Wm. Bast, Wm. Alford, Elizabeth Chapman, Wm. Pullen, Peter Bast, Adam Bast.

Monies Expended: On note on Adam Bast assigned to A. W. McMurty on October 26, 1836 and then assigned to the deceased. Cash paid to T. J. Ellis, G. Waters, A. Shutts, J. Alexander, J. Sosey, Moses Bast. (RD) November 1, 1841, (CLK) John Ralls.

156) First annual settlement of Alexander Buford and Abraham Buford, jr., exrs. of the estate of Abraham Buford, sr., dec. November term, 1841.

Monies Expended: July 8, 1841 cash paid to N. T. Pierce for taxes. Cash paid to Benj. Davis, Allen Brown. (RD) November 1, 1841, (CLK) John Ralls.

157) Final settlement of Gabriel Penn, adm. of the estate of Horatio Penn, dec. November term, 1841.

Monies Expended: I. L. Buchanan. (RD) November 2, 1841, (CLK) John Ralls.

158) Final settlement of William W. Cartwill, adm. of the estate of John Crocket, dec. November term, 1841.

Monies Received: Dr. McElroy, H. Fagan.

Monies Expended: William Martin, Cartwill Crockett, N. T. Pierce, W. Martin, Jackson Crockett, Luke W. Watkins, John Hawkins, Alvin Menifee. (RD) November 2, 1841, (CLK) John Ralls.

159) William Priest, exr. of the estate of John Payne, dec. November term, 1841.

No names given. (RD) November 2, 1841. (CLK) John Ralls.

160) First annual settlement by James M. Leake, adm. of the estate of Joseph Pearielel, dec. December term, 1841.

Monies Received: Sale of personal property October 9, 1840. Cash received from William Leak (sic), Charles Rhodes, Henry Leake, Charles Asher, Benedick Carsies, S.T.T. Haynes, Benedick Gardiner, J. M. Leake, Rosaner L. Piereall (sic). (RD) December 6, 1841, (CLK) John Ralls.

161) Second annual settlement of French Glascock, adm. of Charles Glascock, dec. January term, 1842.

Monies Received: Cash from Joseph Chapman on December 26, 1840, Cash from Marcus Hall on December 27, 1840, Cash from Levi A. Hudson on January 1, 1841, Cash from B. Brizendine on January 1, 1841, Cash from John B. Parris on January 19, 1841, Cash from H. Hopkins on January 19, 1841, Cash from Hansford Brown on February 9, 1841, Cash from Samuel Smith on February 15, 1841, Cash from Allen Dodd on February 15, 1841, Cash from John B. Parris on February 15, 1841, Cash from William Small on February 28, 1841, Cash from Daniel

Brown on March 1, 1841, Cash from William Lmarr on March 7, 1841, Cash from John Biggs on April 5, 1841, Cash from John Ross on April 5, 1841, Cash from Saml. Stowers on June 25, 1841, Cash from William Lmarr on July 7, 1841, Cash from Spencer Glascock on August 30, 1841, Cash from Charles Mills on August 30, 1841, Cash from James R. Garnet on August 30, 1841, Cash from James Neal on June 1, 1841, Cash from William Lmarr on June 1, 1841, Cash from James Cochran on December 21, 1841.

Monies Expended: Joseph Gran, Zed. Merritt, Asa Glascock, K. M. Glascock, Hansford Brown, Joseph Green, --- Loverring, John R. Flowerree, Rob. H. McKay, R. Levering, N. Fuqua, Wm. H. Peake, M. Parker, Wilkinson W. Crawford, Lewis Garnet, N. T. Pierce. (RD) January 3, 1842. (CLK) John Ralls.

162) First annual settlement of Joseph D. Tapley, adm. of the estate of Benjamin Gray, dec. February term, 1842.

Monies Expended: Lewis Tracy, Benj. Robinson, John Ralls, T. D. Tapley. (RD) February 7, 1842, (CLK) John Ralls.

163) Elizabeth Weaver, adm. of the estate of Tilman Weaver, dec. February term, 1842.

Monies Received: William Dowell.

Monies Expended: I. L. Canterbury, H. D. Pariss, A. D. Northcutt, William Priest, A. and W. McMurty, R. H. McKay. (RD) February 7, 1842, (CLK) John Ralls.

164) Final settlement by Richard Boulware, one of the administrators of the estate of Logan Boulware, dec. February term, 1842.

Monies Received: Mary Boulware for the hire of a slave.

Monies Expended: Elizabeth Wilson, Courtney Campbell by Strode & Clayton, A. H. Buckner, John Ralls, Wm. Wright & Horton. There was $5.60 reserved to pay George's demand. No name was stated in this last entry. (RD) February 7, 1842, (CLK) John Ralls.

165) Settlement of James Inlow, adm. of the estate of Peyton P. Wright. February term, 1842.

Monies Expended: Voucher to --- Wright as guardian. (RD) February 7, 1842, (CLK) John Ralls.

166) Final settlement of William Sox, jr., adm. of John Douchimer, dec. February term, 1842.

Monies Expended: Stuart Rainow, John Ralls. (RD) February 7, 1842, (CLK) John Ralls.

167) Settlement of Margaret M. Davis, extrx. of the estate of Robert Davis, dec. February term, 1842.

Monies Received: Malinda Davis, Catharine Davis, Adaline Davis.

Monies Expended: Robert M. Davis. (RD) April 4, 1842, (CLK) John Ralls.

168) Annual settlement of Neal Cameron, adm. of the estate of Joshua Robb, dec. February term.

Monies Expended: Sale of S. P. Pavillion at St. Louis on May 10, 1840, Expenses to St. Louis to settle with S.S. Phelps, Mrs. Robb, Junnus Robb, Saml. Vandergriff. (RD) April 4, 1842, (CLK) John Ralls.

169) Annual settlement of Chapel Carstarphen, adm. of the estate of Wm. R. Brown, dec. April term, 1842.

Monies Expended: W. & S. Thompson, Huntsberry & Walker, A. B. Combs. (RD) April 4, 1842, (CLK) John Ralls.

170) Second annual settlement of John Billings and Geo. Billings, adms. of the estate of Abraham Billings, dec. April term, 1842.

No names given. (RD) April 2, 1842, (CLK) John Ralls.

171) Annual settlement of James McGee, exr. of the estate of James Lee, dec. February term, 1842.

Monies Expended: James H. Campbell, William Lee, John J. Cryler, Silas Crigler, J. H. Leake. (RD) March 7, 1842, (CLK) John Ralls.

172) Second annual settlement of James Culbertson and William H. Vardeman, adm. of the estate of Richard Matson, dec. March term, 1842.

Monies Received: From P.A. Labeaume on May 5, 1839, From Fisher & Rice on September 15, 1839, From Fisher and Rice on September 15, 1840, From Charles Rice on February 19, 1840, From Rueben and H. Low on February 3, 1840, From James L. Fisher on February 4, 1840, From Joseph Hardy on Janary 27, 1840, From A. McGinnis in November, 1829 (sic), From H. Northcutt, From Saul & Davis on December 25, 1840, From -- Saul in April, 1840, From -- Fisher for the hire of Wash. (slave) on February 4, 1840, From T. and I. Lear on May 3, 1840, From Fisher & Davis on September 14, 1841, From Thomas and J. Lear on January 22, 1841, From --- Fisher for the hire of Wash. (slave), From the rent of land in Marion and Ralls Counties in 1841.

Monies Expended: On January 1, 1840 to --- Gerick for cap for Wash. (slave), On January 1, 1840 to --- Eastman for boots for Wash. (slave) on January 1, 1840, On December 30, 1839 to J. Sosey, On February 4, 1840 to J. L Fisher, On February 4, 1840 to J. B. Vardeman, On August 5, 1840 to James L. Fisher, On August 14, 1840 to I. Sosey, On August 14, 1840 to J. L. Fisher, On August 14, 1840 to J. L. Fisher, On November 1, 1840 to N. T. Pierce, On November 1, 1840 to D. Wilcock, On November 3, 1840 to George Fisher, On December 3, 1841 to A. T. Saul, On January 27, 1841 to G. C. Hays, On January 27, 1841 to Joseph Hardy, On February 1, 1841 to A. McMurty, On January 22, 1841 to T. and L. Lear, On June 1, 1841 to R. W. McCreary, On June 21, 1841 to Uriel Wright, On November 7, 1841 to N. T. Pierce, On September 9, 1841 to J. J. Montgomery, On September 9, 1841 to Willis M. Jameson. (RD) March 7, 1842, (CLK) John Ralls.

173) Annual settlement of Stephen Elliott, adm. of the estate of John Elliott, dec. May term, 1842.
Monies Expended: George L. Hardy, James Leake, Aaron Ely, Matthew Elliott, Richard Boulware. (RD) May 2, 1842, (CLK) John Ralls.

174) Second annual settlement of James G. Wylie, surviving administrator of the estate of William Wylie, dec. May term, 1842.
Monies Expended: R. H. Courtney, Wm. B. Wilson, Stephen Glascock, J. Patterson. (RD) May 2, 1842, (CLK) John Ralls.

175) Second annual settlement of Daniel B. Kendrick and Guilford D. Hansborough, exrs. of the estate of Harvey Wilson, dec. June term, 1842.
Monies Expended: --- Seroter, Alfred Wilson, Wm. Wilson, Thos. Brashear, John Houston (sic), John Hauston (sic). (RD) June 6, 1842. (CLK) John Ralls.

176) Annual settlement of Stephen Glascock, adm. of the estate of Harrison Glascock, dec. February term, 1842 (sic)
Monies Expended:To Simon Davis for 1839 school house subscription on November 4, 1838, To A. & W. McMurty on April 7, 1840, To G. C. Hays on February 8, 1842, To A. S. Barley and others as well as Simon Davis, assignee on May 7, 1839, To W. H. Leake on April 7, 1840, To Granville Clayton on September 11, 1841, To --- Eastman on March 13, 1840, To Hansford Brown on February 13, 1840, To A. C. Hawkins on November 13, 1839, To Russel King for coffin on June 6, 1840, To James Gerrish on March 17, 1840, To Luke Watkins on April 6, 1840, To Dr. Robert H. M'Kay on January 3, 1841, To Aaron Kendrick on March 9, 1839, To --- Brackenridge on May 19, 1840, To Jeptha Crasthwait on June 6, 1842.
Unbilled Claims: James Carson, Joseph J. Aldridge, William S. Lofttan, William Shohony, Charles Glascock, C. Rice, B. W. Ralls. (RD) June 13, 1843, (CLK) John Ralls.

177) Final settlement of Robert Sloss, adm. of the estate of Joseph C. Epperson, dec. May term, 1842.
Monies Received: William C. Ford.
Monies Expended: D. Butler, I. Culbertson, James Garrish, Isaac Letter, Drury Eads, C. Carstarphen, David Rice, John Ralls, Joel Ledford, Joseph Wright, Wm. McMurty. (RD) July 5, 1842, (CLK) John Ralls.

178) Second annual settlement of James Epperson, adm. of Joel Taylor, dec. August term, 1842.
No names given. (RD) August 3, 1843, (CLK) John Ralls.

179) Second annual settlement of Otho Brashears and Charles Rice, adm. of the estate of Thomas Hicklin, dec. August term, 1842.
Monies Expended: --- McMurty, Dr. Leake, Lewis Tracy, J. S. Crosthwait, --- Kereheval, Hancesford Brown, John Seely, N. T. Pierce,. (RD) August 31, 1842, (CLK) John Ralls.

180) Annual settlement of James D. Watson, exr. of the estate of John Watson, dec. August term, 1842.
Monies Expended: Wm. Watson, I. D. Palson, Wm. S. Seargeant. (RD) August 31, 1842, (CLK) John Ralls.

181) Second annual settlement of Stephen Glascock, exr. of the estate of Eli C. Galleher, dec. August term, 1842.
Monies Expended: --- McMurty, T. Rhodes, H. Meredith, Caleb N. Galleher, French Glascock, G. C. Hays, Chapman P. Green, I. L. Canterbery. (RD) August 31, 1842, (CLK) John Ralls.

182) Final settlement of Elizabeth Wilson, adm. of the estate of Presley Wilson, dec. September term, 1832.
Monies Expended: Matthew Fife, John F. Hawkins, S. C. Anderson, Elizabeth Wilson. Filed by her agent, J. J. Slosson, (RD) September 5, 1842.

183) First annual settlement of William Forman, adm. of the estate of Mary Parker, dec. September Adjourned term, 1842.
Monies Received: William S. M'Eroy, S. Muldron, estate of Charles Glascock, dec., B. W. Horr, Joshua Mitchell, Charles Lamb.
Monies Expended: Floweree & Mennifee, F. Glascock, A. M. Williams, J. Mitchell, Wm. M. Priest, A. G. Galleher, William Forman, L. Tracy, J. S. Buckhannan, J. M. Johnston, T. Rhodes, George Waller, James S. Dimmitt, Solomon D. Parker. (RD) September 6, 1842, (CLK) John Ralls.

184) Second annual settle of Abraham Buford, adm. of the estate of John Buford, dec. September term, 1842.
Monies Expended: James Dunkin, Francis Conn, T. D. Reed, Jno. F. Hawkins, A. & W. McMurty. (RD) September 6, 1842, (CLK) John Ralls.

185) John Markle, jr. for F. I. Fealze, his guardian.
Monies Expended: O. Markles, --- Floweree, M. Daniel, James Barnet, S. Marsuson, S. Woods. (RD) October 3, 1842, (CLK) John Ralls.

186) Annual settlement of Benjamin Ely, adm. of Thomas Ely, dec. October term, 1842.
Slaves: Jack, Rachael.
Monies Expended: Mention of travel to New London and to Palmyra court in February, March and September of 1841. (RD) October 3, 1842. (CLK) John Ralls.

187) Annual settlement of Joel H. Epperson, adm. of the estate of Richard Epperson, dec. November term, 1842.
Monies Expended: Dr. McKay, Anthony Epperson, Alford Cox, Jas. Epperson, Washington Epperson, Dabney Jones, John Chitwood, William P. Young, Hays & Blair, Pathenia Epperson. (RD) November 7, 1842, (CLK) John Ralls.

188) First annaual settlement of Robert Bayley, adm. of the estate of Charles Bayley, dec. November term, 1842.

Monies Received: On a note from Charles W. Truitt due October 23, 1842, On a note from Arthur Scott due November 28, 1841, On a note from Peter Leonard due August 3, 1841, On a note from George Fisher due December 26, 1841, On a note from George Fisher due December 25, 1842, On a note from George Fisher due December 25, 1843, monies received from James Fuqua, constable.

Monies Expended: T. A. Haden, J. F. Epperson. (RD) November 7, 1842, (CLK) John Ralls.

189) Settlement of of William Priest, exr. of the estate of John Payne, dec. November term, 1842.

No names given. (RD) November 8, 1842, (CLK) John Ralls.

190) Settlement by James Creason, adm. The deceased name was not given. November term, 1842.

Monies Received: Rice Carter, Matthew Brooks.

Monies Expended: Cash paid to Isham Winn on September 22, 1842 for the making of a coffin. (RD) November 7, 1842, (CLK) John Ralls.

191) Second annual settlement of Alexander Buford and Abraham Buford, exrs. of the estate of Abraham Buford, sr., dec. November, 1842.

Monies Expended: On April 26, 1842 to J. Ralls, On November 11, 1841 to J. J. Slosson, On August 23, 1842 to R. H. M'Kay, On January 15, 1842 to A. & W. McMurty, On December 6, 1841 to Wm. G. Johnston, On December 6, 1841 to J. Ralls, On August 5, 1842 to T. S. Purdom, On August 5, 1842 to Tho. S. Miller. (RD) November 7, 1842, (CLK) John Ralls.

192) Third annual settlement of Elizabeth Offutt, adm. of the estate of Thorton F. Offutt, dec. November Adjourned term, 1842.

Monies Expended: Stephen Smith on November 12, 1840 for burial expenses, Flowerre & Neal, J. Dimmint, Mrs. Parker. (RD) December 5, 1842, (CLK) John Ralls.

193) Second annual settlement of James Culbertson, adm. of the estate of Catharine Bast. January term, 1843.

Monies Expended: J. Ralls, J. N. Griffin. (RD) January 2, 1843, (CLK) John Ralls.

194) Second annual settlement by James M. Leake, adm. of the estate of Joseph Pierceall, dec. January term, 1843.

Monies Expended: On June 8, 1841 to R. Pierceall, On June 8, 1841 to J. W. Leake, On November 1, 1841 to J. B. Gore, On November 4, 1841 to Jesse Boarman, On November 5, 1841 to R. J. Pierceall, On October 9, 1840 to Wm. Pulis, On December 18, 1840 to R. J. Pierceall, On December 18, 1840 to J. W. Leake, On December 21, 1840 to C. N. Lynch, On May 10, 1842 to J.I.T. McElory, On May 16, 1842 to Rasanna J. Pierceall. (RD) January 2, 1843, (CLK) John Ralls.

195) Annual settlement of James Inlow, adm. of the estate of P. P. Wright, dec. January term, 1843.

No names given. (RD) February 1, 1843, (CLK) John Ralls.
  196) Annual settlement of Abraham Seely, adm. of the estate of Nelly Johnston, dec. February term, 1843.
No names given. (RD) February 6, 1843, (CLK) John Ralls.
  197) First annual settlement of William Newland, adm. of the estate of John Ross, dec. February term, 1843.
No names given. (RD) February 6, 1843, (CLK) John Ralls.
  198) Final settlement of Neal Cameron, adm. of Joshua Robb, dec. February term, 1843.
Monies Expended: D. M'Creary, Jno. Ralls, S. Buchanan, John J. Slosson. (RD) February 6, 1843, (CLK) John Ralls.
  199) First annual settlement of James G. Wylie, adm. of the estate of Pleasant Cox, dec. February term, 1843.
Monies Expended: John Ralls, George W. Wallers, Harrison Adkins. (RD) February 7, 1843, (CLK) John Ralls.
  200) Settlement of Elizabeth Weaver, adm. of the estate of Tilman Weaver, dec. February term, 1843.
Monies Expended: John Ralls, William Priest. (RD) February 7, 1843, (CLK) John Ralls.
  201) Third annual settlement of French Glascock, adm. of the estate of Charles Glascock, dec. February term, 1843.
Monies Received: Jas. Cochran, William T. T. Swan, John R. Floweree, William Priest, Thos. Priest, Jno. M. Johnston.
Monies Expended: Lewis Garnett, Wm. Bull, J. C. Barrett, Jas. Fisher, B. McPherson, --- Smith, Jesse Carter, Jas. J. Green, S. Glascock, Wm. Beebe, William Lyager, Lucy J. Glascock, Wilkinson Crawford, Sewel Heperon, Thos. P. Norton, Hiram Glascock, George C. Hays, Maria Dodd, Jno. W. Johnston. (RD) February 3, 1843, (CLK) John Ralls.
  202) First annual settlement by Samuel K. Caldwell, adm. of the estate of James D. Caldwell, dec. April term, 1843.
Monies Expended: On June 30, 1842 to Chapel Carstarphen, October 15, 1842 to Lewis Tracy, On August 12, 1842 to James Turley, On August 12, 1842 to G. C. Hays, On June 3, 1842 to Thos. A. Purdom, On August 12, 1842 to Lewis Tracy, On August 12, 1842 to Saml. M'Gowen, On January 15, 1842 to R. C. Caldwell, On December 2, 1841 to Alexr. M'Gaw, On December 4, 1841 to Benedict Little, On December 4, 1841 to H. Northcutt, On August --, 1842 to Hugh Emerson. (RD) April 3, 1843, (CLK) John Ralls.
  203) Final settlement of Chapel Carstarphen, adm. of the estate of William R. Bown, dec. April term, 1843.
Monies Expended: A.B. Combs, A. & W. M'Murty, J. Garrish, G. C. hays, John Ralls, Arthur Menefee. (RD) April 3, 1843, (CLK) John Ralls.
  204) John Newton, ad. of the estate of Gerrard, Newton, dec. May term, 1843.
Monies Received: Land in Marion County mentioned.
Monies Expended: Thos. S. Wilson, N. T. Pierce, Stephen

Smith, James Taylor, James Neal, Gerrard Newton, dec., Dr. E. H. James. John Ralls, John J. Slosson. (RD) May 1, 1843, (CLK) John Ralls.

205) First Annual settlement by James Inlow, exr. of Harvey M'Gown, dec. May term, 1843.
Notes On: Claborn Clark, Harper Wilson, David Clark, Wm. Darvel, Jeptha S. Crosthwait, John A. Woods, Benona Brice, Washington Epperson, Stephen Ems, James Bur, Robt. Sloss, Elmore Haze, James Crosthwait, John Fletcher, Thomas Brooks. (RD) May 1, 1843, (CLK) John Ralls.

206) First annual settlement of Jacob Zimmerman, exr. of the estate of Silas Crigler, dec. May term, 1843.
Monies Recieved: $206.17 cash on hand at the time of death of the deceased on May 1, 1842. Bank of Illinois mentioned.
Monies Expended: John Ralls, R. Wright. (RD) May 1,1843, (CLK) John Ralls.

207) Settlement by George Hardy, adm. of the estate of Wm. Pulis, dec. June term, 1843.
Monies Received: Benjamin Ely, Coleman D. Stone, David Blue, Thomas P. Norton. (RD) June 5, 1843, (CLK) John Ralls.

208) First annual settlement by John A. Wright and Corbin Berm, exrs. of the estate of Joseph Wright, dec. June term, 1843.
Monies Received: Abraham Liter, Job Mace, Wm. C. Wright, J. A. Wright, --- Daniel.
Monies Expended: P. N. Smith, J. Hildreth, T. A. Purdom, John Buford, dec., Wm. Krigbaum, James Hults, James Hawkins, J. Ralls, --- Markle, --- Taliaferro, Wm. Anderson, On June, 1842 to Thomas Cleaver, On June, 1842 to D. Jones, On June, 1842 to R. Vermillion, On June, 1842 to L. L. Smith, On June, 1842 to Wm. O. Young, On June, 1842 to Isaac Dreyfus, On June, 1842 to John J. Ely, On June, 1842 to --- Briggs, On June, 1842 to S. A. Wright, On January 2, 1843 to G. C. Hays, On January 2, 1843 to Dabney Jones, On January 25, 1843 to J. D. Tapley, On January 29, 1843 to N. Ledford, On February 6, 1843 to to J. Buford, adm., On February 9, 1843 to Anderson Briscoe, On September 2, 1842 to A. W. Perdew, On February 20, 1843 to Taylor Jones, On May 14, 1843 to James G. Wylie, On April 4, 1843 to J. J. Slosson, On April 8, 1843 to James Small, On April 8, 1843 to R. S. Wright, On June 6, 1843 to J. A. Wright, On June 6, 1843 to J. Ralls, On June 6, 1843 to --- Smith, On June 2, 1843 to --- Sisk, On June 2, 1843 Heath Jones, On June 2, 1843 to C. Berm, On June 6, 1843 to James S. Ledford, On June 10, 1843 to Wm. Briggs, On June 20, 1843 to J. C. Welbern, On June 20, 1843 to --- Anderson, On June 22, 1843 to J. D. Briggs, guardian of J. S. Ledford, On June 23, 1843 to Wm. C. Wright, On June 24, 1843 to S. B. Wright, assignee of A & W McMurty, On De-

cember 20, 1842 to J. A. Wright, On July 1, 1843 to J. A. Wright, On June 10, 1843 to R. Vermillion, On July 3, 1843 to J. C. Williams, On July 3, 1843 to S. B. Wright, On July 3, 1843 to J. A. Wright. (RD) July 3, 1843, (CLK) J. Ralls.

209) First annual settlement by James Epperson, adm. of the estate of Margaret Ann Mills, dec. David Mills was the former administrator. May term, 1843.

Monies Expended:    James Epperson, William R. Gilbert, Thoms G. Mills, Tyre A. Haden, James Shohong, John Ralls. (RD) July 33, 1843, (CLK) John Ralls.

210) Settlement of Margaret M. Davis, adm. of the estate of her late husband, Robt. Davis, dec. June term, 1843.

Heirs on April 4, 1842:  Malinda Davis, Catharine Davis, Adaline Davis, Robert M. Davis. (RD) July 10, 1843, (CLK) John Ralls.

211) Third annual settlement of Daniel B. Kendrick and Guilford D. Hansboroguh, exrs. of the estate of Harvey Wilson, dec. May term, 1843.

Monies Expended:    Narcissus Wilson, G. L. Hardy, Thos. Brashears, N. T. Pierce, Martin Lyle, Stephen T. Elliott, D. Kendrick, Elizabeth Wilson, John Ralls. (RD) July 10, 1843, (CLK) John Ralls.

212) Final settlement of James Epperson. adm. of the estate of Joel Taylor, dec. August term, 1843.

No names given. (RD) August 7, 1843, (CLK) John Ralls.

213) Settlement of James D. Watson, exr. of John Watson, dec. August term, 1843.

No names given. (RD) August 7, 1843, (CLK) John Ralls.

214) Annual settlement of Benjamin (last name not given- probably - Ely), adm. of the estate of Thomas Ely, dec. August term, 1843.

Monies Expended:  G.L. Hardy. (RD) August 7, 1843, (CLK) John Ralls.

215) First annual settlement of John F. Leake and George L. Hardy, exrs. of the estate of James Leake, dec. August, 1843.

Monies Received:  Y. L. Anderson, J. B. Leake.

Insolvent Notes on May 21, 1842:  E. Poindexter, William Meteers, Robert Irwin, Benjamin Lee.

Monies Expended:  On July 9, 1842 to L. S. Anderson for coffin, On October 14, 1842 to B. Rolandoe, clergyman, On July 16, 1843 to Dr. McLroy, On July 12, 1843 to John D. Biggs, On July 28, 1843 to C. N. Lynch and E. L. Bell, On July 28, 1843 to Benjamin Ely, On July 28, 1843 to J. S. Crosthwait, On August 5, 1843 to Otho Brashear, On February 4, 1843 to F. Bowles, On June 10, 1843 to R. M. Brashears, On June 10, 1843 to William Leake, as an heir, On June 10, 1843 to James B. Leake, as an heir, On August 9, 1843 to James F. Mahan, June 10, 1842 to Wm. Leake, On June 10, 1842

John Blue. (RD) August 14, 1843, (CLK) John Ralls.

216) First annual settlement of James Culbertson, adm. of Isaac Bast, dec. October, 1843.

Monies Received: Adam Bast, William Alfred, Willis M. Jamison, Casper Oardy, One account on Peter and George Bast dated 1820 and 1821, Peter Bast, Thomas Mayhall, Simeon Davis, Moses Bast, George Bast.

Monies Expended: Moses Bast, Catharine Bast, Samuel W. Mayhall, William Bast, Lewis Tracy, John L. Smith, Willis M. Jamison, John Ralls, Isaac Bast, French Glascock, Casper Hardy, John Thomas Mayhall, Peter & George Bast, (RD) October 2, 1843, (CLK) John Ralls.

217) Final settlement of Raphael Leake, adm. of the estate of John R. Gillespie, dec. August Adjourned term, 1843.

Monies Expended: Wm. C. Gillespie; On January, 1840 to Wm. Maddox; On January, 1840 to Joseph Pierceale; On January 25, 1843 to Wm. C. Gillespie; On November, 1842 to Wm. C. Gillespie; On August 6, 1838 to Saml. Smith; On July 5, 1842 to Dr. Jett; On March, 1840 to Wm. Gillespie on a suit before Richd. Boyer; On March 6, 1843 to N. Shannon, J. Ralls, B. Davis, R. Wright. (RD) October 2, 1843, (CLK) John Ralls.

218) Second annual settlement of Joel H. Epperson, adm. of the estate of Richard Epperson, dec. November term, 1843.

Monies Expended: On November 12, 1842 to Dr. Welbourn; On June 19, 1843 to Jacob Sasey; On May 21, 1843 to James Epperson; On September 12, 1843 to Peter Smelson; On August 8, 1843 to James Epperson; On August 8, 1843 to Anthony Epperson; On August 8, 1843 to Richard Epperson; On August 8, 1843 to Parthenia Epperson; On August 8, 1843 to Edmund Bailey, guardian for William Epperson; On July 1, 1843 to John Epperson; On August 8, 1843 to Little Berry Epperson; On August 8, 1843 to Samuel Epperson; On November 6, 1843 to William S. Lofland; On November 6, 1843 to John Ralls.

Bad Notes: James Eals, George Eals, Squire Brothers, A. C. Hawkins, James M. Creason, William Fuqua, Samuel McGowen, Luke W. Watkins. (RD) November 6, 1843, (CLK)John Ralls.

219) Annual settlement of Henry C. Wolfe, adm. of the estate of Ira Sheckle, dec. November term, 1843.

Monies Received: R. Redish, James Figgon. (RD) November 6. 1843, (CLK) John Ralls.

220) Second annual settlement of Robert Baley, adm. of Charles Baley, dec. November term, 1843.

Monies Expended: Robert Bayley (sic), George Fisher, James Shohony, jr., Edmund Baley, Isham R. Winn, Jacob Rouland, John Ralls, (RD) November 6, 1842, (CLK) J. Ralls.

221) Settlement of William Forman, adm. of the estate of Mary Parker, dec. November term, 1843.

Monies Expended: Henry Collins, James & Meredith, James

Withers, William R. Harris, Jacob Long, French Glascock, James S. Dimmitt, David Ford's admr., Hannah Tapley, Wm. Forman, A. & W. Mc Murty, Hays & Blair, Thomas Cleaver, S. McPherson, J. V. D. Bergen, Simon Davis, Jos. Rice, J. R. Garrett. (RD) November 7, 1843, (CLK) John Ralls.

222) Chas. F. Clayton, agent, makes a statement for the administrator. However neither the deceased nor the administrator's name appears in the statement. November term, 1843.

Monies Expended: J. Sasey, French Glascock, Jno. J. Campbell, Jacob Sasey. (RD) November 7, 1843, (CLK) John Ralls.

223) Third annual settlement of Jeremiah B. Vardeman and William H. Vardeman, executors of the estate of Jeremiah Vardeman, dec. November term, 1843.

Monies Expended: Peter Smelson, Dr. James, Dr. Meredith, William Shuck, G.C. Hays, Moses Bast, Thomas O. Rhodes. (RD) November 7, 1843, (CLK) John Ralls.

<u>Lawrence County, Missouri, Liberty Methodist Church Cemetery, Twnshp. 26, Ran. 27, Sec.16, (Note: Persons Born Before 1840 and Who Died Before 1900 Are Not Included In This Listing)</u>

| Name | Birth | Death |
|---|---|---|
| Charles L. Bailey | Feb. 3, 1884 | Mar. 10, 1949 |
| Lottie E. Bailey | Jun. 14, 1889 | Jan. 16, 1970 |
| John R. Bandy | 1872 | 1960 |
| Nancy E. Bandy | 1871 | 1954 |
| Mabel F. Bandy | Feb. 22, 1896 | Aug. 20, 1971 |
| Loren F. Bandy | Apr. 5, 1896 | --- |
| Matilda A. Banta | Oct. 6, 1884 | --- |
| William F. Bauer | Dec. 16, 1883 | May 24. 1969 |
| Henry Bauer | Feb. 21, 1842 | Mar. 18, 1921 |
| Elizabeth Bauer | May 13, 1857 | Oct. 2, 1944 |
| Robert Bauer | Dec. 16, 1890 | Sep. 5, 1918 |
| Mildred Beckett | Jan. 20, 1894 | Jul. 25, 1967 |
| Troy R. Beckett | Oct. 8, 1890 | Sep. 26, 1952 |
| Lillie May Beckett | Nov. 20, 1871 | Oct. 19, 1927 |
| G. W. Beckett | Oct. 3, 1860 | Jan. 5, 1947 |
| John S. Benbrook | Apr. 7, 1842 | Jun. 12, 1914 |
| Susan E. Benbrook | Feb. 3, 1844 | --- |
| John T. Benbrook | 1876 | 1934 |
| Boyd Browning | Sep. 22, 18 (?) | Mar. 3, 1895 |
| Marie Browning | Oct. 19, 1897 | --- |
| Martha C. Caldwell | 1868 | 1969 |
| Frank O. Caldwell | Jun. 30, 1887 | Nov. 23, 1856 |
| Thomas Caldwell | Feb. 12, 1894 | Jul. 4, 1957 |
| Georgia Ann Caldwell | 1861 | 1936 |
| Ollie May Caldwell | Mar. 31, 1892 | Mar. 19, 1966 |
| Samuel R. Cook | Jun. 30, 1894 | Feb. 1, 1972 |
| Stella B. Cook | Nov. 16, 1892 | Mar. 19, 1966 |

| Name | Birth | Death |
|---|---|---|
| Y. E. Costley | 1868 | 1961 |
| Lelia Costley | 1873 | 1958 |
| Opal Costley | Jul. 15, 1898 | --- |
| Merritt Costley | Feb. 18, 1895 | Sep. 24, 1981 |
| Robert E. Costley | Nov. 22, 1893 | May 7, 1974 |
| O. Cresco | 1895 | 1971 |
| William S. Dawson | Oct. 28, 1869 | Dec. 10, 1953 |
| Bertha Dawson | Dec. 21, 1875 | Dec. 18, 1950 |
| Eva May Fennel | May 5, 1887 | Mar. 21, 1976 |
| Thomas J. Fletcher | 1865 | 1948 |
| Martha Fletcher | 1865 | 1943 |
| Emmett Fletcher | Oct. 23, 1896 | Aug. 22, 1959 |
| Lillie Fletcher | Oct. 15, 1899 | Jun. 21, 1959 |
| Zena Jane Fletcher | 1889 | 1937 |
| Frances Fletcher | Jan. 27, 1877 | Jan. 1, 1958 |
| Sam Fletcher | Feb. 24, 1874 | Aug. 29, 1941 |
| Hattie Mae Fletcher | 1899 | 1920 |
| Sam Fletcher | Feb. 24, 1874 | Aug. 29, 1841 |
| Albert R. Fletcher | 1880 | 1973 |
| Edw. Gaydon | May 8, 1887 | Nov. 13, 1957 |
| Lynna G. Gaydon | Aug. 15, 1890 | May 3, 1931 |
| Ernest Gray | 1886 | 1957 |
| Maple B. Gray | 1890 | 1959 |
| Lewtishie Griener | 1864 | 1939 |
| J. C. Harvey | Aug. 25, 1870 | Jan. 27, 1922 |
| Ellen P. Harvey | 1867 | 1918 |
| Enoch A. Hemphill | Aug. 14, 1892 | Mar. 1, 1859 |
| Kate C. Hemphill | Feb. 18, 1892 | Jan. 28, 1977 |
| Chloe Henson | Jul. 26, 1898 | Mar. 21, 1961 |
| John F. Jenkins | 1862 | 1917 |
| Thomas J. Jenkins | 1871 | 1948 |
| Clara Jenkins | 1890 | 1937 |
| Wm. M. Jenkins | Jan. 13, 1865 | Aug. 16, 1957 |
| Caroline E. Jenkins | Jan. 5, 1882 | May 15, 1965 |
| Thomas W. Jenkins | Oct. 18, 1895 | Apr. 30, 1924 |
| Robert L. Jenkins | 1867 | 1941 |
| Ida O. Jenkins | 1868 | 1944 |
| Joseph F. Jenkins | Jan. 24, 1898 | May 13, 1979 |
| Beulah Bell Matthews | Dec. 8, 1888 | Jul. 3, 1964 |
| Rhoda E. Matthews | Feb. 22, 1894 | --- |
| *Robert L. Matthews | May 25, 1843 | 1918 |
| *(Born: Tennessee) | | |
| Elizabeth A. Matthews | 1856 | 1929 |
| Archie B. Matthews | 1882 | 1968 |
| Samuel D. McCormack | Nov. 26, 1865 | Aug. 9, 1937 |
| Mary A. McCormack | Apr. 15, 1868 | Jun. 27, 1915 |
| Samuel M. McCormack | Aug. 25, 1873 | Dec. 17, 1925 |
| Sarah J. McCormack | May 30, 1875 | Feb. 9, 1943 |

| Name | Birth | Death |
|---|---|---|
| Wm. E. McCormack | Jun. 13, 1866 | Jun. 30, 1947 |
| James A. McCormack | Aug. 25, 1889 | Jul. 29, 1964 |
| Ethel M. McCormack | Apr. 17, 1892 | Mar. 20, 1865 |
| Virgil E. McCormack | 1891 | 1966 |
| Mary E. McCormack | 1869 | 1938 |
| Marshall C. McKee | Jul. 30, 1881 | May 22, 1965 |
| August D. Meier | Jan. 31, 1889 | Feb. 24, 1973 |
| Fannie A. Mulkey | Aug. 17, 1870 | Mar. 6, 1922 |
| Loren F. Mulkey | Dec. 15, 1890 | Jan. 30, 1973 |
| Delmer L. Mulkey | May 11, 1896 | Sep. 20, 1944 |
| George D. Mulkey | Dec. 5, 1874 | Sep. 21, 1939 |
| Loren F. Mulkey | Dec. 15, 1890 | Jan. 30, 1973 |
| Sadie J. Mulkey | Nov. 26, 1874 | Sep. 21, 1939 |
| Landon Mulkey | 1890 | 1931 |
| James E. Mulkey | Oct. 21, 1872 | Dec. 7, 1938 |
| Cora F. Mulkey | 1892 | --- |
| Hilda L. Mulkey | Feb. 10, 1878 | Mar. 31, 1954 |
| Gladys G. Mulkey | Apr. 22, 1894 | May 26, 1969 |
| Elmer C. Mulkey | Oct. 26, 1895 | Apr. 17, 1969 |
| Alvey A. Mulkey | 1885 | 1916 |
| Florence P. Mulkey | Feb. 2, 1896 | --- |
| Margaret Mulkey | 1849 | 1927 |
| William H. Mulkey | 1849 | 1940 |
| Ollie B. Mulkey | Sep. 7, 1878 | Feb. 10, 1968 |
| David M. Mulkey | Apr 1, 1880 | Mar. 20, 1947 |
| Nellie Mulkey | Jul. 6, 1873 | Oct. 9, 1908 |
| John W. Mulkey | Sep. 4, 1870 | Aug. 3, 1948 |
| Martin L. Peterson | 1894 | 1969 |
| Gertie Peterson | 1894 | 1928 |
| Susan F. Pharriss | May 27, 1836 | Jan. 22, 1915 |
| Florence F. Smith | Dec. 2, 1894 | --- |
| Frank E. Smith | May 24, 1897 | --- |
| James A. St. Clair | Nov. 30, 1872 | Jul. 5, 1952 |
| Lillian L. St. Clair | Sep. 9, 1881 | Jun. 25, 1863 |
| Ira J. Stockton | Aug. 1, 1887 | Apr. 27, 1950 |
| Edith Stockton | Jul. 1, 1896 | May 21, 1984 |
| Olive M. Strong | Jul. 22, 1899 | --- |
| Ealon H. Strong | Sep. 5, 1897 | Dec. 7, 1969 |
| John D. Thomas | 1878 | 1958 |
| Laura F. Thomas | 1868 | 1954 |
| Robert L. Todd | 1872 | --- |
| Laura B. Todd | 1873 | 1939 |
| Willis M. Todd | Jun. 21, 1899 | Oct. 7, 1954 |
| Harry D. Vantuyl | Mar. 6, 1858 | May 15, 1929 |
| Warren H. Vantuyl | Oct. 11, 1892 | Feb. 8, 1949 |
| Louisa A. Vantuyl | Jun. 20, 1894 | --- |
| Talmage Vantuyl | Oct. 9, 1893 | Oct. 14, 1953 |
| Bernice Vantuyl | Mar. 28, 1897 | Dec. 15, 1982 |

| Name | Birth | Death |
|---|---|---|
| James M. Weldy | 1848 | --- |
| A. J. Weldy | Jul. 30, 1881 | Jun. 1, 1913 |
| James M. Weldy | 1878 | 1941 |
| Eliza J. Weldy | 1845 | 1915 |
| Margaret F. Weldy | 1883 | 1938 |
| Florence Mulkey Wilks | Apr. 3, 1893 | Jun. 8, 1941 |
| Oness W. Wilks | Mar. 28, 1886 | Dec. 20, 1952 |
| May Wilks | Mar. 13, 1890 | Jun. 23, 1955 |
| Herman Wilks | 1890 | --- |
| Cora Wilks | 1891 | 1939 |
| Dee C. Winton | Dec. 15, 1886 | May 22, 1966 |
| Myrtle Winton | Jun. 13, 1888 | Jun. 25, 1968 |
| Barnett C. Wolfe | Aug. 18, 1861 | Aug. 26, 1922 |
| Sarah E. Wolfe | Nov. 26, 1860 | May 15, 1923 |
| Carl B. Wolfe | 1886 | 1943 |

## Cedar County, Missouri, Death Register, 1883 - 1886.

1)   Sarah Clark, single, b. Christian Co., Ill, Lived in Missouri for three months, d. Eldorado Springs, burial by Smith & Simpson, Eldorado Springs, age 19 y, d. July 25, 1883, Dr. J. B. Phipps.

2)   Noah E. Carpenter, b. Bates County, Mo., b. Eldorado Springs, July 25, 1882, age 1 y, 4 m, 13 d, burial by Smith & Simpson at Eldorado Springs, Dr. J. B. Phipps.

3)   Susan J. Ryan, b. Jefferson Co., Tn., Lived in Missouri thirty-six years, d. Eldorado Springs on July 21,1883, age 61 y, 8 m, 13 d, burial at Clintonville by Smith & Simpson, Dr. J. B. Phipps.

4)   Virgil Hansford, b. Texas, d. Eldorado Springs, August 18, 1883, age 4 y, burial in Texas, Dr. W. E. Dawson, Clinton, Missouri.

5)   W. F. Fortney, d. Cedar Co., August 14, 1883, age 5 m, 3 d, Dr. W. C. McMillen.

6)   Thomas Parkasan, d. Eldorado Springs, August 9,1883, age 10 m, 3 d, burial Eldorado Springs by Smith & Simpson, Dr. J. B. Phipps.

7)   John Keiser, b. Cedar Co., d. Box township, July 29, 1883, age 1 y, 9 m, 11 d, burial at Clintonville by Smith & Simpson, Dr. J. B. Phipps.

8)   Aquilla T. Thurman, b. Vernon Co., Mo., d. Box township, July 25, 1883, age 3 y, 4 m, 13 d, burial at Eldorado Springs by Smith & Simpson, Dr. J. B. Phipps.

9)   Nancy M. Smith, married, b. Cooper Co., d. Eldorado Springs, July 28, 1883, age 20 y, burial Eldorado Springs by Smith & Simpson, Dr. J. Phipps.

10)   Isaac Crook, widower, farmer, b. Tennessee, Visiting in Missouri, d. Eldorado Springs, August 22, 1883, age

11) Alta Wayne Enex, b. Stockton, Mo., German nationality, d. Stockton, Mo. September 9, 1883, age 1 y, 7 m, 22 d, burial Stockton by W. F. Dunaway & Co., Dr. R. A. Brown.

12) Cora Ellen Freeman, b. Benton township, Cedar Co., d. Benton township, September 3, 1883 age 1 y, 5 m, burial in Cedar County by Brasker & Ragan.

13) A. M. Pyle, single, male, farmer, b. Cedar Co., d. South Benton township, September 26, 1883, age 20 y, burial at Gum Springs Cemetery, Dr. J. B. Brasher, Jericho Springs.

14) B. F. Mclane, single, male, miner, b. Ohio, Lived in Missouri for 18 years, d. southwest of Jericho Springs, September, 10, 1883, age 24 y, 1 m, 20 d, burial two and a half miles northwest of Jericho Springs by G. M. Wallace.

15) James M. O'Conner, married, farmer, b. Jackson Co., Mo., Lived in Missouri for 52 years, d. Cedar Co. July 31, 1883, age 64 y, 2 m, 3 d, burial in Cedar Co. by Dunaway & Wilderson, Dr. W. B. Perry.

16) Eullia Yager, b. Eldorado Springs, d. Eldorado Spr., october 1, 1883, age 6 m 20 d, burial at Eldorado Springs by Miran Gipson, Dr. Wm. H. Younger.

17) Female baby, b. & d. September 17, 1883, age 1 d, burial at Stockton by Dunaway & Wilderson, Dr. W. B. Perry.

18) Female baby, b. & d. Cedar Co. May 23, 1883, burial st Stockton Cemetery by Dunaway & Wilderson, Dr. W.B. Perry.

19) Wilson S. Curry, b. Mountry (sic) Co., Ill., Lived in Missouri 2 y, 9 m, 2 d, d. Eldorado Springs, October 2, 1883, age 14 y, 5 m, 14 d, burial at Clintonville by J. J. Smith, Dr. Wm. H. H. Younger.

20) Sallee Elizabeth Ryan, b. Cedar Co., d. Eldorado Springs, September 27, 1883, age 1 y, 8 m, 16 d, burial at Clintoville by Smith & Simpson, Dr. J. B. Phipps.

21) Clarence W. Huff, b. Cedar Co., d. Cedar Co., Septe,mber 4, 1883, age; 2 y, 7 m, 27 d, burial at Hebron Cemtery, Dr. M. B. Wooldridge, Bear Creek, Mo.

22) Henry Isham, b. Ceadr Co., d. Cedar Co., July 12, 1883, age 2 y, 3 m, 9 d, burial at Lindley Praire Cemetery, Dr. M. B. Wooldridge, Bear Creek, Mo.

23) James Hess, b. Missouri, d. Cedar Co., July 23,1883, age 1 y, 9 m, 3 d, Burial at Lindley Praire Cemtery, Dr. M.B. Wooldridge, Break Creek, Mo.

24) Sarah Asbell, b. Cedar Co., d. Madison township, November 8, 1883, age 9 m, burial at Lindley Praire Cemetery, Dr. Wm. H. Harris.

25) Elizabeth Routh, widow b. Tennessee, Welch nationality, Lived in Missouri 42 years, d. Five miles south of Stockton, November 7, 1883, age 83 y, 8 m, 6 d, burial at Gum Springs, Dr. R. A. Brown, Stockton.

26) Wm. Osborn, married, farmer, b. Polk Co., Missouri, d. Jefferson township, July 12, 1883, age 38 y, 7 m, burial

27) Walter Ward: b. Cedar Co., d. Madison township, October 6, 1883, age: 8 y, 28 d, buried: Dade Co., Dr. J. E. Alder, Cane Hill, Mo.

28) Lewis M. Beason: b. Cedar Co., d. Jefferson township, July 1, 1883, 2 y, 11 d, buried: Tinker Graveyard, Dr. Wm. H. Harris.

29) B. A. Marshall: married, farmer, b. Mecklenburg Co., Va., lived in Missouri 33 years, d. Madison township, October 31, 1883, age: 82 y, 11 m, 20 d, Dr. Wm. H. Harris.

30) James Moser: b. Cedar Co., d. Madison township, October 2, 1883, age: 1 y, 8 m, 2 d, buried: Lindley Praire Cemetery, Dr. Wm. H. Harris.

31) Thalier E. Rickman: b. Cedar Co., d. Madison township, July 28, 1883, age: 6 y, 11 d, buried: Lindley Praire Cemetery, Dr. Wm. H. Harris.

32) Elly Jane Taylor: b. Cedar Co., d. Madison township, September 1, 1883, age: 1 y, 2 m, buried: Lindley Praire cemetery, Dr. Wm. H. Harris.

33) Fanny Osburn: b. Polk Co., Mo., d. Jefferson township, July 13, 1883, age: 1 y, 16 d, Dr. Wm. Harris.

34) Henruetta Briscoe: married, b. Appomattox Co., Va., d. Stockton, November 6, 1883, age: 58 y, buried: Stockton Cemtery by Dunaway and Wilderson, Dr. Perry.

## Audrain County, Missouri, Taxable Property, 1843, County Roll No. C445.

| Owner | Free Males | Acres | Original Claimant |
|---|---|---|---|
| Edward Beaty | | 80 | A. Day |
| Edward Beaty | | 40 | A. Day |
| Edward Beaty | | 80 | Wm. Reynolds |
| Edward Beaty | | 20 | Levi Day |
| Edward Beaty | | 160 | H. B. Yale |
| Edward Beaty | | 80 | --- |
| Edward Beaty | | 11 | Zach. Ridgeway |
| Jacob Bruce | 1 | | |
| Laben T. Brown | 1 | 80 (2x) | |
| Coleburn Brown | 1 | | |
| Timthy (sic) Barney | 1 | 40 | Andy Still |
| Morton Blankenship | 1 | | |
| Neal Blue | | 40 | |
| Neal Blue | | 80 (2x) | |
| John Blue | 1 | | |
| Martilus Biba (sic) | 1 | | |
| Lawrence Boggs | 1 | | |
| John W. Barnes | 1 | 40 | Thos. Barnet |
| John W. Barnes | | 40 | |
| John W. Barnes | | 80 | |
| William Brown | 1 | | |
| Elizabeth Berry | | 80 | Powel Riggs |

| Owner | Free Males | Acres | Original Claimant |
|---|---|---|---|
| Thomas Brashear | 1 | | |
| Henry Berry | 1 | | |
| William I. Berry | 1 | | |
| Thos. --ckley | 1 | (Note: Corner missing from page) | |
| Moses M. ---ns | 1 | 40 | |
| Moses M. ---ns | | 80 | |
| John Brown | 1 | | |
| Thos. Brown | 1 | 20 (2x) | John Allen |
| Joseph Beaty | 1 | 177 | E. Beaty |
| Isaac Black | 1 | 80 | Jas. Pearson |
| Isaac Black | | 80 (2x) | |
| Isaac Black | | 91 | G. Read |
| Nancy Brown | | 40 | A. L. Reynolds |
| Nancy Brown | | 10 | |
| Thos. Bradley | 1 | 20 | M. Oslin |
| Thos. Bradley | | 80 | J. S. Oslin |
| John J. Bradley | 1 | | |
| Edward Bradley | 1 | | |
| Wm. Bradley | 1 | | |
| Elias Brooks | 1 | (lined out and marked error) | |
| William Byrns | 1 | 40 (2x) | |
| Richard Byrns | 1 | 40 | |
| Ruefus Bruce | 1 | | |
| Joseph Crocket | 1 | 40 | A. Harrison |
| Joseph Crocket | | 40 | A. Harrison |
| Joseph Crocket | | 80 | A. Harrison |
| Saml. Campbell | 1 | 40 (4x) | Mary Campbell |
| John Campbell | 1 | | |
| Reuben M. Canterbury | 1 | 80 | |
| Reuben M. Canterbury | | 40 | |
| Franklin P. Canterbury | 1 | 80 | |
| Franklin P. Canterbury | | 40 | |
| Alfred Cauthorn | 1 | lot in Mexico | |
| Allen Cauthorn | 1 | | |
| Geo. W. Cardwell | 1 | 80 (3x) | |
| Geo. W. Cardwell | | 80 (4x) | Wyet Cardwell |
| Geo. W. Cardwell | | 40 (2x) | |
| Wm. N. Clark | | 160 | W. T. Metcalf |
| John Coil | 1 | 40 | John R. Tenison |
| John Coil | | 40 | Bailey Miller |
| John Coil | | 80 (2x) | Wm. McCormick |
| John Coil | | 40 | Wm. McCormick |
| John Coil | | 40 | Wm. Williams |
| John Coil | | 40 | Wm. Lorton |
| John Coil | | 32 | Wm. Jones |
| Trustee of Maryan E. Lakin | | ? | |
| Guardian of Elizabeth A. Lakin | | ? | |
| John Clark | 1 | | |

| Owners | Free Males | Acres | Original Claimant |
|---|---|---|---|
| Isaac Clark | 1 | 40 | Jas. McCormick |
| Isaac Clark | | 40 | |
| Wm. N. Campbell | 1 | 40 | I. Irvin |
| Wm. N. Campbell | | 43 | Jas. Fields |
| Thos. Couch | 1 | 40 | |
| Thos. Couch | | 80 (2x) | |
| Chas. H. Carter | 1 | | |
| John C. Canterberry | 1 | 40 | |
| John C. Canterberry | | 80 | |
| John C. Canterberry | | 40 | Isham Willingham |
| Benjamin Canterberry | | 40 | |
| Benjamin Canterberry | | 80 | |
| Augustin Creed | | 80 (3x) | |
| Augustin Creed | | 40 (2x) | |
| John Creed | 1 | | |
| Augustin T. Creed | 1 | | |
| Jas. M. Creed | 1 | | |
| James Cauthorn | 1 | 105 | |
| James Cauthorn | | 40 (2x) | |
| Carter Cauthorn | 1 | 40 (2x) | |
| Carter Cauthorn | | 80 (2x) | A. Daniel |
| Carter Cauthorn | | 41 | |
| Carter Cauthorn | | 172 | |
| Lawrence Canterberry | 1 | | |
| John P. Clark | 1 | | |
| Wm. Cardwell | 1 | 188 | |
| Wm. Cardwell | | 80 | |
| Paul Cauthorn | 1 | 40 | |
| Paul Cauthorn | | 80 | |
| Silas Cauthorn | 1 | | |
| Peter Cauthorn | 1 | 40 (2x) | David Cauthorn |
| David Cauthorn | 1 | 40 (3x) | |
| David Cauthorn | | 80 | |
| John Charlton | | 40 (2x) | |
| John Charlton | | 80 (2x) | Lawrence Boggs |
| John H. Charlton | 1 | 80 (2x) | |
| Housen Canady | 1 | | |
| Joel Crosswhite | 1 | | |
| John A. Crosswhite | 1 | 80 | P. N. Mahan |
| John A. Crosswhite | | 80 | |
| John A. Crosswhite | | 40 | William Hukel |
| John A. Crosswhite | | 40 | J. I. Mosley |
| John A. Crosswhite | | 20-1/2 | |
| John A. Crosswhite | | 20 | |
| John A. Crosswhite | | 40 (2x) | |
| Jas. Crosswhite | 1 | 97 | M. Step |
| David Crosswhite | 1 | | |
| Wm. Crosswhite | 1 | 55 | Wm. Freeman |

| Owners | Free Males | Acres | Original Claimant |
|---|---|---|---|
| Wm. Crosswhite | | 55 | John Crosswhite |
| Wm. Crosswhite | 1 | 80 | Wm. Heckel |
| Wm. Crosswhite | | 160 | Wm. Heckel |
| Wm. Crosswhite | | 16 | Michael Step |
| Wm. Crosswhite | | 40 | I. L. Delaney |
| Wm. Crosswhite | | 40 | D. Cooper |
| Wm. Crosswhite | | 182 | |
| Wm. Crosswhite | | 41 | |
| John Creasy | 1 | 80 | |
| Peter Creasy | 1 | 34 | F. Armistead |
| John C. Casidy | 1 | 80 | E. Hall |
| Robert Calhoun | 1 | 184 | M. Dysert |
| Thadius Clendenon | 1 | 80 | M. Dysert |
| James Cook | 1 | | |
| H. I. M. Doan and Phelby Martin, adm. of the estate of John Martin, dec. | | 40 | B. Kilgore |
| Elisha Damsel | 1 | 80 | G. W. Grayson |
| Augustin Damsel | 1 | | |
| Carter & John Dingle | 2 | 40 | T. M. Barnet |
| Carter & John Dingle | | 106 | H. I. M. Doan |
| Carter & John Dingle | | 80 | T. M. Barnet |
| Carter & John Dingle | | 80 | |
| Carter & John Dingle | | 40 | |
| Washington Dilion | 1 | | |
| David Davis | 1 | 40 | Green Johnston |
| Spencer Davis | 1 | | |
| Simeon Davis | 1 | 80 | J. G. Patterson |
| Simeon Davis | | 40 | J. G. Patterson |
| Simeon Davis | | 80 | J. G. Patterson |
| George Davidson | | 60 | S. Paesy |
| Jas. M. Dennis | 1 | 40 (3x) | |
| William Dennis | 1 | | |
| Henry W. Dejaveret | 1 | 41 | E. Brink |
| Henry W. Dejaveret | | 40 | E. Brink |
| Henry W. Dejaveret | | 40 (2x) | |
| William T. Dollins | 1 | | |
| William B. Douglas | 1 | 80 | |
| William B. Douglas | | 72 | |
| William B. Douglas | | 40 (3x) | |
| Guardian of E. H. Douglas' heirs | | 40 | |
| Elijah Davis | 1 | 40 | C. McDonald |
| Elijah Davis | | 40 | J. McDonald |
| Jas. Davis | 1 | 40 | |
| Jas. Davis | | 40 | D. H. Woods |
| Jas. D. Dollins | 1 | | |
| Richard Dollins | - (name only on list) | | |
| Pheby Dollins | | 40 | Charlotte Ellston |
| Pheby Dollins | | 40 | William Dollins |

| Owners | Free Males | Acres | Original Claimant |
|---|---|---|---|
| Wm. Collins | 1 | | |
| H. I. M. Doan | 1 | 80 | Jas. Sims |
| H. I. M. Doan | | 80 (3x) | |
| Lewis Day | 1 | 40 (2x) | |
| Lewis Day | | 80 | |
| Wm. B. Evans | 1 | 40 | |
| Wm. B. Evans | | 40 | Jas. H. Smith |
| Elius Eller | 1 | 40 | John Morris |
| Elius Eller | | 40 | |
| Elius Eller | | 80 | |
| Elius Eller | | 20 | H. McClure |
| Coonrod Ensley | 1 | 21 | Braxon B. Barbee |
| David Eubanks | | 40 | G. W. Willingham |
| David Eubanks | | 40 | J. B. Hatton |
| David Eubanks | | 60 | J. B. Hatton |
| David Eubanks | | 80 | B. Kilgore |
| David Eubanks | | 40 | B. Kilgore |
| David Eubanks | | 40 | Hugh Kilgore |
| David Eubanks | | 40 | John Willingham |
| Simeon Earsom | 1 | 70 | J. Perkins |
| Simeon Earsom | | 80 | J. Perkins |
| Simeon Earsom | | 40 | P. Mahan |
| Simeon Earsom | | 40 | J. Perkins |
| Henry Ess | 1 | 88 | King & Brown |
| Henry Ess | | 80 | King & Brown |
| Jas. M. Earsom | 1 | 40 | A. Smith |
| Jas. M. Earsom | | 40 | W. Robinson |
| Jas. M. Earsom | | 20 | B. McGee |
| Jas. M. Earsom | | 40 | H. Canady |
| Saml. H. Earsom | 1 | 40 | W. Robinson |
| Saml. H. McGee | | 20 | B. McGee |
| Elijah Eubanks | 1 | | |
| John Eubanks | 1 | | |
| Bethiel Eubanks | 1 | | |
| Martin Everheart | 1 | | |
| Isaac Ford | | 40 | J. H. Kilgore |
| David J. Fort (sic) | 1 | 40 | |
| Josiah Fuget | | 80 | Jas. Lamb |
| Josiah Fuget | | 80 | John J. Mithcell |
| Josiah Fuget | | 40 (2x) | |
| Josiah Fuget | | 80 | |
| John Finks | - (name only on list) | | |
| Simeon Finks | 1 | | |
| Beverly Faields (sic) | 1 | | |
| John Flanery | 1 | 169 | W. C. Boon |
| John Flanery | | 85 | W. C. Boon |
| John Fosset | 1 | 40 (3x) | |
| John Fosset | | 40 | Wm. Boon |

| Owners | Free Males | Acres | Original Claimant |
|---|---|---|---|
| Edward Fosset |  | 80 (2x) |  |
| Peter Floyd | 1 |  |  |
| Jas. Griffin | 1 | 320 | Jeremiah Vardiman |
| Alfred Galbreath | 1 | 83 | Mary Kyde |
| Alfred Galbreath |  | 40 | Mary Kyde |
| Alfred Galbreath |  | 40 |  |
| Jas. R. C. Gass | 1 | 80 |  |
| Jas. R. C. Gass |  | 40 (2x) |  |
| Edward Goodnight | 1 |  |  |
| Harison Goodnight | 1 |  |  |
| Elijah Gray | 1 | 40 | C. Hungate |
| John B. Goodnight | 1 |  |  |
| Thos. Grugin | 1 |  |  |
| Isham A. R. Garrot | 1 |  |  |
| John Goatty | 1 | 160 |  |
| John Goatty |  | 40 | J. B. Kilgore |
| Josiah Gant | 1 | 83 |  |
| Josiah Gant |  | 41 |  |
| Josiah Gant |  | 80 (3x) |  |
| Josiah Gant |  | 40 (2x) |  |
| Josiah Gant |  | 81 |  |
| Thos. R. Gant | 1 | 40 | C. McDonald |
| Thos. R. Gant |  | 80 | J. S. Brooks |
| Woodson H. Gentry | 1 | 40 | T. Clendenon |
| Thos. Galph | 1 | 40 | Jas. Wilson |
| Cornelius Garner | 1 |  |  |
| Saml. B. Gass |  | 40 | Wm. Sims |
| Saml. B. Gass |  | 80 | J. E. Fenton |
| Saml. B. Gass |  | 40 | J. E. Fenton |
| Saml. B. Gass |  | 40 | K. Norvel |
| Saml. B. Gass |  | 160 | John Harison |
| Joel Haynes | 1 | 80 | T. T. Stone |
| Milton Hatten | 1 |  |  |
| A. B. R. Hays | 1 | 80 | Jas. Hays |
| William Hall | 1 | 80 | Martha Lockridge |
| Jas. H. Harman | 1 |  |  |
| Wm. D. Harison | 1 | 40 | Jas. Davis |
| Wm. D. Harison |  | 80 | Jas. Davis |
| Wm. P. Harison | 1 | 40 | Hugh Crocket |
| Wm. P. Harison |  | 40 | Wm. Crocket |
| Thos. Hook | 1 | 40 (2x) |  |
| Thos. Hook |  | 49 |  |
| Thos. Hook |  | 20 |  |
| Thos. Hook |  | 80 | Thos. Kilgore |
| Levi Hall | 1 |  |  |
| Elihu Hall | 0 | (0 is correct. There were only 10 free males in the page total. |  |
| Jas. Harison | 1 | 160 |  |

| Owners | Free Males | Acres | Original Claimant |
|---|---|---|---|
| Jas. Harison | | 80 (3x) | |
| Jas. Harison | | 40 (2x) | |
| Jas. Harison | | 40 | T. J. Harison |
| Jas. Harison | | 40 | W D. Harison |
| Jas. Harison | | 80 | W. D. Harison |
| Jas. Harison, adm. of T. Harison, dec. | | lot | In Mexico |
| Thos. Hurdle | 1 | 40 | W. Reynolds |
| Thos. Hurdle | | 80 | John Fost |
| Banks B. Hall | 1 | | |
| Elisha Hall | 1 | | |
| William Harvy | 1 | | |
| S. T. Hayden | 1 | | |
| Thos. Harison | 1 | 80 | Soliman Peevy |
| Jonah B. Hatten | 1 | | |
| Asaph E. Hubbard | 1 | 80 | Geo. Duncan |
| Asaph E. Hubbard | | 80 | |
| Asaph E. Hubbard | | 40 (2x) | |
| Asaph E. Hubbard | | 40 | Wm. Cave |
| Henry C. Hubbard | 1 | | |
| Saml. L. Harvey | 1 | | |
| William House | 1 | 80 | J. H. Welch |
| William House | | 40 | J. Milakin |
| William House | | 70 | J. H. Welch |
| David Hatten | | 80 | |
| David Hatten | | 40 (2x) | |
| David Hatten | | 20 | |
| Joseph Hepler | 1 | 160 | A. Damsel |
| John Hungate | 1 | 80 | |
| John Hungate | | 40 | |
| William Hardin | 1 | | |
| John Houchen | 1 | | |
| Flemming B. Hubbard | 1 | 80 (2x) | |
| Flemming B. Hubbard | | 40 (2x) | |
| William Hukel | 1 | 40 (4x) | |
| William Hukel | | 20 | E. Turner |
| Joseph B. Harris | 1 | 80 | Thos. Wright |
| William Harper | 1 | house and lot | |
| Jas. H. Hobbs | 1 | 40 | J. B. Kilgore |
| Jas. H. Hobbs | | 40 | Solm. Shephard |
| Alfred How | 1 | 40 | D. Woods |
| Alfred How | | 160 | D. Woods |
| John Haley | 1 | 46 | J. J. Gains |
| John Haley | | 46 | J. Johnston |
| John Haley | | 46 | Jas. Reed |
| Saml. Harvey | 1 | | |
| Greenup Jackman | 1 | 40 | Wm. Williams |
| Greenup Jackman | | 40 | |

| Owners | Free Males | Acres | Original Claimant |
|---|---|---|---|
| Greenup Jackman | | 80 (2x) | |
| Adm. of E. Bradford (all listed) | | | |
| Guardian of Adams | 1 | 80 (3x) | |
| Guardian of Adams | | 40 | J. J. Lorton |
| Sanford Jamison | 1 | | |
| John J. Jackson | 1 | | |
| Albert Johnston | 1 | | |
| John Jesse | 1 | | |
| Jas. Jones | 1 | | |
| William James | 1 | 40 | C. McDaniel |
| Levi A. James | 1 | | |
| Isaac Johnston | 1 | 80 | |
| William Jesse | 1 | 40 (2x) | |
| William Jesse | | 20 | M. Aslin |
| Edward Jarmon | 1 | 40 | J. McDonald |
| Edward Jarmon | | 40 | J. Willingham |
| Edward Jarmon | | 40 | Thos. Stricklin |
| Zacariah Jackson | | 40 (2x) | |
| Zacariah Jackson | | 40 | J. Jackson |
| Thomas Jackson | 1 | | |
| James Jackson | 1 | 78 (2x) | |
| Thomas Kilgore | 1 | | |
| Thos. D. Kilgore | 1 | | |
| Jas. W. Kilgore | 1 | | |
| Washington Kilgore | 1 | | |
| Saml. Kilgore | 1 | | |
| John Kieffer | 1 | | |
| Pheby Kilgore | | 40 | John Kilgore |
| Pheby Kilgore | | 80 | John Kilgore |
| Pheby Kilgore | | 157 | John Kilgore |
| Pheby Kilgore | | 77 | John Kilgore |
| John H. Kilgore | 1 | | |
| Philip Kline | 1 | 80 | J. H. Smith |
| Philip Kline | | 80 | J. H. Smith |
| Philip Kline | | 40 | J. H. Smith |
| Philip Kline | | 20 | J. H. Smith |
| Isham R. Kilgore | 1 | 40 (2x) | |
| Isham R. Kilgore | | 40 | J. Goatly |
| Isham R. Kilgore | | 40 | C. McDonald |
| Balus Kilgore | 1 | | |
| Jackson Kilgore | 1 | | |
| Thos. I. Keeton | 1 | 40 | A. L. Reynolds |
| Thos. I. Keeton | | 40 | John Reynolds |
| Thos. I. Keeton | | 46 | J. J. Gains |
| Thos. I. Keeton | | 40 (2x) | |
| Josiah Keeton | 1 | 80 | Joseph McDonald |
| Henry Keeton | 1 | | |
| David H. Luper | | 34 | J. A. S. Anderson |

| Owners | Free Males | Acres | Original Claimant |
|---|---|---|---|
| David Leach | 1 | 40 (2x) | |
| David Leach | | 80 | |
| Wm. Levaugh | 1 | | |
| Wm. H. Lee | 1 | 10 | Mansfield & Smith |
| R. R. Lee | 1 | | |
| Elihu Lockridge | 1 | 80 | G. L. Smith |
| Elihu Lockridge | | 80 | R. Lockridge |
| Elihu Lockridge | | 80 | C. Lockridge |
| Jas. Lockridge, jun. | 1 | 80 | |
| Thos. Lakin | 1 | | |
| John J. Lorton | 1 | 40 | Noah Coyle |
| John J. Lorton | | 80 | Jas. Hays |
| John J. Lorton | | 40 | J. R. Tenison |
| John J. Lorton | | 40 | |
| John Lorton | | 80 | |
| John Lorton | | 40 | |
| George Litrell | 1 | 22 | |
| Garrot Literell | 1 | 62 | H. S. Miller |
| Garrot Literell | | 62 | |
| Jason Levaugh | 1 | 40 (4x) | |
| John T. Miller | 1 | | |
| Thomas McDonald | 1 | 40 | Saml. Wilson |
| Wm. McDonald | 1 | | |
| Arthur McDonald | 1 | | |
| Madison McMullin | 1 | 80 | W. T. Metcalf |
| Madsion McMullin | | 80 | W. T. Metcalf |
| Madison McMullin, adm. | | 40 | Thos. Williams |
| Madison McMullin, adm. | | 40 | W. T. Metcalf |
| Jas. McCormick | 1 | | |
| Bailey Miller | 1 | 80 | J. R. Tenison |
| William Metcalf | 1 | 80 | D. Hunt |
| Lewis Musick | | 80 | John Kincade |
| Robt. C. Middleton | 1 | | |
| William Middleton | 1 | | |
| L. T. Musick | 1 | 40 | W. B. Middleton |
| L. T. Musick | | 80 | J. Herrick |
| William Merrawine | 1 | | |
| Thos. Moor | 1 | 80 | |
| Thos. Moor | | 40 | |
| Robt. C. Mansfield | 1 | 40 | B. A. Field |
| Robt. C. Mansfield | | 40 | E. Beaty |
| Robt. C. Mansfield | | 40 | E. Beaty |
| Neal McSwain | 1 | 40 | (marked throught) |
| Jas. M. McFadden | 1 | 40 | Jas. Wilfrey |
| Jas. M. McFadden | | 80 | Joseph Wilfrey |
| Calvin McCarty | 1 | | |
| Joseph R. Malrey | 1 | | |
| Jas. E. McSwain | 1 | | |

| Owners | Free Males | Acres | Original Claimant |
|---|---|---|---|
| John A. Martin | 1 | | |
| Pheby Mastin (no other information listed) | | | |
| David Mastin (no other information listed) | | | |
| Daniel McSwain | 1 | 40 (2x) | |
| Daniel McSwain | | 80 (5x) | |
| Daniel McSwain | | 80 | E. Brink |
| Daniel McSwain | | 80 | J. R. Tenison |
| Benjamin McCarty | | 83 | E. Brink |
| Benjamin McCarty | | 83 | H. W. Dejevuet |
| Benjamin McCarty | | 80 | --- Lyons |
| Benjamin McCarty | | 41 | W. S. Cave |
| Meredeth Myers | 1 | 80 | Silus Myers |
| Harvy McGee | 1 | 40 | R. Pulus |
| Harvy McGee | | 40 | W. Woods |
| George Moorhead | 1 | 41 | |
| George Moorhead | | 120 | |
| David A. Miller | 1 | 40 | P. Hungate |
| David A. Miller | | 40 | P. Hungate |
| David A. Miller | | 40 | Sanford Doan |
| John Miner | 1 | 81 | |
| J. Do. McRoberts | | 80 | |
| John McRoberts | 1 | | |
| Jas. A. Mahan | 1 | | |
| --- Mahan | 1 | 160 | |
| --- Mahan | | 20 | |
| --- Mahan | | 40 | |
| William Mellon | 1 | 80 | R. Litrell |
| William Mellon | | 40 | R. Litrell |
| William Mellon | | 40 | --- Wilburn |
| Elvinton Malsey | 1 | | |
| Christian Miller | 1 | | |
| Benjamin McGee | 1 | 40 | H. Canaday |
| Benjamin McGee | | 40 | J. Perkins |
| John McDonald | 1 | 40 | |
| Saml. Murry | 1 | | |
| Barnet McDonald | 1 | 40 | Truman Day |
| Barnet McDonald | | 80 | J. Woods |
| Joseph H. Miller | 1 | 80 | Jo. H. Miller |
| Joseph H. Miller | | 80 | Jo. H. Miller |
| Joseph H. Miller | | 80 | Jas. H. Miller |
| William G. Miller | 1 | 80 | Jas. H. Miller |
| William G. Miller | | 40 | Jas. H. Miller |
| Geo. F. Muldroe | 1 | 80 (7x) | |
| Geo. F. Muldroe | | 40 (4x) | |
| Geo. F. Muldroe | | 160 | |
| Geo. F. Muldroe | | 118 | |
| Geo. F. Muldroe | | 38 | |
| Geo. F. Muldroe | | 60 | |

| Owners | Free Males | Acres | Original Claimant |
|---|---|---|---|
| Geo. F. Muldroe | | 81 | Sarah J. Muldroe |
| Stephen Mathery | 1 | 40 | David Myers |
| Margaret Muldrow | | 40 | W. Willingham |
| Margaret Muldroe | | 10 | |
| Margaret Muldroe | | 80 | G. F. Muldroe |
| John G. Muldroe | 1 | 50 | G. F. Muldroe |
| John G. Muldroe | | 80 | G. F. Muldroe |
| John G. Muldroe | | 80 | G. F. Muldroe |
| John G. Muldroe | | 40 | D. Myers |
| John G. Muldroe | | 20 | G. F. Muldroe |
| John G. Muldroe | | 10 | G. F. Muldroe |
| Wm. H. Mastin | 1 | | |
| C. W. McIntyre | 1 | 40 | A. Day |
| C. W. McIntyre | | 40 (2x) | |
| George McIntush | 1 | 40 | L. Day |
| Drury D. Mays | 1 | 80 | |
| Drury D. Mays | | 41 | |
| Drury D. Mays | | 40 | |
| Beverly S. Mays | 1 | 80 | |
| Beverly S. Mays | | 40 | |
| W. W. Mays | 1 | 80 | |
| W. W. Mays | | 40 | |
| John B. Morris | 1 | 40 | R. C. Mansfield |
| John B. Morris | | 80 | J. C. Kilgore |
| John B. Morris | | 160 | Carter Cauthorn |
| John B. Morris | | 18 | Smith & Mansfield |
| John B. Morris | | 80 | Saml. Kilgore |
| John B. Morris | | 40 | W. Wood |
| John B. Morris | | 91 | G. Davidson |
| Thos. J. Mastin | 1 | 40 | S. Shepherd |
| Harison Norvel | 1 | | |
| Thomas Norris | 1 | | |
| David Norton | 1 | | |
| Barnet Newkirk | 1 | 160 | |
| Barnet Newkirk | | 40 | |
| B. M. Newkirk | 1 | | |
| B. Z. Offett | 1 | 80 | M. L. Davis |
| B. Z. Offett | | 80 | Joseph Watts |
| B. Z. Offett | | 23-1/4 | Joseph Watts |
| B. Z. Offett | | 80 | Archibald Geogg |
| Alvin Owings | 1 | | |
| Martin Oslin | 1 | 20 | |
| Martin Oslin | | 40 | |
| Martin Oslin | | 80 | |
| Thos. Odnald | 1 | | |
| John Ogdon | 1 | 80 | Thos. Laurence |
| John Ogdon | | 40 | Thos. Laurence |
| John Ogdon | | 94 | Thos. Laurence |

| Owners | Free Males | Acres | Original Claimant |
|---|---|---|---|
| John Ogdon | | 47 | Thos. Laurence |
| Joshua Owings | 1 | | |
| B. H. Owings | 1 | 20 | |
| Preston Owings | 1 | | |
| Uriah Owings | 1 | | |
| Jas. Oslin | 1 | 20 | M. Oslin |
| Robert Powel | 1 | 80 | Jas. Harison |
| Robert Powel | | 40 | Joseph Brown |
| Robert Powel | | 38 | Joseph Brown |
| Robert Powel | | 40 | |
| Robert Powel | | 80 (2x) | |
| Alford Powel | 1 | | |
| Monroe Powel | 1 | | |
| Alfred M. Petty | 1 | 40 | |
| Solimon Perry | | 40 | G. W. Grayson |
| Solimon Perry | | 20 | |
| John Peery | 1 | 40 | Jas. Speery |
| Thos. Peery | 1 | 40 | B. Canterbury |
| Thos. Peery | | 40 | |
| Joseph A. Peery | 1 | | |
| Richmond Pearson | 1 | 40 (2x) | |
| Richmond Pearson | | 47 | |
| Richmond Pearson | | 93 | |
| Richmond Pearson | | 80 | |
| Wm. Pearson | | 80 | M. (?) Duncan |
| Wm. Pearson | | 80 | D. H. Leeper |
| Wm. Pearson | | 40 | R. Pearson |
| Wm. Pearson | | 80 | |
| Wm. Pearson | | 97 | |
| Wm. Pearson | | 47 | J. O. Pearson |
| Miner Perry | 1 | | |
| Stanfield Porter | 1 | 40 | A. E. Wherry |
| Stanfield Porter | | 40 | A. E. Wherry |
| Thomas Pate | 1 | | |
| Thos. S. Pearson | (no other information given) | | |
| John M. Price | 1 | 80 | |
| John M. Price | | 40 | |
| John A. Pearson | 1 | 80 (4x) | |
| John A. Pearson | | 80 | Joseph Pearson |
| John A. Pearson | | 40 (2x) | |
| Miner Pate | 1 | 166 | |
| Miner Pate | | 40 | |
| John O. P. Pearson | 1 | | |
| John Potts | 1 | 80 (3x) | |
| John Potts | | 160 | |
| Allen C. Reynolds | 1 | | |
| Lewis Russel | 1 | 80 | W. B. Evans |
| Lewis Russel | | 80 | W. B. Evans |

| Owners | Free Males | Acres | Origianl Claimant |
|---|---|---|---|
| Lewis Russel | | 40 | H. I. M. Doan |
| Lewis Russel | | 40 | H. I. M. Doan |
| Lewis Russel | | 40 | D. Norton |
| Lewis Russel | | 40 | D Norton |
| Lewis Russel | | 88 | G. W. Grayson |
| John A. Read | 1 | | |
| Matthew M. Runkle | 1 | 40 (2x) | |
| Matthew M. Runkle | | 40 | Margaret Runkle |
| Oston Reynolds | 1 | | |
| Michael Roberts | 1 | | |
| Jesse Roberts | 1 | | |
| Reason Ridgway | 1 | | |
| Jas. Reed | | lots | Mexico |
| Granville Read | 1 | 40 (2x) | |
| Granville Read | | 40 | J. Adams |
| Granville Read | | 80 | J. Black |
| Henry Shock (no other information given) | | | |
| H. P. L. Shock | 1 | 160 | T. Strickland |
| H. P. L. Shock | | 40 | T. Strickland |
| Henry Shock | 1 | 80 (2x) | |
| Henry Shock | | 40 (2x) | |
| William Sims | 1 | 67 | R. Pulus |
| Eli Smith | 1 | | |
| Joseph Surber | 1 | 40 | Jno. Lockridge |
| Joseph Surber | | 40 | Jno. Lockridge |
| Joseph Surber | | 40 | Jas. Beaty |
| Joseph Smith | 1 | 76 | Jacob Hough |
| Kitty Smith (no other information given) | | | |
| Jas. Straube | 1 | | |
| Christian Straube | 1 | 80 | R. Irvine |
| William Sox (no other information given) | | | |
| William Sox, jr. | 1 | 160 | Isaac Herrick |
| Thomas Sox | 1 | | |
| William Sox, adm. of Will Still, dec. | | 40 | |
| Samuel Sox | 1 | | |
| Jackson Sox | 1 | | |
| Jas. Sperry | 1 | | |
| Jas. Smiley | 1 | 80 | Duncan G. Blue |
| Thos. T. Stone | 1 | 78 | |
| Thos. T. Stone | | 80 | |
| Jas. Smith | 1 | 40 | M. M. Boon |
| Jas. Smith | | 20 | M. M. Boon |
| Jas. Smith | | 80 | M. M. Boon |
| John G. Swindle | 1 | 80 | Jesse Perkins |
| John G. Swindle | | 40 | H. Lynch |
| William Schooler | 1 | | |
| Whorton Schooler | 1 | | |

| Owners | Free Males | Acres | Original Claimant |
|---|---|---|---|
| Elizabeth Schooler (no other information given) | | | |
| Wm. Shepherd | 1 | | |
| Richard Skinner | 1 | 80 | |
| Richard Skinner | | 40 | |
| George Sailor | | | |
| Abraham Smith | 1 | 80 | |
| Soliman Shepherd | 1 | 40 | |
| Jeramiah Shepherd | 1 | | |
| Joseph D. Spencer | 1 | 160 | Wm. Pearson |
| Joseph D. Spencer | | 40 | Joseph Eubanks |
| Joseph D. Spencer | | 80 | Joseph Eubanks |
| Jeptha D. Shields | 1 | 80 | W. D. Harison |
| Jeptha D. Shields | | 26 | W. D. Harison |
| Jeptha D. Shields | | 40 | M. Oslin |
| Jeptha D. Shields | | 30 | A. B. Tinsley |
| Thos. Strickland | 1 | | |
| John Stewart | 1 | 40 | J. G. Reynolds |
| William R. Sims | 1 | 40 | J. Sims |
| William R. Sims | | 183 | |
| William R. Sims | | 45 | |
| William R. Sims | | 40 | |
| William R. Sims | | 45 | |
| Matthew H. Smith | 1 | | |
| Henry Throckmorton | 1 | | |
| Robert Throckmorton | 1 | | |
| Abraham B. Tinsley | 1 | 92 | |
| Abraham B. Tinsley | | 92 | C. Tinsley |
| Abraham B. Tinsley | | 183 | Caleb Tinsley |
| Abraham B. Tinsley | | 160 | Caleb Tinsley |
| Abraham B. Tinsley | | 320 | Caleb Tinsley |
| Hugh Todd | 1 | 80 | John Todd |
| R. L. Thompson | 1 | | |
| Wiley Tally | 1 | 40 (2x) | |
| Wiley Tally | | 80 (3x) | |
| Wiley Tally | | 20 | Danl. Tally |
| Wiley Tally | | 80 | John Tally |
| Wiley Tally | | 80 | John Tally |
| Daniel Tally | 1 | 42 (2x) | |
| George Tally | 1 | 84 | |
| George Tally | | 85 | |
| Jas. M. Tally | 1 | | |
| Berry Tally | 1 | | |
| Judah Tally | | 80 | Wm. Tally |
| Judah Tally | | 80 | Wm. Tally |
| Judah Tally | | 40 | Wm. Tally |
| Andrew Turner | 1 | 80 | John Sailing |
| Andrew Turner | | 40 | John Gee |
| Andrew Turner | | 80 | D. D. Turner |

| Owners | Free Males | Acres | Original Claimant |
|---|---|---|---|
| Andrew Turner | | 40 | D. D. Turner |
| Andrew Turner | | 170 | |
| Andrew Turner | | 40 (2x) | |
| George W. Turley | 1 | lots | Mexico |
| Robert Taylor | 1 | 40 | |
| Jackson Turner | 1 | | |
| John W. Truett | 1 | | |
| John Turner | 1 | 80 | |
| John Turner | | 40 (2x) | |
| John Turner | | 40 | John Fosset |
| Thos. Turner | 1 | | |
| John P. Vance | 1 | | |
| Martin Vaughn | | 80 | Daniel Hunt |
| Martin Vaughn | | 80 | Daniel Hunt |
| Martin Vaughn | | 80 | Daniel Hunt |
| Lewis R. Venable | 1 | 80 | D. D. Turner |
| Jas. Vest | 1 | 40 | J. Oslin |
| Littlebury Watts | 1 | 40 | |
| Wm. Willingham (no other information given) | | | |
| William C. West | 1 | 40 | John C. Martin |
| William C. West | | 40 | Joel Hanes |
| William C. West | | 40 (2x) | |
| William C. West | | 76 | John Willingham |
| William C. West | | 76 | J. B. Kilgore |
| William C. West | | 71 | |
| William C. West | | 48 | |
| William C. West | | 40 | John Kiser |
| Timothy Wooding | 1 | | |
| Jeremiah West | 1 | 47 (2x) | |
| Jeremiah West | | 47 | Nancy Gilpin |
| Jeremiah West | | 25 | W. C. West |
| Grand Williams | 1 | | |
| Caleb Williams | 1 | | |
| Isham I. Willingham | 1 | | |
| Rueben Wilson | 1 | | |
| John Watts | 1 | | |
| Temple Wayne | 1 | | |
| Stanford Watts | 1 | 20 | Roland Watts |
| Gideon P. Williams | 1 | | |
| Joseph Watts | 1 | 80 (5x) | |
| Joseph Watts | | 17 | |
| Roland H. Watts | 1 | 27 | |
| Roland H. Watts | | 47 | |
| Roland H. Watts | | 40 | Stanford Watts |
| Roland H. Watts | | 95 | |
| Roland H. Watts | | 80 | |
| William Woods | 1 | 38 | A. Houp |
| William Woods | | 40 (2x) | |

| Owners | Free Males | Acres | Original Claimant |
|---|---|---|---|
| William Woods | | 160 | |
| William Woods | | 44 | |
| Francis Wisdom | 1 | | |
| John Wilmot | 1 | | |
| David Woodson | 1 | | |
| John J. Weaver | 1 | 47 | |
| Delony Willingham | 1 | 40 | David Hatten |
| Calup V. Williams | 1 | | |
| Isham Willingham, sr. | 1 | | |
| John H. Wilson | 1 | | |
| William L. Wayne | 1 | 80 | M. M. Payne |
| A. H. Wayn | 1 | 40 | M. M. Payne |
| A. H. Wayn | | 20 | M. M. Payne |
| David H. Woods | 1 | 40 | |
| David H. Woods | | 80 (2x) | |
| John Wilson | 1 | 40 | Miner Pate |
| David Wilson | 1 | 40 (2x) | |
| William White | 1 | 40 | William Levaugh |
| William White | | 40 | William Levaugh |
| William White | | 40 | J. W. Levaugh |
| William White | | 40 | J. W. Levaugh |
| William White | | 80 | J. H. Milikin |
| William White | | 80 | J. H. Milikin |
| William White | | 80 | W. B. Evans |
| William White | | 80 | Saml. Dingle |
| William White | | 40 | J. C. Fruit |
| William White | | 45 | H. I. M. Doan |
| William White | | 40 | Thos. Kilgore |
| William White | | 40 | Thos. Kilgore |
| William White | | 80 | Jas. Sims |
| William White | | 40 | W. B. Evans |
| John Willingham | 1 | | |
| George Willingham | 1 | | |
| George W. Wilson | 1 | | |
| Jas. M. Wisdom | 1 | 40 | Nathaniel Cornet |
| Mary Young | | 80 | B. Young |
| Mary Young | | 80 | |
| Thomas Young | 1 | | |
| William Young | 1 | 41 | |
| John Young | | 80 | John Gee |
| John Young | | 80 | D. D. Turner |

<u>Warren County, Missouri, Poll Book, Hickory Grove Township, November 1840, Capitol Fire Documents, CFD 183, Folder 16232</u>
  Thos. Philips, Rufus H, Wadkins, Wm. G. Welch, Robert B. Anderson, Robert Black, Wm. Edwards, David Therman, Isaac T. Daviss, Larken D. Welch, John Mabe, Warren Welch, Henry E. Welch, Jarret Daviss, Ervin Baldridge, Seaton Mathew, Henry

Fadderhase, Alford Mathers, Benjamin Hancock, Andrew Ellis, Charles Thomas, Henry Smith, Joseph Ellis, Jno. W. A. Johnson, Joseph K. Carter, Green Shirez, James Matthews, Joseph R. Plesant, Alexander McKinze, Tandy Collins, Samuel M. Reynolds, Jesse Harnser, Gibson B. Lucket, Silas Wadkins, Henry Abington, Samuel D. Taylor, J. B. Reynal, Gerrymack Sullivan, Charles D. Wright, Jas. W. Simpson, Wm. Collins, Edwin Patterson, Washington Bell, Thos. Burgess, John L. Hubbard, Anthony Graves, Levi Sharp, Thos. Soaper, Jory Therman, Peter Randolph, Henry B. Graves, Vogel K. Pringle, Daniel Martin, Nimrod Darnell, Roger Taylor, Wm. M. Cambell, Wm. P. Handcock, Daniel McGown, Henry Sinker, James Ward, George Jon Collins, Frederick Schuts, Jno. Kirk, Samuel W. Williams, Henry Hetherton, Jno. D. McCullock, Luis Darnold, Wm. Hanley, Wm. Gilkey, Thomas McGaw, William Logan, Plesant Kinnady, Jno. C. Hankock, Rufus Gibson, John K. Williams, Lewis Kinnady, Arthur Langford, Thomas Kinnady, John Duncan, Nicholas Duncan, Wilsher Benton, Jno. R. Carter, A. G. Potter, George Corley, David Sherman, Frances H. Lyles, Robert G. Huston, Harrison Hulbard, James A. Hamilton, Daniel Harding, Joseph Stallard, Eusebuis Bainbridge, James Collins, R. J. Kinnady, Albert J. Arnold, Rufus Fullerton, Arues Brown, Abner Cunningham. Charles Langford, Wm. Dodge, Albert G. Mason, Daniel Z. Sherman, Thomas Moore, Joseph Moore, Jenkin Philips, Wm. Morrison, Moses Edwards, Henry Pritchet, James B. Graves, M. G. Pringle, Preston McRoberts, Jno. A. Murphy, Jno. Rummons, Jno. Brown.

<u>Warren County, Missouri, Pinckney Township, Poll Book, November, 1840, Capitol Fire Documents, CFD 183, Folder 16232.</u>
Samuel Foster, Milton Griswold, Phillip Miller, William Taylor, U. A. Anderson, John Mackinton, James McKee, Felix M. Taylor, Samuel Rogers Hugh Thompson, George W. McNight, Jessey Peek, John C. Massey, Boston Kallahan, F. Sisson, James Penington, John S. Dunham, A. R. Dunham, C. A. Kuntze, A. Hornback, John Ellis, F. Griswold, John Taylor, Benjamin Ellis, William Kullom, William S. Regent, William Clice, James Purrington, Thomas J. Marshal, John H. Posey, Isack J. Ambler, John Marshal, Joshuay (sic) Swagg, John Wright, John Wray, William Wilson, Hinnery (sic) D. Word, Stephen Brown, James Clay, Benjamin Hudson, James A. Carter, Alexander S. Hughes, B. F. Silkey, Theopuilus Floyd, Temple S. Brown, Theodore L. Kingston, Stephen B. Whelon, Rubin Rider, Daniel Morgan, John K. Chamberlin, John W. Browning, John Swinford, James Brown, William Brown, Henery Brown, Andrew Cooper, Dickson Hudson, Lanton P. Brown, Henery Linerber, James A. Riber, Ander. Fort, Milford Clice, Bluford Stone, Pleasent Price, George Anderson, A. D. Fling, James Sharp, Merideth Williams, James Stephens, Joshua McDoneal, Andrew Bencher

Samuel Petteet, Hiram H. Hurmal, Andrew Morland, John Brown, William Ford.

## Lincoln County, Missouri, Poll Book, 1844, Capitol Fire Documents, CFD 183, Folder 16241
### Bedford Township

J. Abbott, J. Anderson, R. T. Anderson, F. Archie, J. B. Author, T. E. Averin, C. H. Bailey, David Baily, William Balin, D. L. Bains, E. Balis, Jno. S. Ball, Eli Bane, Moses Bard, James W. Barber, James Barker Jno. Barker, L. Barker, Saml. Barker, Wm. Barker, P. G. Barns, Willis Barons, Samuel Beckman, Hugh Bettis, A. T. Beck, James Beck, S. E. Beck, F. Bishop,Jas. Black, J. A. Blackmore, S. Blackmore, S. Briles, Jno. Blair, Joel Blanks, Jno. Blanton, R. H. Blanton, Byrent Bonn, Elija Block, A. M. Blunt, Wm. Bowen, Talbott Braff, C. Bronk, Jas. Branson, Saml. Briscoe, Jas. H. Britton, Francis C. Cake, J. Bronk, Harrison Bronk, A, Brown, Levi Brown, Wm. Browning, Wm. Bryent, Jas, Burgen, W. Burkhead, P.G. Burrus, Jas. Callaway, Chesly Calloway, R. A. Calloway, Z. Calloway, Peter Campbell, Isaac Cannon, J. C. Cannon, James L. Cannon, W. Cantrill, Jacob Caps, S. A. Caps, Frank Carr, J. B. Carr, C. L. Carter, James S. Carter, W. T. Carter, James Carty, M. Carty, Wm. Carty, Hiram Chamberlain, Jno. Chandler, Morgan Cofin, S. R. Claggett, T. J. Claggett, F. B. Clane, R. H. F. Clark, D. Clark, W. C. Clark, Wm. Clark, L. W. Coats, James Cockran, G. H. Cofin, T. B, Cofin, F. Collard, Alex Collins, Isaac N. Collian, G. E. Collins, Isaac Collins, C. Compton, Nick Conce, T. G. Conner, A. Cottle, C. Cottle, S. Cottle, E. L. M. Cottle, Orvil Cottle, Y. A. Cottle, A. Couse, Chas. Cox, Alex Creach, Jas. Creach, Jno. Creach, Simon Creach, T. W. Creach, V. Crach, A. B. Crews, J. B. Cropper, A. Crouch, Carty Crouch, Geo. Crow, Jas. Crouch, John Crouch, J. Cruch, Jno. Cruch, David Cups, T. Cups, Joseph Custer, C. Davis, E. T. Davis, Joel A. Davis, Peter Davis, Seymor Davis, Seymor Davis, jr., Silas N. Davis, F. Dawson, David Deney, Jno. H. Duncan, A. Dobbins, W. Doniplant, B. L. Dosirn, James Douglass, N. B. Dudley, P. D. Dudley, David Duff, Levi Duff, A. Dulany, Robt Duff, C. K. Duncan, Hiram Duncan, J.S. Duncan. Jno. H. Duncan, J. T. Dutton, J. Dyer, Jno. Early, Asa East, J. East, L. East, Thomas East Willliam Elam, Jno. Elliot, James Ellis, Jno. A. Elmon, L. T. Elton, D. Erving, David Evans, B. Farmer, H. A. Fisher, J. M. L. Fisher, Thomas Fletcher, M. Forkins, Charles Forbush, Jno. Forkner, A. B. Foster, Jackson Geams, Jas. Foster, B Fostin, Jas. Fostin, J. R. Fostin, J. F. Frazier, E. Galloway, Tho. Gammon, J. D. Gears, Robt Gilmore, Wm. Gears, A. L Geleaned, Jno.Geleaned, S. Gilkey, W. C. Giles, W. Gibson, J. W. Gibson, P. H. Gillehan, Jas. Glenn, Wm. Glenn, A. C. Glover, A. C. Goshon, Glown, W. H. Goodlett, Asop Goodrich, Jno. Goodrich, Jacob

Grant, J. H. Grant, Peyton Graus, J. T. Green, Squire Green, J. Guiliden, J. M. Gunn, Jno. Gurin, T. A. Gurin, Wm. Gurin, Jno. Gwinn, T. A. Gwinn, Chas. Halcomb, N. Hale, A. Hall, D. Hall, Nichos. Hale, Chas. Hall, D. Hall, Henry Hall, Saml. Hall, Lewis Hall, W. M Hall, Jos. Ham, Jas. Hamilton, Jno Hammond, A. Hammon, T. Hammons, George Hanley, W. M. Harper, Exra Harris, Jas. Harris, Olin Harris, B. Harvey, M. Harvey, W. Harvey, Jas. E. Haughton, S. Hefington, John Henderson, L. Henry, S. Henry, C. Hereoll, J. C. Herndon, C C. Hewitt, Asa Hilen, Wm. Hiler, A. Hill, Jas. B. Hobbs, G. W. Homby, Hardin Holcomb Jeff Homely, W. Hopkins, M. Hopkins, Elliot Hughes, A. Howell, T. Howell, Bantor (sic) Hubbard, Henry Hull, Harrison Hubbard Elliott Hughes Wm. Hughsmith Asa Hulen, Lewis Hull, Saml. Hull, Jno. Hunter, Jos. C. Hunter, F. A. Hurt, C. Huston, Geo W. Huston, Saml. Huston, sr., T. G. Hutt, T. W. Hutt, Wm. S. Hutton, William Inis, Yearly E. Jackson, Jacob James, Henry Jane, Jno. Jenkins, Al John, W. H. Jennings, A. Jimerson, J. Johnson, J. B. Johnson, David Keller, A. Keller, Amos Katis Jas. Jones, A. Jones, Benj. Kimar, sr., W. S. Killian, W. S. Killam (sic), Thos. Kimbro, M. Kimbro, Robert B. Kimden Benj. Kinion, Wm. Kinon, James Knox, jr., Huey Knox, Jas. Knox, sr., M. Knox, A. Krathley, S. W. Kyle, Wm. Lambert, L. Lankford, A. Lanfort (sic), Jno. Laughlin, David Lard, M. Layton, E. R. Lenear, Luther Levin, Isaac Linn, P. Logan, L. Lomas, A. B. Louis, M. Lovel, Saul McCammon, Jno. Loving, D. Lynch, G. McCulum, T. McGarver, T. McGowen, David McFarland, S. H. McKay, W. R. McKay, W. W. McKay, G. W. McLoud, H. Maiden, Jno. Manning, W. H. Markam, R. W. Marshall, Alex H. Martin, B. G. Martin, Huey Martin, Jackson Martin, Jas. Martin, M. C. Martin, W. H. Martin, T. P. Massey, M. Mautz, W. W. Merriman, J. W. Miller, S. Moore, Wm. Miller, N. Millsapp, N. P. Minor, R. Mitchell, Jno. L. Moore, James Moore, W. D. More, A. Morris, J. Morris, J. B. Morris, Alex Morrison, Benj. Moss, R. Moulder, Alex Mudd, N. Mudd, Thos. Munford, Jno. Munroe, Mich. Murphy, Wm. Murphy, S. F. Murrey, A. Newchurch, M. Newland, C. Nichols, Elias Norton, J. Nichols, M. Nichols, Grasmist Nolton, G. W. Null, Wm. Nolton, Geo. Null, Jno. Null, Wm. Null, L.D. Oglevie, J. H. Owigs, Henry Owens, Jas. Owigs, Wm. Owigs, K. H. Paddock, Wm. Park, Francis Parker, S. D. Parker, B. Parmer, D. Penny, Wm. Pauk, Perry Pauk, Hiram Parmer, D. Penny, F Perkins, W. Perkins, Jessie Perkins, Benj. Pevis, Danl. Pevis, Chas. H. Porter, Jacob Pollard, B. Pollard, Jas. Porter, L. Pressly, Jno. D. Porter, Levi S. Porter, Wm. Porter, Jos. Powell, D. Pressly, jr., D. Pressly, sr., Jacob Presly (sic), Jas. H. Reid, Wm. Pressly, A. Preston, J. I. Pritchitt, M. Ramsonn, J. W. Randall, A. Reiley, Robert Rickey, T. F. Riddle, F. Riggs, J. O. Riggs, Saml. Riggs, Jos. Rilard, Jno. M. Rinds, Abel Robinson, Levi Robinson, G. W. Roland, W. H. Roper, M.

Ross Martin Rush, Peter Rybolt, S. D. Rybolt, Danl. Sage, J. S. Sallee, Nathan Samons, Geo. Sands, G. F. Scude, Wm. Seagrass, Jno. Shannon, James Shaw, jr., Jno. Shaw, N. Shaw, Armsted Shelton, C. T. Shelton, M. A. Shelton, Ira Sherman, L. Shipp, --- Shirky, J. D. Shitton, G. G. Shrum N. Shrum, sr., Benj. Shuts, Chas. Shuts, N. Simonds, Saul Slater, Jno. Smathan, Thos. Slavens, J. D. Smith, Wm. Smith, William Hugh Smith, Saml. Smithers, Jas. W. Spears, M. Spiers, A. Thomas, Isaac Sprikston, H. Stagner, A. R. Stanly, Jas. Stark, Robt. Stewart, W. B. Stephen, Stephen Stephen, F. S. Sweeny, W. J. Tally, E. Sydmon, Thos. Synder, J. W. Synder, Jacob Taylor, I. P. Thomas, C. M. Thomasson, B. Thornhill, L. Thornhill, Jas. Thornhill, Buford Thornhill, R. Thornhill, Robt. Thornhill, Simon Thornhill, Jos. Thurmond, B. B. Tinnings, Thos. Trail, Jas. Trail, jr., Jas. Trail, Wm. Trail, E. Tuggle, A. Turner, W. Vandover, B. Vankamp, F. Vankamp, Wm. Vaughn, E. Verdin, H. A. Wade, Henry Wade, sr., Jno. Wade, Jas Walker, Hans H. Walker, Telman Well, S. Wallace, Geo. Waine, W. H. Walton, N. Wamble, R. Ware, S. Warren, W. Washam, sr., Thos. Welch, L. Welch, Wm M. Welch, Benjn. West, C. Wheeler, M. Whitehead A. L Williams, A. M. Williams, C. Williams, Wm. M. Welch, N. Wamble, R. Ware, S. Warren, W. Washam, sr., L. Welch, Thos. Welch, Benj West, C. Wheeler, M. Whitehead F. Wing, Jno. Wilson, J.M. Wilson, Alex Wilson, Robt. Williams, L. Williams Jas Williams Jackson Williams, H. B. Wing, J. H. Withrow, Henry Wing Robt. Witt, Jas. Womble, S. Wombles, J. A. Woodfolk, R. H. Woodfolk Shidrick Woodson, M. Wright, T. G. Wright Thos. J. Wright, Jno. Yale, L. Young, William Young, C. Young, I. M. Zimmerman.

### Hurricane Township

Elijah Anderson, A. Alexander, James Alexander, Cary Allen, David Allen, Edwin Allen, H. D. Allen, Ira Allen, J. W. Alloway, A. Anderson, Daniel Barnes, John Barnes, Thomas Barnes, Horatio W. Baskett, J. H. Baskett, Duvel Bedoe R. B. Bell, William Bell, R. B. Belt, Charles Bennet, Alexander Bernier, E. J. H. Bennet, Hery (sic) Blackaly, James Bone, John Blackaly, Benj. Blanton, Wm Boon, Wm. Bosbinden, R. T. Budisill, Parmenus Briscoe, Augustine Bradley, Wm. Butler, Garrett Burklaon, George Burns Bledsoe Butler, Wm. Butler, Thomas Canaday, J. S. Cannon John Cannon, Ephraim Canon, Samuel Carmon, Dabney Carr, J. D. Carr, Wm. Carter, Elijah Cass, Page Cheak, J. E. Clark, McArthur Clark, Jacob Coffey, David Cooper, Nicholas Cooper, Wm. Cooper, Charles Cox, John Cox, Henry Cox, Thomson Cox, Bluford Crenshaw, D. C. Damron, J. B. Cunningham, Andrew Cunningham, John Daniel, Epgraim Davis, J. J. Davis, Johnathan Davis, Malichi Davis, David Diggs, Saml. Davis George Diggs, Thomas Diggs, C.R. Dulany, James Dodson, John Dotson, Andrew Downing, John Downing, R. M. Elliot, G. W. Ellsbury, T. Ellsbury, W. L Ellsbury, W.

L. Ellsbury, W. N. Ellsbury, Samuel Farmer, Thomas Farmer, Charles Ferry, A. R. Finley, Cyrus Finley, Gilmore Finley, Adison Foley, T. F. Foley, James Foly (sic), Sylvander Forbush, D. E. Ferguson, Elias Galloway, John Galloway, Thomas Galoway, J. M. Garner, Goyn Gibson, James Gibson, John Gibson, Joseph Gibson, R. W. Gibson, F. G. Gilmer, Jacob Gray, D. W. Gladney, James Gladney, Samuel Gladney, John Goodman, Herrod Glascock, Wm. Gordon, Thomas Graves, Clifford Gray, George Gray, Wm. Gray, N. H. Griffith, Edward Grimes, A. J. Hammack, B. W. Hammack, Ben Hammack D. A. Hammack, Leander Hammack, John Hammack, J. M. Hammack, Martin Hammack, W. H. Hammack, Wm. Hamon, Francis Harvy, Augustin Hervy, Nicholas Hervy, L. B. Holmes, Spilsby Holmes, David Howdyshell John Hubbard, Wm. Jamison, Bryant Jefferies. Gideon Jewel, Jacob Jewel, Granville Johnson, Abraham Kelling, French Kemper, Ambrose D. Kemper, Octavius Kemph, Martin Kenpin, A.B. King, J. M. King, Ira Kingsbury, Henry Laury, Wm. Leagen, Joseph Lemory, Abner Lewis, Henry Liggin, Wm. Lilly, Zadock Long, David Luckett, F. M. Luckett, J. M. Luckett, Wm. Luckett, J. J. McCay, W. L. McCormack, David McCoy, Darius McDonald, W. W. McGinis, Hiram McDowel, James McDonald, James McKiney, B. N. McTee, David McMalin, Crawford McNeer, Edwin McTee, Lloyd McTee, Henry Maige, Jesse Malin Alexander Martin, F. Gideon Martin, J. P. Martin, John Martin, L. G. Martin, Wm. Moore, T. G. Martin, D. C. Mathews, Rolly Mays, Thomas Moore, Peter Murata, J. H. Morgan, Reasino More, Quinton More, A. H. Poe, Joseph Murry, Elijah Myers, jr., Elijah Myers, sr., Squire Northcutt, David Neele, Alex Nelson, Ira T. Nelson, Auguise New, W. H. Nicklin, Washington Novel, B. W. Obanion, James PaKmen, J. C. Pace, Alexas Palmer, James Palmer, Wm. Parson, John Palmer, J. M. Parsons, James Parsons, Robert Paterson, C. Perpater (?), Wm. Pheobus, John Plumer, A. H. Poe, J. W. Porter, W. F. Price, Alexander Reid, G. W. Reid, George Reid, John Reid, T. S. Reid, C. W. Ricks, J. M. Ricks, David Reid, Francis Rissle, J. S. Rissle, Lewis Rissle, Francis Rissle (sic), Benj. Roberson, Noah Roberson, B.B. Robertson, G. W. Robertson, Wm. Robinson, John Rogers, Saml. Rye, Mordicia Sanders, Wm. Sanders, Mathew Sapp, Wm. Seaton, J. H. Settles, Elijah Shuck, James Smith, C. B. Sitton, F. J. Sitton, J. W. Sitton, James Sitton, Philip Sitton, C.A. Skiner, G. W. Slater, B. P. Smith, G. W. Squires, James Stallard, David Steele, Joseph Steele, T. T. Steele, Thomas Stephens, G. W. Stickelman, Adam Stinebough, Jacob Stinebough, David Stonebraker, A. G. Stout, George Stout, Ira Suddarth, John Suddarth, Lewis Suddarth, Job Taylor, John Thomas. Gabril Thomson, Isaac Thomson, John Thomson, Robert Thomson, John Tiller, Henry Tipton John Trail, Rollins Trail, M. Watts, J. J. Triplet, A. J. Triplett, Benj. Vance, James Vance, Saml. Vance, Theodore Vance, Wm. Waggoner, Sovreigh Wallice,

Richard Wamack, Hines Washen, Nelson Watte, M. Watts, Curtis Wells, Madison Watts, Senica Watts, F. E. Wells, Wm. Wilson, Jacob Whiteside, Howard Wilkerson, John Wilkerson, sr., Wm. Womack, James Wilkinson, Joseph Wilkinson, Robert Wilson, W. T. Wilson, F. Withington, jr., Francis Withington, Madison Zimmerman, C. G. Womack, Hiram Womack, Ephraim Zumatt.

## Monroe Township

George Admire, Squire Admire, Thos. H. Admire, William Admire, James Alexander, Harrison Alexander, Kindle Baley, Levi Baley, A. B. Birkhead, D. F. J. Boanening, Jacob Boone, James Coke, Alvora Cottle, Edward Cottle, Warren Cottle, John Crauch, Philip Creumes, Johnathan Crume, B. C. Crump, John Daulton, Littleton Dryden, Willis Elston, F. W. Rose, Samuel Ezzell, Ely Y. Foxwell, Saml. Galaway, Alford Gorden, McCol Gravens, George Hardesty, Isaac Hauston, Wilis Huttan, Thomas Hilton, William Hilton, Robt. Jamersand, Birther (?) Jamerson, James Lindsey, John H. Lindsey, Charles McIntosh, Joseph McIntosh, Robert McIntosh, Charles W. Martin, Thomas Mauzy, James Olive, John T. Overall, William Overall, Geo. Parsons, Jeremiah Page, Berry Perkins, John Pollard, William Pollard, George Potter, Elisha Scott, James Shanon, Lawrence B. Sitton, William Sitton, William C. Sitton, Abraham Smith, William Snead, James Stewart, William Tailor, Chancy Tuttle, Johnathan Tipton, James Turnball, George Turnball, Thomas Witsan, W. W. Wise, Joseph Wright.

## Union Township

J. W. Appleton, John T. Bell, A. J. Blair, Harison Blair, Laton Bradley, Augustus Briles, George Briscoe, Thos. Britt, J. M. C. Briscoe, David Cantrol, George Clare, Jas. Clarke, M. N. Clarke, Allan Cleve, Andrew Cochran, Jos. Cocchran, Samuel Cochran, Wm. Cochran, John Colbert, Robt. Cook, Geo. Coon, Nathan Cortney, G. H. Dejarnatt, E. Downing, Daniel Draper, M. Drumheller, M. M Duff, Samuel Dunn, J.C. Duvall, George Fenton, Richard Fenton, jr., Richard Fenton, sr., F. L. Hally, Andrew Finly, Jas. Finly, Denis Galaway, Richard Gladney, Peter Galway, M. R. Gallehad, Robt. Gillerlaid, Wm. Gladney, John R. Gordon, Jas. Green, Thos. Green, Thos. J. Hamony, W. F. Hally, Thos. Hally, Edward Hawkins, Jerymiah Henry, R. H. Hill, John Hines, Jos. Houdershell, jr., Jos. Houdershell, sr., Thos. B. Hutt, W. A. Jackson, Carson King, George Jimerson, Lemuel Kimon, David Laferdy, Isaac Lea, O. C. Liles, Thos. Lewis, Samuel K. Lilford, W. H. Long, Ezekel McDonold, Benj. McGowin, J. P. D. McGuire, Henry Mackmahan, Thorito (sic) P. Mathews, Fountain Meriwether, Israll Moris, Henry H. Mourts, Henry T. Mudd, John L. Mudd, F. L. Nally, Robt. Mudd, jr., Thos. Nally, W. F. Nally, J. W. Patterson, C. E. Perkins, Robt. C. Prewitt, jr., P. Raney, John Ray, M. Read, John Ray, jr., Robt. Ray, Thos. Ray, Wm. Ray, Benjamin Right, Hansford Richards, Thos. Reid, Jas. Reid, A. H. Stom,

Ludwell Ross, Robt. Sammons, John Samons, Milton Sanford, T. D. Sandford, John Shipley, Nicholas Shrum, S. B. Sitton, A. H. Stone, John Smiley, Elijah Stephens, Biless Stom, Thos. Stone, William Surgain, Jas. Suttles, William Suttles, William Swingain, Archibald Tailor, Wm. Taylor, Andrew Teague, D. Teague, Jas. M. Teague, Peter Teague, Jas. Telfird, Jos. W. Thomas, Fulton Thompson, Thos. Triplet, Jas. Tucker, Wm. Tucker, Lemuel Tucker, Edward Tugler, --- Humphries, Waner Verdier, Van Verdier, Jefferson Verdier, Jas. Verdier, sr., Washington Verdier, John Waldenblade, J. B. Waugh, Thos. S. Wells, G. N. Wells, Haden Wells, J. S. Wells, P. T. Wells, Joel Wheler, J. E. Whitesides, Wm. Whitesides, Robt. Wilbun, L. G. Williams, A. R. Willson, David Willson, Jas. Willson.

## Waverly Township

Samuel Abbott, G. L. Adams. James Alexander, Robert B. Allen, Mathew Anderson, George Anson, A. L. Armstrong, S. B. Baird, James Baird, David Baird, William Baird, P. B. Bell, Joshua Bartlett, James Belbro, Leston Bell, P. B. Brant, James Brown, John Brown, Robert Brown, Samuel Brown, John J. Burkhood, Washington Brown, Edward Chasten, Robert Chasten, William F. Clear, William C. Cobb, H. J. Cochran, O. N. Coffey, Jacob Copenhaven, John Copenhaven, John C. Cornwall, Dayton Crider, Peter Cullep, Colman Downs, Isaac Downs, John Estes, James Dudley, William Dudley, George Dull, Lewis Duncan, George Dyer, jr., Jacob Willman, A. Edelen, John L. B. Fendley, Alonzo Edlen, A. P. Elmore, Enoch Emerson, Elbert Ernest, Thomas Ernest, John Estes, Richd. Estes, S.B. Henry, Jacob Edleman, William Estes, Thomas Farriss, C. F. Findley, John P. Ficklen, Henry Findley, Job Flemming, Cary Fulton, C. W. Gillum, Granville Gillum, John Gillum, Thomas Grason, Zachrah Gunison, Robert Haislip, John Halcom, Slado Hammond, Thomas S. Hammet, William Hammond, Thornton Hancoch, William Haygood, John Harriss, Burk Haygood, Samuel Hickeson, Henry Holoway, Jacob Hoss, Charles Hudson, Isaac Hudson, Thomas M. Hudson, Thomas Hudson, William Hudson, John F. Huekstop, George W. Hughs, E. Huntsman, Jarrard Ingram, Johnathan Ingram, Samuel Ingram, D. S. Jamison Samuel Jamison, James Johnson, John Johnson, Willis Joiner, E. K. Jones, William J. Lovil, Caleb Kimble, J. T. Kimble, Laiken Lawrence, John Logan, Nelson Locker, C. B. Lewis, Theophilus Lomax, Carter Lovelace, Z. R. Lovelace, E. F. Lovil, William T. Lovil, H. B. McFarland, Philip Maberry, Caleb McFarlan, M.H. McFarlan, T. S. McGinnis, John F. McNutt, Milton Maginnis, William D. Mitchell, S. R. Manlay, Markwood Marrett, Ross Martin, Jas. Merrett, James Miller, J. E. Moore, J. F. Moore, E. Y. Moss, Arthur Moping, C.R. Morriss, James Y. Morriss, Francis Mudd, Jesse Morriss, Lawrence Morriss, Nicholas Morriss, William Morriss, George L. Mudd, H. P. Mudd, Harris Murphy, Joseph Myers, J. J. Nichols, Caton Nunn, A. C. Parish, Jas. Parke,

Peter Parish, Benjamin Parsons, David Parsons, John Parton, Jesse Parsons, Nathan Parsons, Peter J. Parsons, L. H. Paxton, James R. Paxton, Nathan Penny, James Reason, Thomas Reed, sr., G. R--s (?) Reeds, David Reynolds, V. G. Sanders, Woodson Reynolds, Callestenes Sandford, Wesley Scobee, L. O. Scott, F. Shackleford, F.Shackleford, jr., Jesse Shaw, John Shrum, Thomas Shaw, S. M. Shaw, John W. Shrum, G. G. Sitten, Hankerson Sitten, William B. Sitten, John Sparrow, William Spradling, H. W. Sperry, Stephen Stephens, David Stewart, Thomas Stubblefield, Christopher Suddeth Jacob F. Swoet, Bolden Taliferio, Charles Taliferro, Lott Tarance, Robert Tompson, M. L. Thomas, G. Thomas, Samuel Trulove, Armsted Uptigrove, Isaac Uptigrove, jr., Isaac Uptigrove, sr., Wm. Uptigrove, William Uptigrove, jr., A. B. H. Victor, Buttell Vincent, Russell Vincent, James L. Walker, Micajah Wheeler, William White, James W. Williams, John C. Williams, James Wilson, Nathaniel Williams, John Wood, James A. Wren.

Hickory County, Missouri, Durnell Chapel Cemetery, State Rt. O and County Road 290 Southeast of Weaubleau, Missouri.

| Name | Born | Died |
|---|---|---|
| W. B. Downs | Apr. 3, 1883 | May 4, 1958 |
| Effie D. Downs | Jul. 30, 1893 | Feb. 24, 1973 |
| John W. Lockhart | Apr. 1, 1855 | Dec. 15, 1929 |
| Sarah Durnell | Jun. 28, 1854 | Dec. 16, 1961 |
| Jesse Durnell | Dec. 1, 1892 | May 26, 1896 |
| James E. Bullington | Dec. 22, 1896 | Feb. 4, 1972 |
| Ura Bullington | Aug. 25, 1897 | Dec. 31, 1972 |
| William Pruett | Feb. 25, 1866 | Feb. 23, 1945 |
| G. H. Richter | Jan. 22, 1865 | Apr. 4, 1902 |
| Bertha Allen | Mar. 10, 1886 | Mar. 17, 1916 |
| Francis K. Brown | May. 27, 1842 | Apr. 1, 1906 |
| Nancy R. Brown | Jan. 21, 1853 | Mar. 5, 1926 |
| ---- Chaney | --- | --- |
| George W. Durnell | 1870 | 1956 |
| Maggie Durnell | 1874 | 1946 |
| Cleo Durnell | Jul. 28, 1893 | Dec. 11, 1947 |
| Ethel Durnell | Feb. 21, 1894 | Feb. 3, 1928 |
| Mary E. Durnell | Jun. 2, 1862 | Feb. 3, 1938 |
| Thomas S. Durnell | Nov. 9, 1865 | Feb. 5, 1928 |
| Sarah Hunt | --- | --- |
| Elizabeth Hunt | --- | --- |
| Opal Hunt | Oct. 7, 1893 | Jan. 23, 1978 |
| Mary Johnson | Dec. 27, 1840 | Feb. 22, 1921 |
| Mordica McCracken | Oct. 2, 1853 | Mar. 8, 1930 |
| Josephine McCracken | Nov. 13, 1855 | May 1, 1948 |
| Cicero C. McCracken | 1880 | 1948 |
| Sarah E. Murry | Dec. 8, 1855 | Feb. 5, 1855 |
| Olin Murry | Feb. 1, 1877 | Mar. 2, 1877 |

| Name | Born | Died |
|---|---|---|
| David M. Floyd | Jul. 30, 1864 | Nov. 7, 1868 |
| Ardelia Hunt | 1873 | 1957 |
| Calvin Hunt | 1865 | 1944 |
| Bluford Hunt | Aug. 26, 1866 | Jan. 2, 1957 |
| Evelina Hunt | Jul. 4, 1873 | Nov. 4, 1942 |
| Curtice L. Hunt | May 12, 1892 | May 27, 1894 |
| Laura Hunt | 1863 | 1898 |
| W. C. Hunt | --- | --- |
| Lurana Hunt | --- | Dec. 4, 1886 |
| Thomas C. Durnell | 1860 | 1947 |
| Ophelia Durnell | Aug. 17, 1858 | Jun. 16, 1923 |
| Olen Durnell | May 22, 1892 | May 28, 1892 |
| Ronie Durnell | Jun. 28, 1892 | Mar. 24, 1897 |
| Benjamin A. Brown | Dec. 27, 1871 | Apr. 24, 1959 |
| Charles Home Cauthon | Aug. 26, 1895 | Jan. 1, 1964 |
| Naoma Virl Cauthon | Jan. 5, 1897 | Jun. 25, 1942 |
| Cuba Williams | 1897 | 1933 |
| Grant Thomas | Jan. 21, 1898 | Jun. 7, 1969 |
| Gustava Thomas | Aug. 21, 1897 | Dec. 13, 1959 |
| Alva C. Swicegood | Aug. 4, 1896 | Nov. 17, 1974 |
| Sarah Swicegood | Mar. 17, 1871 | Feb. 3, 1950 |
| William Swicegood | May 9, 1861 | Aug. 21, 1932 |
| Nancy A. Stokes | Jan. 3, 1840 | Mar. 28, 1910 |
| Robert Stokes | Jan. 13, 1879 | Oct. 8, 1927 |
| Celestie Stokes | Aug. 15, 1883 | Jun. 16, 1956 |
| Timothy Stokes | Jul. 2, 1898 | Dec. 15, 1978 |
| Cordelia Stokes | Oct. 30, 1872 | Apr. 1, 1910 |
| Jacob Stokes | Apr. 20, 1869 | Sep. 23, 1950 |
| Susan Marilla Ross | Feb. 8, 1856 | Dec. 23, 1950 |
| John R. Ross | Sep. 24, 1856 | Jan. 30, 1920 |
| Barney W. Pruett | Jul. 3, 1890 | Oct. 24, 1909 |
| Robert D. Pruett | May 5, 1868 | May 16, 1943 |
| Viola Pruett | Aug. 25, 1870 | May 6, 1954 |
| Thomas Neff | 1849 | 1927 |
| Thomas Hunt | Sep. 8, 1899 | Aug. 1, 1966 |
| Myrtle Hunt | May 19, 1899 | Dec. 17, 1973 |
| Clara Hunt | 1885 | 1972 |
| S. D. Hunt | Sep. 5, 1876 | Dec. 10, 1954 |
| Dona May Miller | Sep. 6, 1888 | Jul. 4, 1961 |
| James A. Miller | Aug. 23, 1887 | Aug. 10, 1874 |
| Margaret A. Miller | 1861 | 1934 |
| Barton S. Miller | 1861 | 1928 |
| Henry C. McDaniel | Sep. 6, 1844 | May 4, 1921 |
| Eliza W. Leibli | Jul. 4, 1856 | Oct. 24, 1946 |
| Anton F. Leibli | Apr. 20, 1859 | May 10, 1933 |
| Arminta Hunt | Nov. 14, 1880 | Feb. 14, 1944 |
| Henry William Gerke | Oct 27, 1893 | Jul. 21, 1968 |
| Harriett Fitzhugh | Jan. 12, 1863 | Jan. 24, 1902 |

| Name | Born | Died |
|---|---|---|
| George A. Fitzhugh | Mar. 15, 1861 | Dec. 29, 1927 |
| Blanche Durnell | Nov. 13, 1894 | Aug. 1, 1954 |
| Mittie Durnell | Aug. 8, 1895 | Mar. 19, 1915 |
| Virgie D. Durnell | Oct. 2, 1899 | May 26, 1902 |
| William B. Brown | Nov. 17, 1864 | Aug. 26, 1932 |
| Claude E. Brown | Dec. 11, 1897 | Dec. 25, 1971 |
| Nona Brown | Oct. 28, 1897 | Apr. 15, 1976 |
| James D. Chaney | 1873 | 1945 |
| Charlotte M. Chaney | 1886 | 1962 |
| James M. Chaney | Feb. 16, 1880 | Feb. 16, 1938 |
| Lee C. Crawford | 1886 | 1954 |
| Ina May Crawford | 1886 | 1946 |
| Otto Durnell | May 6, 1893 | Dec. 30, 1915 |
| Zoa Durnell | Dec. 23, 1890 | Jul. 21, 1905 |
| Lillie Downs | Nov. 13, 1897 | Feb. 24, 1973 |
| Noble Downs | Sep. 13, 1891 | Nov. 29, 1964 |
| Arthur Dehart | Jan. 18, 1885 | Sep. 5, 1969 |

<u>Monroe County, Missouri, Poll Book, November, 1844, Capitol Fire Documents, CFD 183, Folder 16241</u>

### Indian Creek Township

John G. Buckman, Joseph Buckman, John Calhoon (sic), John D. Fields, B. Carrio, Ignatius Carrico, A. B. Cornes, Samuel Dyer, Joseph Corrico, J. Edwards, James Elder, Ely Green, Q. T. Hand, George Forrest, Joseph Forrest, Thos. Forrest, John D. Green, Alexander Gelmer, George Gelmer, Joshua Gentry, E. Goodnight, John Gilmer, Leonard Green, Edward Hardesty, John S. Ireland, Hilery Hardesty, William Haresty, Riley Henry, Jasper Higgins, Joseph Higgins, Henry Jennurson, William T. Leake, William Lawrence, Jonathan Judge, Jabez Lewellen, R. Liewellen (sic), John Lewellen, Jabez Liewellen (sic), John Parres, (sic) James C. Parris, William Loff, William Melton, henry Miles, Richard Miles, A. R. Moorhead, A. Mudd, James Murphy, James C. Parsons, Elijah Peck, William Penn, Joseph Purcall, G. Purcall, Jannus Piercall (sic), E. Q. Riley, J. Riley, Richard Riley, Clement H. Roth (sic), Clement H. Rott (sic)(?), John S. Rubison, John Short, Michael Shuck, Henry Vermilion, A. Wimsell, Jacob Wright, Davis D. Yates, Raphael Yates, Thomas Yates, Vincent Yates, M. Young, Francis E. Zagar.

### Jackson Township

J. P. Acriff, Geo. Adams, Otho Adams, Thos. Aikin, David Ashby, J. Alexander, W. Allison, D. Anderson, T. B. Archer, N. L. Appleget (sic) Wm. Armstrong, H. Arnold, Wm. Arnold, Wm. Arnold, sr., A. Arnot, Wm. Atterberry, R. Baker, Marrice Baker, Jas. Atterbery (sic), J. Barker, Bela Barnes, Squire Barton, N. Barnes, T. M. Barnet, H. Barnett (sic), Taylor Barton, T. L. Barrett, S. Barton, J. M. Bean, John Bellmar,

Saml. Bellmar, Solomon Blessing, Benj. Bluebald, M. Bodin, H. A. Bondine, R. D. Bodine, H. W. Bookwood, E. W. Boon, S. J. Bound, N. B. Bowen, R. C. Bower, A. J. Boyd, Eli Bozarth, Peter Bramber, Wm. Bridgeford, C. J. Britton, Wm. Britton, C. Brown, Wm. Brown, C. W. Brwoning, Jacob Bruce, D. Bryant, E. Bryant, Geo. Bryant, J. Bryant, Jos. Bryant, S.L. Bryant, M. Bryant, Saml. Bryant, W. S. Bryant, W. A. Buckman, G. M. Buckner, F. Buckner, Theophilus Bullen, J. H. Bussey, Robt. Camel, Ambrose Bush, J. E. Campbell, W. B. Campbell, Wm. H. Carr, Wm. Campbell, S. W. B. Canage, H. C. Carder, George Cardwell, John Carroll, J. H. Carry, Wm. Carry, A. Carter, C. H. Carter, G. W. Carter, J. L. Carter, Peter Carter, Wm. S. Carter, Saml. Cartwright, D. Cawthorn, Wm. Chapman, C. C. Chinn, C. S. Clay, C. J. Collins, J. G. Coldwell, F. Combs, J. S. Conyers, S. W. Conyers, D. L. Cooper, John Cooper, J. W. Coopage, Isaac Coopage, M. Coppage (sic), Mason Coppage (sic), Simeon Coppage (sic), John Couch, J. S. Covington, J. V. Cox, J. M. Craig, J. S. Craig, W. M. Craig, John Crim, C. Crimm, Stephen Crimm, Saml. Crow, sr., W. W. Crump, O. Dry, A. Crutcher, Thos. Crutcher, Wm. Crucher, J. S. Cunningham, J. M. Curry, Wm. Curry, B. F. Davis, Benj. Davis, J. J. Dry, J. H. Davis, Wm. Davis, J. S. Dawson, Wm. Deaning, Eli Dry, J. W. Dearing, John Deering, S. J. Denison, Rho. Dever, Geo. Dickson, Phillip Divers, S. J. Dooley, Jas. Dowell, Mathew W. Evans, H. Dry, J. E. Dry, John Dry, Tho. Dry, J. H. Ford, A. G. Duckworth, G. H. Duckworth, G. W. Duckworth, J. England, W. G. Duckworth, G. M. Dulaney, John Dulaney, Garrod Fowkes, W. S. Dulaney, David Duncan, J. Duncan, P. Ellison, D. M. Ellison, Thos. Ellison, Jesse Ellsbury, A. A. Evans, John Farthing, Thos. Ferrel (sic), Wm. Ferrell (sic), C. W. Flanagan, Danl. Ford, J.H. Ford, Jacob Ford, sr., V. Fowkes, Tiry (sic) Ford, W. H. Forman, John Forsythe, J. S. Fowkes, Jos. Fowks (sic), J. C. Fox, Jas. Fugate, C. Furguson, Wm. Furguson, J. Gabbert, W. Garnet, Henry Gasscock, W. A. Geer, O. P. Gentry, Henry Gibson, Saml. Gilbert, T. J. Gillaspy, Geo. Glenn, E. T. Goe, O. Goings, Wm. Gooch, John D. Goodnight, A. Goodrich, E. Goodrich, M. P. Goodrich, A. E. Gore, Jonathan Gore, F. Gosney, Wm. Gosney, Wm. J. Gosney, Wm. B. Grant, T. G. Grant, Jos. Goss, John Graves, James Greening, R. Greening, Thos. Greening, S. W. Greer, S. C. Hackley, A. Grimes, S. Gross, A. Groves, Wm. Guttire, Wm. Haines, C. W. Hanagen, Wm. Hall, J. Hardick, G. W. Harlow, M. Harlow, L. Harris, G. C. Harrow, Trueman Hart, E. Hayden, C.W. Hawkins, J. P. Hawkins, Benj. Heathman, J. Heathman, J. T. Heathman, M. Heathman, S. Heathman, W. Heathman, Flem. Helms, H. Hill, J. W. Helms, Jos. Helms, Thos. Helms, P. Henneger, Thompson Holliday, J. H. Hill, Jas. Hill, John Hocker, Jos. Holliday, Horatio Hollingsworth, G. W. Holloway, John Howe, E. Hunt, W. J. Howell, Jos. Hutchison, J. R. Jacks, A. Jackson, Eli

Jackson, Wm. Jackson, A. James, Jos. James, A. Johnson, Geo. Jones, A. Jones, B. Jones, Wm. Jones, Wm. Jones, jr., G. M. Jorden, H. Jordon (sic), Martin Judy, H. Kelly, John Kipper, snr., J. C. Kipper, J. Kirkendall, A. Kirkland, G. S. Lake, J. G. Kirkpatrick, Malsey Larmer, P. Linton, Benjn. Long, W. M. Long, Joshua Long, E. W. McBride, P. H. McBride, Thos. C. McKarney, P. McCams, R. D. McCann, P. McCarns, J. McCarty, F. McChord, J. B. McChord, J. S. McFadden, J. McFarland, H. J. McGee, J. G. McGee, J. L. McGee, J. S. McGee, John McGee, Jos. McGee, sr., Josiah McGee, Josiah McGee, R. McGee, R. H. McGee, Wm. McGee, C. McGrue, Jos. McGrue, J. C. W. McKenny, W. G. McKey, H. McManama, J. C. McMurty, D. W. Major, Wm. Major, B. Mallory, Saml. Mallory, jr., M. Mappin, H. Martin, J. S. Marr, Levy J. Marr, Abm. Mason, G. G. Mason, R. Mukes, M. F. Mason, W. H. Mason, G. A. Mattox, Jesse Mattox, W. C. Mattox, I. Maupin, Boaz Maxcy, John J. Maxcy, D. A. Miller, Walter F. Maxcy, Samuel Miller, W. H. Miller, S. Million, B. F. Minor, Tho. Mills, Wm. E. Minor, A. P. Moore, T. Mosley, Austin Moore, J. C. Moore, J. H. Moore, R. H. Moore, Stephen Morrison, T. C. Moore, W. Mosely, G. M. Moss, T. T. Moss, R. Mukes, Wm. Mupin, Thos. Nelson, Samuel Nesbit, A. Newsom, N. Newsom, John Nichol, Robert Nichol, A. H. Nise, H. Noonan, Thos. Noonan, William T. Noonan, William Orr, L. Page, Thos. Palmer, G. F. Palmer, Burton Palmer, C. P. Parish, H. Poag, J. H. Parish, B. M. Parks, O. L. Parks, J. N. Parsons, J. M. Patrick, L. G. Patrick, A. Patterson, S. Patterson, J. Pool, Wm. J. Patterson, Geo. Peercy, Nathan Pieffer, S. Pickle, F. A. Poag, Jos. Poage, F. G. Pool. S. Pool. Thomas Pool, J. E. Power, P. W. E. Power, H. Powers (sic), John Powers (sic), M. N. Powers, R. D. Powers, G. W. Price, W. M. Priest, Benj. Raney (sic), Martin Ramey (sic), Santfor Ramey (sic), W. B. Ransdall, J. M. Ray, A. C. Rice, W. Rice, Elias Riley, James Rogers W. Robison, Wm. Rogers, A. E. Rucker, Wm. Rucker, J. B. Rundicil, Wm. Runkle, W. H. Russell, W. C. Sadler, Milton Saling, Jas. Saling, J. Saling, Bedford Saling, C. Sally, H. Sanders, John Sally, John Sallyng (sic), Wm. Sanders, Wiley Sandes (sic), John M. Sanizer, John Sayres, S. Scobee, David Shanks, Davis Scott, Thos. P. Sharp, Wm. M. Sharp, H. Simms, J. H. Sherman, J. H. Shott, James Shoot, A. G. Shortridge, Robt. Sikin, J. B. Simpson, R. Simpson, E. H. Smith, Geo. W. Smith, Geo. Smith, H. Smith, I H. Smith, J. B. Smith, J. H. Smith, J. P. Smith, J. R. Smith, John Smith, Jos. H, Smith, Josephus Smith, O. C. Smith, Samuel H. Smith A. C. Smithee, A. Smithee, Granville Snell, P. G. Snell, R. M. Snell, Jos. Sparks, J. I. Sparks, H. Sparks, M. Sparks, S. Sparks, Jos. Sprowl, W. M. Spencer, J. Speed, J. E. Sprowl, Wm. Stalcup, David Steel, Wm. Steel, Wm. Stephens, J. Stewart, R. Stice, Peter Stice, J. Stover, J. Strain, jr., T. Stribling, David Thomas, S. Tate, Maxsey Tanner, Thos. P. Thomas, G. Tuggle,

David Thomas, Dennis Thompson, John Thompson, S. Thompson, Jos. Thompson, Smith Thompson, Wm. Threlkeld, sr., Harrison Vaughn, Geo. Therlkeld, Wm. Therlkeld, H. Tillett, J. Trout, W. Tribbee, M. Trumbo, J. Twyman, W. R. Vanarsdall, Francis Williams, J. P. Vaugh, John Vaughn, Jos. Vaughn, sr., Saml. Walls, S. F. Vaughn, W. M. Vaughn, Jos. Veach, M. Vivion, A. H. Walden, Wm. Waller, Larkin Walters, M. C. Warren, B. S. Webb, Thos. Welch, Jos. West, R. F. West, R. M. West, Samuel West, Jesse White, H. L. Wigginton, M. Wiles, Peter Wiles, P. Wilkerson, Ferd. Williams, J. W. Williams, J. Willis, W W. Williams, John Willis, Jos. Willis, Lee Willis, C. Wills, D. Wills, J. W. Wills, J. B. Wilson, John H. Wilson, Hugh Withers, R. W. Wilson, W. Wilson, Wm. Wilson, W. Withers, F. Wood (sic), J. H. Woods, Jas. Woods, John Woods, B. Woodson, S. Woodson, A. Wright, A. J. Wright, John Wright, W. Wright, R. G. Wright, W. T. Wright, Charles Yakee, William Young, John Yowell.

## Jefferson Township

Jno. Allred, John Anderson, J. Banister, E. Barnes, T. A. Beall, C. Bear, A. K. Bell, Jas. Bell, Thos. Bell, K. Boggs, Robt. Blackbirn, Jas. Bond, F. Bowles, Ben Bradley, A. Bush, Felix Bradley, J. M. Bradley, S. G. Bradley, S. P. Bradley, Jas. Bryant, R. H. Buchanan, J. R. Buckman, R. C. Carter, A. Cartwell, S. P. Cason, T. J. Chowning, Jno. Cissell, Jno. M Crawford, P. Clapper, Joe Coal, Ben Cowherd, Wm. Cowherd, T. J. Crawford, Jas. Cox, Jon. Cox, G. W. Creed, Jerry Crigler, T. J. Creed, Joel Crigler, Jonas Crigler, J. Crockett, Jno. C. Crow, Jas. Dale, Marshal Damrell, E. Daniel, Noel Dayton, Wm. Decross, A. C. Donaldson, T. J. Donaldson, Job Dooley, Job Dooley, jr., S. Dooley, Geo. Dye, J. Dye, Jno. Dye, Rama Dye, Chas. Eales, Wm. Ealy, Hiram Engle, John L. Engle, Jas. M. Ferguson, Sandy Fagan, Jno. Fowler, J. W. Gathright, John Gatson, R. B. Goodwin, Joseph Greening, J. A. Grimes, Alexr. Hickman, B. Haines, R. Hanna, W. Hargood, T. N. Haycraft, A. Haynes, John C. Heizer, C. Herndon, E. Hewett, A. Hickman, H. A. Hickman, R. Hickman, James Hinson, R. Hirby, J. Ivie, Thos. Hurd, jr., Thos. Hurd, sr., W. Huston, G. Huteson, S. W. Johnson, J. W. Ivie, John Jordan, J. K. Keath, John Luke, B. Lawrence, G. B. Leachman, A. M. Leake, Saml. Leake, Jacob Lewis, John Lewis, Luke Lewis, Michael Lewis, Edmund Long, Jno. Long, Wm. Long, Wm. Lupton, Jno. Lyons, G. W. McGown, Henry S. McClure, A. McLabish (sic), Jno. McNutt, S, Maunce, R. W. Magruder, M. Manning, N. H. Marders, R. S. Marr, Wm. Middleton, E. M. Moffett, B. H. Morton, J. T. Morton, Jacob Painter, J. W. Orr, S. Norman, S. Nesbitt, James Nesbitt, Morgan Paris, Mos. (sic) Paris, T. Parker, Geo. Paynter, C. E. Penn, Wm. N. Penn, Jas. Phelps, Darius Poage, R. Poage, G. E. Poage, J. E. Poage, Thos. Poage, Harrison Prewitt, B. F. Price, Jno. A. Quarly, Drury Ragsdale, Saml. Ready, Thos.

C. Rice, Jerry Rouse, U. Rouse, William Samuel, Willis Samuel, John Scobee, Robert,Scobee, S. Scobee, jr., John Scott, Jesse Searcy, L. B. Sharp, C. Shatluck, Jas. S. Simms, R. L. Simms, Robt. Simpson, E. Smalley, David Snider, A. Steevett, James Stevenson, R. P. Stout, P. H. Swinny, Jno. Thomas, J. L. Thompson, R. D. Tuner, Richard H. Turner, Robert Turvis, Jno. Upton, E. Underwood, R. T. Underwood, William Upton, A. Utterbeck, Henry Utterback, R. Utterback, John Vandevanter, M. A. Violette, Henry Walton, B. G. White, J. M. White, John White, Joseph White, M. Wilkerson, Milton Wilkerson, Morgan Wilkerson, Wm. O. Wilkerson, S. P. Williams, T. Williams, W. W. Williams, C. Williamson, E. C. Wilson, W. G. Woodson, A. Wright, G. G. Young, H. Young, M. Young, Thomas Young, E. Yowell.

## Marion Township

William Adams, Gal. Alexander, Garland Alexander, Jno. M. Alexander, Thos. Allred, Wm. Alsbury, Daniel Arterbury, Wm. Baker, George Ash, Willis H. Atterbury, George Bagley, Isaac Baker, Elisha Baker, Moses Baker, Wm. N. Bassett, David E. Bryan, Alfred Boulware, Simpson Boulware, Jno. Briscoe, Baily, Brown, G. A. Brown, Jas. Brown, Rob. Brown, Sam. Bryan, Vincent Bryan, Jno. Buchannan, Nathaniel E. Bullock, Hernden Burton, Jno. Burton, R. B. Burton, Simeon Burton, Jno. Capp, Joseph Calaway, Andrew Capp, Charles Capp, David Capp, William Capp, Peter Capp, Charles H. Carter, Levi Caters (sic), Wm. Chandler, Fountain Chandler, Jno. W. Claybrook, Jno. Davis, Boulin Coats, Medad (sic) Comstock, Coonrod Creasman, Geo. Cunningham, Archibald Cruise, Bluford Davis, Evan Davis, J. H. Ellis, D. D. Embree, Evan Davis, senior, James G. Davis, Jno. Davis, James W. Davis, Jefferson Davis, Lewis Davis, Matison Davis, Richard A. Davis, Thomas Davis, Edward A. Dawson, W. W. Embree, John W. Dawson, Jno. Dearbourn, Elias Deyoung, J. W. Eubank, Samuel Dickerson, Lander Dodge, Martin Dorrell, J. C. Foreman, Willis Duncan, David B. Enoch, Richard Eubank, Jas. H. Evans, Joel Farrell, Tandy Farrell, Wm. Farrell, jr., Thoms. Farthing, Zacheriah Ford, Thomas Gaines, Washington Hays, Anderson Garnett, S. B. Garnett, Doctor S. H. Gaston, I. U. Harris, Jno. M. Glenn, James P. Grove, Martin Grove, John Grove, Robert Gwin, Handsford Haney, Saml. Harper, Sylvester B, Holmes, Henry Harris, Robt. Harris, Enoch Hayden, Liman Hockins, Francis Henson, Wm. H. Holliday, Jno. A. Holloway, Joshua Hutcherson, Vincent Jackson, Jesse Jinnings, Michael Klugh, Peter Peter Johnson, James M. Kiney, Edward King, Anderson Marders, William H. King, Jas. Love, C. P. Love, Jno. McNeal, B. F. Noel, Jno. Manion, Jesse W. Marell, Gilson (sic) Martin, Sandford Matthews, Wyate Maxfield, Jno. N. Meals, Jos. D. More, Jas. H. Milikin, Hugh Miller, Jno. Miller, Jno. Milhouse, Gideon Moberly, Wm. G. More, B. F. Noel, Garnet Noel,

Leroy Noel, Moses Noel, Thomas Noel, Bery Overfelt, V. R. Waller, Charles Overfelt, David Overfelt, Jno. Pendleton, Squire Patterson, Allen Phillips, Wm. Pickett, Jas. Porter, Samuel M. Quirey, Dr. N. Ray, Phillip Roberts, John Sanders, Squire Roberts, Achiles Rogers, Jacob Sanner, Henry Sharp, Mortimer Sharp, Wm. Sawyer, Levi Shortridge, Wm. Smith, Wm. Standford, Layton H. Smith, Wm. Snidow, Edward A. Stephens, Jas. Stephens, Jno. Stephens, sr., Jno. A. Stephens, John D. Stephens, Joseph Stephens, Phillip Swatts, James Swindell, Wm. Swindell, Wm. C. Swindell, Chesley Swinny, Henry Swinny, Henry Swinny, sr., Harvy Thompson, Waller Wethers, Benjamin Willson.

## Otto Creek Township

Martin Attbury, Thos. Attbury, Elishah Attebury (sic), Wm. Dry, Carter Baker, William Baker, Marion Bigs, John Bush, Amos Coats, Willis Duncan, Benjamin Dye, Wm. F. Gainst, Wm. Holder, Alexander Genings, J. M. Hagons, Perry Hamton, S. D. Hodge, George Hand, George Harnes, Stephen Hill, E. D. Holder, F. F. Holder, Wm. Hord, Henry Howell, James King, John Lindlay, Comadore McFarling, Joseph McRenolds, Henry Miller, Benjamin Mason, Monroe Million, Ervin Millon (sic), William Sanders, Edward Ridgby, Wiley Sanders, Morgan Sherman, C. G. Shoot, Walter Shopher, Wm. A. Sparks, Theoflas (sic) Vinson, William Webb, David Wetherford, James Williams, J.B. Willis.

## South Fork Township

James R. Alexander, Thomas J. Atkinson, Garland G. Biby, John Biby, jr., John S. Bibey (sic), Norman Biby, William Biby, sr., Wm. Blankenbaker, D. G. Blue, James F. Botts, Dr. John Bybee, Paton Botts, James Briggs, John W. Briggs, Allen Caruthers, Allen Cawthorn, Benjamin Carder, James Camplin, G. W. Clayton, Abraham Clement, Jacob Cox, Augustin Creed, James E. Crawford, Austin Creed, James Creed, William Creed, Wilenson (sic) Creed, Michael Crigley, George Crigley, D. L. Davis, Lewis Crigley, William Davis, Wm. Dollard, Abraham Finks, Samuel Drake, John Finks, Simeon Finks, Enoch Fruit, Robert Gray, Benjamin Hanna, David Hanna, James Hanna, John Hanna, Wm. Hanna, jr., William Hanna, sr., Daniel H. Heer, John Heer, John Hiscate, Joseph Hiser, Robert Hiser, Asaph E. Hubbard, J. B. Holloway, Clay H. Hubbard, Wm. Lamb, W. S. Lampton, Henry Lell, Mitchel Mateer, Edward Mosley, William Oldam, John Ogden, H. J. Peek, Wm. Perrin, James Powel, John Scoby, Hiram W. Powell (sic), T. G. Price, A. D. Reid, John Seaby, James S. Sinclair, James Sterrit, John Stuart, Daniel H. Theen, John Theen, James M. Vaughn, John J. Wever, James Wilfley, James Williams, William Yowell.

## Union Township

Charles Allin, Charles Balow, John Bell, John Boulerean, Joseph Bell, Simeon T. Blever, Larkin Brannon, Henry Burnam, Larkin Branum, Richard Branum, Waymack Brashers, James M. S.

Bury, Eliza G. Brody, Hudson Brodis, John R. Brodis, Peter M. Burras, Charles Burton, Jeremiah Burton, Charles Bury, Stephen M. Calloway, David Croswhite, Daniel M. Cruise, Wm. G. Dulaney, James Cunsley, Henderson Davis, Baily Dent, John Forman, Alexander Doyle, George H. Dulany, Joseph S. Dulany, William H. Dulany, Caleb M. Embree, Milton J. Embree, Robert Ferrel, Thos. Embree, Ezekiel Evans, Anthony Faucet, Joseph Fuch, Greenbury Featherstone, John Fuch, James A. Galbreth, Joel Gannet, Isham Garret, Sidney O. Gentry, Wm. Givings, S. W. B. Gideons, George Giddions (sic), Tandy B. Giddions, Wm. S. Lain, Thos. Grugin, John M. Harris, Joseph B. Harris, J. G. C. Milligan, John B. Hays, Martin Heathestone, George L. Hersman, Sandford Hedges, Joseph Hersman, Fleming Hubbard, Robert Hunter, John Jones, Aaron W. Lane, William Lightner, George Litteral, William H. Lowery, Martin Luttle, Lewis H. Mays, Edmund Madox, Isaach (sic) Martin, J. G. C. Milligan, Cornelus Nelson, Alexander Oldham, James Ounsby, Nicholas Rea, Christopher C. Reed, Anderson W. Reid, John Reid, Thos. J. Joseph M. Reid, William Reid, Joseph Roberts, Absalom W. Stephens, Michael Roberts, William Roberts, John Shaffer, Theodore, John A. Snell, William Stephens, Wm. R. Stephens, John G. Swindle, Joseph D. Swiney, Austin Swinney, Harvey A. Swinney, Preston Swinney, William Thomas, John Thompson, May B. Thompson, Isaach (sic) Thompson, Edward T. Tucker, Andrew Turner, Edward Tydings, Thos. M. Tydings, Little B. Waid, William Walter, Benj. Whitenburg, Daniel Whitenburg, Joseph Whitenburg, Thos. C. Wirt, Henry Wolf, William L. Wood.

## Washington Township

Geo. Adriaen, N. Allbert, H. Ashcraft, Sam Banks, Isaac Banks, B. Bounds, R. Bowlin, R. Bowlin, sr., Wm. Boyd, W. H. Burgess, P. Burgess, W. Burford, Carter, O. Carter, John R. Davis, J. Chaney, J. Chavez, James Collins, H. Condiff, J. Coomme, Jas. Cox, J. Crook, R. Crook, Wm. Davis, J. M. Dian, Jas. Deaver, H. Dooley, C. Edwards, Alex Fowler, L. Fowler, J. W. Fowler, W. Fowler, sr., W. C. Fowler, O. Gerry, G. B. Gough, Wm. Gibson, W. Gilbert, B. Gough, Jas. N. Gough, Wm. M. Gough, Joseph D. Gough, Wm. M. Gough, J. D. Green, Levi Green, A. M. Greenwell, Wm. Haringer, Charles Harrison, Wm. Harneger, Lee Harrison, N. Harrison, Wm. H. Hawkins, A. J. Haukins, W. Henderson, J. W. Henndon, D. Henniger, Wm. Jett, D. Henniger, Jno. Henniger, Adam Hichart, J. Kirkland, Jno. Kirkland, J. Lewis, A. Linberry, Richard G. Little, D. Luck, Jos. McGill, Thos. McGill, William McGruder, H. McNeel, John W. Martin, Thomp. Manuel, Tho. McPherson, Q. T. Martin, Jas. S. Parks, R. Martin, sr., C. G. Maupin, Thos. Maupin, James Raglans, Vincent Moreland, C. Parkwood, A. Penn, S. Penn, G. Penn, jr., G. Penn, E. Perkins, G. F. Phage, Sam Pollard, L. Price, R. Price, W. Prichett, Wm. Purchell, J. M. Quigley, N. M. Ragland, T. B. Ragland, J. Ragsdale, H. Roe, A. White,

A. G. Saunders, W. A. Saunders, C. Shraur, Nicolas Sickles, Jos. Sidner, Thornton R. Smith, R. Sparks, John Strayer, S. G. Styles, Wm. Styles, Tho. Swain, Tho. Swann, W. Thomason, S. Searinger, Thos. Searinger, Alex. Thompson, E. Watts, C. Wood, Robinson Thrailkell, Jos. M. Vansarsaall, L. Zigler, R. Vanschoike, Saml. Vanschoike, Geo. W. White, A. G. Williams, F. Williamson, Geo. Williamson, Jacob Williamson, Lisa Williamson (?), Wm. Williamson, Fielder Wood, Vincent Worland, Jas. Wood.

Perry County, Missouri, Licenses Granted, February Term, 1840, Capitol Fire Documents, CFD 31, Folder 1352.

| To Whom Granted | Commencement | Termination |
|---|---|---|
| Joseph Pratte & Son | Jan. 14, 1839 | July 14, 1839 |
| Robt. M. Tucker and Jas. Cashion | Nov. 9, 1839 | May 9, 1840 |
| Isaac G. Whitworth | Nov. 9, 1839 | May 9, 1840 |
| Morris Block | Nov. 9, 1839 | May 9, 1840 |
| Moritz Behrle | Nov. 12, 1839 | May 12, 1840 |
| Tinnon & Daly | Nov. 13, 1839 | May 13, 1840 |
| Anson P. Norton | Nov. 14, 1839 | May 14, 1840 |
| Ferdinand Rozier | Nov. 18, 1839 | May 18, 1840 |

Cass County, Missouri, 1848, Tax List.
T. D. Akin; Wiley M. Akin; Stephen Acres; Wm. B. Agnew; Cornelius R. Anderson, 40 a, 80 a, (OC) Cornelius R. Anderson; John Amint, 18 a, (OC) J. C. Berryman; John C. Agnew; Robinson C. Anderson; John R. Ashcraft; John Antill; Thomas W. Ament, 67 a, (OC) J. C. Berryman; James R. Ament; Henry Adams; Ervin Alderson; Elihu Ashcraft, 40 a (OC) Elihu Ashcraft; Robert Acres; Mary Anderson; James Anderson; Robert Anderson; Otho L. H. Ashcraft; Alfred Ashcraft; Squire L. Allen; Sidney Adams, 40 a, 40 a, 80 a, 80 a, (OC) Sidney Adams; Sidney Adams, 80 a, (OC) Thos. M. Hood; Sidney Adams, 160 a, (OC) John Pettyman; John Adams; Jesse Ashcraft; John Ashcraft; Jacob Arnett; Anderson Allen; Alexander Arnett; Isam Adams; Jesse Auldridge; William Adams, 74 a, (OC) Thos. Hobbs; John Adams; Nathan Auldridge; James Akin; Thomas B. Arnett, 11 a, (OC) Thomas B. Arnett; Wyatt Adkins; Benj. C. Adkins; James M. Adkins; Gideon B. Arnett; W. J. Andrews; Jacob Allen; Andrew Allen; Elijah Atkinson; Mauzey Q. Ashby, 155 a, 160 a, 159 a, 79 a, 320 a, 240 a, 320 a, (OC) Mauzey Q. Ashby; Thomas Alexander, 40 a, (OC) John Hicklin; Robert Aull, 80 a, (OC) John Hicklin; Wesley H. Arnett; Jas. Adams; Stephen Abstan (sic); Alex. Armstrong; John M. Armstrong; E. L. Beck; John H. Beck, 80 a, (OC) Samuel Orr; Joseph Brooks; Thomas H. Brown; George W. Beck; P. D. Brooks; Joseph Beets; John Blackstone; James Barrett; David Bennett; James Butt; Henry Brooks; Wm. C. Burford, 80 a, 160 a, (OC) Wm. C. Bur-

ford; John L. Brooks, 80 a, 160 a, (OC) John L. Brooks; Jas. Blakeley; William Baldridge; Jehu Bouse; William Butram; Job Bouse; James Barnard, 80 a, (OC) James Barnard; Alexander Barnard, Isaac Blazer, 79 a, 80 a, 40 a, 40 a, (OC) Isaac Blazer; Silas Bouse; Frederick Bouse; John Bouse; Richard D. Berry, 40 a, (OC) Richard D. Berry; Wm. Bickerstaff; Thomas Burris; Hamilton Burris; Elias Burris; Thos. F. Bryant; Ira Bedwell; P. J. Burrow; James Brooks; John Brady; Elizabeth Barker; Isiah Brown, 80 a, (OC) Sanford Porter; James Bayse, 160 a, (OC) Evan H. Buck; Wm. C. Brown; John Ballard; Hannah Barnett; William Boyer; Robert Bicketts; Moses Brumfield; H. B. Bouton; John Brasfield; Wm. J. R. Bailey; Wm. L. Burton; Alfred Bybee, 80 a, 40 a, 40 a, 40 a, (OC) Alfred Bybee; Wm. Bullock; Alfred Bybee, 160 a, (OC) James Black; John Best; Walter Bradberry; Wm. L. Burton; Evan H. Buck, 38 a, 80 a, (OC) Evan H. Buck; Minerva Brooks, 40 a, 80 a, (OC) Lynch Brooks; John Burford, 80 a, (OC) Joseph Beets; Josiah Best; Alexander Blair, 40 a, 40 a, 80 a, (OC) Alex. Blair; William Bailey; Isaac Blowing; John Bedwell, 40 a, (OC) Joseph Prigmore; James Bones, 40 a, (OC) James Bones; Elias O. Brooks; J. M. C. Bullock, 37 a, 79 a, 79 a, 80 a, 40 a, 80 a, 40 a, (OC) J. M. C. Bullock, David B. Combs, Peter Welch; Benjamin Britton; Jouden Bennett; Fields Bledsoe; Wm. Brandon; James B. Bailey; James Bailey; Wm. Blackburn, 160 a, 80 a, 80 a, 40 a, 40 a, 80 a, 80 a, 40 a, (OC) Wm. Blackburn, Hiram Davis, Alex. Blair; Levi G. Boren; Leonard Bradberry; Alex. A. Burney; John Briscoe; Wm. M. Briscoe; Chas. G. Briscoe; John Belcher; Nancey Belcher; Daniel Belcher; Mastan Burris; Jas. A. Burney; Michael Burkhart; Isaiah Burris; Perry G. Brock; William Butram, jr., Newton P. Brooks, 80 a, (OC) Newton P. Brooks; Andrew W. Black, 40 a, (OC) Henry F. Baker; Henry F. Baker; David Burris, jr.; John Bones; Moses Bailey; Abram Bolejack, 40 a, 40 a, (OC) Abram Bolejack; Jacob Butram, Wm. Bradshaw; Johua (sic) Bayse; John P. Barnaby; Samuel Blakey; Robert A. Brown, 36 a, (OC) John Cook; Wiley Bailey; Samuel Bargin; Pleasant Barley; Wm. Bradshaw; Hiram Bicketts; Isaac Bledsoe; Lindsay Burney; Wm. P. Burney; William Bedwell, 40 a, (OC) Joseph Prigmore; John Baker, 160 a, 80 a, (OC) Henry Pemberton; Zachariah Benson, 80 a, 80 a, 160 a, 160 a, 80 a, 80 a, (OC) Wilson Adams; John W. Briscoe, 40 a, 40 a, (OC) John W. Briscoe; Martha Bunn, 80 a, (OC) Martha Bunn; Jacob Bouse; Simon Bradley, on the middlefork of the Grand River, a (?), (OC) Simon Bradley; Cornelius Butram; William Bailey; John Brandon; Beverly Burton; William E. Boswell; William Bartram, jr.; John Cummins; Nathl. Chamblis; Abram Cassel; John Clayton; John Cougherour, 80 a, 40 a, (OC) Henry F. Baker; John F. Calloway; A. J. Coots; James H. Calloway; David Cook; Thomas Campbell; Widow Cole; Wm. T. Cole; Samuel Cole; Lucy Cochom; Jas. Cusick, 80 a, (OC) Jas. Cusick; Almond G.

Copley, 40 a, (OC) A. G. Copley; Chris. H. Clark; Blackston Cornett; David Cook, 40 a, (OC) Samuel Porter; Elijah Cook, dec.; Lucas Corlew; William Childers; Wash Childers; David Cooper, 40 a, (OC) Henry Cooper; George Cooper; dec.; Nathan Cornett; Joseph Cathey; Jackson Childers; Christian Cooley; William Curran; Joseph Clymer, jr., 160 a, 80 a, (CO) Joseph Clymer; Allen Clymer; Robert Crays; Aaron Case; Henry Cook; Lucretia Coatney; Volentine B. Cook; David M. Cook; Thomas Cummmings; Benjamin Cummings; George W. Cockrell; Alexander Conway; Simon Cockrell; Theren Crossland; William Conner; Mary Charles, 40 a, (OC) Mary Best; Samuel Cornett, 80 a, 80 a, 80 a, 40 a, 40 a, 40 a, 40 a, 80 a, (OC) Robert Cornett, Isaac Cornett, Joseph Sterling; Isaac Carter, 158 a, 160 a, (OC) Isaac Hutchins and Isaac Carter; Volentine M. Cook, 80 a, (OC) John Cook; Joseph Cusick, 80 a, (OC) Joseph Cusick; Peter Carnell; Covington Cooper; Alexander Cockrell, 160 a, (OC) William Davis; Henry Corlew; James A. Corlew; James A. Corlew, sr.; Robert Corlew; William Chilton; Wm. Carmichael; James Caruthers; Geo. Carmichael; William Crawford; Stephen Cassell; Jane Cook, 160 a, 83 a, 80 a, (OC) John Cook; James L. Cook; Thomas Cook; Joana Carter, William Y. Cook, dec., 26 a, 26 a, (OC) John Cook; Green Collins; John B. Cook, 40 a, (OC) John Cook; John Colbern; Joseph H. Carter; Thomas E. Clayton; Joel D. Campbell; Achilles Cook; John Calloway; Wm. Cary; Madison Cary; Saml. Cunningham, 80 a, (OC) Saml. Cunningham; Wm. Cunningham, 80 a, (OC) John Hicklin; Jefferson Cary, 37 a, 40 a, 37 a, (OC) Jacob Spainhour, Martin Rice; Jacob Carpenter, 80 a, 40 a, 80 a, 38 a, (OC) Jacob Carpenter; James Cox, 20 a, 40 a, 20 a, (OC) J. Stone, J. Henderson; H. L. P. C. Calloway; William Carter; Harvey Cameron; Monroe Cameron; Jas. C. Copeland; Thomas Collins; Hamilton Carmichael, 80 a, (OC) Hamilton Carmichael; F. M. Chadowing; John M. Clark, 40 a, 80 a, 40 a, (OC) Abram Hendricks; John C. Christian; Milton Creek; Andrew Collins; Edward Carrol, 80 a, (OC) Edward Carrol; James Clark; John Cole; Estate of Morgan Cockrell, 160 a, 80 a, 76 a, (OC) Morgan Cockrell's estate; John Cook, 26 a, 26 a, 26 a, (OC) Minor heirs of John Cook; Thomas Calloway, 80 a, 74 a, 78 a, 80 a, 79 a, 70 a, 79 a, (OC) Benj. Thomas, Jacob Thomas, Thomas Calloway; Jesse Carton, 80 a, (OC) James Fletcher; Lindsey T. Cook, 80 a, (OC) John Cook; Josiah Carter, 80 a, (OC) Stephen Easley; Hiram Campbell; John Chrisman; James Cook; James Doland; Wm. H. Duncan; Richard J. Dejarnett 80 a, 80 a, 80 a, 80 a, 40 a, (OC) Richard J. Dajarnett; C. J. Dejarnett, 40 a, 80 a, 160 a, 80 a, 40 a, (OC) C. J. Dejarnett; Richard H. Dickson; Jourden Dulaney; Griffin Dulaney; Hugh Dunbar, 40 a, (OC) D. J. Floyd; Lorenzo E. Dickey, 110 a, (OC) Samuel Porter; John Dice, 40 a, 40 a, (OC) John Dice; Jesse Davison, 80 a, (OC) Jesse Davison; Harrison Davis, 160 a, 160 a, (OC) Harrison

Davis; William Day; Charles Duncan; Edward Dale; Volentine Daniels; James Demasters, 41 a, (OC) William Demasters; Wm. Davis, 80 a, (OC) William Davis; Barnett Dudley; Christena Duncan; David Davis; James Duncan; Josiah H. Davison; James L. Duncan; Aquilla Davis; Richard Dickson, sr.; Wm. Dickson; Charles Dickson; Wm. H. Duncan; Thomas Dickey; John Dickey, 40 a, (OC) Martin Rice; James Dickey; Peter Daniels, 50 a, (OC) Allen James; John Daniels; John Davis, 40 a, 80 a, (OC) Harrison Davis; Eli Dodson; B. F. Davis; Eleazor Dickson, 149 a, (OC) Eleazor Dickson; Chas. Davison, free negro; Wm. S. Dudley; Orrien Derby, 160 a, (OC) Orrien Derby; Humphrey Dickson, 40 a, (OC) James Vanslike; James Davenport; Julius Davenport; Alexander Elliott; Elisha Evans, dec., 80 a, 80 a, 80 a, 40 a, 80 a, (OC) Wm. L. Evans, John Evans; Martha H. Erwin; Hiram Edwards, 80 a, (OC) Hiram Edwards; William Erwin; Enos Ellis, 80 a, 80 a, 40 a, (OC) James McKill; B. K. Erwin, 80 a, (OC) Young Ewing; Andrew M. Eisle; Emeline Enos; Isaiah Evans, An-- (?) Edmundson; Wm. Edmundson; John W. Estes, dec., 40 a, 40 a, 80 a, 40 a, 200 a, (OC) Watson Lynch, John Hicklin, John W. Estes; Wm. C. Estes, 80 a, 40 a, 39 a, 40 a, 80 a, (OC) Elbert Lynch, Wm C. Estes; William Enos, dec., 40 a, 40 a, 80 a, 79 a, 79 a, (OC) Peter Welch, James Bullock, Wm. Enos; Harris Estes, 40 a, (OC) Andrew Lower; Rufus C. Edmunson, 40 a, 40 a, 40 a, 40 a, (OC) William Edmunson, Anthony Hines; Thomas Emmerson; Sarah Easley, 38 a, (OC) Chas. S. Easley; Charles Easley, 36 a, (OC) Stephen Easley; Wm. H. Ewing, 40 a, (OC) Wm. H. Ewing; Peter Franse; Joshua Flinn, 134 a, (OC) Joshua Flinn; Arthur Fulton; David Fulton, 80 a, 80 a, 80 a, 80 a, (OC) Arthur Fulton, L. P. Stacey, Thos. R. Simpson; James W. Feely; Hannah M. Foster; Marvin Foster; James Foster; Martin Foster; John Franse; Nancy Frost; Abraham Fonda, 80 a; Gardner Farmer, 80 a, (OC) Wm. Hufft; Wm. Ferrell, 40 a, 37 a, 60 a, 40 a, (OC) P. M. Frost, J. B. McFerren, H. Davis; John Ferrel; Elihu W. Fox; Joseph C. Ferrel; James Fulton; Comodore Fulton; Oliver Fulton; Edmund Findley, 80 a; Lewis Findley; Willis Feely; Alexander Feely; David Findley; John Feely; William Farmer; John Freeman; Russell Ferguson; P. Foster; Martin P Foster; Andrew Freshour; Lienten Fowler, 156 a (OC) John Job; Wilson Feely; Charles Fleetwood; Thomas F. Freeman; James Flemming; Frederick Farmer; John M. Farmer; Thos. J. Fristoe; John B. Flemming; Violinda Flemming; David Flemmng; Henry Farmer; H. Finey; John T. Franklin, 38 a, 19 a, (OC) Jas. Tucker, J. T. Franklin; Andrew Farmer; Andrew Farmer; Moses Farmer; Martin Furguson; Fleming H. Fulton; William Fleming; Calvin Foster; Nancy Farmer; William Fry; John Fine; John Fewson, 80 a, 80 a, (OC) Thomas Burris, sr.; M. W. Flouney, 40 a, 160 a, 80 a, 160 a, 80 a, 40 a, 80 a, (OC) Dewit Pritchett, Wm. Fine, Mathew Flourney, Edley Hooper; William Frost; Miles Griffin;

William Farmer, jr.; Creed T. Fulton; Gunnils Jackson; H. G. Glen; Glen & Ostrander, 40 a; Wm. Gilbreth, 40 a, (OC) John Evans; Jesse Gasaway; John Golding, 38 a, 19 a, (OC) James Tucker; John Franklin; Macomb Gregg; Chesley Gates, 40 a, 80 a, 40 a, 40 a, (OC) Samuel Pile, Jas. R. Gates; John Green; Alexander Gilham; Widow Gomlen; William Gunnels, dec.; John Gilmore; Sarah Griffith, 40 a, 80, a, 80 a, 40 a, 80 a, 40 a, 0 a, (OC) Samuel Pruett, Robert Griffith; Alex Griffith; Charles E. Griffith; John Griffith; Nathan Gregg; Pleasant Gowing; John Gregg, 40 a, 40 a, 40 a, (OC) Isaac Strong, Jos. Prigmore; Aaron Gregg; James Gregg, 160 a, 80 a, 40 a, (OC) Robert Cornett, James Watts; Joseph Glass; George W. Gowing; John A. Green; John Gray; Aquilla Graham; Lauretta Glascock, dec., 80 a, (OC) Asa Glascock; Grunt Lawson; Hiram Grunt; Hiram Graham; A. J. Gibson; John Gibson, 37 a, 37 a, (OC) C. McKnight, Isaac Gibson; Owen; Jos. S. Hansbrough; H. B. Hawkins, 80 a, (OC) Andrew McAlexander; Aaron Harless; William L. Harris; Flemming Harris; Barnet Holloway; George Hackler; Flemming Holloway; John Hobbs; Anne Hobbs; Lawson Holloway; John Holloway, jr.; Thomas Holloway; David Halloway; James Holloway; Joseph Holloway, 40 a, (OC) Wm. Taylor; William Holloway; John Hammontree; James Hoouchins, 80 a; H. M. Hansbrough, 80 a, 40 a, 80 a, 166 a, 164 a, (OC) Needham Hamby, John Cook, G. D. Hanbrough; Enoch Hansbrough; Elijah Hansbrough; Wm. T. Hatfield; C. O. P. Hatfield; John Hickum; Benjamin Hiser; Elisha Hendricks; Hiram Harris; John Hubble, dec., 160 a, 110 a, 80 a, (OC) A. J. Ashcraft, J. Hubble; Lewis Highley; John Harbert, 40 a, 40 a, 80 a, (OC) Samuel Pyle, J. Harbert; James Harbert, 40 a; James M. Hill, 40 a, 40 a; Martin Hackler; James F. Hackler; Samuel Herril; Jacob A. Hamby; Anderson Herril; Needham Hamby, 80 a, 38 a, (OC) Thomas B. Arnett, Jackson Childers; John J. Hensley; William Hensley; James B. Hensley; William T. Hensley; Wm. W. Hensley; Middleton Hensley; John Hensley; David Hufft; Humphrey Hunt; David Hufft; Widow Hufft; William Hufft; Hugh Horton; Jarvis Hayden; David N. Horton; Thos. M. Horton; John Ham; John Haislip; Bluford Haines; Agness Harless; Michael Hiser; Amanda Hendricks; Jacob Hiser; Reuben Hiser; Geo. W. Henry; Giles Hutson; John Houston, 80 a, 80 a, 40 a, 40 a, (OC) Wm. A. Vowel, John L. Vowel, John Houston; William R. Harris, 40 a; Jefferson Harris, 40 a, (OC) Jas. Bones; Charles Hughes, 160 a, 80 a, 40 a, 40 a, (OC) Jas. H. Hughes, Chas. Hughes; Thos. J. Harris; Judith Harris, dec.; Josiah Harrison, 80 a, 40 a, (OC) Peter Welch; Eli S. Harris; Joseph Hall; Charles Hamilton, 79 a, 99 a; Estate of Samuel Hamilton, 79 a; Hugh Hamilton, 159 a; Robert Hamilton; Absalom Hicks; John A. Hicks; John B. Hook, 56 a, (OC) Jobe & Hook; John C. Hughes; James Hughes; Jacob Horn; James Hamilton; Abner C. Houchens; Samuel Hannor; Joseph Hughes; James Hurndon; James Highton;

Samuel Hamilton; N. E. Harrelson; John Hail; Henry J. Hail; Mastin V. Hornsby; Henry Hincle; John Hincle; James Hincle; Edwin Hincle; Thomas Hincle; Nathan Haines; Joshua Hansen, 37 a, 80 a; Shadrick Holcomb; Thomas Holcomb, sr.; Thomas Holcomb, jr.; A. Hocker; Estate of Elijah Hooper; William Henderson; Edley Hooper, 40 a, (OC) Chas. A. Goshen; Samuel Henderson; James Henderson; Barnett Hall; Elijah Hooper; G. D. Hansbrough; Benjamin F. Hays; Ana Howel; William Heath; William Huntsucker; Elijah Hill; George Harrison; Miles Harless; Elijah B. Hicks; John C. Henderson; William Hagans; T. M. T. Jackson; Joseph Howard, 40 a, (OC) Worham Easley; Alex Iddings; Martin Houston, dec., 40 a, (OC) William Powell; H. C. Jackson; Benjamin Hinshaw; Allen Ingle, 53 a, 160 a; Wm. Ison; Parmelia Ison; Morris Ison; Robert Irvin; Green Ison; William Idson (sic); Jeremiah Jones, 80 a, (OC) Jas. Black; Thomas J. Jennings; Jehu Jackson; Allen Jackson; Elizabeth Ann James; John Jackson, 40 a, 40 a, 40 a, 40 a, 40 a, 40 a, 40 a, 40 a, (OC) Wm. M. Settle, L. A. Settle, Wm. O. Taylor; Frances Jackson; Isaac Jackson; Jane James; Martha J. James; Jesse James, 40 a, 40 a, 80 a, 160 a, (OC) William Powell; Eli Joes, 160 a; Thomas Jackson, 40 a, 80 a, (OC) John Hicklin, T. Jackson; H. C. Jackson; Henry Jobe, 71 a, 35 a, (OC) John Jobe, Jobe & Hook, Henry Jobe; Wm. A. Jack; James C. Jackson; Linsey Jackson; Berry James, 20 a, 40 a, 80 a, (OC) Allen James, Berry James; Solomon Johnson; Wiley Jones; John Kerr; Abner L. Jones; Jeremiah James, 40 a, 40 a, 40 a, 80 a, (OC) John Daniels; Wash. Jones; Joseph Kelly; Isaac King; Nathan King; William King; Miles Keeton;Emberson Keeton; Wm. Keeton, sr.; John Kelly, 80 a, 80 a, (OC) Nancy Frost; Perry Knighton; Asbury King; Joseph Kimberland, 39 a, 80 a, (OC) Henry Rider; Elizabeth Kincaid; James R. Kincaid; John Lyon; William Knight; John M. Keeton; David Keeney, 40 a, 40 a; H. M. G. Kinkaid; Josiah Keeran, 160 a, 80 a, 80 a, 40 a, 40 a, (OC) John Farmer, J. Keeran; William Kupper; Margaret Lucas; Jesse F. Lee, 80 a, 80 a, (OC) Elias Burris, Thos. Burris, jr.; Daniel Lyon; Lewis Lee; Henry L.Lyon; Oliver Little; J. D. Lowery; Jesse Lay; John M. Lewis; Thomas Launnon; George Ludwick, 80 a, 40 a, 40 a, 40 a, (OC) Geo. Ludwick, Thos. J. McDaniel; William Lowery; Solomon Lynch; Widow M. Lynch; Wm. Lynch, on Big Creek; Hiram Lewis; Richard Longacre; John E. Lightner; George Long; William Long; Louis Lassconte, 40 a, 40 a, (OC) James Noland; Creed Lundy, 40 a; William Lynch; Henry Landers; Wesley W. Lynch, 39 a, 40 a; Aaron Lynch, 40 a, 40 a, 40 a, (OC) Spencer Rice, Thos. Hughes, A. Lynch; B. W. Meadow; John Lynch, 80 a, 20 a, (OC) Thos. Hughes; James Lawrence; James Lynn; Hardin Leach; Manuel Laws, negro; Adam Lammon, 80 a, 80 a, 40 a; Harvey E. Lawrence; J. C. Morris; Wm. R. Maxwell; Jesse Moriss; Sandford J. Morriss; Joseph McMullin; James C. McClelan; John O. McFerrin; Thomas J. D.

Moffett; Christian Miller; Robert S. Morriss; J. C. Morriss; Patrick Murphy; Rev. Alexander Majors; Wm. T. McCleland; B. L. McFerrin, 80 a; Juliann McCord; John Murry; James McKee; John McKee; B. L. McFerrin, 80 a; C. P. McColough; Joseph L. Maxwell; George Mills, 40 a, 35 a, (OC) Thomas Patton; John Mills; Lewis Musick; Ephraim Musick; John Majors; Estate of Samuel Moor, 80 a, 160 a; Marion Martin; James McCool, 40 a, (OC) Jas. R. Gates; Joseph McCord; Widow Mitchell; Nathan H. McKinney, 79 a, 79 a, 39 a, (OC) Nathan H. McKinney; Robert Means, 780 a, (OC) Sanford Porter; Joseph Means; Robert Miscal; Thomas Murry; Daniel Med; John W. Montgomery; Allen B. Mathia, 40 a, (OC) Riley Frost; Joseph L. Maxwell; John S. McCrawl; Sarah McCrawl; John Millsap; M. A. E. Morris, 40 a, (OC) E. S. Payne; Elizabeth McAlexander; Robert McAlexander; Samuel T. McAlexander; Samuel M. Majors; David Majors; John Miller; Daniel Miller; James W. McCleland; Abram Murry; Abel Massey; Jesse G. McDonald; Henry Massey; John S. Meador; R. M. Miller; Jesse V. Meador; John P. Moor; Thomas McCord; Wm Moffett; Logan McReynolds; Samuel McAninch (sic); William S. Norton; John Mathew; John Majors, 40 a, 40 a; Peter Majors; Absalom Majors. 40 a; James Moor, 40 a, (OC) Edwin Hincle; Squire Majors; John Mulkey; James Melone, 40 a, 40 a, 39 a, 80 a, 40 a, (OC) Jasper Hopper, Thos. McKnight; John Miller; George Miller; Jacob Miller; John McClung, 80 a, 40 a, 30 a, (OC) John Gibson, Alen James; Charles Mires, jr.; Archibald McGuire; James Miller; James Miller (sic); David C. Moor; William Mills; Joseph Montgomery, 80 a, 80 a, 80 a, 80 a, 80 a, 40 a, 80 a, 80 a, (OC) H. C. Davis, J. B. Sears, J. Montgomery; H. C. Meek, 80 a, (OC) Hiram Harris; J. B. McFerrin; Isom Majors, 80 a, (OC) Isham Majors; John McElvain; Jarret McClain; Benjamin McClain; Benjamin McClain; Henry Newman; William McClain; Stephen McReynolds; Hosea H. Nunnally; John Nix; Widow Newman; Joseph Newman; Angeline Nelson; Fountain Nailor; Isaac Nolen, 80 a, 81 a; Wid. A. Nailor, 59 a, 37 a, 39 a, (OC) Hiram Davis; Liborn Nailor; Jesse Newman; Edmond Nelson; Benjamin Nicholes; David Obrian, 82 a, (OC) William Erwin; Elias Owens, 40 a, 40 a, 80 a, (OC) Thomas Owens; Wm. Oldham; Abagail Owens, 160 a, (OC) Solomon Acres; Alfred W. Oldham; Samuel Orr; Aaron Oxley, 30 a, (OC) Danl. Floyd; W. J. Parker; James W. Oldham; Noah Oneal; John Oneal; Tarply Oldham; William Ousley; William R. Owens, 80 a, 80 a, 40 a, 40 a, 40 a, 40 a, 80 a, 80 a, (OC) Thos. J. McDaniel, Morris Malone, Jas. Sulivan; John Oliver; Samuel C. Owens, 40 a, 40 a, 40 a, (OC) Joseph McCraw; George Oldjam, jr.; Richard E. Price; A. S. Pullam, 40 a, 40 a; Henry Payton, 80 a, 80 a, (OC) Rubin Nelson; Edward Payton; Silas Price, 149 a, (OC) Wm. L. Wilson; John Potter; Peter Potts; Thomas Patton, 152 a, (OC) Thos. Patton; George M. Pettygrew; William B. Poage, 80 a, (OC) G. W. Patrick; Richard L. Pettis, 160 a, 40 a, 40 a, 80 a, 40 a, (OC) Octine Evins; Samuel Pyles, 40 a; Estate of John Pyle, 40 a, 40 a; Henry Palmer; Nicholas C. Poague, 160 a, 40 a; Cyrus Potts; Elisabeth Potts, 80 a, (OC) Hosea Ashcraft; Charles Potts; David Phipps; Jacob E. Peck; Robert Picketts; James Parsons; George W. Peck; John Prettyman, 40 a; Joseph Peyton; John W. Pulliam; Thomas Prettyman; Milton Parker; E. S. Payne, 80 a, 80 a, 40 a, 40 a, (OC) John Newton, E. S. Payne; Enoch L. Pettit, 40 a; Hillory Philips; George Preston, 80 a; James W. Porter, 40 a, 40 a, 40 a, 40 a, (OC) James W. Porter; James Preston; Mary Paul; William H. Palmer, 40 a; Hugh Paxton; William Parker; Enos Pilcher; Greenbury Parker; William C. Parker; James B. Parker; John T. Philips; Callaway Prigmore; Henry Philips; Samuel Potter; Edward Pleasants; William G. Pleasants; John T. Pleasants; Thomas Pursiville; Theopholus Powell, 160 a; Harris Ralls; Edwin Pursiville; Mordica Philips; John M. Philips; Ruphus (sic) Pilcher; William Purket; William Pursiville, 40 a, 40 a, (OC) William English; Robert Persille, 40 a; William C. Porter, 40 a, (OC) J. B. McFerrin; R. L. G. Peyton; John Y. Porter, 80 a, 40 a, (OC) Samuel Porter, Wm. C. Porter; David M. C. Pettigrew; Daniel Prigmore, 168 a; Winchester Payne, 77 a, 160 a, (OC) James Black, F. H. Fulton; G. W. Peyton, 80 a, (OC) Wm. C. Black; A. B. Palmer, 160 a, (OC) Samuel Potter; Minor heirs of Catharine Palmer; James Philips, 40 a; (OC) S. W. Pilcher; Estate of Henry Pemberton, 40 a, (OC) Samuel Carter; Jesse Purkins, 40 a, (OC) John Cook; Calvin Powell; Robert E. Price; William Philips; William M. Rider; Jackson Quisenberry, 80 a, 160 a, (OC) Alexes Freeman; Widow S. Reed; Bassil Robin, 160 a; Harris Ralls; Jesse Ragan; P. A. Smith; Levy Russel; Henry Rider; James Rider; Estate of A. R. Rayburn; Ellinor J. Rayburn; John Ragan; John Rawlins; Joseph Reader; Austin Reader; Benjamin Reynolds; Alexander Rice; George Roads; Philip Ruby; Joseph A. Rice; George Rowland; Charles Rector; William Rector; Mathew Robertson, 40 a, (OC) Thomas Collins; Charles Rice, 39 a, 80 a, 49 a, 83 a; 40 a, (OC) Charles Rice; Martin Rice, 60 a, 80 a, 40 a; John Reed, 75 a, 74 a, 20 a, 40 a, 75 a, 37 a, (OC) Jeremiah James, Jas. Burris, Allin James; John Read, William O. Gibson; Hankinson (sic) F. Read; Robert Read; Jesse P. Rolland; Medford; James Reynolds; Farlow Read; Samuel Ramsey; Jackson Riddle; Tyree Riddle; James Riddle; Simpson Riddle; Richard R. Ress, 80 a; Riley Riddle; Samuel Roads; Abraham Redfield, 80 a, 80 a, 40 a, (OC) William B. Charles; David Rice; James Read; Nicolas Roberts; Samuel E. Rowdon, 159 a; Aaron Smith; John H. Rolen; David Reed; Lewis Reed; Alvin Stephens; John Shively; William Spain; N. T. Shaylor; Robert Shelton; Henry Shirley; Levi P. Stacy; Alexander Smith; Alfred Shelton; H. B. Staniford; James Sears; Anderson W. Smith, 40 a, 80 a, 80 a; Charles Sage; Temple Smith; Francis Simpson, 80 a, 80 a,

(OC) Alexes A. Freeman; Thomas Short, 40 a, (OC) David Urie; Michael Shupe, 40 a, 40 a, (OC) James Vanslike, D. Urie; A. M. Steeples; Elmador (sic) Staley; William Swift, 80 a, 160 a; Abraham Staily, 80 a, 40 a, (OC) Jacob Coffman; Thomas R. Simpson; John Staily, 40 a; Stephen Staily; Jess Stephens; John Strong, 80 a, 40 a, 80 a, 80 a, (OC) Moses Strong; John W. Stateler; Moses Strong; Hiram Stephens, 100 a, 99 a, 80 a, (OC) Moses L. Ashby, Wm. Jackson; Benjamin Stephens, 100 a, 99 a, 80 a, 80 a, 160 a, (OC) James Black, Jos. Chambers, Ferdinand Leob; Thomas Simpson; William Scott; John Sears; William Shuster; John C. Striffin; John Sheuster; James See; Henry Shuster (sic); Chance Smith; George Smith; Jesse Sims; Joshua Smith; James Sims; William Stephens; Lucy Stephens; William Smith; Thomas Steepleton; Tolbert Shiply; Larkin A. Settle; George F. Settle; David F. Settle; David W. Smelser, 55 a, 54 a, 210 a, (OC) Alexes Freeman, Wm. Smelser; Samuel Sharp; John Sterling; B. W. Saunders; John Shelly; Alfred G. Sloane, 80 a, 80 a; Gay Smith; Ames M. Simpson; William See; Joel Snider; Jesse Snider; Silas Sorense; Edward Smith; John W. Smith; Mark H. Shumater, 80 a, 40 a, 40 a, (OC) Martin Rice, Allin James; David Steward; James Steward; Edward D. Sullens; Martha Sullens; Hileman Stine; Caleb Stork; William Stinson; Isaac Smith, 40 a; Austin Smith, 40 a, 40 a, 40 a, (OC) W. W. Wright; Solomon Sinclair; Thomas D. Smith; Sarah Streaklin; Hesekiah Smith; W. F. Stone; Thomas Stone, 80 a, 80 a, 80 a, 80 a, (OC) David R. Carson; Jeremiah Sloan; John Sease; Solomon Stewart, 36 a, 40 a, 40 a, (OC) John Gibson, Jas. Gibson, William Gibson; Jacon Spainhour, 151 a; Mathew W. Sparks; Isaac Sparks; Mathew Sparks, jr.; Charles Smith; Joseph H. Slease; Margaret Sellers; Green E. Story; William Stephens, Big Creek; James Smith, 40 a, (OC) Jas. Reynolds; Wiley Scott; James Savage; Charles Sims, 80 a, (OC) Daniel Ratcliff; James E. Stephenson, 80 a; James B. Sears, 80 a, 80 a, 40 a, 80 a, 40 a, 160 a, 40 a, 80 a, 160 a, 80 a, 80 a, (OC) Franklin Sears, Francis Sears, J. B Sears; Franklin Sears; Joel Sears, 80 a, (OC) Ezekiel Evans; Isaac J. Smith; William A. Scott, 49 a; William Shipley; Richard Snead; John A. Tuggle; William A. Temple; William Taillor (sic); James Teague; W. G. Templeton; William Tull; Henry Tull; Benjamin Tharp; John Tailor; Atha (sic) Tull; William Tharp; William D. Tuggle; Benjamin Tharp; D. M. Tabor; William Tompson; A. J. Tackett (sic); S. W. Tackitt (sic); Mathew Todd; Robert Tompson; Elijah Tompson; William Thomas; John Tucker; Thomas Tucker; Ann Tucker; Henry Tarrent; Solomon Teague; Joseph W. Tarkington, 32 a; Elihu Teague; John Tally, 40 a, 40 a 37 a, 40 a; Paterick Talbott, 160 a, (OC) Ellisshas (sic) Shelton; Joshua Talbott; Serena Tidwell; Hanah Tarkington, 80 a, 160 a, 62 a, (OC) Hanah Tarkington; Sarah A. Tarkington; Wm. S. Taylor; James W. Tarkington, 32 a; Robert P. Tarkington,

32 a; Ocavia (sic) Tarkington; John T. Thornton; --- Tate's Estate, 80 a, (OC) Barnard James; Samuel Taylor; Andrew H. Urie; Charles Thomas; David Urie, Jackman Underwood; David Urie, 40 a, 40 a, 40 a, (OC) Daniel Vanslike; Westley Underwood; John Underwood; Moorman Vaughn; George Vanwinkle; John H. Walker; Clayton Vannoy, 40 a, 157 a; Robert Vannoy; Hiram Wilson; Thomas Vestal; Joseph D. Willmott; Thomas Walker; B. E. Williamson, 80 a; Nathaniel Willett; Fletcher A. Willett; George A. Wade; Andrew Wilson; William Wilson; James White; James H. Williams, 40 a, (OC) D. J. Gloyd; Joseph Williams, 79 a, 20 a, (OC) P. D. Brooks, Hanah Tarkington; Edward J. Wheeler; Isaac Woolard; John Watts, 40 a, 40 a; M. M. Watts; William Wair; Thomas Wilborn; Richard Wilborn; H. M. White, 80 a, (OC) Alexes Freeman; Powell Williams; Joseph Williamson, 80 a; Samuel Winston; Oliver Westover; James A. White; Timothy Whitehead; William Wilson; Henry Wilson; Cyrus Ward; Samuel Wilson; William Watkins; William Wilson (sic); Thomas Watts, 40 a, 40 a; Pleasant Whiteworth; M. M. Watts; Alfred L. Watts; Lot Watts, 80 a, 40 a, (OC) S. E. Rowdon; Joseph Warson; James Watts, 77 a, 40 a, (OC) T. R. Dawson; Walker & Dickson; Bloomer White; James A. Wilson, 80 a, (OC) Michael Masters; David Wilson, 40 a; Barton L. Wilson, 100 a, (OC) Joel D. Campbell; Madsion Walrand, 40 a, 40 a 40 a, 40 a, 40 a, (OC) Mockbee Cathbirt (sic), R. D. McSpadden, William W. Ewing; Calvin Walker; Jehehiel (sic) Williams, 77 a, Geo. Preston; James White; James Warren; Phebee Warden; John B. Wheeler; Henderson Wilson; Benjamin Westfall; Thomas White; Tillman M. West; Tandy Westmoreland; Samuel Whiteman; James Williams; William R. Wilmott, 160 a, (OC) Arias J. Talbot; Malinda Wright, 77 a, 80 a, 40 a, 40 a, 40 a, 36 a, 80 a, (OC) John H. Edminson, Jacob Coffman, W. W. Wright, Benjamin Dulany, Saml. T. McAlexander; Harrison Williams; William M. Williams; Hosa Williams; Roswell Wright; James Williams; J. D. Walker; Joseph Walters; James Walters; Mary Wheeler; John S. Wheeler, 80 a, (OC) Henry F. Baker; J D. Walker; Mahala Weathers; Luke Wilborn; J. D. Walker; Hardin Wooten, 40 a, 40 a; Benjamin White; James Wood; Luke Williams; Moses Weed, 40 a, 20 a, 20 a, (OC) Jas Conner, Jos. Henderson, Jeremiah Sloan; John Willet; Joel Warren; William Wilson, 40 a (OC) John Cook; Estate of Andrew Wilson by Green E. Story exr.; George W. Wallis; Tolman Warren; Granville Wilson; James H. Williams; John Weir; Samuel Wilson, 77 a, 79 a, (OC) James Black; Noah Williams, 153 a, 28 a, 77 a; Cook Warden; John Webb; John M. Williams; Jesse Williams; Edward Wilbourn, 80 a, 80 a, (OC) David R. Carson; George W Walker, 40 a, 40 a; Pleasant Walker, 160 a, 80 a 160 a, (OC) Pleasant Walker; Felander Whitlesey, 80 a 39 a; Richard Wall, 40 a, 80 a; Wm. P. Walter, 40 a, 40 a; Abner Williams; Uriah Young; Mathew Yocum's estate 40 a, 40 a; Jesse Yocum, 40 a, 40 a 40 a;

Mark Yocum; Westley Yankey; Norchester (sic) Wilson; Thomas York; Allin Yocum.

## Jackson County, Missouri, Delinquent Tax List, November, 1840, Capitol Fire Documents, CFD 31, Folder 1383.

John Aea, Joshua Anderson, Benjamin Allen, Jas. Anderson; Saml. H. Ayers; John R. Ashcraft; Joseph and William Adair; Abner J. Adair; William P. Allen; Michael Arthur; Arthur & Samuels; Christopher L. Bladen; Thomas Bradley, sen.; Thomas W. Bradley; James M. Briscoe; Charles Blythe; Given Bradley; John Bell; Felix Beauchamp, admr. of R. Gibson and Nicholas Burris; Francis Brvin (?); Thomas J. Boggs; Abner Beurs; Willis Bledsoe; Lewis Burlow; Thomas G. Bennett; Felix Braden; Peter Boothe; Hanson Bingham; John Q. Berry; James Baxter; Noah Baxter; John Baxter, jr.; Wm. H. Chatham; William Ceroly; Nicholas Crenshaw, jr.; Julius W. Clarkson; John H. Carter; Isaac Crabtree, jr.; Thomas Constable; William Constable; Thomas G. Clarkson; Calvert Clanton; James L. Cox; Charles Cantrell; William W. Cross; Willis Cox, sr.; Rueben D. Collins; Edward Constable; John Dodds; Wayan Bennis; Wm. S. Denning; Bowles Denning; Robert Dunlap; Thorton Dulany; John W. Doub; Antoine Delerier; Drury Dodson; John George; Joseph Godwin; William Graham; Nicholas Gentry; Eli Green; Robert C. Given; David J. Gwin; F. D. Greenwood; David Hunter; John Hubbard; Saml. D. Hulse; James Gray; John F. Gibson; Fletcher, McGirk & Reed; George W. Forman; Halen Fry; Halen Fry, sen.; John Fitzhugh; Robert Fitzhugh; Benjamin Hubbard; William Haynes; Isaac Hutchens; Edward Hopper; John Hopper; William B. Hawkins; Wiley Hall; Richard C. Harris; Nicholas Hopper; Eljah Hill; William L. Irwin; Alfred Justin; Michael Johnson; James L. Jessin; John James; Albreath W. Keonig; Joseph Kirk; Rachel Kunsey; Peter Kevanaugh; Joel Lipscomb; Jacob Kanatzer; Joshua Lana; George Lance; William Lackey; Jonathan Lee; Samuel Loomis; Newton N. Lynch; Kinsey Linham; William Lynch, Big Creek; Maturim (?) Letramtre; Wm. Miles; Joshua Lewis and heirs; Burrell Mullins; John McGuire; Andrew G. McDaniel; Squire Moody; Joseph McCraw; Charles B. Messick; Gabriel Morriss; Anna Moberly; John McDowell; James G. McIlhaney; George W. McCraw; Richard McCarty; Eli Nutt; John McIlhaney; John McGlothler, sen.; James Miller; Alfred Matthews; David Magan; Jacob McMaghan; Thomas Newton; James Noland; John P. Nicholas; James B. O'Toole; Gilbert Pointer; Thomas Padas; Hugh Patton, sen.; Francis Philabar; Haren (?) Philip; William Poe; William Price; Richard Ragan; Lenoard H. Reinick; Benedict Reaux; Farlow Reed; Luther Rinnick; Wm. Sheppard; Bozzle Simmons; Mathias Speed; John W. Spencer; Andrew Sikes; James Sheppard jr.; Wm. T. Sheppard; Richard Sawyers; Elias Smith; John M. Smith; Thomas Simmons; James B. Tomlin; John Sears; Peter Stallcup; David Smith; Rueben

B. Fulkerson; James Thomas; John C. Tharp; J. F. and D. L.
Stuart; Ayle M. Tamley; George G. Tandy; Francis P. Toller;
Thomas Taylor; John L. Tamly; Therese, Indian Woman; Joseph
Vanleferelle; James White; Saml. Whiteman; R. Clark Willam
(sic); John Watson; Philip William; George W. Noah Williams;
Saml. W. Walker; James M. Young; Jas. R. Yocum; John Yocham;
Hiram Young.

Montgomery County Missouri, Delinquent Tax List,March term,
1840, Capitol Fire Documents, CFD 31, Folder 1389
    George W. Bishop; --- Bystalf; Jefferson Bill; Marmiduke
Mays; Andrew Henry; John C. Fields; Charles Charles Filses;
William A. J. Martin; William McDonald; James Newlin; Henry
Smith; Jacob Sipes; Henry Sipes.

St. Louis County, Missouri, Delinquent Tax List, December,
1840, Capitol Fire Documents, CFD 31, Folder 1394.

| Name | Total Value | Poll | Comments |
|---|---|---|---|
| James Adams | $ 190 | | Insolvent |
| John Anderson | 189 | 1 | Not Found |
| Price Arnold | 92 | 1 | Macon |
| Joseph Asbury | 40 | 1 | Insolvent |
| Jacob Ashlemon | 82 | 1 | Not Found |
| John Armstrong | | 1 | Not Found |
| William Acres | 42 | 1 | Insolvent |
| James Anderson | 50 | 1 | Insolvent |
| Smiley Barnard | 40 | 1 | Not Found |
| Edward Brooking | 100 | | Insolvent |
| Zachariah Barr | 15 | 1 | Insolvent |
| Loving Ballard | 42 | 1 | Insolvent |
| John Baxter | 30 | 1 | Insolvent |
| John H. Bryant | 40 | 1 | Not Found |
| Isaac Briggs | | 1 | Insolvent |
| Dudley Barnes | 12 | 1 | Insolvent |
| Taylor Barnes | 45 | 1 | Insolvent |
| Enoch Barnes | | 1 | Insolvent |
| David Barnett | 37 | 1 | Macon |
| Samuel Briggs | 92 | 1 | Macon |
| Walter Baker | | 1 | Insolvent |
| Thomas Baker | | 1 | Insolvent |
| Jesse Better | 75 | 1 | Not Found |
| Phillip Burress | 104 | 1 | Macon |
| Joel Bradley | 144 | 1 | Macon |
| John Buckhannon | | 1 | Insolvent |
| George W. Broy | 12 | 1 | Insolvent |
| John Bound | 30 | 1 | Gone |
| Mat. Cummins | 60 | 1 | Gone |
| Jesse R. Cox | 20 | 1 | Gone |
| Jerry Crook | 65 | 1 | Insolvent |

| Name | Total Value | Poll | Comments |
|---|---|---|---|
| Charles Cook | $ 92 | 1 | Gone |
| Alxr. Colvin | 120 | 1 | Macon |
| Joshua Cox | 114 | | Not Found |
| Young Colvin | | 1 | Macon |
| Alexr. Collier | 52 | 1 | Macon |
| Charles Carter | 52 | 1 | Macon |
| Aaron Chamber | 50 | 1 | Insolvent |
| William Creasey | | 1 | Insolvent |
| William Cook | 24 | 1 | Insolvent |
| Luke Church | 12 | 1 | Insolvent |
| James Clark | 12 | 1 | Insolvent |
| James David | | 1 | Insolvent |
| Joseph Dobson | 25 | 1 | Insolvent |
| Peter Davis | | 1 | Insolvent |
| R. H. Downing | 80 | 1 | Insolvent |
| William Downing | 12 | 1 | Insolvent |
| Absalom Downing | 110 | 1 | Insolvent |
| Madison Downing | 40 | 1 | Insolvent |
| John Day | 28 | 1 | Shelby |
| Elizabeth Davis | 275 | | Not Found |
| John Dunn | 160 | 1 | Gone to Ill. |
| Jesse Daviss (sic) | 80 | 1 | Gone |
| Hezekiah Doane | 52 | 1 | Insolvent |
| Henry Downing | 620 | | Macon |
| John S. Davis | | 1 | Insolvent |
| Henry Downing | 72 | 1 | Macon |
| Andrew Darnell | 236 | 1 | Macon |
| Aaron Dunn | 12 | 1 | Insolvent |
| Joseph Davis | 50 | 1 | Insolvent |
| William Davis | | 1 | Insolvent |
| James Dwarf | | 1 | Insolvent |
| Frosty English | 52 | 1 | Insolvent |
| Abraham Ellis | 12 | 1 | Insolvent |
| John I. Falkner | 50 | 1 | Insolvent |
| John Franklin | 370 | 1 | Shelby Co. |
| Thomas Fox | 100 | 1 | Insolvent |
| David Frigley | | 1 | Gone |
| John M. Fish | 60 | 1 | Macon Co. |
| James Frowbank | | 1 | Insolvent |
| John Fincher | | 1 | Macon |
| Charles Fryener | 92 | 1 | Ioway T. |
| William Flenner | 50 | 1 | Decd. |
| Daniel Griffith | 10 | 1 | Insolvent |
| William Gilson | 50 | 1 | Not Found |
| Wilson Gentry | 30 | 1 | Shelby |
| John Gault | 66 | 1 | Macon |
| Alexander Givens | 2290 | 1 | Macon |
| Bird Gilbert | 52 | 1 | Macon |

| Name | Total Value | Poll | Comment |
|---|---|---|---|
| D. H. Goodnoe | 117 | 1 | Insolvent |
| John F. Glass | | 1 | Insolvent |
| King Hoback | 50 | 1 | Insolvent |
| George Hainez | | 1 | Insolvent |
| John Hainez | 50 | 1 | Insolvent |
| Henry Haines (sic) | 12 | 1 | Insolvent |
| Walter Hudson | | 1 | Insolvent |
| Peter A. Hall | 65 | 1 | Insolvent |
| Thomas Hicks | | 1 | Insolvent |
| Thomas House | | 1 | Insolvent |
| Henry Harrison | 184 | 1 | Gone |
| James Hall | 99 | 1 | Gone |
| Joseph Hudson | 12 | 1 | Not Found |
| Samuel Harris | 50 | 1 | Insolvent |
| James Hardin | 104 | 1 | Macon |
| Alexr. Hays | | 1 | Macon |
| Henry Higby | 410 | 1 | Macon |
| William Haydon | 50 | 1 | Inslovent |
| Benjn. House | 50 | 1 | Insolvent |
| I. S. Hasmon | | 1 | Not Found |
| Thos. Haydon | | 1 | Insolvent |
| John Hamilton | | 1 | Insolvent |
| Henry Isaac | 115 | 1 | Macon |
| Ralph Joseph | 130 | 1 | Gone |
| John Johnson | 205 | 1 | Not Found |
| Benjn. Jones | 50 | 1 | Shelby Co. |
| Jeremiah Johnson | 12 | 1 | Insolvent |
| Ruebin Jenning | | 1 | Insolvent |
| Stephen Knowlton | | 1 | Not Found |
| Richd Kinnemon | 62 | 1 | Insolvent |
| Edwin Layton | | 1 | Insolvent |
| William London | 122 | 1 | Macon |
| C. M. H. London | 59 | 1 | Macon |
| John Laux | | 1 | Insolvent |
| Mat. J. Lowe | 40 | 1 | Macon |
| John Lancaster | 124 | 1 | Kentucky |
| Daniel Leadford | | 1 | Insolvent |
| John Lowdermilk | 42 | 1 | Insolvent |
| Jasper Lewis | | 1 | Not Found |
| Cornelius Malone | 89 | 1 | Gone |
| Benjn. Mudd | 184 | 1 | Gone |
| Hinson McGlanthlin | | 1 | Macon |
| John McPherson | 40 | 1 | Insolvent |
| William Mathews | 57 | 1 | Not Found |
| Daniel McClaine | 144 | | Decd. |
| Lyrd March | 92 | 1 | Macon |
| John March | 104 | 1 | Macon |
| Thos. McDowell | 80 | 1 | Not Found |

| Name | Total Value | Poll | Comment |
|---|---|---|---|
| George Taylor | 175 |   | Insolvent |
| Thomas Taylor | 65 | 1 | Insolvent |
| M. B. Tompkins |   | 1 | Gone |
| James Taylor | 504 | 1 | Shelby C. |
| Wisdom Upton |   | 1 | Insolvent |
| Salmon Umphrey | 24 | 1 | Insolvent |
| Henry Umphrey | 57 | 1 | Insolvent |
| George Woodson | 99 | 1 | Insolvent |
| Andrew Williams | 10 | 1 | Insolvent |
| Hiram Williams | 40 | 1 | Insolvent |
| Ignetius Wheeler | 104 | 1 | Macon |
| David Wadkins | 46 | 1 | Insolvent |
| Josiah West | 12 | 1 | Insolvent |
| William Wilton | 80 | 1 | Macon |
| John Williams | 40 | 1 | Macon |

Grundy County, Missouri, Hatton Chapel Cemetery, Hwy. 63 N. and Rt. A NW (Note: Only Person Born 1840 and After.)

| Names | Born | Died |
|---|---|---|
| Caroline V. Graham | 1851 | 1936 |
| John A. Graham | 1849 | 1928 |
| Lulu H. Graham | 1882 | --- |
| Henry W. Graham | 1880 | 1918 |
| Anna Bell Ratliff | Dec. 15, 1875 | May 31, 1963 |
| John R. Ratliff | May 12, 1852 | Oct. 23, 1939 |
| Elvira C. Ratliff | Jan. 16, 1857 | Nov. 28, 1904 |
| Estelle B. Moore | 1885 | 1888 |
| James M. Moore | --- | Jun. 1, 1880 |
| Louenna Moore | 1860 | 1947 |
| Luther B. Moore | 1847 | 1894 |
| Wilbur L. Moore | Nov. 21, 1888 | Dec. 15, 1963 |
| Besse M. Moore | Jan. 24, 1888 | Dec. 15, 1963 |
| Minnie Moore | 1886 | 1957 |
| Harry E. Moore | 1881 | 1900 |
| David Marrs | Feb. 13, 1865 | Apr. 16, 1930 |
| Susie M. Marrs | May 20, 1868 | May 30, 1912 |
| Edee G. Marrs | 1874 | 1941 |
| Sarah I. Marrs | Jan. 25, 1846 | Apr. 3, 1900 |
| Anna Blue | Oct. 19, 1839 | Dec. 14, 1927 |
| William B. Tabor | Feb. 21, 1816 | Jul. 31, 1884 |
| Charity H. Tabor | Sep. 1, 1816 | Feb. 1, 1890 |
| Hulda L. Shafer Pryor | Apr. 23, 1865 | Jan. 22, 1954 |
| James D. Pryor | Apr. 8, 1858 | Oct. 2, 1917 |
| Sarah A. Hoffman | Oct. 14, 1866 | Feb. 4 1884 |
| Blanch L. Brown | 1888 | 1916 |
| Louisa E. Brown | 1844 | 1917 |
| J. H. Brown | 1840 | 1900 |
| Lettie E. Brown | 1871 | 1949 |

| Name | Born | Died |
|---|---|---|
| A. K. Brown | 1868 | 1961 |
| C. B. Olyer | Mar. 17, 1890 | Dec. 21, 1945 |

Buchanan County, Missouri, 1840 Tax List, Roll No. C974.

Lewis C. Anthony, A. K. Argyle, John G. Allen, Singleton Asher, Ely Arnold, William Allnutt, James Anderson, Thomas Auxier, Isaac Auxier, Everhart Antle, Argyle & Boyd, George Buck, John Brittain, Ennis Burris, David Burris, James Boyd, Morris Baker, John Burris, John Black, George Brittain, Asia Boyd, Michael B. Balieu, Thomas A. Brown, Aurey Ballard, Wm. B. Brown, Kinzey G. Bond, Henry H. Bruce, Weston H. Bruce, Daniel Blevens, Jesse Blevens, James M. Burnett, Loyd Bell, John Bohannon, James Briles, Elisha Brown, Wm. Bragg, Jacob Bohart, James Barnes, Brinsley Barnes, Martin Berry, Silas W. Berry, Kennard Blackstone, Gideon S. Brown, John Burgess, Samuel K. Burgess, Manuel Best, John Best, Zebadiah Baker, Charles Boyer, Walter Bivens, Andrew Baker, Thomas Brinter, Stephen Blevens, Jonathan Blevens, William Boidstan, William Berryhill, Benjamin Becket, Thomas Boidston, Josiah Brawley, Isaac Brown, Edward Brown, Jacob Bittle, Valentine Bledsoe, John Berryhill, Jackson Berryhill, John Berryhill, Azariah Berryhill, Peter Bark, Jesse Barnett, James Barnett, William Bledsoe, Austin Bledsoe, Stephen Bedford, Richard Bagley, J. W. Brigmore, John E. Bedford, Archibald Bedford, John Belk, John Butler, George Bittle, Manuel Bittle, Peter Boyer, John Barmont, Henry Boyer, Peter Boyer, jr., George Boyer, David Barrow, Jacob Boyer, David Barrow, John Barmont, John Belk, John Barmont, jr., Jesse Barber, Jesse Butler, Daniel Boyer, John Bombarger, Robert S. Boyd, Thomas Bilderback, Archibald Chittick, James Blakely, Henry Cook, Thomas Chittick, James D. Campbell, James A. Cochran, Joseph Cromwell, Abel Coplen, Frederick Cogdale, Daniel Cogdale, Levi Cromwell, Jos. Cromwell, Thomas Bunten, Stephen Blevens, Jonathan Blevins, William Boidston, William Berryhill, Benjamin Becket, Valentine Bledsoe, Thomas Boidston, Josiah Brawley, Isaac Brown, Jacob Bittle, Edward Brown, John Berryhill, Azariah Berryhill, G. W. Bridgeman, Peter Bark, Jesse Barnett, James Barnett, Wm. Bledsoe, Austin Bledsoe, Stephen Bedford, Archibald Bedford, John Bedford, John Butler, Wiliam Clasley, Benjamin Catlet, John Crey, William Carl, Alfred Coats, Charles Cates, George W. Chadd, Benjamin Carnes, Johnson Coplen, John Clasley, Asa Curl, Newton Cowan, James Curl, Noah Curtis, Jacob Cogdale, William Cogdale, Bartlet Curl, Jonathan Cox, Wm. Connell, Squire S. Connell, Richard James Chany, Daniel K. Clark, Wm. Crocket, Richard Chany, James Carpenter, Eli Copelin, Joel M. Clanton, Isaac Clanton, James Carsner, Wipple Carpenter, John R. Clark, John Coplen, Adam Cook, John Cleek, William J. Clark, James Carns, Rachel Cleek, Jacob Combs, Benjamin

Cornelius, Joseph Combs, Barnes Clark, Danah Chapel, Michael Carnes, Leroy Coffman, Daniel Devoss, jr., John J. Devoss, Joseph Devoss, Daniel Devoss, Joseph Duncan, John D. Davis, William Dunning, Alexander Dunning, Mathew S. Davis, James Dorrel, Frances Deshain, James Donovan, Voluntine Day, Lucus Dawson, Henry Dillen, John Durham, George W. Daniel, Sarah Davis, Robert Donnell, Enoch Dixon, Tanner (?) Davidson, Edward M. Davidson, Reason Davis, John W. Davison, Robert W. Donnell, John Davis, James Davis, John Daniel, jr., Morgan Dryden, John Daniel, John Dryden, Ishmael Dacks, Jas. Dacks, onnell & Jones, Powel Dean, J. and B. K. Dixon, Robert Duncan, James Davis, Nathaniel Daugherty, Mary Dekart, William Dotson, Robert English, Samuel English, William English, Abner Enyart, Samuel E. Edwards, Willis Elliott, John Enyart, Aumphrey (sic) P. Elison, John Ellison, James Ellison, John Ellison, jr., William Ellison, John A. Ewell, Wm. Edwards, Robert C. Ellesrit, Ealy (sic) Edwards, John English, William Estes, William Edwards (sic), William K. Elliott, Westen S. Everett, John M. Evans, William S. Earixson, John Earixson, Harison Earixson, David M. Edwards, Jones S. Edwards, Dennis Earley, David E. Ewing, William Fulk, Jesse Finch, Stephen Fields, William Flanery, John W. Freeman, Isaac Farris, William Flanery, James Finch, Nathaniel Finch, Humphrey Finch, William C. Frakes, Jefferson Ferrell, William Feeler, Nathan F. Frakes, Joseph Fugate, Samuel D. Finch, Jonathan Fugate, Sanford Feland, Zachariah Kenney, K. S. Fitzgerald, Henry Foster, Richard Fallen, John Fletcher, Ezekiel Fidler, Charles Fletcher, James Fidler, jr., James Fidler, Wm. Fowler, jr., John Fowler, John Fidler, Alexander Fudge, Solomon Fraizer, Lewis Garrett, John Good, Lewis Grism, John P. Gibson, Thomas S. Gillet, Samuel Gist, Anderson Gilmore, James Gilmore, Bradford Glascock, Robert Gilmore, Price B. Gess, Aaron Groom, James Groom, jr., Benjamin Guinn, Milford Gilmore, Wilson, John Gan, William Guinn, Kenny Gill, Zachariah Garton, Uriah Garton, Isam Gardner, Michael Gabbert, Nathan Gates, Isaac Gan, George S. Gibson, James Gibson, jr., Jos. Gladden, James Keys, Joseph Huff, Hugh Kays, Stephen Hawley, Harlow Kirkston, Henry Hays, Thomas Horton, Isaiah Hughes, Willliam Hughbanks, Samuel C. Hall, Henry W. Hinson, James W. Keys, Jacob Geshore, Samuel M. Gilmore, John Garret, Hugh Glen, Andrew B. Greggory, Abraham Groom, Solomon Groom, Jas. Gibson, George Gibson, jr., Wm. S. Gibson, George Gibson, John Giddens, William Giddens, Joseph Groom, Isaac Givens, Silvester Keys, Richard Hancock, Wm. Harrington, sr., Joseph Hughes, Richard Hull, Lyman Hide, Andrew J. Hunter, Joseph Hill, Aleck Harrington, Edmund Herring, Wishy Hunter, Thomas Hickman, Eli Hubble, John Hill, James Hedgsbeth, Simon Hunsucker, Joel Hedgsbeth, William Harrington, Jesse G. Henderson, Lovett Horn, David Henderson, John Harrington, Gilford

Henderson. Silas Hughes, Henry W. Hensley, John Kargrove, John Keys, George W. Hudspeth, John Harris, Andrew Hall, Charles Huddleston, Widdow (sic) Henderson, James Hall, Joseph Hall, Kenley Humphrey, Joseph Hall, Jeremiah Kimbro, James Kanan, Noah Hickman, James R. Holman, John Holland, John Huntsucker, John Kiney, Absalom Kiney, William Hudson, Silvester Hughlitt, Robert Henderson, Thomas Huntsucker, Wm. Huntsucker, Lewis Kanes, Noah Henderson, Joseph Kendrick, Isaac Hanes, Caly Kisamore, John Hardy, Robert Hardin, A. M. Johnson, Ephraim Igo, Robert Levin, Jonathan Jones, Nelson Jonas, Andrew Jordan, Welsey Jinkins, M. Johnson, Eli Judah, George Jeffers, Stephen Jones, William Jones, David Johnson, Lewis Johnson, James Jones, Nancy Jones, Robert Jones, Levi Jackson, Benjamin Jones, Elijah Jenkins, James James, Andrew Jones, Kerrington Johnson, John M. Jacks, Dudley Kees, Abel Kenner, William Kirkman, Peter Keefer, Jacob Kissler, James J. Karnes, Simeon Kemper, John King, Peter Kirk, David Lee, John W. Kirk, John Kirk, George Lacy, Thomas Linville, Geo. K. Linville, Jacob Lower, Henry Lower, Charity Linville, O. K. P. Lucas, Zachariah Linville, R. J. E. Linville, Joseph Lady, Hugh Luther, John Lewison, David Linch, Silvester Lanham, David Lothrop. Robert Louland, Edmund Lane, Hardy Lasater, Peter Lilley, Charles Lewis, Thomas L. Lasater, Joseph Layman, Benjamin Lane, Hardy Lasater, Thomas Langley, Edward Lawles, Samuel Lisle, Thomas Ladingtin, Alton Lacefield, Wm. McRay, Thomas Martin, Thomas Mills, Job Mcnames, Brightberry Martin, John Mcnames, John H. Markesack (?), John Mars, John V. Mansfield, Joseph Marks, Spurgeon Mansfield, Drury Moore, Benjamin McCary, John Martin Thomas V. Montgomery, Presley Montgomery, Elisha L. Montgomery, John Morris, Saml. Morrow, James F. Mulkey, K. M. McPherson, James Mitchel, Logan Maxwell, Samuel Martin, William Moore, Silas McDonald, William McDowal, James McQuire, William McDowel, Jacob Miller, Nancy Moberly, Christopher Martin, Jacob Miller, Starling Morgan, Joshua Michael, David May, Abraham Martin, Daniel Mulkey, Elisha Mulkey, Marhal Martin, Robert McCatchen, Samuel May, Silas Moreland, Gilford Montray, James Montray, Noah Mast, William McQuire, Carnelius (sic) McQuire, Robert McCain, Wm. McCarty, John McCarty, David McCarty, Francis I. Meadows, Walter Murphey, Absalom Munhoss, P. P. Madgett, Wilson Madgett, Ambrose D McDaniel, George Maffty, Daniel McCray, Wm. McDaniel, James McQuinn, Margaret Miller, Jabez McCrkle, A. F. Noland, Jesse Miller, George W Means, Jacob Mann, John P. March, Alexander McCorkle, Isaac Miller, Philip Marker, Jeremiah McHourn, William McNeel, Robert Modrel, Robert M. Nivens, Robert Modrel, John Modrel, Wilson Modrel, John Norris, Abner Norris, J. F. Noland, Moses Noland, Joseph Nash, Clabourn Neil, William M. Owen, John Owen, Benjamin F. Owen, James B. Otoole, Nicholas Owens, Powel S. Owlsey, Wm. Poe,

Thomas Oldham, William Obannon, Peter Price, Smith Pike, A. C. Patten, Claiborn Palmer, Samuel Poteet, James Powel, Wm. S. Portis, Simon Pickrel (?), Jacob T. Price, Rufus Patchen, William Poice, Joel S. Penick, William Powel, Isaac Poulton, John Paeley, Ephraim Porter, Nathan Price, Ann Philbert, Wm. Pearson, Morris Pete, Obadiah Persinger, Lewis Persinger, George Patterson, Elizabeth Pearson, James Pearson, William Poice, Thomas Potet, Conrad S. Petters, Stephen Parker, Jos. Rabidoux, Julian Rabidoux, Frances Rabidoux, Michael Rogers, Frances Rabidoux, jr., Nelson Rector, James M. Rector, David Rutledge, George W. Recor, Manuel Robertson, James Roberts, Hiram Roberts, Richard Roberts, John Robinet, Tapley Ralph (sic), Stuart Reynolds, John D. Robert, Hiram Rogers, John Robb, Cornelius Roberts, Andrew Russel, Robert R. Russel, Jefferson Ragsdale, Thomas B. Ridgeway, John Rodes, Hugh B. Reynolds, Jas. Ross, John Rousey, John Rutledge, John Robinson, Nathan Robinson, John Richardson, James Russel, Samuel Roundtree, John Russel, Elijah Russel, Joseph Roberts, John Ross, John Ritcher, William H. Ray, John Ray, Rochild, Jesse Reams, Adam Rangle, George F. Reynolds, George Ray, Jeremiah Reynold, John Ridgway, Alred M. Recor, Lewis Rederick, Jas. Sharp, Williams, James I. Reynolds, Nicholas Roberts, Joseph Rawls, Frederick Rasetel (?), William W. Reynolds, William Southland, George Shanks, John H. Shanks, John Silvers, John shays Elijah Smith, Anderson Smith, John Singleton, Timothy Snel, John Stenger, Elijah W. Smith, Jr., Alexander Sheen, Isaac Smith, Benjamin Sampson, Glen Sampson, Elijah Smith, Henry Sellers, John Sampson, Benjamin Sampson, jr., William Stevens, Robert M. Stuart, James Spencer Wm. Silvers, John Sun Elisha Smith, Charles Stuart, Ezekiel Stuart Archibald Stuart, John Sipe, Eli Sipe, James Stalls Metalf Smih, Samuel Sum, Josiah Shelton, James Sales, Mary Scott, Wm. Scott, O. M. Spencer, Joshua Skinner, Oglesby Smith, John Silvers, John Silver, Jacob Shepherd, Elias Sellards, Robert Swinney, Elizabeth Stuppleban, Joseph Sherwood, Jonathan Smith, Hugh Silvers, Vincent Snelling, Daniel Snelling, James Smith, Wm. Strickland, Golden Silvers, George Smith, jr., Edwd. Snider Thomas Strickland, George Smith, Allen Stephens, Wm. Stephenson, Martin Shultz, Burden G. Smith, Joab G. Shults, John Slaybaugh, Jacob Shanleaver, George W. Sims, Brice Summers, Thomas Sollers, Alfred Tipton, James Taylor, L B. Torannce, Turpen T. Thomas, George W. Taylor, Jesse B. Thompson, Elias Taylor, John A Thompson, James Sugnor (?) Taylor, Alfred C. Taylor, Give B. Taylor, James P. Thompson, David Thorp, John Thurman, Isaac Thompson, Nathan Tuner Geoge Tinker, Larkin Thompson, Washington Tanner, Jesse Thomas, Moses Thompson, David Tithrow, Elder Teague, John Thorp, John Tobin, John J. Tinsley, Tyron Thorp, David Thomas, James Thornbaugh, David K. Thompson, Samuel Thornbaugh, Stephen Trimble, William Underwood, Isaac Thorton, John Thorton, Charles Thurman, John Underwood, James Vaughn, William Vert, Daniel Varble, Daniel K. Vestal, Alexander Vaughn, Samuel Vessor, John Vangundy, W. Voorhies, Benjamin Vanmeter, Philip Walker, Isaac Womack, Abram Womack, Levin Wooton, James W. Whitehead, John C. Whitsett, David Winkler, Stephen L. Waymire, James Wilson, Jas. K. Williams, Michael Walis, James Web, Samuel Whitsler, Ross Wilkerson, Jasper Wilson, Thomas P. Williams, Jinkin Williams, Henry Williams, John Williams, Wm. Williams, John Witley, Thomas Willis, Jesse Watkins, Charles Wright, Nelson Will, Harrison Watson, Anderson Wilhelm, David Worcester, Alexander Williams, Hiram Wilburn, Joseph Wounderley, John H. Whitehead, William Young, Plesant Yates, John P. Younger, Thomas T. Ziegler.

Henry County, Missouri, Drake Chapel Cemetery, 1-1/4 Miles Northeast of Lewis, MO., Deek Creek Township.

| Name | Born | Died |
| --- | --- | --- |
| Alex B. Griffith (3rd. Lt., Co. D, 10th MO Cavalary, CSA) | | |
| Louisa B. Garrett | 1862 | 1898 |
| Norman Finks | 1877 | 1909 |
| Thomas Dalton | 1855 | 1929 |
| Emma M. Dalton | 1862 | 1940 |
| Wiliam A. Dodson | --- | --- |
| Susan E. Dodson | Mar. 4, 1846 | Nov. 15, 1914 |
| K. D. Dodson | Mar. 4, 1846 | Nov. 15, 1914 |
| William F. Chapman | 1856 | 1934 |
| Merida Floyd Chapman | 1867 | 1916 |
| Laura B. Chapman | 1860 | 1948 |
| Lulla Carroll | Feb. 24, 1869 | Sep. 9, 1902 |
| *Lena Burch | Feb. 6, 1890 | Nov. 5, 1890 |
| *(Infant daughter of G. M. and B. I. Burch) | | |
| George M. Burch | 1859 | 1939 |
| David Arthur Burch | 1896 | 1946 |
| Boadicia T. Burch | 1863 | 195 |
| Louisa Bentz | Aug. 23, 1894 | Jul. 28, 1917 |
| Louise Bentz | 1851 | 1939 |
| Maggie E. Bentz | --- | Jan. 29, 1878 |
| John Bentz | 1851 | 1931 |
| *Jenny Lay Allen | 1872 | 1946 |
| *(Florence, Mo) | | |
| *Dr. James Thomas Allen | 1864 | 1929 |
| *(Lexington, Mo) | | |

Vernon County Missouri, Qualified Voters List, November, 1866, Capitol Fire Documents, CFD 182, F. 16188.

### Deerfield Township

William S. Burd, Phillip H. Huffman, Thos. F. Clay Lewis Keeper, Daniel Williams, Oscar McGinnis, Peter Brown, Joseph

Grant, B. F. Humphrey, J. H. Requa, Isaac Taylor, Friederick W. Folks, W. B. McGinnis, David Reelfield, G. M. Miller, E. S. Weyand, W. J. Scoield, John Pitman, C. Guinn, James Alexander, W. H. Hergford, Jesse F. Nelson, James Fleenor, Pres. G. Rule, W W. Murphy, E. M. Heryford, W. H. Hurst, Henry K. Hogan, David Hogernsen, Rueben Bare, James T. Thornton, J. Beard, T. B. Furgeson, Asaa (sic) Hinds, James H. Tilman, G. W. Smith, John Linn, John McGinis, W. P. King, A. H. Logan, N. McColugh, J. H. Murphy David Hogan, jr., M. W Lambert.

### Center Township

Samuel Austin, William Adams, Daniel Austin, F. P. Anderson, T. H. Austin, Albert Badger, James Bryant, Elish Boyd, J. T. Birdsye, H. S. Bryant, T. T. Buch, John Brown, Benton Dean, Barnett Bulware, H. W. Corker, F. S. Chambers, Willson Davenport, J. B. Callway, Mikenel Charles, J. B. Carpenter W. T. Davis, John Dean, Elias Dean, J. N. B. Dodson, Richard Elkins, E. I. Fishpool, Sylvester Fuller, A. J. Gregory, B. F Howard, F. M Hasselton, James Hooper, S. C. Hall, Joshua Hightower, Comodore Howard, Hiram Johnson, Lewis C. Jones, A. L. Journey, P. A. Logan, B. F. Long, J. R. Midler Joseph Moore William Morris, F. M. Myre, Collumbus (sic) Morris, George Mullins, Joseph Nipp, C. M. Nillson, A. A. Pitcher, W M. Poland, A. W. Prueket, Thomas Paine, J H. Pepers, Anderson Roberts, W. B. Randolph, Theodore Rea, J. M. Ruford, L. J. Shaw, John Scot, John Stark, J. M. Smith, Levi Turner, J. M. Sample, J. W. Thomas, Clinton Thomas, Samuel Thomas, S. H. Thomas, W. H. Woods, Roland Wright, Daniel Ward John Wray, J. G. H. Wehmeyer, T. C. Williams.

### Montevellow Township

Monroe Agnew, Henry E. Bankson, Wm. S. Burk, Even Lipes Compton G. Bandy, Nathan Creek, W. P. Carter James Dickson, Curnelus Galvern, James Harris, Wm. F. Haines, John Haynes, Isam Hatfield, W. L. Haynes, V. W. Kimball, J. W. Kiethly,W. T. Mitchell, Even Lipe, Wm. Montgomery, Benjamn Meisner, J. H. Mitchell, Jacob Neff, William Prichard, R. T. Parks, Wm. Rians (sic), D. W. Snyder, J. C. Snyder, T. A. Snodgrass, N M. Tracy, John L. Thompson, Peter Walker,.

### Clear Creek Township

Micajah Brown, A. H. Caruthers, John B. Eidson, D. Guill, H. P. Mobley, W. D. Mitchell, Z. F. Moncrief, J. C. Willson, D. H Mitchell.

### Henry Township

Andrew Bogn, Thompson Bogan, Wm. Bogan, Jerry Brown, John G. Daniel, J. H Cox, Joseph Crumbell, Green Cline, Charles Phillips, R. K. Daniel, D. G. Glascock, A. B. Hall, Gorlin Kirk, Jefferson Jent, H. T. Jent, Henry Jent, Richard Meeks, J. T. Jones, Jacob Killer, Richard Kirk, A. J. H. Kidney A. J. Philips, W. L Phillips, T D. Palsgrove, James B. Reed Richard Pryor, C. N. Ryan, William Smith Arthur Smoot, John

A. Sartonions, Andrew Townsend, H. T. Tayor, William Vail, Edmond Wade, John Webber, Jasper Williams, Marion Woodall.

### Bacon Township

R. M. Armstrong, Samuel Chesnut, A. H. McKee Leventine Plummer, J. W. Westfall.

### Harrison Township

J. Baily Wiliam Hiller, W. S. Paynes, H. D. Patton, M. D. Hall, James T. Willson, Eli Phillips B. E. Hummell, Adam Huffman, Henry Chabi, Joseph McFarland, Adam Huffman, Newton White, G. H. Dollard, H. D. Corker, E. M. Ansley, A. Rosenbaum, John N. Comer, J. K. Gammons John Rohrer L. Shubin, A. N. Corley, S C. Meinken, Levi Kenoley, John Ellis.

### Little Osage Township

D. F. Downey, Peter Vanton, Dr. D. Perry, J. J. Williams, A. B. Wallkins, A. Cameron Reubin Stinson, Joseph Bunt, W. L. Summers, M. D. Cephers, W. H. Morris, J W. Walker, J. W. Wright, George W. Charles, John S. Willson, T. J. Swartz, R. C. Anderson, Elbert Walker, Humphrey Dickson, John Grant M. M. Clough, Mathew McColuck Daniel A. Robinson, W. W. Tibbs, John H. Dodge, J. M. Austin, W. Waltrip S. F. Dodge, James Maloy, S. J. Base, T. S. Dodge R. W. McNeal jr., Nathaniel Robinson W. J. Nollingham, B. J. G. Parker, G. R. Summers, F. K. Summers, O. L. David, John H. Reinberg J. W. Rule, G. M. Rule, John G. Dryden, Jacob Son, W. Nilack, John Foster, Mathew Lambert, Jacob Foland, A. Kuhn, Andrew Steinback, J. V. Ellis, J. Steinback, S. M Davis, C S. Gorton, Mitchell Burch, J. C. Sickel, John Richardson, J. W Carles, Joseph H. Charles, M. M. Swinney, Elijah Rea, John Hill, Alexander Pennington, David Hurst, Fritz Russman, George Smith, J. P. Smith, John Smith, John Dallis, John Pennington, Anson Dickson, John Henry Tuttle.

Atchison County, Missouri, County Home Cemetery, Clay Township, Rock Port, MO.

| Name | Born | Died |
|---|---|---|
| *Frank Waste | Dec. 31, 1859 | Nov. 28, 1938 |

*(b. Keokuk, IA, d. age 78 y, son of Frank Waste and Sarah Nelson.)

| +R. C. Wall | Jul. 9, 1877 | Jun. 6, 1932 |

+(d. 54 y, son of W. H. Wall and Mary Lucas.)

| #Dr. P. A. Talley | Jun. 15, 1845 | Mar 29, 1927 |

#(b. Norway, d. age 81 y, 9 m, 14 d)

| *Harry C. Snodgrass | May 1, 1876 | Jul. 13, 1938 |

*(B. Morgan Co., IN, d. 62 y, son of J. B. and Orella Snodgrass.)

| +John Payne | Aug. --, 1848 | Jan. 17, 1920 |

+(b. Ohio, d. age 71 y, 5 m, son of Bill Payne and Matilda Bigley.)

| #Charles H. Moody | Jan. 18, 1852 | Jun. 19 1928 |

| Name | Born | Died |
|---|---|---|

#(b. Cincinnati, OH, son of W. H. Moody and Hannah Traust.)
\*W. R. Johnson	Aug. 19, 1853	Feb. 19, 1926
\*(d. 72 y, son of Joseph Johnson and Elizabeth Pool)
John Humes	(d. 70 y) ---	Jan. 4, 1902
+Thomas Faubion	Nov. 4, 1861	Apr. 8, 1942
+(b. Worth Co., d. age 80 y, son of John J. and Nancy Jane Faubion.)
#William Andrew Dishong	Feb. 5, 1847	Mar. 26, 1928
#(b. Ohio, d. age 81 y, 22 d, son of Andrew and Elizabeth Dishong.)

Callaway County, Missouri, 1840, Poll List, Presidential and Vice Presidential Election, Capitol Fire Documents, CFD 182, Folder 16220.

### Auxvasse Township.

William Adams, Willis T. Alexander, Mikul Alkin, Samuel Alkin, William Alkin, Mitchell Atterberry, John Austin, John Blackburn, Samuel Atterberry, Edmund W. Baker, James Bell, James W. Baker, Robert C. Baker, Thomas H. Baker, Jefferson B. Benson, Moses Ballard, David Bardon, Ben. F. Berry, Geo. Bradford, Edward Berry, Thomas Berry, Samuel Bethill, John Blackburn, Robert Blackburn, William Blackburn, Saml. Boom, Joshua M. Boom, Edward Booker, Geo. Bradford, Wm. A Brite, Nathaniel Bradford, Frank Brantram, Benjamin Brashear, Levi Brashear, William Brashear, Ewill Brook, Joseph T. Bryan, Felix Bryant, Pleasant Bunch, Samuel Bunch, Wm. Callicotte, David P. Calvin, Elisha Chace, Hiram Coats, Lemuel B. Coats, Marshall S. Coats, William Coatss, Mark Cole, Stephen Cole, Brice D. Collins, Joel B. Cook, John Cook, Williamson Crews, Lorenzo Cook, Daniel M. Dame, George Dame, Simon Dame, John Davis, Johnathan Dvis, Jos. G. Davis, Ackley Day, Charles A. Day, Truman Day, John Dodds, William S. Dodds, Wm. Dudley, Peyton J. Duley, Stephen Dudley, Fred W. Duncan, Joseph C. Duncan, Jeroam B. Duncan, Onslon Duncan, Dangerfield Dunn, William Dyson, Louis Eno, John Estes, Thomas Estes, Andrew Ferrier, Samuel Ferrier, Thomas H. Ferrier, John Fish, G. W. Ferrill, Thos. Ferrin, Thomas Flood, Edward Foster, Thomas G. Fox, Leonard Frederick, Augus Galbreath, Wm. B. Garrett, Maryland H. Garrett, Aaron Gee, Standford Gee, Presley Gill, James Gilbert, Kemuel C. Gilbert, Michael Gilbert, William H. H. Gilbert, William J. Gilman, John Gipson, Thomas Goff, William Glover, James M. Glover, John Gregory, jr., William Grisham, Lewis Griffin, Henry Hall, George Hamblin, William J. Jackson, Robert Harper, George Harris, John Harris Peter Harris, Mastus Harris, A. H. Henderson, Benjamin Hill, John H. Hull, Robert C Hill, Samuel Hooker William Hudson Jas. Jillet, Welton Hull, Perry Hunter, Richard B. Jackson, James

Law, Horatio Jones, Jordan Kemp, William Kemp, Randolph W. Kidwell, Thomas Kitchen, John B. Leeper, jr., John N. Lewis, James E. McCall, Peter H. McCall, William S. McCall, William McCarven, James McKinney, John McKinney, Jonathan McKinney, William McKinney, Isham McMahan, Jesse McMahan, Newton Moon, Richard McMahan, Harvey McRobaras, James Maimes, James Martin, Britain Mathews, Gabriel May, Henry H. May, William B. Miller, Moses G. Meadows, Henry Mitchell, John Moseley, Benjamin Neil, Joseph Neil, Bartet (sic) Nichols, Robert Orme Daniel Nichols, George Nichols, John E. W. Offutt, Benj. A. Oliver, James M Orme, William Patton Jackson Petty, Joseph Pica, Charles Phelps, Zachariah Petty, Francis H. Pothoff, Thomas L. Powell Thomas J. Pratt, William Pratt, William A. Scott, Stephen Quick, Thomas G. Rankin, Otho Rannebarger, A. J. Shobe, Allen D. Ranney, Hiram Rawlings, James Saunders, Allen Scott, James Scott, William A. Scott, John Shobe, John K. Seale, James Shannon, James A. Simpson, Joseph T. Sitton, John Smith, Peter S. Smith, Richard Smith, William H. Smith, John Smithey, John Sparks Samuel Sparks, Henry J Spud, Wm. Stewart, Henry J. Sped, Garrett N. Stewart, James Stewart, Rueben Stewart Benjamin Stookey, John Stricklen John Suggett, Minte (sic) Suggett, Volney Suggett, Calet W. Tate, Thomas Swearingen, Calvin Tate, John G. Tate James Taylor, Nathaniel N. Tate, Thomas Taylor, Hiram S. Thomas, Alexander Tucker, Joel Tipton, Zachariah Tucker, Henry Tutt, William Underwood, Jesse Van Cleave, Edward Walker, sr., William A. Wrenn, Young C. Walker Joseph C. Wells, Lewis Welton, Moses Welton, David L. Whaley, Samuel Wicks, Saml. Williams, A. S. P. Winsor, Thomas R. Winn, Douglas J. Winul, Oliver Wright, Ignatius Wright.

### Bourbon Township

Andrew Adair, John Aair, Joseph Adair, jr., Jonathan Aldersson, Joel J. Adcock, Walker Allen, Henry Atkinson, Jas. A. Baker, Isaac Baker, Benj. Baker, Jas. A. Baker, Thomas Baker, William F. Baker, William M. Baker Thomas H. Benton, H. M. Branham, Hiram Brown, Preston Byers, Creed C. Carter, Robt. Carter, John Combs, Henry Coons, Joseph Coons, Samuel R. Crump, John Crosswhite, Jacob Crowson, Robt. L. Davis, John Davis, Philip Davis, Abel Dodd, John Duncan, jr., John Finley, George W. Duvall, Abrm Ellis, Daniel Esham, Michael Fannon, Patrick Fleming, Joseph Freeland, John Gee, Silas W. Gee, Nathan Glassgow, John Gooden, Walker Gooden, Joseph W. Jolly, John A Griffith, Martin Griffith, John Hanah, Samuel Hanah, John Huston, Peter Isonhour, Calvin Jackson, Thomas Jamison, Levy James, B. F. Jones, Stephen N. King George W. Morris, William Little Isaac Loyd, John McClelland, Jas. W. McClelland, Robt. McCleeland, Thomas McClelland, Wm. Martin, Thomas McCutchen, Elisha McKine, Joseph M. McKine, William Miller, Abram Miller, Noah Martin, Arthur Neal, John Neal,

Thomas Besbit, Saml. Newland, John C. Pemberton, Jas. Price, Oscar Poindexter, Thomas Poindexter, Calvin Renfro, William Renfro, Ninian Ridgeway, Thomas Ridgeway, Robert S. Russell, jr., Jas. Ryan, Isaac Sally, Cephas (sic) Selby, Jas. Selby, John Selby, Joshua Selby, Lewis V. Selby, Benj. Sheets, Wm. Smith, Pneuman B. Starks, W. E. Stephens, W. B. Stone, Benj B. Taylor, David Stoplet, John Steward, Wm. Stephens, Thomas P. Stephens, John L. Stephens, Joseph D. N. Thompson, Thomas J. Trigg, William Tomlinson, Thomas Truett, Jas. E. Turley Jas. Turner, Thomas S. Tuttle, Abram Vantricht Asbury Vest, Garland A. Vier John Vivion, Jas. R. Ward, Robt. M. Wells, John M. Ward, John West, Jas. Woods, Alexander Wright.

### Cedar Township

William Alexander, Appleton Allen, Joseph Allen, Kindred Baily, Wm. Armstrong, J. J. Ausborne, William T Bass, Joel A. Bennett, John Bellows, Andrew K. Bell, Samuel H. Beevers, John Baysinger, Charles H. Baynham, John Bennett, Smith A. Brandon, Joseph Bennett, Milton Bennett, Moses Bennett, John Blythe, John Boyd, Micajah Boyd, Thomas Boyd, sr., Thomas P. Bradley, A. P. Bradley, F. B. Bradley, G. E. Bradley, John T. Bradley, Abner H. Brandon, Thomas H. Branham, Charles K. Brown, James Brocks, Robert Brocks, Thomas Brocks, Richard Bullard, Mosley Brown, John Brown, James Brown, Wm. Cayson, John Bunhett, Benjamin Cayson, Aqullia Burnett, Hawkin Cayson, John D. S. Burnett, Samuel Burnett Larkin Cayson, JOhn H. Childs, Rubin Chaney, Parke I. Chaney, James Clatterbuck, Cazeby Clatterbuck, Sauel Citerley, John Clatterbuck, Leroy C. Clatterbuck, Richard Clatterbuck, Wm. Clatterbuck, Thomas D. Conger, John Conger, Leroy C. Colton, Abraham Coonce, Wm. Criswell, Dabney H. Crank, Henry Crank, Nathaniel H. Crank, Samuel Crews, Thomas P. Crews, George Criswell, James Criswll, jr., James Criswell, sr., John Curry, William Curry, Henry Davis, James Davis, Thomas J. Davis, Ezekiel Day, Paul H. Dooley, Samuel Day, Solomon Day, Thomas Day, Wm. Dosier, Charles Dougherty David Duane, William F. Dunn, John Fry James W. Edge, Elias I. Emmonds, Gibson U. Emmons, James D. Fisher, Joseph Ennett, Erastus Evans, Josiah Faulkner, John J. Foster, James D Fisher, Larkin Fleshman, Perry Fleshman, Alexander Ford, Robert Ford, James T. Foster, Wm. H. Foster, John Fry, James Furgison, T. J. Furgison, James S. Gray, Wm. Hayden, John B. Gray, Thomas F. Grear, Ambrose Gregory, Geo. Gray, David Griffith, Samuel T. Guthrie, John Hale, Mathew Hall, Samuel Hall Josep Ham, Hiram C. Harkins, sr., Alford E. Hart, Rawlenger Hayden, William Hayden, Henry Hene, John Hinton, Walker D. Heeling James A. Henderson, Daniel Hiller, James Hirtlin, Jacob G, Hisey, Abner Holt, Hiram Holt, Abner C. Holt John Holt, John D. Holt, Robert Holt, William P. Holt, jr., William P. Holt, sr., Arealas Hoover, Abraham Jinson, Perry Hoover, Isaac P. Howe, Thomas Howe, Harrison

Jinson, John Hudson, James Hudson, Thomas Hudson, George W Jinnings, David Hoduston, J. B Huffington, John Humphries, James G. Jones, Alsolem Kemper, George King, Jessey E. King, John B. King, Coley Langley, James Langley, sr., Samuel B. Long, Moses Langley, John Leapard, T. W. Longley (sic), J. W. Lyons, Washington Lyons, Charles McArlin, John McDonald Charles McAslin Joseph McCulough, James D. McGary, William R. Mcgary, James McKamey, James I. McKamey, Robert McKamey, William H. McKamey, Weden Major, John W. Martin, Bird Moore George Maupin, Bird Milliams, John B. Moore, William Morgan, Goke (sic) Moores, Augustus H. Murphy, Andrew R. Murray, W. H. Obertson, Enoch Murray, Abram Narfleet, Alford Nash, Robert Nickles, Bery Olds, William Olds, Benjamin Oliver, John S. Pulliam, Isaac Oliver, Isaac Oliver, sr., Benjamin Overton, Thomas H. Oliver, Sisney Parker, Charles L. Powell, Asa Puliam, James H. Powell, Henry Pulliam, Levi Pulliam, James P. Reynolds, Washington Ramsey, John H. Rensome, Alexander D. Scott, John Rawley, Howard Reeves, John Reynolds, Bedford Reynols, James Reynolds, George W. Rucker, David Sage Rubin Stanley, Richard Shacleford, Benjon (sic) Sheley, Singleton Sheley, Horace Sheley, Reason Sheley, Van Sheley, Benjamin D. Sugett, William Stanley, Henry W. Stokes, James Stone, Henry H. Suggett, James Suggett, sr., Joseph R. Suggett, M. Tindel, Thomas S. Suggett, Wily G. Tatum, James Thomas, John H Tutt, James M. Thackston, D M Tucker, Martin G. Turner, Daniel Waggoner, John Waggoner, John Waggoner, Mathias Waggoner, Stokeley Waggoner, William Wallace, Lewis White Bird Williams, Daniel Williams, John Williams, Wm. S. Williams, Eli B. Wilson, Joel Wiseley Thomas E. Wood, David Yount, Joseph Yount, Abraham Zumwalt, Anthony Zumwalt, Frederick Zumwalt, David Zumwalt, Isaac Zumwalt

### Cote San Dessein Township

A. J. Baker, Floyd Baker Thomas F. Baker, A. G Bennett, Rufus E. Berchard Rober (sic) Boyce, Baptist Capten, David Cheatham, John L. Cheaney, Milton Cleveland, Stephen D. Conger, John H. Cora, Joseph H. Croa, Barnabus C. Davis, Robert Davis, Thomas Davis, Francis Denoier, Cyrus Dixon Wm. Grey, Haw Dority, Matthew Dority, Francis Ernos, George Evans, Wm. Evans James Evans, Jesse Evans, jr , Jesse Evans sr., John Evans, Jesse Farmer, John Farmer, Joseph Farmer, Archibald Gilmore, John L Ferguson, Moses Ferguson, Thomas Feree, N. B. Furgerson, Ebeneser Finly, J. W. Finly, Francis Fory, W. P. Furgerson Swan Furgerson M. W. Gathright, Wm. Grey, R. S. Hornbuckle, Hansen L Gray, Thom. Hampton, Nathaniel Harler, Richard L. Hard, Edward Harper, Green Hazlerig George B. Hopkins Alexander Hoard, Thomas Humphreys, Henry Jones, Isaac Langley, William R Langley, Lewis Laplant, Abraham Luzoeder, Isaac Leroy, Edward McDonald, H. H. McGarry, John B. Moor, Thomas N. Ming, Moses T. Miller Samuel Mason, Wm.

Major, Joseph Mahar (sic), Alfred Mangfed, Allen Nash, Wm. Nash H. W. Neill Henry Neill, John Oxier, James Pace, John Pace, Benjamin Perkins, John Perry, John W. Pulliam, James Saunders, Euel L. Ramsy, John Reed, Peter Rudy, Frederick Saunders, Jonithan (sic) Ramsy, Wm. B. Saunders, John Wadly, Moses L. Simpson, James Slaughter, James A. Smart, Richard Williams, Robert Tarter, Benidict Turman, Joseph Vincan, J. P. Young, Nathan Wainscot, John Wansly, Patrick Ward, Daniel White, John W. Wayner, George Williams, Wm. Williams, Joseph Williams, Peyton Williams, Richard Williams, Thomas Yancy.

## Fulton Township

W. J. Acre, Josepgh Adair, Benjamin Adams, Ransom Agee, Michael Alderson, Arct. (sic) Allen, Hugh Allen, Jas. Allen, Jesse R. Allen, C. G. Anderson, William Armstrong, Daniel W, Bagby, James Atkinson, Absalom Austin, James W. Bagby, John Baker, Richard Bagby, Samuel Bagby, Waddy C. Bagby, Theodore Beavin, Benj. Bailey, Charles Bailey, W. A. Bailey, James H. Baskin, Henry Baily, Jas. H. Baker, John Baker, Alfred Barrow Thos. H. Baker, George Bartlett, John Bartlett, William Belamy, John Belamy, James Belamy, Zadock Beavin, Eden Benson, John C. Baskin, Rueben Belamy, Thomas Bernard, Richard Berry, sr., Ginns Berry, Robert Berry, Marcus Bird, Thompson Blair, John W. Blackwell, Phillip Blackenburg, A. Bledsoe, John W. Blount, Samuel Blount, Richard H. Bogguss, Mathew D. Bogguss, David Bond, Edwd. Bond, V. D. Boone, William Booth, Daniel Boulware, Stephen C. Boulware, Theodrick Boulware, G. W. Brailey, Robert Boyd, David Bright, Henry T. Bright, N. D. Broadley, Willim Broadwell Pleasant D. Brooks, Cornelius Burnett, John Burdit, Franklin Burt, Jordan Bush Robert A. Caldwell, J. H. Calbraith, Thomas Caldwell, Thomas Callaway, Thomas H. Caldwell, Joseph P. Callaway, Thomas Campbell, Wm. Campbell, Joseph Carr, Wm. Carrington, Claibourn Cheatham, David L. Cheatham, Harrison L. Cheatham Leonard Cheatham, Lewis Cheatham, Luther Cheatham, Turley Cheatham, Carter T. Craig, Joseph Chick, Abram Childers, James H. Clanton, John Coats, Thomas Clark Thomas Collier John A. Collier, John A. Comer John H Cook, James Coons William Cooper William Craig, J. T Craig, Larkin Craig, Isaih Craighead, Samuel D. Dickerson, Isaih W. Craighead, J R Craighead, M. V. Davis, James L. Craighead, John Craighead, Robert Craighead, Jesse P. Craige (sic), Solomon Craighead, Stephen Craighead, John Crooks, W. A. B. Craighead, William Craighead, George W. T. Davis, George Davis, David B. Davis, Gerrard Davis, James M. Davis, James Davis, Mathew Davis, John Davis, John B. Davis, Rufus Davis, W. C. Davis, Richard Daviss (sic), Tho. Dulin, Benj. Dawson, Elijah Dawson, George Dawson, James A. Dawson, Martin Dawson, Robert Dawson, Daniel T. Day P. E. Day, W. T. Day, John Debo, Isaac DeHavan, Adam Dickerson, James H. Dirskill, Thos. L. Douglass, John Douglass, John Duckworth,

D. L. Dunagan, John Duncanson, Daniel Dunham, David Dunlap, sr., David M. Dunlap, Robert Dunlap, John Dyae, James Elam, Abram Ellis, John Ennet, B. P. Evans, James Eweing, Patrick Eweing, William H. Eweing, David S. Faber, Joseph Faber, Wm. Fariss, A B. Fant, James Fair, John R. Ferguson, Alexander Fitzhugh, Joseph Fisher, James Fletcher, John Fletcher, John F. Fletcher, Joseph Fletcher, Peter F. Fort, Robert Foster, William Foster, William Freeman, Edward P. Gaines, Gideon Gaines, Alfred George, William M. George, John Gibbony, John Gladwill, C. I. Gibbs, Robert F. Gibbs, Samuel Gibbs, Thomas J. Gibbs, P. D Gilbert, James Gilmore, Robert Gilmore, W. H. Gilmore, W. R. Givens, Chesley Glover, Jesse Glover, John Cohagen, Robert Glover, Israel B. Grant, James Grant, James Grey, William Green, W. H. Greor, James A. Griffith, Stephen Guerramt, John Griffith, John Guy, S. B. Ham, Robert Hanse, James C. Hamilton, John Hamilton, jr., James Hamilton sr., Robert Hamilton, William B. Hamilton, Allen Hammond, John A. Hannah, Archibald Hanley, Elihu Harden, George Harden, Moris Harden, William Harden, N. D. Harper, John Harrison, M. V. Harrison, Mathew G. Harrison, George W. Harriss, Hamilton H. Harriss, Thomas B Harriss, Thos. D. Harriss, Samuel Hayden, John Hays, G. C. B. Hedges, David Henderson, Jas. S. Henderson, William Henderson, Samuel Hensley, George Herring, John Herring, James C. Herring, John B. Herring, Charles Hill, J. O. Hockaday, Nathaniel Herring, John Hill, Morgan Hill, John Hockaday, Richard Hill, Willis Hill, Isaac N. Hockaday, sr., James Hockaday, Henry Holeman Peter H. Hollend, Thoms Hook, William Hook, Zadick Hook, Alfred Hornbuckle, Heny Houf, J. H. Hughes, Harden F. Hornbuckle (2x), David Huff, Samuel A. Hunter, Samuel Humphreys, James Humphreys, Peter Huff, John Hutcherson, William M. Hunter, Lorenzo Hutz Simpson Hyton, James Jameson, Samuel Jameson, Sandford Jameson, Jefferson F. Jones, Alex D. Jeans, John Jones, Thomas G. Jones, George T. Johnson, William Jones, A. H. Johnson, Geo. T. Kee, Tho. Johnson, Harrison R. Kelsoe, Andrew L. Kemp, George W. Kemp, Jordon Kemp,sr., Michal Kemp, Nathan Kemp, Robert Kemp Walter Kemp, William Kemp, Adomjah (sic) Key, Martin Key, Silas King, Lewis Kiger, George Kibler, John Kinnon, James Knight, William Knight, Nathan Kouns, Cornelius Langley, John Levit, James Langley, John Langley, sr., William Langley, Arbuckle Langtree, Henry Laramore Robert Lawson, W. S. Letcher, John McClanahan, James Logan, R. P. Long, E. N. Loveless, James McCampbell, William McCarty, James McClanahan, John McClure, I. H. McClure, Samuel McClure, Thomas McClure, John McGowan, William McClure, Joel McConnel, Otho McCracken, John Malone, Wm. H. McCulloch, George McFarland, Benjamin McGee, William McGee, John McIntire George McIntosh William McKinney, Wm. Moore, Andrew McLaughlin, James McLaughlin Larkin Maddox, Sherwood Maddox, Isaac Magard, John Martin Russell Martin,

Robert H. Martin, Wesley Mazingoe, Allen D. Miller, Daniel Miller, Martin Miller, Robert W. Miller, Samuel Miller, Jas. B. Moore, James W. Moore, William Moore, Benj. L. Mosley, Wharton H. More (sic), John Moss, Jerrimiah (sic) Muir, John Nevins sr , William H. Neal, James Nelson, Thomas Nelson, Samuel Nesbit, James Nevins, Thomas Nevins, Robert Newsom, John Newton, Felix G. Nichols, Alfred Newson, Jesse Nichols, Frederick Nichols, Garrett Nichols, William Nichols, George A. Nicholson, Daniel Nolley Jesse D. Oldham, Wm Oldham, W. H. Pace, James Oliver, Eli M. Overfelt, James Overton, Louis Overton, R. B. Overton, Robert Paine, Joel Palmer, John Peyton, Thomas Patton, Eli M. Overfett (sic), Edmond Pemberton, J. B. Pemberton, John Petross, Zachariah Petty, Cyrus Price, Daniel Phillips, James Pierce, Waddy T Poindexter, James R. Porter, John Pugh, Reuben Pulis, Elisha Ralekin, Preston B. Read, Edmond Randolph Robert Randolph, James Rawson, Robert Read W. C. Reed, Henry T. Renoe, James W. Reynolds Thomas W. Rhodes, Absolam Rice, Jonathan Rice, Joseph Rice, Samuel Riley, Benjn. Roberds, Jackson Roberds, John Robinson, John A. Robinson, James Rogers, Robert F. Roll Thomas Roll, Jas. Sage, Thomas Sales, Edward Sallee, Joseph Salle John Smart, W. P. Sallee, John Sampson, James M. Scott, Martin W. Scott, George Secre, Isaih Selby, John W. Selby, William P. Selby, Warner W. Sheets, James K. Shelby, William Shrtridge, T. T. Shuteman, James Simpcoe John Simpcoe, Reuben Simpcoe, Ezra B. Sitton, Wharton Simpcoe, Robt. W. Sinclair, Edmond Smart, William Smart, Bethel A. Smith, Elkanama (sic) Smith, John M. Smith, Tartan Smith, Thomas Smith, Robert Snedicor, John Snell, W. W Snell, Elias Spicer Lewis Stark Elijah Steel, Samuel Steel, William Stever John H. Stone Richard Swan, John P. Suggett, George Talbot, Benj. F. Talley, Isaac Tate, Calvin Tate, James Tate, John Tate Ira Tatman, James A. Terrell Thomas Tatum, George S. Terry, Basil L. Tharp, John Thatcher, E. N. Thatcher, D. N. Thatcher, Wm. S. Thatcher, George Thomas, James Thomas, Presley Thomas, Wm. Trueman. R. W. Thurman, Mthew O. Throgmorton, Hiram Thralkill Charles B. Thornhill, Samuel Thornhill Cabel Tinsey, John Trimble St. George Tucker, Thomas F Turley Henry S. Turner, James Underwood, Daniel Vanbibber Francis Vanbibber, Irvine Vanbibber, William Wadery, Thompson Walton. William Walton, Wm. H. Wells, Russell Ware, Tho B. Warren, Francis H. Watkins, John K. Watson, Aron Wells, John I. Wells, Nathan Well, John White, Frederick White, Thomas West, Peter White, John Wilson, Sauel White, Newton Whittaker, Amos Wilcoxson, Harvey Wilcoxson, John Wiley, William Wiley, Joseph Wifley, Henry Wilkerson, Hiram Wilkerson, Moses Wilkerson William Wilkerson, Asa Williams, Peyton Williams, Thomas Williamson, David H. Woltz, William Willings, John Wilson, Thomas I Wilson, Richard Wise, John Wolery, John L. Yantis, Joseph D. Young,

Hiram Yates, Joseph D Young.

## Liberty Township

Elija Adams Wiiam Allen David P. Booze John C Flint Nathaniel Creag, Jacob Eler, Arthur Forguson Thomas Glendy Samuel Glency, John Grimes, John Hendison, Thomas Hendison, William Hendrick, Henry Jeffers, James Larrence, William C. Leeper, David Leeper, James A. Loapen, Archbald McClintic Isom McDaniel, James McIndear, James McKinney, John Price, Thomas McLinton, Samuel Martin, William R. Martin, William Pleage, William N. Pleage, Robert Murfey, David Murfa, Jacob Weaver, G. G. Pleage, Joseph Price, Thomas Riche, George L. Smith, William Riley, John Rothwell, John Scot, Mathew Scot, George Sheates, John Sheates, Greenip Snell, Chrles Tibs.

## Nine Mile Prairie Township

Chas. P. Allen, Thos. N. Allen, James C. Anderson, Robin Arnold, Robert Ansel, Thomas Austin, Robert Bailey, John K. Barry, Wm. Bell, Calieb (sic) Berry, William Blanton, James M. Boone, John Board, John W. Blunall, Rodolpho Boone Minor Boswell, Matthew Boswell, John B. Bragg, Isaac Branham, Jas. T. Bryan, N. E. Branham, Saml. L. Bryan, William Buchannan, George Burt John A. Burt, James Callison, William Callison, Francis Chick, Barba Collins, Melchindec (sic) Covington, J. Crump Noah Covington, James Cox, Elijah Coyle, George Craig, Solomon Coyle, Samuel Craig, Benedict Crump. D. W. S. Crump, Jas. S. Crump, John Crump, Marmadue (sic) Dallas, Francis B. Garrott, Isaac Davis, James Davis, Joseph Davis, John Dearing, John S. Dillard John Dyer, John H. Ellis, John French Joseph Everheart, Philip H. Felkores, William Foxworthy, W. Grant, John Green, John B. Gregory, Richard J. Gregory John K. Grey, William Gregory, Wilson H. Gregory, John Hamblin, Andrew Hamilton, James L Hamilton, John C. Hamilton, Elias H. Harding, William Hamilton, Andrew L Harrison, Wm. Hays Harmon Hays, Samuel Hensely, Armstead Hickiston, Geo. E. O. Hocksaday, Wm. H. Hill, John Hostler, Basdell Holt, Stephen A Hunt Elisha Hughes, John Hughes, Rees Hughes, Benj. P. Jones, Daniel Hunt, William Jones, David Kennedy, Robert H. McCall, Joseph Larch Oliver Little, Charles Love, Charles M. McKenney, Daniel McIntyre A. McCubbin, James McCormick, David McCormick, James McMurty, Levy McMurty, John Matheny, John P. Martin, Absalem Meredith, John Meteer, Sam Meteer, William Meteer, Bailey Miller, James Mosby, B. G. D. Moxley, James Myers, John Myers, Lewis Myers, Alien Nance, Fielding Oliver, Philip Owen, William Penn, William Peyton, Hezekiah Price, Thos. H. Polly, Jesse Potter, Nicholas S. Purvis, W. H. Wilson John A Read, Josephus Robinson William Robinson, Griffin P. Sanders, Jesse Scholl, John Scholl, Joseph Scholl, James Scott, Reuben Scott, Benjamin Sisk John T. Spear, Sihon Spencer, John Steel, William Thacker Stephen Tucker, Mastin Vaughan, Francis M. Weems, Curtis Wilburn,

John Wilburn, Alexander Williams, Bryden Wilson, Calbrath Wilson, John Wilson, W. H. Wilson, Wm. H. Wilson, Henry C. Wood, Joseph Wood, H. D. Woodsworth, Jeptha Yates, John N. Yeldell, John Yates.

## Round Prairie Township

Wm. B. Arthur, Gasper Barger, Henry B. Barger, James C. Barger, JOhn Blount, Andrew Bowen, James Bowen, Joseph Boyd, Thos. Boyd, John Carrington, Samuel Carrington, Simeon R. Crago, Robert Criswell, Joseph R. Daniel, Thompson Daniel, Elisha Davis, Wm. H. Davis, John Harvey, Charles Hays, John W. Johnston, Nehemiah Honley Joseph H. Howe, W. W. Howe, R D. Renoe, Stephen H. Hyten, Emanuel James, Wm. Martin, John D. Nevins, Nicholas P. Martin, Wiett Pace, Robert Randolph, Thomas Scrogham, Daniel Scrogham, Samuel Shaw, George Smith, Willis Smith, John Smoot, Wm. Suggett, George C. Thompson, David H. Thompson, Jesse B. Thompson, Wm. N. Thompson, Tilman G. Vaughan Holley Wilkerson, Joseph Wilkerson.

## Hickory County, Missouri, Nemo-Bethel Missionary Church Cemetery, Intersection of Hwy. NN and Hwy 64, Nemo, Missouri.

| Name | Born | Died |
| --- | --- | --- |
| W. B. Jones | Mar. 15, 1842 | Jan. 29, 1904 |
| Sarah Jones | Jul. 12, 1844 | Apr. 6, 1913 |
| Mintie Depew | Apr. 25, 1881 | May 4 1908 |
| Una Hare Miller | Jul. 20, 1886 | May 26, 1941 |
| Hoyt Adkins | Oct. 19, 1898 | May 20, 1975 |
| Ora King | Jul. 21, 1899 | Aug. 23, 1965 |
| Wm. A. Ferguson | Aug. 17, 1868 | May 8, 1914 |
| Margaret Ferguson | Sep. 24, 1868 | Oct. 16, 1948 |
| George A. Alexander | Apr. 16, 1856 | Oct. 21, 1931 |
| Mary M. Eads | 1855 | 1896 |
| Edward W. Wuertz | Sep. 11 1892 | Dec. 9 1976 |
| Carrie G. Simmons | 1880 | 1964 |
| Margaret C. Cady | 1857 | 1913 |
| Jonas B. Ihraig | Oct. 24, 1891 | Dec. 11, 1948 |
| William D King | 1863 | 1953 |
| Ida B. Wrinkle | May 23, 1871 | Oct. 9, 1942 |
| Luther S. Wrinkle | Mar. 17, 1873 | Oct. 23, 1959 |
| Lewis Alvin Sawyers | Nov. 1, 1883 | Jun. 30, 1978 |
| Lucy Irene Sawyers | Jan. 21, 1889 | Jan. 15, 1967 |
| Samuel K. King | 1880 | 1960 |
| Katie King | 1889 | 1987 |
| Ben F. Crawford | 1875 | Jul. 15, 1950 |
| Martha Crawford | Jul. 22, 1877 | Jul. 15, 1915 |
| Henry J. Hooper | Jul. 14, 1886 | Feb. 7, 1967 |
| *Donna B. Hooper | Apr. 11, 1885 | Feb. 28, 1964 |
| *(Married September 2, 1916) | | |
| Jesse Tolliver | May 9, 1891 | Oct. 11, 1940 |
| John Robert Carter | Dec. 16, 1870 | Aug. 8, 1934 |

| Name | Born | Died |
|---|---|---|
| John C. Hitson | Dec. 26, 1856 | Jan. 4, 1929 |
| William Dennis King | Jan. 11, 1863 | Apr. 3, 1953 |
| Flossie Butcher Crawford | May 3, 1889 | Dec. 18, 1966 |
| Cornelius Ferguson | Jun. 2, 1883 | May 12, 1956 |
| Gussie G. Ferguson | Feb. 29, 1884 | Aug. 17, 1924 |
| Cora Belle Tylor | Feb. 24, 1880 | Feb. 8, 1959 |
| Lewis Winfield Taylor | Oct. 2, 1877 | Mar. 11, 1953 |
| Bert McQuerry | Jun. 17, 1882 | Jul. 21, 1958 |
| Catherine E. McQuerry | Nov. 11, 1881 | Oct. 6, 1958 |
| Wm. Claude Patterson | Nov. 15, 1899 | Jan. 7, 1982 |
| *Lucy Patterson | Jun. 22, 1896 | Apr. 12, 1975 |
| *(Married Dec. 1917) | | |
| Robert I. Russell | Nov. 28, 1894 | Mar. 22, 1981 |
| Nathan Edde | Jan. 13, 1862 | Apr. 19, 1943 |
| Eliza R. Alexander | May 23, 1858 | Jan. 1, 1949 |
| Lonnie J. King | Jul. 16, 1882 | Jan. 31, 1930 |
| Cora May King | Jun. 13, 1890 | Nov. 25, 1948 |
| W. R. Hare | 1840 | 1905 |
| Sarah E. Hare | 1849 | 1916 |
| J. W. Toliver | 1851 | 1936 |
| Amanda Toliver | 1852 | 1893 |
| Tennie Meadows | Jan. 4, 1884 | Mar. 1, 1971 |
| Edward H. Bewly | 1895 | 1980 |
| *Minnie Bewly | 1891 | 1986 |
| *(Married May 8, 1915) | | |
| Theodosia Fisher | Aug. 22, 1884 | Jan. 21, 1923 |
| Joe E. Crawford | Feb. 29, 1885 | Nov. 21, 1967 |
| Harrison R. Reser | Sep. 3, 1888 | Feb. 19, 1960 |
| Mabel E. Reser | Apr. 5, 1895 | Jul. 16, 1984 |
| Francis E. Taylor | Aug. 26, 1884 | Jan. 7, 1928 |
| Vina King | Dec. 21, 1877 | Feb. 21, 1960 |
| Thomas F. King | Jan. 13, 1869 | Mar. 15, 1930 |
| Oscar D. Darby | May 21, 1885 | Nov. 2, 1971 |
| Vira Darby | Oct. 5, 1884 | Mar. 24, 1967 |
| Wesley N. Nelson | Mar. 13, 1889 | Jan. 17, 1974 |
| Nancy E. Knight Crawford, wife of W. R. | May 16, 1878 | Dec. 30, 1907 |
| Lennie J. Hitson, son of J. L. and M. J. | Mar. 5, 1898 | Aug. 19, 1900 |
| Lester Dorman | Dec. 19, 1891 | --- |
| J. R. Huckaby | 1883 | 1920 |
| H. E. "Ed" Taylor | Aug. 31, 1895 | Jul. 26, 1974 |
| *Lettie M. Taylor | Dec. 5, 1895 | Jun. 27, 1970 |
| *(Married Feb. 2, 1917) | | |
| Samuel Mitchell | Jan. 26, 1855 | Mar. 1, 1923 |
| Bennie F. Crawford | 1891 | Nov. 7, 1959 |
| Mary S. Crawford | 1898 | 1953 |
| John Andrew Hooper | Sep. 8, 1897 | Feb. 21, 1987 |

| Name | Born | Died |
|---|---|---|
| Robert Simmons | 1890 | 1918 |
| George W. Crawford | Oct. 14, 1896 | May 14, 1914 |
| Atha King Crawford | Oct. 24, 1889 | Sep. 23, 1980 |
| Tennie A. Ferguson | Dec. 4, 1873 | Dec. 23, 1963 |
| Geo. W. Ferguson | Dec. 31, 1870 | Dec. 20, 1943 |
| Eller F. Ferguson | Dec. 16, 1873 | May 3, 1903 |
| Jerusha King | 1862 | 1950 |
| *Walter Lee Blackwell | Oct. 12, 1893 | Nov. 14, 1986 |
| *(Pvt. U. S. Army WW I) | | |
| Frances E. Mitchell | March 22, 1861 | Dec. 23, 1947 |
| Jno. Wrinkle | --- | Jan. 20, 1899 |
| John S. Pitts | Aug. 14, 1876 | Nov. 9, 1954 |
| Maud M. Pitts | Jun. 15, 1882 | Sep. 30, 1972 |
| Tennie A. Taylor, wife of H. D. | Aug. 11, 1896 | May 4, 1923 |
| Lois J. Blowers | Mar. 7, 1850 | May 17, 1905 |
| Chabod A. Blowers | Mar. 2, 1849 | Sep. 19, 1915 |
| *Wm. M. Dobbs | 1844 | 1922 |
| *(Civil War Veteran) | | |
| Daniel Hooper | Jun. 30, 1846 | Aug. 12, 1927 |
| *Isabelle Hooper | Mar. 28, 1859 | Aug. 15, 1933 |
| *(Married July 22, 1877) | | |
| Eliza G. Russell | 1868 | 1899 |
| Arthur Nelson | Mar. 13, 1885 | --- |
| Stella Nelson | Feb. 15, 1890 | May 11, 1967 |
| Robert E. Meadows | Jul. 24, 1875 | Aug. 6, 1943 |
| Lee Brown, son of A. E. and Eliza | Jun. 13, 1885 | Oct. 13, 1910 |
| David Crawford | Feb. 9, 1884 | Apr. 18, 1946 |
| Martha E. Crawford | Feb. 28, 1883 | Dec. 16, 1971 |
| Cyndy Fisher | Aug. 24, 1859 | Feb. --, 1931 |
| Wood Fisher | Jul. 24, 1852 | Aug. --, 1930 |
| Susan E. Lower | Apr. 28, 1847 | Mar. 13, 1936 |
| Aaron W. Nelson | Dec. 2, 1856 | Jun. 2, 1912 |
| Sarah F. Nelson | May 16, 1872 | Nov. 2, 1954 |
| Wm. Elmer Simmons | 1880 | Nov. 5, 1951 |
| Goldy King | Mar. 27, 1899 | Feb. 17, 1901 |
| John Cady | 1852 | 1915 |
| Ethel I. Grisham Dorman | Jan. 1, 1892 | Apr. 27, 1978 |
| Della F. Mallott | Jul. 21, 1887 | May 1, 1968 |
| Chas. A. Mallot | Jul. 17, 1875 | Aug. 11, 1945 |
| Florence Dorman | Apr. 17, 1870 | Dec. 7, 1947 |
| *Eugene Dorman | Feb. 3, 1866 | Dec. 15, 1944 |
| *(Married Feb. 2, 1888) | | |
| Georgeann Meadow Edmondson | Mar. 6, 1847 | Dec. 31, 1935 |
| John T. Ferguson | Aug. 24, 1843 | Jul. 30, 1931 |
| Susan A. Ferguson | Jun. 25, 1848 | May 12, 1925 |

| Name | Born | Died |
|---|---|---|
| *James F. Hare | Sep. 22, 1888 | Sep. 21, 1923 |
| *(Co. B, 110th Engineers) | | |
| Tennessee Parolee Ferguson, daughter | | |
| of J. T. and Susana | Mar. 12, 1877 | Jul. 19, 1894 |
| John E. King | Sep. 5, 1874 | Jul. 29, 1947 |
| Margaret L. King | Apr. 29, 1884 | Dec. 20, 1959 |
| Hattie E. King | Sep. 7, 1878 | Feb. 6, 1901 |
| Jasper J. Knight, son of | | |
| M. E. and J. W. | Apr. 10, 1894 | Jul. 9, 1897 |
| Sherman Wrinkle | Mar. 3, 1876 | Dec. 31, 1985 |
| Mary E. Knight | Aug. 24, 1841 | --- |
| Martha Wrinkle | Nov. 8, 1882 | Apr. 1, 1988 |
| Eliza J. Knight | Jun. 17, 1876 | Aug. 4, 1899 |
| John Landreth | Apr. 20, 1858 | Mar. 31, 1930 |
| Margarett --- (?) | Sep. 5, 1860 | Mar. 27, 1918 |
| Sarah E. Taylor | Sep. 20, 1862 | Jun. 11, 1937 |
| Dennis D. Taylor | Jan. 17, 1859 | Dec. 25, 1938 |
| John Henry Nelson | Apr. 15, 1885 | Oct. 19, 1961 |
| Charles Franklin Nelson | Nov. 4, 1890 | Nov. 24, 1967 |
| A. J. Taylor, son of | | |
| Elvira and E. N. | Nov. 26, 1860 | Jul. 26, 1908 |
| John E. Taylor | Sep. 11, 1874 | May 20, 1953 |
| *Effie L. Taylor | Apr. 22, 1879 | Dec. 30, 1879 |
| *(Married Dec. 24, 1901) | | |
| Luke Taylor | Oct. 2, 1877 | Mar. 11, 1953 |

Jackson County, Missouri, Westport School Tax List, 1869.

Wm. Adams, Albert Ashcraft, L. A. Allen, Charles Aimes, Josephine Adams, James Agan, John Adams, Joseph Arnduff, A. M. Allen, Widow Adams, J. E. Adams, August Baumeister, Rufus Bradshaw, Estate of Mr. Balls, Sam Bucher, J. O. Boggs, John Bailey, George W. Braint, W. C. Brown, Jack Booth, Phillip Becker, H. H. Baber, D. W. Brown, A. Bevis, agent for Mrs. Vogel, A. C. Blue, Thomas Bennett, Geo. K. Briant, Francis Gallop, J.O. Boggs, Burris Balis, I. M. Blue, W. H. Bent, H. C. Buerkman, Wm. Bent, Mildrige Boggs, Minnette Deval, John Black, G. C. Bryant, Mary Blue, John C. Ballagh, J. J. Blue, Joab Bernard, F. H. Booth, James Brice, W. R.Bernard, James Bass, Clark Brown, Peter Beham, Casper Barth, Wm. Burns, Wm. Butter, Lottie Bucher, Julius Baber, James Baird, Sam Hays, Mrs. Blaylock, Harris Brown, James Bridger, Joseph Bance, C. Charley, Wm. R. Bernard, J. A. Coggshile, J. F. Crutchfield, Calvin Carter, Sam Collins, Phillip Conboy, J. I. Crane, Wm. J. Dillon, T. F. Cardom, Talton Crutchfield, Sam Davenport, James Childs, Anderson Case, Ben Fogel, E. W. Dill, Patrick Curran, Michel Dixon, Irwin Case, W. A. Coggshile, Thomas A. Kirkpatrick, Jack Dominick, Jerry Collins, J. M. Duff, Jacob Endres, Hugh Dixon, John Consor, August Charles, Mary Gable,

J. Cheyene, Winston Dillard, Z. Coggshile, J. D. Gregg, G. W. Daggett, Ambrose Key, Peter Divinney, John Davis, Roxanna Erwin, Mrs. E. Davis, Andy Davis, Chas. Grall, Ira Emmons, Salomon Houck, C. F. Helm, Wallace Law, James Kirkpatrick, J. Patton, George Houck, Augustus Jay, W. F. B. Grigsby, J. W. Hedges, Conrad Eckhart, Jerome Graham, Elijah Johnston, E. Lehay, Jacob Endres, Jacob Endres, jr., J. Isom, Charles Heyle, Theodore Case, Fred Eslinger, Margaret Eisle, Charles Fink, M. H. Eisle, Mary Gluntz, Mrs. Chris Hedding, James C. Hunter, Thomas Norman, Henry Stine, Mr. Coffee, Catherine Weideman, V. S. Ford, Ed. G. Goforth, Levin Louis, Leonard Peers, Mary Howard, John Frazier, Perry Fristo, A. M. Price, J. H. Langworthy, John Harris, J. A. Farrell, Gregg Faux, F. A. Kratlow, W. S. Poole, Thos. Gillespie, A. A. Goodman, Wm. Woodson, Benjamin Miller, Estate of -- Glunz, M. J. Graham, Mrs. Findlay, Thos. A. Goforth, Finis Farr, Joseph Fritz, J. G. Hamilton, Dr. H. F. Hereford, Martin Hamilton, Geo. Keck, August Horning, J. J. Hittebridle, Sam Justice, J. M. Wells, Antony Heberle, Godfrey Horning, C. C. Huffaker, Wm. Olden, John Harris, jr., John Jackson, Francis Hahn, Z. Truitt, Wm. Melease, Frank Hutmacher, Norman Hamilton, Lydia Hampton, H. Finney, Clement Dall, Ed. Price, Albert Kinger, Wm. Kald, B. F. Simpson, James Keel, C. E. Kearney, Estate of -- Klaber, Jno. Y. Kinkaid, Joel Liscomb, John Klaber, Robert Sey, Geo. Walker, Mr. Curtis, J. W. White, Mrs. Kelsey, Thomas Mastin, Martin Stegmiller, Phillip Knowles, John Lurson, Wm. Phelps, Easte of -- Coates, Fred Langeman, R. I. Lewis, Louis Leon, Geo. London, Morris Leon, Isabel Logston, John Laight, John Phelps, Joseph McDonnell, James Shell, Jas. Goodwin, August Robert, Theobald Werry, James Turner, A. Goodman, Ferninand Wiedelich, Thos. Peers, Wm. Gillis, John Majors, Baptiste Mahoney, Henry Sager, August Garber, Mrs. Hornbuckle, Joseph Tilton, Richard Swain, L. A. Garrett, J. A. Garrett, Fannie Smith, Wm. Moriarty, Adam Smith, Alex Moore, Ed. Herron, A. P. Warfield, J. G. Hamilton, John Docking, G. R. Montgall, John Harris, John S. Harris, H. C. Millsaps, John Soda, Dr. Hunter, Geo. W. Cutter, J. W. McFadden, Tracy Spencer, Thos. M. Hunter, John Mastin, James McDonnell, M. Moore, Estate of -- Porter, August Meyer, Wyatt Webb, Estate of -- Gluntz, J. McCarty, Thos. Mastin, J. C. Price, Wm. Heltzall, Wm. Matny, James M. Hunter, John Weidman, E. J. Maguire, A. J. Talley, London Morton, A. B. H. McGee, Seth Ward, M. A. Moore, John C. Morris, Alfred Price, Mobillion McGee, J. F. McCormick, J. P. Moore, R. F. Moore. Dr. Morgan, Dr. Morris, L. B. Palmer, William Weidman, Wm. Mattingsby, Chas. Mattingsby, John Thoes, Francis McComas, Sam Rucker, Judge Tate, Wm. Warren, Jacob Walsh, B. F. Robinson, Jessee Thomas, J. L. Mize, John McCoy, Henry Richardson, Ellen McGurk, James Warrington, J. W. Thompson, Jacob Dimerlich, --- McKutchin, M. McCarty, W.

R. Shotwell, John Wear, Henry Madison, M. T. Osgood, Henry Moppins, Wm. Pentze, Joseph Stagmiller, Edmund Smith, Estate of Purdom,A. D. Rhodes, Andres Patel, Wm. Ramsay, Wm. White, Wm. Souenschein, Frank Theobald, John Regan, Michel Riordan, Riley & Curtis, Jacob Ragan, Herman Souenschein, John Smith, Susan Wright, S. Thorton, Dwight Spencer, D. P. Riley, James Tobin, Katy Stuart, Alex Waskey, Sarah Schoeph, Mrs. Stockton, Ulan Stin, Mrs. Mize, T. H. Rosser, Jacob Ragan, Chris Sautter, Wm. Rensch, John Smith, M. A. Stotts, J. H. Sweeny, Duke Simpson, John Taylor, Larch Truitt, Catherine Spence, George Vogel, Geo. Weideman, Mrs. Sharkey, G. W. Weidman, W. H. Wilson, Christ. Weideman, Jacob Weideman, Louis Vogel, J. M. Piper, Moses Wolf, Fred Wagner, Harris Wilson, W. H. Wilson, M. E. Woodford, Frank Wieland, Bernhard Wurz, Ravell & Herrigan, David Slater, Wm. Stewart, Henry Sager, Milton J. Payne, G. M. Waltice.

## St. Clair County, Missouri, Grand Jury, May term, 1856.

Harvey C. Douglass, Wm. L. King, Peter Stephens, Thomas Calvin, Hezekiah Thompson, Lewis Metcalf, James C. Culbertson, James C. Price, Rueben S. Nance, Jacob Coonce, Josha W. Ellis, James M'Agee, Robert F. Gardner, Wilson Garrett, Jas. H. Simms, James H. Justus, Hiram Sweet, Stinson S. Stevens.

## Maries County, Missouri, 1880 Mortality Schedule (Note: Only Those Persons Born 1840 Or Later Are Included).

Euseha Breeden: 1 yr, female, white, single, b. Missouri, Father b. Missouri, Mother b. Missouri, d. March, Twp. Miller, Dr. Powers, Resided. 1 year

Mary A. Menecke: 30 yr, female, white, single, b. Missouri, Father b. Arkansas, Mother b. Arkansas, d. December, Twp. Miller, Dr. Bowles, Resided. 9 years.

Nancy A. Brandon: 11 yr, female, white, single, b. Missouri, Father b. Tennessee, Mother b. Illinois, d. November, Twp. Miller, Dr. Barnet, Resided. 11 years.

Judah Helton, 23 yr, female, white, single, b. Missouri, Father b. Tennessee, Mother b. Missouri, d. March, Twp. Miller, Dr. Wilson, Resided. 23 years.

Leona Schell: 9 days, female, white single, b. Misouri, Father b. Baden, Mother b. Hanover, d. September, Twp. Miller, Dr. Bumpass, Resided. 9 days.

--- Cooper: stillborn, male, white, b. Missouri, Father b. Missouri, Mother b. Missouri, d. September, Twp. Miller, Dr. Powers.

--- Bird: 2 months, male, white, b. Missouri, Father b. Indiana, Mother b. Indiana, d. October, Twp. Miller, Dr. Bumpass, Resided. 2 months.

J. W. Scotty: 40 yr., male, white, married, b. Indiana, Father b. Indiana, Mother b. Indiana, d. November, Twp. Miller, Dr. Wilson Resided 1 year.

T. J. Mitchell: 1 yr, female, white, b. Missouri, Father b. Indiana, Mother b. Missouri, d. March, Twp. Miller, Dr. Bumpass, Resided. 1 year.

Ellen Stephens: 25 yr, female, white, married, b. Missouri, Father b. Missouri, Mother b. North Carolina, d. December, Twp. Miller, Dr. McGregor, Resided. 5 years.

Thomas Shaver: 36 years, male, white, married, b. Kentucky, d. January, Twp. Miller.

Olive Copeland: 1 year, female, white, b. Missouri, d. September, Twp. Miller.

Wiseman Copland: 8 yr, male, white, b. Misouri, d. September, Twp. Miller.

Dora Veasman: 18 yr, female, white, single, b. Missouri, Father b. United States, Mother b. United States, d. January, Twp. Miller, Dr. Bumpass.

J. Nelson: 26 yr, female, white, married, b. United States, Father b. United States, Mother b. United States, d. August, Twp. Miller, Dr. Hickman.

Anna Lubbert: 1 year, female, white, b. Missouri, Father b. Prussia, Mother b. Bavaria, d. November, Twp. Boon, Dr. Bowles, Resided. 1 year.

Wilhelmina Weil: 13 yr, female, white, single, b. Missouri, Father b. Prussia, d. February, Twp. Boon, Dr. Wiry, Resided. 13 years.

Anna Bax: 2 yr, female, white, single, b. Missouri, Father b. Prussia, Mother b. Missouri, d. July, Twp. Boon, Dr. Bowles, Resided. 2 years.

Lorenzo D. Burns: 7 months, male, white, b. Missouri, Father b. Missouri, Mother b. Missouri, d. December, Twp. Boon, Resided 7 months.

Harrison Champain: 8 days, male, white, b. Missouri, Father b. Missouri, Mother b. Missouri, d. December, Twp. Boon, Resided. 8 days.

John H. Clark: 31 years, male, white, married, b. Missouri, Father b. Missouri, Mother b. Missouri, d. March, Twp. Boon, Dr. Bumpass, Resided 31 years.

Charles O. Rowden: 6 months, male, white, b. Missouri, Father b. Missouri, Mother b. Missouri, d. December, Twp. Boon, Dr. Bumpass, Resided. 6 months.

Henry Freund: 32 yr, male white, married, b. Prussia, Father b. Prussia, Mother b. Prussia, d. November, Murdered, Twp. Boon, Sr. Stadtler, Resided 19 years.

A. Thompson: 2 yr, male, white, b. Missouri, Father b. United States, Mother b. United States, d. August, Twp. Boon, Dr. Scott.

Susan Riges: 6 yr, female, white, b. Missouri, Father b. Missouri, Mother b. North Carolina, d. September, Twp. Dry Creek, Dr. Apley, Resided. 8 months.

Philip Grayham: 22 yr, male white, single, b. Missouri, Father b. North Carolina, Mother b. North Carolina, d. April, Twp. Dry Creek, Dr. Wilson, Resided. 15 years.
Robt. Osborn: 25 yr, male, white, b. Tennessee, Father b. Tennessee, Mother b. Tennessee, d. April, Twp. Dry Creek, Drs. Apley and Glover, Resided 4 months.
Joseph Vaughan: 15 yr, male, white, single, b. Missouri, Father b. Kentucky, Mother b. Missouri, Twp. Dry Creek, Drs. Wilson and Jones, Resided 15 years, d. May
Jas. G. Duncan: 18 yr, male, white, single, b. Missouri, Father b. Missouri, Mother b. Missouri, d. December, Twp. Dry Creek, Drs. Wilson and G;ove, Resided 18 years.
Fanny Gather: 33 yr, female white, married, b. Missouri, Father b. Missouri, Mother b. Missouri, d. November, Twp. Dry Creek, Dr. Bowles, Childbed Fever, Resided. 6 years.
Mary S. Maneghe: 25 yr, female, white, married, b. Tennesee, Father b. Tennessee, Mother b. Tennessee, d. December, Twp. Dry Creek, Dr. Bowles, Resided. November.
Charles McCuen: 1 month, white, male, b. Missouri, Father b. Ireland, Mother b. Ireland, d. October, Twp. Dry Creek, Resided 1 month.
Mary Blackwell: 25 yr, female, white, b. Missouri, Father b. Kentucky, Mother b. Virginia, d. February, Twp. Dry Creek, Resided 15 years.
--- Blackwell: 5 months, male, white, b. Missouri, Father B. Tennessee, Mother b. Virginia, d. February, Twp. Dry Creek.
Mary E. Brumley: 23 yr, female, white, married, b. Missouri, Father b. Virginia, Mother b. Missouri, d. May, Twp. Dry Creek, Dr. Apley, Resided. 10 years.
Leonia Copling: 1 yr, female, white, b. Misouri, Father b. Missouri, Mother b. Tennessee, d. August, Twp. Dry Creek, Drs. Apley and Jones, Resided. 1 year.
--- Freeze: female, white, B. Missouri, Father b. Massachuetts, Mother b. Arkansas, d. January, Twp. Dry Creek, Dr. Apley, Stillborn.
--- Fulkerson: 5 months, female, white, b. Missouri, Father b. Missouri, Mother b. Missouri, d. January, Twp. Dry Creek, Dr. Apley, Resided. 3 days.
Luette Robberson: 16 y, female, white, b. Missouri, Father b. Missouri, Mother b. Georgia, d. September, Twp. Dry Creek, Dr. Jones, Resided. 16 years.
--- McNinn, : female, white, entered twice, twins ?, b. Missouri, Twp. Dry Creek, stillborn, d. September.
Charles O. Skyles: 1 yr, male, white, b. Missouri, Father b. Tennessee, Mother b. Missouri, d. September, Twp. Spring Creek, Dr. Merryweather, Resided. 1 year.
--- Snodgrass: female, white, b. Missouri, Father b. Missouri, Mother b. Missouri, d. August, Twp. Spring Creek, Dr.

Prigmore, Stillborn.
I. E. Honeay: 3 months, male, white, b. Missouri, Father b. Kentucky, Mother b. Kentucky, d. December, Twp. Spring Creek.
Oliver Honeay: 3 years, male, white, b. Missouri, Father b. Kentucky, Mother b. Kentucky, d. March, Twp. Spring Creek, Dr. Hutcheson, Resided. 1 month.
Mary M. Feeler: 17 yr, female, white, single, b. Missouri, Father b. Indiana, Mother b. Tennessee, d. June, Twp. Spring Creek, Dr. Bowles, Resided. 17 years.
Elley Fenton: 19 yr, female, white, married, b. Missouri, Father b. United States, Mother b. United States, d. March, Twp. Spring Creek, Dr. Fetzar.
Sophia Loop: 22 yr, female, white, single, b. Illinois, Father b. Indiana, Mother b. Indiana, d. May, Twp. Jackson, Dr. Bowles, Resided. 7 months.
Elizabeth Loop: 2 months, female, white, b. Missouri, Father b. Missouri, Mother b. Illinois, d. May, Twp. Jackson, Dr. Jones, Resided. 2 months.
Dennis Hagerty, jr.: male, white, b. Missouri, Father b. Ireland, Mother b. Ireland, d. February, Twp. Jackson, Dr. Bowles, Stillborn.
John Hickam: 19 yr, male, white, single, b. Missouri, Father b. Missouri, Mother b. Missouri, d. March, Twp. Jackson, Dr. Bowles.
Hannah Hickam: 17 yr, female, white, single, b. Missouri, Father b. Missouri, Mother b. Missouri, d. April, Twp. Jackson, Dr. Bowles, Resided. 17 years.
Catherine Russo: 21 yr, female, white, married, b. Missouri, Father b. North Carolina, Mother b. Tennessee, d. August, Twp. Jackson, Dr. Bowles, Resided. 21 years.
M. J. Russo: 1 yr, male, white, b. Missouri, Father b. Illinois, Mother b. Missouri, d. September, Twp. Jackson, Dr. Bowles, Resided. 1 year.
Sarah Reynolds: 17 yr, female, white, single, b. Missouri, Father b. Tennessee, Mother b. Illinois, d. October, Twp. Jackson, Dr. Bowles, Resided. 17 years.
Coen Jones: 1 yr, female, white, b. Missouri, Father b. Missouri, Mother b. Missouri, d. May, Twp. Jackson, Dr. Jones, Resided. 1 year.
James Crismon: 21 yr, male, white, single, b. Missouri, Father b. Missouri, Mother b. Missouri, d. November, Twp. Jackson, Dr. Barnett, Resided. 21 years.
Rosa Stockton: 1 month, female, white, b. Missouri, Father b. Missouri, Mother b. Missouri, d. May, Twp. Jackson, Dr. Jones, Resided. 1 month.
Josephine King: 1 month, female, white, b. Missouri, Father b. Pennsylvania, Mother b. North Carolina, d. May, Twp. Jackson, Resided. 1 month.

J. F. Hutchison: 34 yr, male, white, married, b. Missouri, Father b. Tennessee, Mother b. Tennessee, d. May, Twp. Jackson, Dr. Bowles, Resided. 2 years.

Joseph Bailey, 39 yr, male, white, single, b. Tennessee, Father b. North Carolina, Mother b. North Carolina, d. October, Twp. Jackson, Dr. Jones, Resided. 1 year.

Edward Riley: 20 yr, male, white, single, b. Missouri, Father b. Illinois, Mother b. Illinois, Twp. Jackson, Dr. Bowles, Resided. 2 years.

--- Weyer: 4, female, white, b. Missouri, Father b. Prussia, Mother b. Prussia, d. April, Twp. Jackson, Resided. 3 years.

Barabara Zimmer: 12 yr, female, white, b. Missouri, Father b. Prussia, Mother b. Prussia, d. November, Twp. Jackson, Dr. Hughs, Resided. 2 years.

Agness Zimmer: 11 yr, female, white, b. Missouri, Father b. Prussia, Mother b. Prussia, d. November, Twp. Jackson, Dr. Hughs, Resided. 2 years.

Emily Crider: 1 month, female, white, b. Missouri, Father b. Missouri, Mother b. Missouri, d. February, Twp. Jackson.

Emily Lovelace: 1 month, female, white, b. Missouri, Father b. Missouri, Mother b. Missouri, d. May, Twp. Jackson.

Sarah Nakin: 28 yr, female, white, married, b. Missouri, Father b. Tennessee, Mother b. Tennessee, d. May, Twp. Jackson, Dr. Jones, Resided. 20 years.

Geo. M. Poor: 8 months, female, white, b. Missouri, Father b. Tennessee, Mother b. Indiana, d. February, Twp. Jackson, Dr. Jones, Resided. 8 years.

Catherine Watts: 8 months, female, white, b. Missouri, Fatherb. England, Mother b. Missouri, d. April, Twp. Jackson, Dr. Jones.

Francis Buschoff: 5 yr, female, white, b. Missouri, Father b. Prussia, Mother b. Prussia, d. April, Twp. Jackson, Dr. Bowles.

Joseph Buschoff: 3 yr, male, white, b. Missouri, Father b. Prussia, Mother b. Prussia, april, Twp. Jacksom, Dr. Bowles.

James Winson: 2 yr, male, white, b. Missouri, Father b. Missouri, Mother b. Missouri, d. March, Twp. Jackson, Resided. 1 year.

Ella Littleton: 21 yr, female, white, b. Ohio, Father b. Ohio, Mother b. Ohio, Twp. Jackson, Resided. 1 year.

Jacob Brockman: 20 yr, male, white, b. Switzerland, Father b. Switzerland, Mother b. Switzerland, d. May, Twp. Jackson, Resided. 4 months.

--- Stokes: male, white, b. Missouri, Father b. England, Mother b. Missouri, d. September, Twp. Jefferson, Dr. Bowles, Stillborn.

John Branson: male, white, single, b. Missouri, Father b.

Missouri, Mother b. Missouri, d. September, Twp. Jefferson, Dr. Jones, Resided. 12 years.

James Rogers: 26 yr, male, white, single, b. Missouri, Father b. Virginia, Mother b. Missouri, d. March, Twp. Jefferson, Dr. Jones, Resided. 7 years.

--- Cofer: 1 day, male, white, b. Missouri, Father b. Illinois, Mother b. Missouri, d. December, Twp. Jefferson, Dr. Jones.

Fred McQueen: 18 yr, male, white, single, b. Missouri, Father b. New York, Mother b. Maryland, d. February, Twp. Jefferson, Dr. Jones.

Sarah Ritter: 33 yr, female, white, married, b. Missouri, Father b. Missouri, Mother b. Missouri, d. Kentucky, Twp. Jefferson, Dr. McGregor, Resided. 33 years.

Alfred Travis: 7 yr, male, white, b. Missouri, Father b. Tennessee, Mother b. Missouri, d. March, Twp. Jefferson, Dr. Bowles, Resided. 7 years.

Sarah Gaither: 1 yr, female, white, b. Missouri, Father b. Tennessee, Mother b. Missouri, d. November, Twp. Jefferson, Dr. Jones,

Lewis H. Miles: 2 yr, male, white, b. Missouri, Father b. North Carolina, Mother b. North Carolina, d. June, Twp. Jefferson, Dr. Bowles, Resided. 2 years.

Joseph Hutchison: 4 yr, male, white, b. Missouri, Father b. Tennessee, Mother b. Missouri, d. September, Twp. Jefferson, Dr. Bowles, Resided. 4 years.

--- Cox: No age, male, white, single, b. Missouri, Father b. Missouri, Mother b. Missouri, d. February, Twp. Jefferson, Dr. Bowles.

Arietta Hutcheson: 10 months, female, white, b. Missouri, Father b. Tennessee, Mother b. Missouri, d. July, Twp. Jefferson, Dr. Bowles, Resided. 10 months.

Hana Cowden: 5 months, female, white, b. Illinois, Father b. Mississippi, Mother b. Illinois, d. January, Twp. Jefferson, Dr. Miller, 5 months.

Mary Harrison: 19 yr, female, white, b. Missouri, Father b. Missouri, Mother b. Missouri, d. March, Twp. Jefferson, Dr. Meriwether, Resided. 19 years.

Nora Givens: 1 yr, female, white, b. Missouri, Father b. Virginia, Mother b. Virginia, d. October, Twp. Jefferson, Dr. Bowles, Resided. 1 year.

--- Terrill: male, white, b. Missouri, Father b. Missouri, Mother b. Missouri, Twp. Johnson, Dr. Elder, Stillborn.

--- Mizell: female, white, b. Missouri, Father b. Missouri, Mother b. Illinois, d. January, Twp. Johnson, Dr. Bowles.

John Bullock: 21 yr, male, white, single, b. Missouri, Father b. Tennessee, Mother b. Missouri, d. january, Twp. Johnson, Resided. 20 years.

Frances Welch: 40 yr, male, white, married, b. Missouri, Father b. Missouri, Mother b. Tennessee, d. February, Twp. Johnson, Dr. Meriwether, Resided. 12 years.

--- Harrison: 1 day, female, white, b. Missouri, Father b. Missouri, Mother b. Missouri, d. February, Twp. Johnson, Resided. 1 day.

Margaret F. Shinkle: 18 years, female, white, b. Missouri, Father b. Indiana, Mother b. Missouri, d. September, Twp. Johnson, Dr. Headler, Resided. 18 years.

Anna Walker: 23 yr, female, white, single, b. Illinois, Father b. Kentucky, Mother b. Kentucky, d. June, Twp. Johnson, Dr. Grammis.

Emma Lindner: 1 yr, female, white, b. Missouri, Father b. Missouri, Mother b. Missouri, d. August, Twp. Johnson.

Belinda Fritta: 34 yr, female, white, married, b. Missouri, Father b. Kentucky, Mother b. Kentucky, d. October, Twp. Johnson.

--- Richardson: 3 days, female, white, b. Missouri, Father b. Illinois, Mother b. Missouri, d. December, Twp. JOhnson, Dr. M. Richardson.

William Harrison: 2 yr, male, white, b. Missouri, Father b. Missouri, Mother b. Missouri, d. July, Twp. John, Dr. Elder.

Lydia Bailey: 10 days, female, white, b. Missouri, Father b. Missouri, Mother b. Missouri, d. March. Twp. Johnson, Dr. Meriwether.

Eliza C. Walker: 31 yr, female, white, married, b. Virginia, Father b. Virginia, Mother b. Virginia, Twp. Johnson, Dr. Meriwether, Resided. 12 years.

--- Barnwell: male, white, b. Missouri, Father b. Missouri, Mother b. Tennessee, d. December, Twp. Johnson, Stillborn.

Margaret Harkins: 9 days, female, white, b. Missouri, Father b. Missouri, Mother b. Missouri, d. September, Twp. Johnson, Dr. Elder.

<u>Clark County, Missouri, Will of John M. Reed, Mason County, KY, Filed in Will Book Q, Page 357, Mason County, KY, Dated November 7, 1854, Proven February, 1855.</u>

Heirs/Children: Isaac S. Reed, Armedda Glidewell, Nancy Frampton, Mary Ball, Judith Weeder, Susan Wheeler, late wife of Aaron H. Wheeler.

Heirs/Grandchildren: Ann and Judith Lacy, children of daughter, Elizabeth Lacy, dec.; Frances Glidewell; Benjamin Leonidas Clark.

Heirs/Brother: Wm. Reed, Clark Co., Missouri.

Executor: Isaac Shelby Reed, son, and Emery Whitaker.

Witnesses: Luke Dye, James Varndinburg, James S. Bratton, Emery Whitaker.

Johnson County, Shawnee Mound Cumberland Presbyterian Church
Session Records, Chilhowee, Missouri.

## Register of Adult Baptisms.

| Name | Date | Reverend |
|---|---|---|
| Mary Moore | Aug. 20, 1869 | B. F. Thomas |
| Mary Jane Guian | Aug. 20, 1869 | B. F. Thomas |
| Peter Smiley | Aug. 20, 1869 | B. F. Thomas |
| Ferdinand W. Crooks | Aug. 23, 1869 | B. F. Thomas |
| Ellen Thresher | Aug. 23, 1869 | B. F. Thomas |
| William P. Moore | Nov. 19, 1869 | B. F. Thomas |
| Daniel Grey | Nov. 19, 1869 | B. F. Thomas |
| Margaret Jane Wade | May 22, 1870 | B. F. Thomas |
| Margaret Gowens | Aug. 21, 1870 | B. F. Thomas |
| Martha J. Hays | Aug. 22, 1870 | B. F. Thomas |
| Julie F. Glasgow | Aug. 22, 1870 | B. F. Thomas |
| Joseph Mays | Aug. 22, 1870 | B. F. Thomas |
| Martha Grey | Aug. 22, 1870 | B. F. Thomas |
| Carry Powers | Aug. 18, 1870 | B. F. Thomas |
| Jacob Wiseman | Aug. 22, 1870 | B. F. Thomas |
| Anna Wiseman | Aug. 22, 1870 | B. F. Thomas |
| Andrew Russell | Aug. 22, 1870 | B. F. Thomas |
| Amanda Cassy | Aug. 22, 1870 | B. F. thomas |
| Robert B. Smith | Aug. 22, 1870 | B. F. Thomas |
| Margrett E. Smith | Aug. 22, 1870 | B. F. Thomas |
| Susan J. Crabtree | Aug. 22, 1870 | B. F. Thomas |
| Susan Kimsey | Aug. 22, 1870 | B. F. Thomas |
| Geo. W. Maze | Aug. 23, 1873 | B. F. Thomas |
| Josie Burgess | Dec. 23, 1874 | B. F. Thomas |
| Alphonso Hickinson | Dec. 27, 1874 | B. F. Thomas |
| Frank S. Sharp | Sep. --, 1874 | B. F. thomas |
| Thomas P. Clagett | Sep. --, 1874 | B. F. Thomas |
| Mrs. Jennie Semson | Sep. --, 1874 | B. F. Thomas |
| Mrs. Emma Wolf | Sep. --, 1874 | B. F. Thomas |
| Sarah R. Frelden | Dec. 20, 1875 | B. F. Thomas |
| Robert C. Frelden | Dec. 20, 1875 | B. F. Thomas |
| Noah Hickerson | Aug. 8, 1877 | S. H. McKlane |
| A. F. McCall | Aug. 8, 1877 | S. H. McKlane |
| J. C. Hubbard | Aug. 8, 1877 | S. H. McKlane |
| Joseph Orkins | Aug. 12, 1877 | G. L. Moad |
| Mrs. Fannie Orkins | Aug. 12, 1877 | G. L. Moad |
| Master F. A. Whitenack | Aug. 12, 1877 | G. L. Moad |
| Miss M. F. Moore | Jul. 29, 1877 | S. H. McElvain |
| Mrs. Mary F Maize | Nov. 17, 1878 | Y. W. Whitsett |
| George W. Brown | Nov. 17, 1878 | Y. W. Whitsett |
| Mr. C. R. Rice | Nov. 24, 1878 | Y. W. Whitsett |
| Miss Virginia Winehope | Nov. 24, 1878 | Y. W. Whitsett |
| William Hinton | Nov. 20, 1879 | J. Cal. Littrell |
| Mr. M. R. Glasgow | Nov. 20, 1879 | J. Cal. Littrell |
| Mrs. Sarah A. Hinkle | Nov. 20, 1879 | J. Cal. Littrell |

## Register of Adult Baptisms

| Name | Date | Reverend |
|---|---|---|
| Walter Nickelson | Nov. 20, 1879 | J. Cal. Littrell |
| John R. Hinkle | Nov. 20, 1879 | J. Cal. Littrell |
| James Hinkle | Nov. 20, 1879 | J. Cal. Littrell |
| John L. Moore | Nov. 20, 1879 | J. Cal. Littrell |
| Miss Sarah H. Jones | Nov. 20, 1879 | J. Cal. Littrell |
| Miss Della Hickerson | Nov. 20, 1879 | J. Cal. Littrell |
| Miss Belle Hickerson | Nov. 20, 1879 | J. Cal. Littrell |
| Bettie Moore | Dec. 7, 1879 | J. Cal. Littrell |
| Mary J. Boling | Dec. 7, 1879 | J. Cal. Littrell |
| Katie Guion | Jan. 2, 1881 | J. H. Houx |
| Ida V. Mills | Nov. 4, 1881 | J. H. Houx |
| Luie Casey | Nov. 14, 1881 | J. H. Houx |
| Sarah O. Elliott | Nov. 14, 1881 | J. H. Houx |
| Minnie Lee Casey | Nov. 14, 1881 | J. H. Houx |
| Minnie A. Eagleson | Nov. 14, 1881 | J. H. Houx |
| Lottie M. Mills | Nov. 14, 1881 | J. H. Houx |
| Mary E. Smith | Nov. 14, 1881 | J. H. Houx |
| Mattie A. Eagleson | Nov. 14, 1881 | J. H. Houx |
| Nellie A. Mills | Nov. 14, 1881 | J. H. Houx |
| Eugene Wolff | Nov. 14, 1881 | J. H. Houx |
| Thomas W. Moore | Nov. 14, 1881 | J. H. Houx |
| Llewellyn G. Wolff | Nov. 14, 1881 | J. H. Houx |
| John S. Casey | Nov. 14, 1881 | J. H. Houx |
| Sarah Holt | Dec. 4, 1881 | J. H. Houx |
| John W. Bond | Nov. 5, 1882 | J. H. Houx |
| Francis E. Comer | Sep. 11, 1885 | J. B. Fly |
| H. J. Cook | Sep. 11, 1885 | J. B. Fly |
| Elmo Maize | Sep. 11, 1885 | J. B. Fly |
| Jasper N. Cale | Sep. 11, 1885 | J. B. Fly |
| Anna Zarragar | Sep. 11, 1885 | J. B. Fly |
| Andrew M. Comer | Sep. 13, 1885 | Z. T. Orr |
| Clarrance McCann | Sep. 13, 1885 | Z. T. Orr |
| Jennie Bemis | Sep. 13, 1885 | Z. T. Orr |
| Robert Hawkins | Aug. 29, 1886 | Z. T. Orr |
| Walter Runner | Aug. 29, 1886 | Z. T. Orr |
| Moses E. Watkins | Aug. 29, 1886 | Z. T. Orr |
| James M. Barrager | Aug. 29, 1886 | Z. T. Orr |
| Daniel Barrager | Aug. 29, 1886 | Z. T. Orr |
| Sarah E. Watkins | Aug. 29, 1886 | Z. T. Orr |
| Carrie L. McCann | Aug. 29, 1886 | Z. T. Orr |
| Zerelda Barrager | Sep. 1, 1886 | Z. T. Orr |
| James H. Roser | Sep. 1, 1886 | Z. T. Orr |
| Maggie S. Whittaker | Sep. 2, 1886 | Z. T. Orr |
| Ida Whittaker | Sep. 2, 1886 | Z. T. Orr |
| John W. Hood | Sep. 5, 1886 | Z. T. Orr |
| Della Hood | Sep. 5, 1886 | Z. T. Orr |
| Georgia E. Whitside | Sep. 12, 1886 | Z. T. Orr |

## Register of Adult Baptisms

| Name | Date | Reverend |
|---|---|---|
| Cynthia N. Bailey | Sep. 12, 1886 | Z. T. Orr |
| Della M. Bailey | Sep. 12, 1886 | Z. T. Orr |
| James Bailey | Sep. 12, 1886 | Z. T. Orr |
| Allice (sic) Moore | Sep. 11, 1887 | Z. T. Orr |
| Effa Casey | Sep. 11, 1887 | Z. T. Orr |
| Clara A. Wade | Sep. 11, 1887 | Z. T. Orr |
| Bertha Whitsides | Sep. 11, 1887 | Z. T. Orr |
| Lulia Watkins | Sep. 11, 1887 | Z. T. Orr |
| Ella Wolff | Sep. 11, 1887 | Z. T. Orr |
| Samuel T. Lycook | Sep. 11, 1887 | Z. T. Orr |
| Thomas Hincher | Sep. 11, 1887 | Z. T. Orr |
| George W. Elliott | Sep. 11, 1887 | Z. T. Orr |
| Luella Murray | Sep. 7, 1888 | Z. T. Orr |
| Ada G. Smith | Sep. 7, 1888 | Z. T. Orr |
| Anna M. Tilman | Sep. 7, 1888 | Z. T. Orr |
| Eli D. Bradshaw | Sep. 9, 1888 | Z. T. Orr |
| Melissa C. Webb | Sep. 9, 1888 | Z. T. Orr |
| Clara V. Hicks | Sep. 9, 1888 | Z. T. Orr |
| M. C. Dunn | Sep. 10, 1888 | Z. T. Orr |
| Wm. R. Hicks | Sep. 11, 1888 | Z. T. Orr |
| Lucy M. Casey | Nov. 24, 1890 | Z. T. Orr |
| Lullie Moore | Nov. 24, 1890 | Z. T. Orr |
| Annie Lee Casey | Nov. 24, 1890 | Z. T. Orr |
| Cliff H. Kensinger | Nov. 24, 1890 | Z. T. Orr |
| George Barker | Nov. 24, 1890 | Z. T. Orr |
| Frank Trissemiter | Nov. 27, 1890 | Z. T. Orr |
| Laura Trissemiter | Nov. 27, 1890 | Z. T. Orr |
| Mattie E. Andrew | Nov. 27, 1890 | Z. T. Orr |
| Clara E. Bradshaw | Nov. 27, 1890 | Z. T. Orr |
| Etta M. Bradshaw | Nov. 27, 1890 | Z. T. Orr |
| Minnie Wade | Nov. 27, 1890 | Z. T. Orr |
| Merodith Wade | Nov. 27, 1890 | Z. T. Orr |
| Lena Tilman | Nov. 30, 1890 | Z. T. Orr |
| Warren Wickham | Nov. 30, 1890 | Z. T. Orr |
| James Heckter | Dec. 20, 1891 | Z. T. Orr |
| Allice (sic) Bailey | Nov. 20, 1892 | Z. T. Orr |
| Dora Snodgrass | Nov. 20, 1892 | Z. T. Orr |
| Della Wade | Nov. 20, 1892 | Z. T. Orr |
| Miss Lise Gains | Aug. 8, 1894 | Z. T. Orr |
| Etta M. Powers | Nov. 2, 1894 | L. R. Nichols |
| George F. Crooks | Nov. 2, 1894 | L. R. Nichols |
| James C. Commer | Nov. 2, 1894 | L. R. Nichols |
| George W. Comer (sic) | Nov. 2, 1894 | L. R. Nichols |
| John H. E. Elliott | Nov. 2, 1894 | L. R. Nichols |
| Henry C. Descombs | Dec. 23, 1894 | L. R. Nichols |

## Register of Adult Baptisms

| Name | Date | Reverend |
|---|---|---|
| John W. Woolf | Dec. 23, 1894 | L. R. Nichols |
| Albert Scott | Sep. 20, 1895 | B. Margeson |
| Lewis F. Waldridge | Sep. 20, 1895 | B. Margeson |
| John C. Whiteman | Sep. 22, 1895 | B. Margeson |
| Lela J. H. Elliott | Sep. 23, 1895 | B. Margeson |
| Mary Hathaway | Sep. 23, 1895 | B. Margeson |
| Wm. W. Bailey | Sep. 23, 1895 | B. Margeson |
| Roy Whitesides | Jul. --, 1895 | L. R. Nichols |
| Edward Bailey | Jul. --, 1895 | L. R. Nichols |
| J. G. Beaty | Sep. 30, 1895 | L. R. Nichols |
| Miss Hattie Lewis | Sep. 30, 1895 | L. R. Nichols |
| Lewis Bradley | Jun. 21, 1896 | Y. W. Whitsett |

## Register Of Deaths

| Name (Deceased) | Death Date | Reverend/Service |
|---|---|---|
| James Kimsey | Jul. 9, 1870 | |
| Mrs. Martha J. Hays | Feb. 23, 1872 | |
| Mrs. Cary Baker | Aug. 17, 1876 | B. F. Thomas |
| Mrs. Nancy Murray | Feb. 12, 1879 | Y. W. Whitsett |
| Mrs. Mariatta Whitworth | Mar. 27, 1888 | Z. T. Orr |
| Jane Morgart | Feb. 12, 1897 | J. A. Murphy |

## Register of Marriages

Cary Allen Eager and Margaret Jane Wade, (MD) July 31, 1870, (JP) J. H. McCan.

Ferdinan Crooks and Mary DaComb, (MD) November 27, 1872, (REV) B. F. Thomas.

Frank S. Sharp and Nancy E. Evans, (MD) December 3, 1874, (REV) B. F. Thomas.

George W. Maize and Sallie W. Martin, (MD) December 17, 1874, (REV) B. F. Thomas.

W. L. Roy and Mary A. Davis, (MD) December 31, 1874, (REV) B. F. Thomas.

John B. Barker and Carrie L. Powers, (MD) May 6, 1875, (REV) B. F. Thomas.

Henry Hinton and Susan Kimsey, (MD) October 17, 1875, (REV) B. F. Thomas.

Wm. Tuttle and Mrs. Jemima Darling, (MD) July 20, 1875, (REV) B. F. Thomas.

Wm. Whitworth and Mrs. Marieth Crooks, (MD) Not given, (REV) J. H. Gillespie.

J. R. Maize and Mary Neal, (MD) Not given, (REV) B. F. Thomas.

John R. Barker and Amanda E. Casey, (MD) November 27, 1879, (REV) B. F. Thomas.

Thomas Zarnes and Mattie A. Eagleson, (MD) Not given, (REV) S. Finis King.

David Williamson and Elizabeth Sharp, (MD) Not given, (REV) Z. T. Orr.

## Register of Marriages

C. H. Kensinger and Minnie Eagleson, (MD) January 28, 1891, (REV) Z. T. Orr.

Johnson Kesinger and Clara A. Wade, (MD) March --, 1892, (REV) Z. T. Orr.

## Register of Elders

| Name | Ceased To Act | Ordained |
|---|---|---|
| P. W. Moore | | 1850 |
| Daniel Grey | Sep. --, 1876 | Feb. 20, 1876 |
| Mosses (sic) E. Watkins | | 1867 |
| --- Fitzwater | Mar. --, 1873 | |
| Saml. H. Elliott | | Sep. 20, 1874 |
| Geo. W. Maize | Mar. 9, 1878 | Sep. 20, 1874 |
| John W. Broraugh | | Mar. 5, 1882 |
| Robert Sharp | | Mar. 5, 1882 |
| G. W. Watkins | | Feb. 22, 1894 |
| Frank S. Sharp | May 18, 1878 | Mar. 12, 1876 |
| Llevellyn Wolff | | Feb. 22, 1891 |
| Dr. J. G. Beaty | | Nov. 8, 1897 |
| Wm. Hinton | | Nov. 8, 1897 |
| C. L. Crooks | | Nov. 8, 1897 |

## Register of Deacons

| Name | Ceased To Act | Ordained |
|---|---|---|
| Geo. M. Casey | | Sep. 20, 1874 |
| Ferdinan Crooks | | Sep. 20, 1874 |
| Andrew Russell | Mar. 11, 1877(Died) | Sep. 20, 1874 |
| Jacob Wolf | | Mar. 12, 1876 |
| James Eagleson | Mar. 1, 1895 | Mar. 5, 1882 |
| Wm. Hinton | Nov. 8, 1897 | Mar. 5, 1882 |
| Mrs. Wm. Hinton | | Nov. 8, 1897 |
| Alice Powers | | Nov. 8, 1897 |

## Register Of Infant Baptisms

Sallie A. Whitsett, (PRTS) Mr. and Mrs. Y. W. Whitsett, (BD) November 19, 1878, (REV) W. W. Brannum.

Ollive B. Maize, (PRTS) Mr. and Mrs. J. R. Maize, (BD) November 19, 1878, (REV) W. W. Brannum.

Charles L. Crooks, (PRTS) Mr. and Mrs. F. M. Crooks, (BD) November 19, 1878, (REV) W. W. Brannum.

George F. Crooks, (PRTS) Mr. and Mrs. F. M. Crooks, (BD) Novbember 19, 1878, (REV) W. W. Brannum.

Delia A. Crooks, (PRTS) Mr. and Mrs. F. M. Crooks, (BD) November 19, 1878, (REV) W. W. Brannum.

William Sharp, (PRTS) Robert and Alice Sharp, (BD) February 28, 1888, (REV) Z. T. Orr.

Joseph Sharp, (PRTS) Robert and Allice Sharp, (BD) February 28, 188, (REV) Z. T. Orr.

Ava Lee Hinton, (PRTS) Wm. and Lizzie L. Hinton, (BD) November 24, 1890, (REV) Z. T. Orr.

Emeline Hinton, (PRTS) Wm. and Lizzie L. Hinton, (BD) No-

## Register of Infant Baptisms
vember 24, 1890, (REV) Z. T. Orr.
 Fannie S. Nichols, (PRTS) Rev. L. R. and Hattie M. Nichols, (BD) August 8, 1894, (REV) Z. T. Orr.
 Edna Isabella Kensinger, (PRTS) Mr. and Mrs. Johnson Kensinger, (BD) September 7, 1897, (REV) J. A. Murphy.

## Building Fund Pledges, March 23, 1871

G. M. Casey, Philip W. Moore, Wm. Adair, John R. Powers, Joseph Sharp, F. W. Crooks, J. H. McCann, Wm. Tuttle, Danl. Grey, Geo. W. Murray, F. W. Bleil, W. T. Wilson, D. B. Whidbee, C. E. Powers, George Arnold, Wm. Paul, Wm. Hinton, John Woolfolk, Wm. P. Moore, Bedford Tuttle, Frank Crooks, Frank Kemp, Chas. DesCombs, Joseph Williams, Jane Stone, William J. Ferel, William Freeland, D. B. Lambert, Isaac Adair, N. B. Moore, Robert Harwood, David Snodgrass, Rebecca Neil, V. J. Moore, Jacob Fingle, Jacob Thrasher, Sarah Kimsay, Robert Sharp, sr., P. DesCombs, Max McCann, Mary F. Moore, H. Caldwell, Frank Caldwell, D. P. Kimsey, M. E. Watkins, Joseph Cole, Jas. H. Carter, Willis Helm. John Coppage, Joseph Berger, W. D. Wash, Elias Tuttle, W. J. Butler, G. Townsler, R. F. Ceicil, Emma Wolff, W. A. Bryson, A. Judge, E. C. Gillam, N. H. Fitzwater, B. F. Thomas, W. E. Foster, P. R. Webster, J. D. Wiseman, Alexr. Miller, John J. Mason, A. J. Bailey, J. W. Hariger, G. Y. Salmon, D. C. Stone, F. H. Land, Jacob Wolff, John Curtis, Philip Land, A. C. Comer, Robt. Allen, R. F. Stevenson, Herkett & Brother, Ed Curtis, H. Riehl, N. D. Land, Haysler & Bro., B. L. Quarrels, John Raglan, E. A. Covington, Geo. Barker, Salmon & Stone, S. D. Garth, F. W. McFarland, W. G. Rogers, --- McCollins, R. W. Cressy, Wm. S. Stone, B. G. Boone, Roberts & Bro., Robert Lewis, Jas. Webb, Jacob Goldsmith, Andrew Russell, R. B. Smith, R. T. Lindsey, Robt. Gilbert, Miles Weeks, R. B. Casey, Sarah Jane Holt, Y. G. Culley, Jack Johnson, John C. Culley, G. D. Wright, T. J. Wright, J. D. Farr, E. H. Askew, W. R. Culley, P. P. Embrey, Saml. R. Brown, John R. Johnson, W. P. Huff, Arthur Hand, W. J. McFarland, J. D. Williamson, N. W. Norris, J. F. Loyd, S. V. Turner, D. W. Bennzette, Myron Wallace, T. N. Carpenter, R. R. Walls, John A. Townsend, Jas. G. Turk, W. S. Wantland.

## Henry County, Missouri, Huntingdale Cemetery, Shawnee Township, Huntingdale, MO.

| Name | Born | Died |
|---|---|---|
| Sallie E. Bradford | Dec. 17, 1870 | Jun. 6, 1872 |
| Wm. W. Bradford | Apr. 30, 1876 | Jul. 5, 1880 |
| George E. Ellington | Dec. 11, 1884 | Jul. 14, 1886 |
| Garrott J. Freeman, son of Garrott and Sallie age: 3 yr, 2 d | --- | Mar. 11, 1871 |
| H. A. Freeman | Sep. 3, 1846 | Jun. 6, 1877 |
| Inez Adelia Freeman | Oct. 3, 1892 | Nov. 23, 1900 |

| Name | Born | Died |
|---|---|---|
| James M. Freeman | 1844 | 1923 |
| Philip S. Freeman | age: 15 y, 2 m, 19 d | Jan. 26, 1881 |
| Wm. R. Freeman | Feb. 24, 1871 | Mar. 23, 1907 |

Benton County, Missouri, Delinquent Tax List, December 1, 1869.

H. H. Dodd, J. Y. Middleton, Joseph Baker, Henry Hearst, C. H. Hanson, W. Powell, Richard Carpenter, Wm. S. Jabes, Y. S. James, Daniel Henbricht, John James, O. E. F. Londsey, J. W. Cardwell, Jesse Smith, Wm. R. Ash, Wm. H. Bernay, John H. Black, W. Carpenter, Felix Chancey, Wm. H. Crabtree, John H. Doss, Jesse H. Dyer, John H. Douglas, Absolem Flippen, Chas. C. Goat, Creed Ingram, Wm. Y. Ingram, Presley Leslie, Joseph McMerty, W. Leslie, Schuyler M. McFarland, Robt. Nicholson, Thos. Nicholson, Henry Shull, Wm. Stephens, Yo. W. Weisner, Isaac E. Smith, John Pierce, Newton Goss, Rich. H. Edwards, John R. Ayers, Wm. R. Anderson, Mary Bomer, T. M. Bomer, C. C. Bomer, Elijah A. Bomer, Eleazor Brooks, James Brooks, John Brooks, Verdeman Caffee, Isaac N. Dadel, James Gardner, Edward Crenshaw, Chas. F. Irwin, Geo. W. Ganeway, Benjamin Summers, Nancy Honeycut, Hugh S. Johnson, Wm. M. Chester, Jacob Kiefer, Peter Nichols, Joseph Reed, Wm. A. Reed, John Sally, Wm. Salsbery, John W. Weatherford, James Jinkins, J. F. Moeymold, Newell E. Britt, Hiram Franklin, Nathan Swift, Herman Hubricht, Lucinda Summers, John Bishop, John Wills, Jesse Williams, Thos. C. Williamson, William Wallace, Jesse Williamson, John C. Walace (sic), Claus Stiljus, Wm. Budd, Dedrich Stiljus (Claus' son), James R. Donaldson, Thos. I. Garry, Geo. Cooper, John Jackson, William Lowry, Christian Kuntz, Joseph Lowry, Dolphus Orenbery, John J. White, John B. Young, Theodore Mesler, J. A. Jones, Claus Thaken, Albert Meyer, Cord Wallers, Henry Busholts, Henry Bochlman, Robert Helnuch, Claus Brandt, Meta Boschen (a minor), John Boling, John Clansen, Est. of Fred Detzen, Henry Feldman, Catharine Feldman, John F. Feldman, Catharine Goetz, Henry Harms, John D. Harms, H. H. Harms (Big Belly), Claus Husterbery, Peter Holtszen (son of Daniel), Geff Hajse, Cord Holtzen, Peter H. Holtzen, Peter E. Holtzen, John Intleman, Paul Marten, Cord Meyer, Yost Meyer, John Reifsel, Fred Berhner, Peter Jagles, John D. Wiese, Jos. Graffenrath, Est. of Claus Gerken, Floyd E. Bush, Est. of Hughs Allison, Pleasant Byrd, E. W. Babbit, J. W. D. Belt, Isaac A. Cattrell, Robert Cusic, Wm. T. Crawford, Jos. C. Cassland, Elj. B. Cisney, Geo. W. Combs, W. B. W. Cardsell, Allison Douglas, Wm. C. Danson, Adron Echle, D. A. Logen, Isaac England, Milley England, Harrison Johnson, A. Parsley, Marion Kerby, Thos. E. Gevis, Job Logan, Noah Martin, Leroy Millans, Jno. McCall, Walter McFarland, Asa Tolson, Wm. A. Phegley, Joel R. Reeves, A. J. Sally, James R.

McFarland, Susan Salsberry, Giles T. Thomas, Eli C. Thomas, James M. Thurston, John Wheeler, Joseph Weaver (a minor), E. T. White, Frank Whittington (a fugitive), Calvin Williamson, Alonzo Goff, Tolly Goss, Joseph Combs, J. J. Bird, Franklin Proctor, John Hines, James B. Chesser, G. F. Smith, James W. Chesser, Jordan G. Shoner, Blueford Bybee, William Byrd, Wm. Gorrell, Gremill Bryant, Lataman Caywood, John S. Caywood, Grey Cook, Sidneyhem Cook, Green Cook, Albert Dauson, Robt. W. Neuell, Mathew Davis, Sarah S. Dauson, John Davis, Julia Fagg, W. D. Galbreath, John S. Grashon, Mary Grashong, John R. Galbreath, Thos. Haskin, Stephen Horn, Geo. Johnson, Wm. T. Kays, S. T. Jones, Wesley Harris, Benjamin Kearnes, W. F. Kearnes, Hugh Kilgore, Wash Kilgore, Abner Neal, John Sally, Jehu H. Purnell, Wilson Quinby, Thomas Reed, Joseph Sharp, James M. Riddle, James Rainwater, Temperance Swift, Francis M. Skaggs, Thomas A. Swift, James Sandford, John Wickliffe, Sarah G. McCall, Thos. Bradley, Spencer Blundell, William E. Deins, Ashley Benjamin, J. C. Berry, John C. Bomer. Matilda Carico, John Burns, William Burns, Henry Bishop, F. W. Barr, Est. of Jas. Q. Carico, John Dobbs, Sarah J. Dillon, W. Dillon, Wilson Estes, Abraham Eldridge, Leonard Tailer, Lucinda Farr, John H. Garrison, Phebe Jeemes, William Kullman, Philo Millius, John Mertens, E. N. Price, Jackson Price, Benjamin Ross, Jacob Snahel, W. S. Smith, Sterling Sueringen, William Smith, Mernerner (sic) Smith, Melzer Schuyler, Thos. Skaggs, Isaac Templeton, Westley Walthal, Wm. O. Brown, Henry Berry, Lewis J. Dillon, D. A. Barnes, Henry Berry, Wm. E. Barley, Jesse Crunya, John H. Dewitt, Lewis England, John Eckoff, W. H. Shull, Eliza Fuller, David Shull, C. F. Shull, Jno. H. Tigg, James Tigg, John Vandever, C. S. Vance, Geo. L. Byrd, Wm. H. Williams, Ezekiel P. White, Wm. Alexander, W. D. Allen, Jacob Burns, Hiram Brown, Robert Brady, Sarah Baily, T. Gash, James H. Brown, Ruben P. Bailey, Robt. H. Bibb, Benj. R. Bristoe, Thos. Bristoe, Robt. H. Bibb, Jas. H. Bailey, W. W. Smith, Mark T. Cook, Isaac Dalby, John B. Fort, Francis L. Jay, John F. Gibson, Vinson Gwin, John M. Heedson, Josiah Ingram, Francis Hoover, Joe M. Huffefinger, John W. Ingram, Vatek (?) Light, Caleb Lindsay, Wm. J. Light, Jonathan Martin, John E. Morgan, Jerry McCormak, Wm. H. Orr, David Reed, Jas. L. Rawlins, John L. Stewart, Isaac R. Smith, Wm. Bush, Edward See, John H. Towns, Thomas Trent, W. H. H. Wickliffe, Chas. Wickliffe, Anderson Warren, Samuel Wharton, Saml. and Gus Webb, Samuel Webb, Will S. Whitten, Samuel Wharton, Clem Antricth, Pat Atkinson (black), Jonathan Autricth, William Adams, Geo. W. Barber, John L. Brock, Vina Bush, Wm. H. Balwin, B. G. Blair, Sam. Bagwell, Alexander Blair, Calvin Sellers, Joseph Cochran, Edward G. Cook, --- Craft, Calvin Cook, Jesse Drake, Lewis H. Dehshout, Mark M. Davis, Isaac N. Giffens, Mothe (sic) Giffens, --- Glazebrook, Major Hodges,

Henry F. Green, William Groshong, A. J. Hart, jr., Elizabeth Huff, J. J. Hedgepeth, W. J. Hains, Thos. B. Huff, Hugh F. Haryman, F. M. Knowls, D. P. Knowls, Lewis Keunalt, Fletcher Lemon, jr., Amos Knootz, Samuel Miller, Wm. B. Means, Samuel D. Miller, John M. Miller, Elizabeth Miller, Walter Richardson, Wm. Remky, John L. Smith, Hiram Stratton, W. B. Thomas, S. C. Stratton, Lewis Tucker, Luke Wilson, Mathew West, Geo. W. Wallace, E. Wright, J. J. Welhoff, L. Wright (negro), Wm. Young, Fred Weimen, Elbert Wright, Walter H. Barshold, John Y. Carpenter, Fred Bohmer, A. Bernes & Co., A. R. Fain, John R. Fain, Masten Fain, James M. Holland, Charles Harvey, Fred Kriesler, Henry Kesseman, Henry Kerr (black), August Jagles, Lewis Hollyman, John Knapp, Benjamin Minter, Chas. Rambam, Charles Mitchell, Rev. E. Mackinson, Thos. McMurdough, Moses Phillips, Wm. Pemberton (black), Wash Shock (black), Antorie Wunch, Sept. Wise, E. M. White, Townsend, John Anspaugh, Wm. H. Alberts, Henry Alberts, Sam. Coates, John W. Eastwood, W. R. Neal, John Neal, James R. Rand, Eli Patterson, M. Allen, Mathew Allen, W. E. Ashinurst, J. T. Ashinhurst, Henry Capp, W. C. Ashinhurst, Joshua G. Ashinhurst, Wm. Alexander, James Alexander, James S. Bailey, Smith Bailey, Robt. Capp, Wm. J. Horn, Jos. W. Chancellor, John S. Feaster, Chas. W. Gish, W. Joplin, Milly Hamard, John Horn, Thomas Johnson, Geo. Smart, Lucinda Means, Selector Martin, James S. Means, Mary Mathew, Gras (?) Pouell, Benj. McClaren, James McClaren, V. Newell, Saml. McClaren, Thompson Stewart, James Smart, C. G. Heath, Neoma Stewart, Edward Stilles, A. M. Suiter, A. H. Scott, Wm. Wendall, Isaac J. Weaver, Sarah Wright, James Tipton, Martin M. Suenay, A. H. Scott, Martha J. Weaver, Edward Weaver, Wm. Miller, Isaac M. West, Salma Wisdom, Samuel H. Weaver, John W. Baily, Charles Martin, Alfred Bishop, Peyton Brown, Jacob Dobbs, Nathaniel Brown, A. J. Cockran, Jas. H. Cunningham, Noah Cooper, M. W. Downing, John Feaster, jr., Isaabella S. Ferguson, M. D. Feaster, Elias Gerkey, John M. Hatfield, C. G. Heath, Pollard M. Hayne, Jas. L. Heath, W. A. Inlow, John B. Haryman, Abraham Jenkins, James Kidwell, Jas. F. Land, W. H. Newbill, Joseph Monroe, Chas. Morton, Ambrose Loveless, James Niece, Wm. Platt, John Paulson, Wm. H. Peal, Burdette Osburn, John M. Poson, Lundie Parks, Benj. Reed, Wm. Tailor, Morgan Stewart, C. M. Scott (black), Edward Turner, James Tailor, John L. Tailor, James Warren, John Wingate, Velorius Chastain, Eliza Young, exr., John Bran, John Claycomb, Levi Claycomb, Daniel Carpenter, T. B. Cornwell, H. H. Freeman, Robert E. Freeman, Eluza Freeman, Jas. R. Graham, Wm. Walls, Wm. Graham, John J. Graham, Saml. R. Graham. Geo. W. Guinn, F. Gregory, James Gorrell, Wm. Hartell, Jas. M. Hughs, C. M. Hartell, Samuel Johns, Citey Kennedy, John G. Miller, James A. Miller, Jane Phillips, Rowland Berry, John Suratt, John M. Sutton, Wm. Summers, Montavill Scott, Jonathan Truax, W.

Chauncey, George Vincent, Talton Weldon, Eugene Anderson, Henry Braugher, Henry G. Brown, John Braugh, B. Corrinder, Jas. W. Davis, M. A. C. Davis, Mary Davis, Thos. Eaton, John Greggs, J. E. Griffith, Morford Gorden, Samuel E. Gunn, J. W. Griffith, Jesse Hudson, James Hunt, Philip Huson, Mary Howard, James Johnson, Walter M. Junoll, A. W. Lryman, James Oliver, Edmond Littlee, Cal M. Littlee, Wm. H. Miller, John Makisson, Wm. Moreland, John Newman, A. G. Nixon, Wm. Ray, Geo. W. Overshiner, John F. Pogue, John Ralston, Cyrus Red, David Ralston, Ander. Ralston, Wm. Ralston, Geo. C. Smith, James C. Story, Josiah Shrum, James Sherer, John Q. Smith, Wm. Shumnell, Benj. Summers, James Sands, Valentine Sands, James Scrivener, E. J. Tompson, J. C. Vanpool, E. F. White, E. E. Williamson, J. W. White, Samuel Pogue, Henry Beral, D. Hustain, Saml. Dasher, John W. Ellis, James J. Ellis, John Gibson, Walter Hiphery, Wm. J. League, Thos. J. League, John Sassen, Benjamin Lingle, Lewis Sassen, G. W. Sassen, James E. Tindell, Wm. Willard, Martin Amos, J. A. Bernette, David Bishop, Isaac Burns, John Bernett, J. A. Crawford, Theodore Edmondson, Henry Davis, Isaac Campbell, John Clark, Jerry Ferguson, Thos. W. Fressna, Richd. Ferguson, Harris, Farmer & Co., Cole G. Farmer, T. B. Harzrider, John Holland, Wm. L. Harris, Peter Jackson (black), Isaac J. Knight, John Lemon, C. B. B. Knight, L. Y. Lemon, John M. Linglie, Geo. Ogden, Geo. McElurath (col.), Wm. A. McClain, Jas. B. Phillips, G. N. Whaley, Ed-- Byam, John Byam, Sem. Soyster, Jas. Sutherland, Wm. Southerland (gone), Elizabeth Scott, Jonathan Armstrong, Anthony Stratton, J. H. Trammel (gone), W. Heurman, Jas. A. Adams, G. N. Whaley, John H. Baker, C. A. Carter, T. J. Korber (dead), Henry Michales, Henry Steurhman, Jonathan Armstrong, Chas. Wright, Eleazer Owens, Fred Feldman.

## Mono County, California, Great Register, (Note: Only Listed Persons Showing Missouri As Their Birthplace).

Charles Severe Anderson: 42 yr, b. Missouri, miner, r. Benton, Jun. 6, 1875.

John W. Bagby: 23 yr, b. Missouri, farmer, r. Antelope Valley, August 15, 1873.

Lafayette Brooks: 31 yr, b. Missouri, laborer, r. Benton, Sep. 2, 1872.

David Cingcade: 28 y, b. Missouri, famer, r. Antelope Valley, August 27, 1873.

Jasper M. Harney: 38 yr, b. Missouri, ranchman, r. Antelope Valley, Jul. 11, 1866.

Samuel Hays: 28 yr, b. Missouri, farmer, r. Antelope Valley, Jul. 11, 1866.

Henry Lovelady: 28 yr, b. Missouri, farmer, r. Bridgeport, Oct. 15, 1873.

Thomas C. More: 23 yr, b. Missouri, farmer, r. Antelope

Valley, Aug. 18, 1873.
    Wharton T. More: 42 yr, b. Missouri, farmer, r. Antelope Valley, Aug. 15, 1873.
    John F. Owen: 23 yr, b. Missouri, farmer, stockman, r. Antelope Valley, May 12, 1875.
    Barnabas Peeler: 33 yr, b. Missouri, farmer, r. Bridgeport, Aug. 25, 1869.
    James W. Pew: 22 yr, b. Missouri, laborer, r. Antelope Valley, Jul. 15, 1867.
    James M. Stone: 21 yr, b. Missouri, farmer, r. Antelope Valley, Oct. 2, 1871.
    Levi Perry Stone: 27 yr, b. Missouri, farmer, r. Antelope Valley, Sep. 29, 1868.
    Rueben Terry, 26 yr, b. Missouri, farmer, r. Antelope Valley, Jun. 27, 1867.
    Joseph G. Wiley: 36 yr, b. Missouri, farmer, r. Antelope Valley, Oct. 22, 1872.
    Benjamin J. Short: 23 yr, b. Missouri, farmer, r. Antelope certificate, Alpine Co., Aug. 15, 1875.

**Missourians in "History of Santa Clara County," California, 1881 by Ally, Bowen & Co.**

| Name | County |
|---|---|
| John Trimble | Montgomery Co. |
| Thos. Reynolds | Lewis Co. |
| Jos. Awbrey | St. Charles Co. |
| M. O. Stanley | Clark Co. |
| Gilbert E. Shore | Crawford Co. |
| Jos. E. Rucker | Howard Co. |
| John J. Roberts | Missouri |
| Benj. T. Bubb | Washington Co. |
| Wm. Henry Bubb | Washington Co. |
| Zadoc A. Riggs | Boone Co. |
| Royal Cottle | St. Charles Co. |
| Caleb Brown Crews | Boone Co. |
| Spencer P. Fine | Lafayette Co. |
| George Givens | Callaway Co. |
| Milton T. Holsclaw | Howard Co. |
| Andrew Jackson Pitman | St. Charles |
| Jas. F. Phegley | New Madrid Co. |
| Samuel T. Moore | Dade Co. |
| J. C. Morris | Warren Co. |
| J. M. Ogan | Boone Co. |

**Passengers On The Ship, Wieland, From Bremen To New York, Arriving April 28, 1853, That Gave Their Destination As Missouri.**

| Name | Age | Sex | Occupation | From | Going To |
|---|---|---|---|---|---|
| L. S. Baergen | 24 | m | Merchant | Hanover | St. Louis |

| Name | Age | Sex | Occupation | From | Going To |
|---|---|---|---|---|---|
| Heinrich Ennst | 25 | m | Farmer | Hanover | Missouri |
| Christian Deneke | 33 | m | Farmer | Hanover | Missouri |
| August Deneke | 9 mo | m | Infant | Hanover | Missouri |
| Amalie Birner | 27 | f | Unknown | Hanover | Missouri |
| Ludewig Berlin | 40 | m | Farmer | Hanover | Missouri |
| Christian Schuette | 28 | m | Joiner | Hanover | Missouri |
| Dorothee Schuette | 22 | f | Servant | Prussia | Missouri |
| Conrad Dodbach | 20 | m | Laborer | Schwarz-burg, Sonderhausen | Missouri |

Passengers On The Ship "Herime" From Bremen To NY, Arriving September 27, 1852, That Gave Their Destination As Missouri.

| Name | Age | Sex | Occupation | From | Going To |
|---|---|---|---|---|---|
| Chr. Hartung | 41 | m | Farmer | Hanover | St. Louis |
| Wilhelmine Hartung | 39 | f | Unknown | Hanove | St. Louis |
| Wilhelm Hartung | 16 | m | Unknown | Hanover | St. Louis |
| August Hartung | 14 | m | Unknown | Hanover | St. Louis |
| Regine Hartung | 12 | f | Unknown | Hanover | St. Louis |
| Georg Hartung | 10 | m | Unknown | Hanover | St. Louis |
| Carl Hartung | 8 | m | Child | Hanover | St. Louis |
| Heinr. Hartung | 6 | m | Child | Hanover | St. Louis |
| Louise Hartung | 3 | f | Child | Hanover | St. Louis |
| Doretha Hartung | 6 mo | f | Infant | Hanover | St. Louis |
| Henriette Buehren | 26 | f | Unknown | Hanover | St. Louis |
| Dorethe Buehren | 4 | m | Child | Hanover | St. Louis |

Index Of Election Returns, Missouri, 1842, Capitol Fire Documents, CFD 183, Folder 16234.

| Name | Office | County |
|---|---|---|
| ALonzo Abernathy | Representative | Perry |
| Joseph T. Abernathy | Representative | Perry |
| Robert E. Acock | Senate | --- |
| John C. Adams | Justice | Bates |
| Henry D. Aden | Representative | Platte |
| Andrew Alexander | Representative | Osage |
| Corbin Alexander | Representative | St. Francois |
| John Alexander | Justice of Peace | Ray |
| James Allcon | Representative | Howard |
| Bethel Allen | Representative | Platte |
| James Allen | Justice | Bates |
| John Alley | Representative | St. Francois |
| James C. Anderson | Representative | Callaway |
| William C. Anderson | Senate | --- |
| Thomas Andrews | Representative | St. Louis |
| Moses Anglin | Justice | Jasper |
| Hugh C. Armstrong | Senate | --- |
| Mathew R. Arnold | Representative | Boone |
| Charles H. Ashby | Senate | --- |

| Name | Office | County |
|---|---|---|
| Henley Ashby | Senate | --- |
| Walker Austin | Justice | Macon |
| Thomas N. Awbrey | Representative | Grundy |
| Absolem B. Bailey | Representative | Stoddard |
| William C. Baker | Justice | Johnson |
| Bland N. Ballard | Representative | Pulaski |
| Ira Barbee | Justice | St. Louis |
| Joseph Barclay | Coroner | St. Louis |
| Richard M. Barkhurst | Representative | Holt |
| --- Barnes | Justice | Cooper |
| Hugh Barnett | Representative | St. Clair |
| Peter D. Barrada | Justice | St. Louis |
| John S. Barrett | Justice | Ste. Genevieve |
| John C. Bart | Representative | Montgomery |
| William W. Bassett | Senate | St. Louis |
| John Baxter | Sheriff | Clay |
| William V. N. Bay | Representative | Franklin |
| Henry Bazile | Justice of Peace | Jefferson |
| James A. Beale | Justice of Peace | Jefferson |
| John H. Bean | Senate | --- |
| Moses Bean | Representative | *Kinderhook |

*(County renamed to Camden on Feb, 23, 1843.)

| Name | Office | County |
|---|---|---|
| Jasper N. Bell | Sheriff | Livingston |
| Moses Bean | Senate | --- |
| Nathaniel Bell | Representative | St. Clair |
| Henry B. Belt | Coroner | St. Louis |
| A. G. Bennett | Senate | --- |
| William Berry | Justice of Peace | Ray |
| John R. Berryman | Congress | --- |
| Thomas Biggs | Justice of Peace | Ray |
| William Biggs | Senate | --- |
| William A. Blackwell | Coroner | Jasper |
| William G. Blake | Representative | Dade |
| William R. Blythe | Senate | --- |
| Lilburne W. Boggs | Senate | --- |
| Jesse C. Bouyer | Coroner | Linn |
| G. B. Bower | Congress | --- |
| Gustavus B. Bower | Congress | --- |
| J. M. Bower | Congress | --- |
| James B. Bowlin | Congress | --- |
| Talbot Bragg | Justice | Lincoln |
| Robert Branaugh | Senate | --- |
| Daniel Branstetter | Representative | Ray |
| John Brawley | Representative | Shannon |
| Robert D. Brewington | Representative | Pike |
| John B. Brinker | Representative | Crawford |
| Alvin Brooking | Justice | Jackson |
| Jeremiah Brower | Justice Co. Ct. | Adair |

| Name | Office | County |
|---|---|---|
| Anderson Brown, sr. | Justice | Marion |
| John R. Brown | Representative | Franklin |
| Rolin Brown | Representative | Platte |
| Wilie D. Brown | Sheriff | Jasper |
| James Browne | Senate | --- |
| James S. Brumwell | Representative | Chariton |
| Ben Bryan | Representative | Montgomery |
| Samuel H. Bunch | Sheriff | Polk |
| --- Bullock | Representative | Barry |
| Samuel Burch | Justice Co. Ct. | Chariton |
| James Bunton | Assessor | Chariton |
| Eldridge Burch | Representative | Lafayette |
| Joseph Burden | Representative | Greene |
| Fabius M. Butler | Justice of Peace | Johnson |
| Jonathan B. Butler | Sheriff | Johnson |
| John C. Calhoun | Congress | --- |
| John Calvert | Assessor | Marion |
| John J. Campbell | Senate | --- |
| John P. Campbell | Congress | --- |
| William Campbell | Congress | --- |
| Samuel R. Campbell | Representative | Andrew |
| Elisha Cameron | Justice | Clay |
| William Carson | Representative | Marion |
| --- Carter | Justice | Cooper |
| Robert Carthcart | Sheriff | St. Louis |
| John C. Cavanah | Justice Co. Ct. | Chariton |
| Edward L. Chauteau | Representative | Bates |
| James Chiles | Senate | --- |
| John Chilton | Representative | Ripley |
| Tho. J. Chowning | Representative | Monroe |
| Peyton H. Clark | Congress | --- |
| Thomas L. Clark | Justice | Osage |
| Wm. P. D. Claybrooke | Justice | Marion |
| Beriah Cleland | Congress | --- |
| Thos. P. Coats | Representative | Randolph |
| John A. Cobbs | Representative | Marion |
| L. D. Cockerell | Justice | Bates |
| Joseph Coffman | Representative | Ste. Genevieve |
| Thomas Cohen | Justice | St. Louis |
| William T. Cole | Representative | Morgan |
| John B. Collier | Representative | Platte |
| William H. Collins | Justice of Peace | Johnson |
| Jacob Comegys | Assessor | St. Charles |
| William W. Compton | Representative | Carroll |
| Samuel M. Coolley | Justice | Jasper |
| Owin Cooper | Justice of Peace | Johnson |
| Edward Corder | Justice | Johnson |
| Campbell G. Cowan | Representative | Barry |

| Name | Office | County |
|---|---|---|
| John C. Cox | Sheriff | Jasper |
| Jeremiah Cravens | Senate | --- |
| John E. Crawford | Representative | Pettis |
| Temple Crews | Representative | Howard |
| William W. Crook | Representative | Morgan |
| Louis Criglon | Sheriff | Howard |
| James Cummins | Coroner | St. Louis |
| William Curl | Representative | Buchanan |
| A. W. Daggett | Representative | Clark |
| Jas. B. Dameron | Representative | Randolph |
| David G. Davenport | Congress | --- |
| James B. Davenport | Justice | Jackson |
| John Davis | Justice | Marion |
| James A. Davis | Justice | Livingston |
| John M. Davis | Sheriff | Chariton |
| John W. Davis | Representative | Pike |
| Wm. R. Dawson | Justice | St. Louis |
| Foster Demasters | Representative | Johnson |
| Clement Detchemendy | Senate | --- |
| Wm. Dixon | Representative | Benton |
| Daniel H. Donovan | Representative | St. Louis |
| John Doxey | Assessor | Chariton |
| William E. Dudley | Sheriff | Lincoln |
| John Duncan | Representative | Pulaski |
| Leroy C. Duncan | Justice of Peace | Johnson |
| Alonzo J. Edward | Justice of Peace | Pettis |
| John C. Edwards | Congress | --- |
| Phillip L. Edwards | Representative | Ray |
| W. B. Edwards | Representative | *Niangua |

*(Name changed to Dallas Dec. 10, 1844)

| Name | Office | County |
|---|---|---|
| William R. Ellett | Senate | --- |
| Robert Elliote | Representative | Andrew |
| Robert B. Ellis | Senate | --- |
| William Ellis | Representative | Lewis |
| James Ellison | Representative | Lewis |
| Elkanah English | Coroner | St. Louis |
| Thomas B. English | Representative | Cape Girardeau |
| Garad Erwin | Representative | Warren |
| Jesse Essa | Justice of Peace | Ray |
| Frances Estes | Congress | --- |
| Samuel Farnanats | Sheriff | Livingston |
| Absolem Farris, jr. | Representative | Stoddard |
| Baldwin H. Fine | Justice | Johnson |
| Abner Finnell | Sheriff | Chariton |
| Chas. W. Flanagan | Representive | Monroe |
| Edgar Flory | Representative | Linn |
| Lawrence Flournoy | Justice | Jackson |
| Wm. Fort | Senate | --- |

| Name | Office | County |
|---|---|---|
| Joseph Fowler | Justice of Peace | Pettis |
| Thomas Fowler | Representative | Holt |
| William Foxton | Justice of Peace | Jefferson |
| Charles French | Justice | Scotland |
| Richard Frestoe | Justice | Jackson |
| John Fulton | Justice | Scotland |
| Charles Funk | Justice of Peace | Ray |
| Joseph Funk | Senate | --- |
| Louis D. Gamache | Justice of Peace | Jefferson |
| Archibald Gamble | Justice | St. Louis |
| Justus Gamble | Justice of Peace | Jefferson |
| Samuel Gardner | Representative | Chariton |
| Jesse W. Garner | Justice of Peace | Ray |
| Joshua Gentry | Senate | --- |
| Henry O. Geyer | Congress | --- |
| Robert Giboney | Representative | Stoddard |
| John Gilleland | Representative | Daviess |
| Cornelius Gilliam | Senate | --- |
| William Gilpen | Congress | --- |
| Isaac Gilstrap | Co. Ct. Justice | Adair |
| Mathew Given | Representative | Pike |
| Eli Glascock | Justice | Jackson |
| Aldin A. Glasscock | Senate | --- |
| D. O. Glasscock | Congress | --- |
| Peter G. Glover | Senate | --- |
| James Gordon | Sheriff | St. Louis |
| Henry Madison Gorin | Justice | Scotland |
| Samuel M. Grant | Representative | Marion |
| Samuel T. Greer | Justice of Peace | Jefferson |
| John F. Grider | Justice of Peace | Ray |
| John C. Griffin | Representative | Grundy |
| William Griffin | Senate | --- |
| J. C. Gullett | Representative | Dade |
| Harrison Gwinn | Representative | Saline |
| John Gyer | Coroner | Linn |
| Saml. B. Hall | Coroner | Jasper |
| Thomas Hamilton | Justice of Peace | Ray |
| Brice W. Hammack | Justice | Lincoln |
| John Hammond | Justice of Peace | Jefferson |
| John W. Hancock | Senate | --- |
| William Hare | Representative | St. Louis |
| Charles Harper | Senate | --- |
| Tyre Harris | Senate | --- |
| William Harris | Coroner | St. Louis |
| James Harrison | Representative | Audrain |
| Robert C. Harrison | Representative | Cooper |
| Thos. H. Harvey | Congress | --- |
| Henry Hatcher | Coroner | St. Charles |

| Name | Office | County |
|---|---|---|
| William B. Haynes | Representative | Bates |
| Gilmore Hays | Representative | Saline |
| John G. Heath | Justice | Gasconade |
| Joseph Helterbrand | Representative | New Madrid |
| John Hempstead | Representative | St. Louis |
| John Hempstead | Senate | --- |
| John H. Henderson | Justice of Peace | Pettis |
| Joseph W. Henderson | Justice | Johnson |
| Abraham Henline | Surveyor | Bates |
| Franklin Hickox | Representative | Cole |
| David B. Hill | Representative | St. Louis |
| William Hines | Representative | Linn |
| Peter A. Hitt | Surveyor | Clark |
| Nathaniel Holcomb | Representative | Newton |
| N. B. Holden | Justice | Johnson |
| Lucius S. Hollenbeck | Justice of Peace | Jefferson |
| Allen W. Holloman | Justice | Ste. Genevieve |
| D. B. Holman | Representative | Holt |
| G. B. Hopkins | Representative | Callaway |
| George W. Hough | Representative | Cole |
| William T. Howell | Representative | Monroe |
| Elijah H. Hudson | Representative | Ozark |
| Thomas B. Hudson | Representative | St. Louis |
| Ayres Hudspeth | Senate | --- |
| Andrew S. Hughes | Senate | --- |
| James M. Hughes | Congress | --- |
| Litel Hughes | Senate | --- |
| William Hughes | Representative | Pulaski |
| Lytle Hughes | Senate | --- |
| John M. Hughs | Congress | --- |
| Abraham hunter | Senate | --- |
| Logan Hunton | Representative | St. Louis |
| George Hurd | Representative | Pettis |
| George W. Huston | Representative | Lincoln |
| John H. Hutchison | Sheriff | Cooper |
| John Hyer | Representative | Crawford |
| Clabourn F. Jackson | Representative | Howard |
| James Jackson | Representative | Audrain |
| William James | Justice | Ste. Genevieve |
| John Jameson (sic) | Congress | --- |
| John Jamison (sic) | Congress | --- |
| David Jenkins | Representative | Linn |
| Jesse John | Representative | Scotland |
| Andrew Johnson | Senate | --- |
| Gabriel J. Johnson | Justice | Jefferson |
| Vincent Johnson | Justice | Pettis |
| Benjamin Johnston | Justice of Peace | Jefferson |
| William F. Johnson | Coroner | St. Louis |

| Name | Office | County |
|---|---|---|
| William Johnston | Representative | Ripley |
| David Jones | Representative | Cooper |
| John Jones | Representative | Newton |
| William Jopling | Justice of Peace | Pettis |
| C. C. Kavanaugh | Representative | Jackson |
| William R. Kemp | Sheriff | Pettis |
| Henry Kemper | Representative | Madison |
| Ferdinand Kennett | Representative | St. Louis |
| Wm. C. Kennett | Congress | --- |
| W. G. Kirkpatrick | Representative | Caldwell |
| Isaiah King | Representative | Gasconade |
| John King | Representative | Jackson |
| John B. King | Representative | St. Louis |
| John B. King (sic) | Surveyor | Bates |
| Joshua M. King | Justice | Lincoln |
| Charles Kumle | Sheriff | St. Louis |
| William Lair | Justice | Marion |
| Samuel Lanan (sic) | Representative | Henry |
| Samuel Landes (sic) | Representative | Henry |
| George H. Lanham | Representative | St. Louis |
| Eloy LeCompte | Justice | Ste. Genevieve |
| James Levingston | Senate | --- |
| John W. Lewellwen | Justice | Clark |
| Stewart Lewis | Justice | Jackson |
| John Lindsey | Representative | Pike |
| Campbell G. Link | Assessor | St. Louis |
| Isaac Lionberger | Sheriff | Cooper |
| Dr. Livingston (sic) | Senate | --- |
| James Livingston (sic) | Senate | --- |
| Alton Long | Sheriff | St. Louis |
| Hezekiah Long | Representative | Franklin |
| John W. Long | Representative | Shelby |
| Archibald Lovelace | Justice of Peace | Pettis |
| Hugh C. P. Lucas | Representative | Jefferson |
| James Lusk | Representative | Adair |
| James C. Lynch | Justice | St. Louis |
| Joseph McClary | Assessor | Johnson |
| Michael T. McClellan | Representative | Jackson |
| Jordan M. McCormick | Justice | Marion |
| Allen B. McCresey | Coroner | Jefferson |
| Henry McCullough | Justice | St. Louis |
| William Mcdaniel | Senate | --- |
| Jacob McDonold | Coroner | Chariton |
| William J. McElhiney | Representative | St. Charles |
| Caleb McFarlan | Justice | Lincoln |
| Rueben A. McFarland | Justice of Peace | Pettis |
| William S. McGinnis | Justice | Jasper |
| Joseph C. McGonnigal | Congress | --- |

| Name | Office | County |
|---|---|---|
| John McHenry | Representative | Bates |
| E. Y. McKee | Justice | Cape Girardeau |
| Allen McLain | Representative | Platte |
| Nicholas McMinn | Representative | Polk |
| Benjamin P. Major | Senate | --- |
| Francis Mallet | Coroner | St. Louis |
| George Manship | Justice | Bates |
| James Marshall | Representative | Madison |
| Littleberry Mason | Senate | --- |
| Benjamin F. Massey | Senate | --- |
| James A. Matthews | Justice | Gasconade |
| Joseph Matthews | Justice | Johnson |
| Stuart Matthews | Representative | St. Louis |
| Hannaneoh P. Maulsby | Representative | New Madrid |
| Robert Maxwell | Constable | Johnson |
| Richard M. May | Representative | Boone |
| Samuel Meley | Representative | Jasper |
| John Menafee | Congress | --- |
| William Milburn | Sheriff | St. Louis |
| Hugh W. Miller | Senate | --- |
| John G. Miller | Representative | Cooper |
| William A. Miller | Justice | Pettis |
| Adam L. Mills | Senate | --- |
| Thomas J. Minor | Representative | St. Louis |
| William G. Minor | Representative | Cole |
| John N. Mitchell | Representative | Stoddard |
| Robert P. Mitchell | Coroner | Clark |
| William C. Mitchell | Representative | Shelby |
| William Monroe | Representative | Kinderhook |
| William Monroe (sic) | Senate | --- |
| --- Montgomery | Sheriff | Marion |
| Wm. Montgomery | Representative | Niangua |
| Joseph Moon | Justice of Peace | Jefferson |
| Martin Morgan | Assessor | Chariton |
| Solomon R. Morley | Justice | Lincoln |
| Jefferson Morrow | Justice | Macon |
| Mark Moss | Sheriff | Jefferson |
| Woodson J. Moss | Representative | Clay |
| Mirun Mudget | Justice of Peace | Jefferson |
| Richard Murphy | Representative | St. Francois |
| Andrew R. Murray | Sheriff | Clay |
| Robert Murray | Justice of Peace | Ray |
| Abraham H. Neal | Justice | Cooper |
| Robert Neal | Justice | Jasper |
| George H. Netherton | Senate | --- |
| John G. Newbill | Justice of Peace | Pettis |
| Nathaniel A. Newbill | Assessor | Pettis |
| Ezekiel Norman | Justice | Livingston |

| Name | Office | County |
|---|---|---|
| William Nutt | Senate | --- |
| W. O'Bannon | Justice | Cape Girardeau |
| William Ogle | Justice | Jefferson |
| Alexander R. Oldham | Representative | Monroe |
| John Onich | Sheriff | St. Charles |
| James Overstreet | Justice | Bates |
| William G. Owsley | Justice | Ste. Genevieve |
| J. Lawrence Page | Representative | Platte |
| William B. Pennell | Justice | Gasconade |
| Jonathan Paris | Representative | Dade |
| Samuel Parks | Co. Ct. Justice | Chariton |
| Joseph Patterson | Assessor | St. Louis |
| Joseph Pearson | Representative | Newton |
| Joseph Persinger | Senate | --- |
| Ashby Peters | Sheriff | Clay |
| John S. Phelps | Congress | --- |
| Jerimiah Phillips | Sheriff | Linn |
| Enos Pipkin | Representative | St. Louis |
| John Pitcher | Justice | St. Louis |
| Belfield J. Porter | Justice of Peace | Pettis |
| Joseph A. Porter | Assessor | St. Louis |
| Samuel C. Potts | Coroner | Pettis |
| Arjalon (sic) Price | Justice of Peace | Johnson |
| C. F. M. Price (sic) | Representative | Callaway |
| F. M. Price (sic) | Representative | Callaway |
| John Price | Representative | Johnson |
| Sterling Price | Representative | Chariton |
| Elias Priest | Justice of Peace | Ray |
| William Priest | Representative | Ralls |
| Isaiah Prigmon | Justice of Peace | Pettis |
| John Pritchett | Justice | Jasper |
| William Proffitt | Justice | Bates |
| Alfred H. Puckett | Senate | --- |
| Daniel S. Purcell | Representative | Kinderhook |
| James J. Purdy | Justice | St. Louis |
| James S. Quisenberry(sic) | Representative | St. Louis |
| David H. Quesenberry(sic) | Justice of Peace | Ray |
| Henry Rains | Justice of Peace | Pettis |
| J. H. Ralph | Congress | --- |
| J. Ramsay | Representative | Callaway |
| Charles S. Rankin | Representative | Jefferson |
| J. Ranny (sic) | Congress | --- |
| Nathan Ranny (sic) | Congress | --- |
| Robert D. Ray | Representative | Carroll |
| William A. Rebard | Representative | Boone |
| Abraham Redfield | Justice | Bates |
| Walker P. Redford | Justice of Peace | Johnson |
| Harmon Reed | Representative | Stoddard |

| Name | Office | County |
|---|---|---|
| Isham Reese | Sheriff | Johnson |
| J. H. Relfe (sic) | Congress | --- |
| James H. Relfe (sic) | Congress | --- |
| James H. Requa | Justice | Bates |
| George W. Rhoades | Representative | Jackson |
| James B. Richardson | Assessor | Jefferson |
| Benjamin Ricketts | Justice | Clay |
| Alfred M. Riley | Representative | Clay |
| H. W. Riley | Representative | Pulaski |
| Albian Roberson | Justice of Peace | Pettis |
| Roysden Robinson | Justice | Osage |
| Louis Robion | Representative | Howard |
| Thomas C. Rogers | Representative | Shanon |
| Upton Rohrer | Representative | Andrew |
| John F. Ross | Representative | New Madrid |
| Henry Rothrock | Justice of Peace | Ray |
| Frederick Rowland | Justice | Macon |
| William Rowland | Representative | Boone |
| Henry M. Rubey | Justice | Pettis |
| James W. Rucker | Representative | Morgan |
| Elijah Ruggles | Senate | --- |
| Joseph Sale | Justice | St. Louis |
| Edmond Sales | Justice of Peace | Jefferson |
| J. K. Salsy | Representative | Callaway |
| Abel Sanders | Representative | Newton |
| Bryant Sanders | Representative | Lafayette |
| Alfred Sanford | Representative | St. Louis |
| Hartly Sappington | Justice | St. Louis |
| Richard Saye | Sheriff | Polk |
| William Sayers | Representative | Scott |
| Charles Scott | Representative | Howard |
| Felix Scott | Representative | St. Charles |
| John Scott | Senate | --- |
| William Scott | Justice | Pettis |
| Henry Shannon | Co. Ct. Justice | Chariton |
| John D. Shannon | Representative | Taney |
| Pines H. Shelton | Representative | St. Charles |
| Jonah H. Shepherd | Coroner | Howard |
| William Shields | Representative | Cooper |
| Seth Shoemaker | Justice | Jasper |
| James D. Shrader | Representative | Stoddard |
| Michael T. Simmons | Representative | Andrew |
| Leonard H. Sims | Representative | Greene |
| Jonathan D. Skaggs | Coroner | Clay |
| John Skidmore | Representative | Caldwell |
| J. M. Slack | Coroner | Linn |
| William Slack | Representative | Livingston |
| Robert G. Smart | Representative | Jackson |

| Name | Office | County |
|---|---|---|
| Anderson W. Smith | Representative | Van Buren |
| Charles H. Smith | Justice | Cooper |
| Francis Smith | Justice | Clark |
| J. Smith | Senate | --- |
| John Q. Smith | Representative | Clinton |
| Lawrence Smith | Justice | Jasper |
| Rueben Smith | Justice | Cape Girardeau |
| Thomas Smith | Coroner | Chariton |
| Thompson Smith | Representative | Clinton |
| William Smith | Assessor | Johnson |
| William Smith | Representative | Boone |
| Wm. Smith (sic) | Senate | --- |
| Wm. W. Smith (sic) | Senate | --- |
| W. W. Snell | Senate | Callaway |
| Aaron Snider | Representative | Cape Girardeau |
| Henry Snively | Justice | Clark |
| Dain Snowden | Justice of Peace | Ray |
| Richard D. Stanley | Justice | Jackson |
| Robert Q. Stark | Representative | Clark |
| Robert Steel | Assessor | Johnson |
| David D. Stockton | Sheriff | Polk |
| Jno. H. Stone | Representative | Callaway |
| John M. Strickland | Justice | Jefferson |
| Jacob Sulsenhiser | Co. Ct. Justice | Bates |
| Eli Tabor | Congress | --- |
| Francis Talbert | Justice of Peace | Pettis |
| George W. Tate | Representative | Jackson |
| Tho. N. Tatlon | Congress | --- |
| Reuben Terrill | Justice | Osage |
| Martin Thomas | Representative | St. Louis |
| J. L. V. Thompson (sic) | Senate | --- |
| James L. V. Thompson(sic) | Senate | --- |
| Jesse B. Thompson | Representative | Buchanan |
| T. V. Thompson (sic) | Senate | --- |
| Merit Tillery | Representative | Clay |
| Peringoine Tippett | Representative | St. Louis |
| Alfred Tracy | Representative | St. Louis |
| Hayden S. Trigg | Justice of Peace | Ray |
| John W. Tucker | Representative | Livingston |
| Jos. H. Tuel | Representative | Callaway |
| Warrick Tunstall | Representative | St. Louis |
| --- Turley | Justice | Cooper |
| Benjamin Turner | Representative | Johnson |
| Joel Turnham | Justice | Clay |
| David C. Tuttle | Representative | Marion |
| Felix Valle | Justice | Ste. Genevieve |
| Cornelius Van Ausdale | Justice | St. Louis |
| Nathaniel Vincent | Justice | Clay |

| Name | Office | County |
|---|---|---|
| Thacher Vivion | Representative | Jasper |
| Anthony S. Walker | Justice | Cooper |
| John K. Walker | Justice | St. Louis |
| William G. Walker | Justice of Peace | Jefferson |
| Henry Walton | Justice | St. Louis |
| Zephaniah Warren | Representative | Kinderhook |
| Richard C. Warner | Justice of Peace | Johnson |
| Thomas Wash | Representative | St. Louis |
| Thomas Wasson | Justice | Pettis |
| Thomas Watson | Congress | St. Charles |
| John W. Weaver | Justice of Peace | Jefferson |
| John C. Wellborn | Senate | --- |
| Harvey Wellman | Representative | Ralls |
| Carty Wells | Representative | Lincoln |
| James Wells | Representative | Adair |
| Joseph B. Wells | Representative | Warren |
| John L. West | Representative | Miller |
| J. Weston | Congress | --- |
| Theodore D. Wheaton | Representative | Andrew |
| Lemuel C. Whedbee | Justice of Peace | Ray |
| Samuel H. Whipple | Representative | Benton |
| John A. White | Representative | Platte |
| Robert M. White | Representative | Johnson |
| Thomas B. Whitledge | Representative | Pike |
| Eli Wiley | Justice of Peace | Jefferson |
| Wm. Wilkinson | Senate | --- |
| Peter H. Willard | Representative | Ste. Genevieve |
| John A. Williams | Representative | Davies |
| John C. Williams | Representative | Howard |
| John W. Williams | Representative | Henry |
| Landon Williams | Justice of Peace | Jefferson |
| Olly Williams | Representative | St. Louis |
| George M. Willing | Coroner | St. Louis |
| David Willock | Justice | Marion |
| Andrew Wilson | Representative | Van Buren |
| Joseph Wilson | Co. Ct. Justice | Adair |
| Robert Wilson | Senate | --- |
| James Winston | Congress | --- |
| John Wolfskill | Senate | --- |
| Richard Womack | Sheriff | Lincoln |
| Martin M. Wood | Representative | Stoddard |
| Wm. C. Woodson | Co. Ct. Justice | Chariton |
| Gilber (sic) Woolsey | Justice | Livingston |
| Samuel Workman | Justice of Peace | Johnson |
| John Wray, jr. | Representative | Taney |
| A. J. Worthley | Representative | Cole |
| Johnson Wright | Representative | Adair |
| James B. Yager | Justice | Jackson |

| Name | Office | County |
|---|---|---|
| Thomas D. Yeats | Justice | St. Louis |
| Louis Yosti | Senate | --- |
| Jos. L. Young | Representative | Polk |

Randolph County, Missouri, Warranty Deeds Recorded From January, 1896 to June, 1896, Capitol Fire Documents, CFD 68, Folder 6427.

| Grantor | Grantee |
|---|---|
| Wm. & Hattie S. Elliott | D. Peeter |
| Thos. A. & Mary E. Morgan | J. T. Lingo |
| J. T. & Sarah E. Lingo | Mrs. Mary E. Morgan |
| J. C. Bounds (single) | Hattie S. Hulen |
| Margaret J. & D. M. Frazier | Cyrus Frazier |
| Wm. E. Robertson & Isebelle R. | Wm. & Julie B. Wilson |
| S. M. & Lucy W. Eatherton | Wm. E. Robertson |
| H. M. Kilgon (single) | J. M. Bergstresser |
| Oro & G. T. Rothiwell | J. W. Manning |
| Joseph & Violetta Chapman | James Jobson |
| Geo. E. & Cornelia A. Marshall | J. F. Ridgeway |
| Jno. E. & Laura (?) Dawkins | G. O. Edwards |
| Geo. O. Edwards | Jno. E. Dawkins |
| M. M. Burton | Geo. W. Evans |
| W. F. & Susie Hammes | Reeese D. Davis |
| Julius Crause & wife | Jno. H. Krones |
| Jno. R. Terrill | Saml. A. Michaels |
| Granville N. Wilson | Thomas Kitchen |
| Jno. T. & M. E. Smith | Eliza B. Sears |
| Mrs. R. B. Wilson & D. W. Wilson | Robert A. Radford |
| J. G. Stockton & wife | Henry Hamilton |
| Henry Hamilton & Sallie B. (sic) | J. G. Socton (sic) |
| C. G. Mitchell & wife | J. G. Bell |
| T. D. & Ada Sayre | J. T. Crews |
| Thomas V. Christy & wife | Sallie A. M'Culhy |
| Geo. W. & Bessie Sparks, & N. M. Buschell | Alfred R. Scott |
| M. Murphy | Jessie Hare |
| Harvey L. Terry & wife | Jno. A. Lowry & G. W. Rice |
| Ralph Potter & wife | Norbert Hubet |
| Wm. & Theresea Segar | A. S. Haynes |
| A. S. Haynes & wife | Wm. Seger (sic) |
| Gus Chandler & wife | E. M. Edwards |
| Jno. S. Switzer & wife | M. F. Switzer |
| W. H. Thirty | W. B. Settle |
| Mary E. Birchard | Charles Quale |
| L. Randle & wife | A. L. Bassett & wife |
| Samuel Paul & wife | Mrs. Frankie Rucker |
| Geo. A. Coulter & wife | A. O. M'Canne |

| Grantor | Grantee |
|---|---|
| Alve W. & Susie C. Talman | Wm. G. Newman & wife |
| J. D. Hammett & wife | Geo. Barnes |
| O. H. & M. J. Bagly | B. F. Bagly |
| J. B. Freeman & wife | W. F. Turner & wife |
| Mitty L. & J. S. McKinney | W. L. Burton |
| Josiah Huntsman & Fannie B. H.(sic) | Geo. Hinshaw |
| Waller D. & Carrie Malone | G. P. Dameron |
| D. W. Sly & Elizabeth Sly | J. B. Heathman |
| Chas. T. Atkins & wife | W. M. Chamberlain |
| W. S. & Mary C. Jean | Rhoda E. Crose |
| L. T. & Esther C. Burton | Kate V. Satterbee |
| Joseph & Sallie Allin | O. A. Skinner |
| R. G. & Mattie Duncan | J. L. Warford |
| J. W. Smith & wife | Sarah J. Osborne |
| Moses & Agnes Barnes | Enoch & Chas. Brandenburg |
| G. H. Wilson | James Hess |
| E. W. & Eva L. Chapman | Geo. W. Ficklin |
| M. Murphy | Wm. H. Vincent |
| Jas. H. Mary E. Bagly | Jno. M. Lawrence |
| Lizzie & Oswald Rutzer (sic) | Lucy Whitman |
| Oswald & Lizzie Rutzer (sic) | Lucy Whitman |
| Elizabeth J. Jackson | Jno. T. Tillerson |
| J. W. & Mary Hammett | Geo. W. Dameron |
| Emaunel Dill | J. A. Fowler |
| T. J. & Rose Molinari | Lutie C. Bolinger |
| Oswald & Lizzie Rutzer | Mrs. E. Mathieu |
| Moritz Oswald & Lizzie Oswald (sic) | Mrs. E. Mathieu |
| Jacob & Barbara Dean | Louis Shipp |
| Taswell & Bell Gray | Andrew J. Phipps |
| Taswell & Bell Gray | J. P. Carter |
| Dennis Tierney (single) | Medley Burton |
| W. Y. & Ithena Mason | W. B, Toombs |
| B. T. Hudson | Irvin Ratliff |
| B. T. Hudson | J. F. Harlan |
| J. E. & M. E. Hubbard | ---- |
| Wm. & Ella Rice | J. W. King & F. L. Sweeney |
| S. E. & Lankford Cook; Elise L. & Leotine V. Bragdon | Roger T. Carson; & P. J. Staats |
| Wm. C. & Mary M. Cross | Marvin E. Cross |
| Mrs. Ida M. Booth & L. E. Booth | Jno. Nebergall & A. J. Gee |
| W. H. & Bettie Stark | Wm. H. Thompson |
| A. J. Romesburg & wife | Wm. M. Evans |
| S. M. & Bena Hirsch | Bena Hirsch |
| G. R. & K. E. Reynolds | Phoebe Bain |
| Saml. & Martha E. Daniels | Geo. Berdio |

| Grantor | Grantee |
|---|---|
| J. C. & Lillie Miller | A. P. Bradley |
| Alfred & Lizzie Graves | Jno. E. Dawkins |
| J. E. & Laura A. Dawkins | W. J. Brogan |
| J. W. & Addie Skivin | Jno. Pelkington |
| D. W. Cibbage | Harriet McDowell |
| Geo. A. & Ida M. Schnack | M. E. Mayo |
| J. J. & Mary E. Bradley | Samuel Daniels |
| J. J. & Mary E. Bradley | Chas. Evans |
| Edwin & Julia Edwards | Ashford J. Hendron |
| Hendrick & Mann R. E. & Bdlg. o. | Morris Sale |
| Wm. H. Thompson & wife | Rudolph H. Williams |
| G. O. & Margaret Lillie | Chas. C. Erwin & Saml. C. Stevenson |
| Lafayette & Mary C. Coulter | W. D. & Bell Coulter |
| James & Alice Daggs | Henry B. Cubage (sic) |
| Anthony & Susan Fox | Anthony Fox |
| Hugh J. McCanne | Edgar P. Hutchinson |
| Blanche & W. T. Botts | T. H. Dinwiddie |
| Mary B. Kolman | Wm. H. Stark |
| E. M. & M. E. Terry | Gid. W. Rice |
| Jno. N. & Nannie Terry | Gidein (sic) W. Rice |
| Oswald & Lizzie Rutzer | Elizabeth Mathieu |
| Isaac & Nancy Giles | Luta Frances, Mary Jane, Martha Lee, & Victoria Giles |
| M. M. Carter & Mollie E. Carter | S. P. Rico |
| R. T. & K. S. Christian | Monitar & Mary Bailey |
| Charles F. Ware | Jno. J. Morris |
| Harvey & Minerva Robb | Wm. T. Smith |
| Jno. S. & Ortha Hanly | L. H. & J. P. Cross |
| M. M. & Mary E. Carter | W. D. Halliburton |
| Robt. L. Murphy | Isa Polson |
| Thos. F. & Ida Polson | Robt. L. Murphy |
| Lena B. & Michael McCabe | Minnie D. Harlan |
| R. O. & Etney J. McCanne | Jno. H. Coulton |
| P. J. Christian | J. E. Terrill |
| Joseph C. & T. C. Samuel | E. G. Coyley |
| J. W. Adams & wife and Chas. Eranso & wife | R. G. Duncan |
| The Moberly B. & L. Asso. | H. H. Kent |
| Fannie T. & P. P. Shaw | F. W. & W. A. Smith |
| J. A. & Mariah B. Heathes | J. P. Hamilton & wife |
| J. K. McLean & wife | C. F. McLean |
| J. K. McLean & wife | W. H. McLean |
| Cuddie & Frank Boyd | Samuel S. Jean |
| Jno. H. Swetman & wife | W. T. & Mary E. Fullington |
| Jno. S. & Ortha Hanly | J. E. Hubbard |

| Grantor | Grantee |
|---|---|
| Wm. C. & Mary M. Cross | G. S. Crow |
| Hannibal & St. Joseph R. R. Co. | Geo. G. Levick |
| Joseph A. W. Halterman & wife | Geo. G. Levick |
| J. J. & Alice Graves | R. M. Dameron |
| J. A. Bright & wife | L. W. Ficklin |
| Slater & Annie Zfrazier | Jas. M. Kirkpatrick |
| T. B. Kimbraugh and Carrie & Lucinda Seaman | Enoch P. & Wm. Sutliff |
| Arthusa & Jas. E. Emerson | C. C. Hagar |
| America & Jacob Brown and Fannie Stevens | C. C. Hagar |
| C. C. & Hester A. Hagar | J. D. Rutherford |
| S. T. G. Smith | E. O. & W. O. Doyle |
| Mrs. L. C. Samuel & J. C. Samuel | Mrs. Cynthia A. Cockrill |
| V. S. & Catharine Clark | Claton Clark |
| Mary Ellen & Samuel Rupp | Jno. T. Haley |
| Jno. T. & Agnes E. Haley | Mary Ellen Rupp |
| Luther Noel & L. B. Williams (sic) | L. B. Williams |
| Miss Ella E. Campbell | Jas. H. Smart |
| Sarah Kenappe | J. R. L. Clarkson |
| J. H. & Elizabeth Reagan | Peter Foster |
| J. R. L. Clarkston | Sarah Kenappe |
| J. W. & Ella Lewis | F. A. Purinton |
| H. H. & Anna B. Wayland | Harriet J. Lawless |
| H. H. & Idella Kent | Moberly B. & L. Assoc. |
| Jno. H. & Mariah Roberts | Maggie R. Haley |
| Sophia Brown | Annie Fint |
| Theresa B. & Saml. Bowman | Margaret M. Chapman |
| W. R. Samuel & wife | Mary A. Bradney (sic) |
| Michael & Mary Murphy | Harry Wood |
| Jno. A. & E. C. Hinton | Geo. W. Johnston |
| Henry & Martha Wilson | Judge Jackson |
| Denie B. & Jno. B. White | Mollie J. Rains |
| Elijah & Eliza Martin | James Martin |
| Jno. & Lou Ann Thomson | Stirling P. Thomson |
| Opeliah & Napoleon B. Tritch | Everett Tritch |
| Wm. & Margaret M. Chapman | G. M. Nichols |
| James D. Manning | Jno. R. Campbell & Mary L. (sic) |
| James D. Manning | Henry A. Manning & Luella (sic) |
| Harvey A. Manning & wife and Wm. J. Barney et al | James D. manning |
| Thos. L. & Mary L. Davis | Eliza Maple |
| L. N. & Ida Miller | James Painter |
| James & Nora Painter | Ida Miller |
| Mrs. Susan C. Owen | J. W. & Clara Frazier |

| Grantor | Grantee |
|---|---|
| Geo. W. & Bessie Sparks and N. M. Baskett | Jacob & Amanda Jacobson |
| Thomas & Margaret McSweeney | Anna Danley |
| J. W. Frazier & wife | Susan C. Owen |
| Jas. M. & Kate Kirkpatrick | Jno. G. & Maud S. Sandison |
| J. F. & Orla Holman | B. T. Hudson |
| N. C. & Etta A. Williams | Joseph Patton |
| James & Sarah Anna Capp | E. M. Capp |
| C. W. & Mary A. Puffer | W. P. White |
| Mary E. & L. A. Pope | Wm. Burke |
| Wm. & Maru Burke | Mary E. Pope |
| Enoch P. Sutliff & wife | Elizabeth Mathis |
| Abe & Mary Burton | John Turner |
| James D. Manning | Willie N. Bruvrr (?) |
| Geo. N. & J. J. Ratliff | Wm. Cunningham |
| Wm. & M. A. Cunningham | G. N. Ratliff |
| Annie E. Smart | J. H. Smart |
| Frances E. & J. H. Smart | Annie E. Smart |
| Mrs. J. M. Yerwill | Wm. Quayle |
| Robert Shipp | M. B. Shipp |
| Wm. J. & Hattie Buchanan | Geo. Tedford |
| Geo. Tedford | Katie Buchanan |
| Frank P. & Bettie B. Wiley | James S. & Mattie L. Roberts |
| Joseph H. & Nancy E. Durham | Robert Shipp |
| Richard & A. E. Owings | Lou O'Neal |
| james H. Cunningham & wife | Lucy Ellen Wirt |
| S. P. & R. B. Rice (wife) | Jno. T. Singleton |
| E. P. (wife) & W. H. Sutliff | A. J. Romesburg |
| Wm. & Rose Blaine | Geo. Schwabe |
| James N. Cottingham & wife (2x) | Sarah M. Cottingham |
| James H. Cottingham & wife | Earnest Cottingham |
| Ernest (sic) Cottingham | James H. Cottingham |
| Joseph Bartee | Lula Hines |
| G. L. Hasset & wife | Isaac Weisberg |
| Sarah L. & Wm. C. Rutledge | Joseph Haley |
| B. H. & Susan E. Ashecom | M. J. Blanke |
| James L. & Manda F. Polson | James W. Dowling |
| James W. & Martha F. Dowling | Geo. W. Biney |
| A. T. Douglass & Mrs. Clara A. Douglass | E. R. Eichenberger |
| Wm. P. White & Mrs. L. A. White | J. D. Bridensdolph & C. W. Puffer |
| R. A. & Annie R. Reynolds | T. A. McVay |
| Wm. & Phoebe Morgan | Geo. L. Hassett |
| Chas. P. & Friederika M. Baender | J. J. Border |
| Josephine & A. P. Terrill | Geo. M. C. Mallery |

| Grantor | Grantee |
|---|---|
| Vallentine & Mary J. Miller | Annie Nunn |
| Mra. Lara Semple | Maria B. Huther |
| Wm. P. & Elizabeth Wade | Frank Hisofelder |
| J. W. & E. C. Stark | Ella C. Hountz |
| Saml. & Sarah L. Cobb | James H. Lynn |
| Clara E. Robinson | Geo. W. & Mina Morsey |
| Hedrick & Marrs R. E. & Bldg. Co. | J. L. Hammett & Beu. H. Ashern |
| L. S. & Mary A. Harlan | Julana D. Vaughan |
| Wm. H. Lawley | John Stewart |
| P. C. & Rachel A. Epperlt | Irving S. Botts |
| Leny & P. J. Tedford | R. F. Wheeler |

St. Louis County, Missouri, Bill of Costs, Criminal Court, March Term, 1860, Capitol Fire Documents, CFD 68, Folder 6430.

B. Balthouse, G. Becker, G. Brown, G. Beatty, J. Benner, J. Bowlin, W. Connelly, N. Childs (2X), J. Casey, J. Dwyer, C. Enson, H. Feenan, C. Gallagher, C. Hatsburgh, F. Kemper, J. Hussbeth, C. A. Jones, J. Kelly, S. Kelly, C. Pothiff, J. Martin, G. Lynn, J. Leibert, M. Kelly, T. Malloy, P. Smith, C. Redbaugh, C. Ramelsburg, J. Schaffer, M. Stafford, F. Nebo, P. Schaffer, C. Turenne (2X), H. Versserman, J. Wilcox, J. Wilson, A. Wepke, C. Zink, J. Augustine, J. Ray, M. Harley, E. Boulin, J. Barry, J. Cummings, A. J. Coombs, E. Gruber, V. Flanz (sic), E. Hammon, F. F. Kealing, M. Kavanuagh (2X), T. Kelly, G. Laurence, W. Phillips, D. A. Rawlings, J. Reddy, W. Schaeffer, C. Schlie (2X), A. J. Warner, G. Goetz, C. A. Wallace, T. Ammel, J. Hertzing, D. H. Brown, W. Stein, A. Gertzer, L. Mathews, W. Clark, P. Lester, G. Scott, H. O. Hawkins, J. Turner, N. Adams, J. Berhard, W. Edwards, M. Amber, C. Meyer, F. New, E. Picker, A. Preston, E. Flannigan, J. Stommell, H. Volkman, J. Sullivan, F. Clark, J. Sharack, E. Flannigan, O. S. Meeker, J. Clark, W. Hanlon, A. Alexander, F. Butler, M. Batter, J. Burns, H. Bancroff, R. Cooper, H. Collins, M. Campbell, J. Debo, H. Dabel, N. Gunn, M. Gibbons, M. Gallenham, J. Hyman, -- Johnson, J. H. Ketham, H. Lambers, C. McCarty, F. Mikhal, J. Donnell, D. Purdy, J. Quiley, B. Priester, H. Bustick, J. Ryan, A. Sherman, M. Wibber (sic), A. Sharf, M. Schel, R. Wesley, J. Welsh.

## Justices' Fees
Brown, Bowlin, Kelly, Pethaff, Adams, Bernhart, Edwards, Hawkins, Meyer, Pecher, Stommell, Volkman, Flanigan, Sullivan.

Correspondence To Michael K. McGrath, Secretary Of State, Regarding The 1870 Census, Capitol Fire Documents, CFD 182, Folder 16199.

| Name | Date | County |
|---|---|---|
| E. Brayton | Feb. 24, 1877 | Andrew |
| L. C. Christian | Feb. 23, 1877 | Atchison |
| Lemuel Mills | Feb. 24, 1877 | Butler |
| Sam Russel | Mar. 1, 1877 | Caldwell |
| S. F. Sacket | Feb. 24, 1877 | Clark |
| Wm. W. Cook | Feb. 23, 1877 | Cass |
| G. W. Burris | Mar. 2, 1877 | Clay |
| Geo. R. Ray | Mar. 1, 1877 | Clinton |
| T. B. Morrow | Feb. 27, 1877 | Dallas |
| E. T. Butler | Feb. 25, 1877 | Dent |
| Chas. R. McCune | Feb. 23, 1877 | Franklin |
| J. D. Vanbibber | Mar. 6, 1877 | Greene |
| D. C. Pugh | Mar. 6, 1877 | Grundy |
| Ben L. Quarles | Feb. 22, 1877 | Henry |
| Sid B. Cunningham | Mar. 1, 1877 | Howard |
| S. C. Major, jr. | Mar. 8, 1877 | Howard |
| A. Mayer | Feb. 14, 1877 | Jackson |

Land Patent With Certification By Sam. B. Cook, Secretary Of State, 1903 (sic), Capitol Fire Documents, CFD 183, Folder 16208.

Patent issued to James H. Hancock oh July 18, 1848. Recorded in Volume 3, Page 976 for 500,000 acres as an U. S. Grant. Certified by Saml. B. Cook, Mar. 13, 1903. (sic)

Carroll County, Missouri, Grand Inquest, March term, 1842, Volume A, Page 354.

Thomas G. Winfrey, John B. Winfrey, Joseph Mead, William Crockett, John Hull, John Corley, Hugh M. Caton, William R. Creel, Benjamin Ely, Joshua F. Tomlin, Thomas Minnis, Samuel Brook, John Pile, John Daugherty, Pascal Early, Wm. Drake, Roland Adkins, Reesee Paynton.

Lewis County, Missouri, Index To Circuit Court Records, Volume Two, August, 1841 to May, 1851.

| Case No. | Case and Page Numbers |
|---|---|
| 641 | Alexander, Goff & Peterson vs. Glinn and Rees, (P) 2. |
| 647 | Abernathy vs. Richardson, (P) 7. |
| 579 | Agee vs. Moore, (P) 22. |
| 681 | Askin & Walten vs. Love & Moore, (P) 73. |
| 810 | Anderson, T. L. vs. Tate, C. B. (P) 82. |
| 817 | Anderson vs. Owsley, A. B., (P) 89, 486. |
| 809 | Asbury vs. Magge, (P) 100. |
| 770 | Ammermon vs. Broy, (P) 105, 145, 162. |

| Case No. | Case and Page Numbers |
|---|---|
| 804 | Anderson vs. Smith, admrs. & others, (P) 118, 128, 37, 165. |
| | Anderson, Thos. L. to Sheriff, deed, (P) 198, 199, 200. |
| 914 | Anderson, Rob. vs. Seeber, (P) 215, 246 |
| 773 | Anderson, Rob. vs. Kendrick, (P) 221, 258. |
| 975 | Anderson, Rob. vs. Carter, (P) 221, 258. |
| 974 | Anderson, Rob. vs. Smith, (P) 221, 254. |
| 976 | Anderson, Rob. vs. Bradshaw, (P) 221, 258, 345 |
| 1084 | Anderson, T. L. vs. Martin & others, (P) 279, 345. |
| | Abernathy, James R., Commn. Cir. At., (P) 304. |
| | Anderson, K. P. from Tate, Shf., deed, (P) 311 |
| 1131 | Anderson, T. L. vs. George S. Marks, (P) 334, 369. |
| 1184 | Ammermon, Saml. vs. Shumate, James, (P) 369, 377, 382, 418, 426, 464, 508, 523, 575, 580. |
| 1192 | Anderson & Easton vs. Ammerson, Sam., (P) 371. |
| 1187 | Abbott & Peake vs. Parsons, J. B. & Co., (P) 386, 395, 400, 440, 459, 509, 534, 555. |
| 1188 | Same as Case No. 1187. |
| 1189 | Same as Case No. 1187 |
| 1191 | Ammerman, Saml. vs. Oyster, Abraham, (P) 377, 384, 417, 427, 463, 496. |
| 1194 | Abbott & Peake vs. Parsons & Crooker, (P) 396, 400, 441, 459, 509, 534, 556. |
| 1218 | Anderson, Thos. L. vs. Richart, A. L. (P) 409. |
| 1227 | Archer, E. E. vs. Bourne, D., (P) 415, 426, 464, 493. |
| 1230 | Ammermon, S. vs. Oster, A., 2nd Case, (P) 418, 427, 477, 496. |
| 1309 | Allen, Wm. A. vs. Hayman, P., (P) 449. |
| 1327 | Ammerman, S. vs. Smith, guardian for M. I. Smith, (P) 481, 496. |
| 1362 | Adams, C. vs. Poage, L. (P) 504. |
| | Anderson, admr. Frazier vs. Redding, (P) 523, 561. |
| | Anderson, admr. Frazier vs. Robinson, (P) 543. |
| 1425 | Abbot & Peake use Tate vs. Haygood, admr. James, (P) 559. |
| | Ammerman vs. Wallace, Jno. & J. Shumate, (P) 575. |
| | Ammerman vs. Tolls. N. J. Shumate, (P) 580. |
| | Anderson, K. P. vs. Lowen, Francis, (P) 589, 608, 654. |
| | Able, D & B. vs. Lane, W. & others, (P) 596. |
| | Amos, Jas. F. vs. Hutton, Jno., (P) 600, 615. |
| | Atwood, H. vs. Durlee, H. J., (P) 619, 637. |

| Case No. | Case and Page Numbers |
|---|---|
|  | Anderson, Thos. L. vs. Sutton, J. M., (P) 633, 639 |
|  | Anderson vs. Sutton, garnishee Ousley, (P) 667, 697. |
|  | Amos, Josh vs. Hay, Turner, (P) 676. |
| 646 | Bates vs. Tuttle, admr. of Sloan, (P) 2, 40, 67. |
| 669 | Banks pet. for mill, (P) 2, 55. |
| 608 | Bank vs. Hamilton, Hughes, (P) 6, 35. |
|  | Bixen, Thomas pet. for naturalization, (P) 11. |
|  | Buckland, Thomas A. pet. for naturalization, (P) 24, 272. |
| 560 | Bontz vs. Miller, (P) 27, 37, 47. |
| 636 | Bank vs. Morris, Judg., (P) 37. |
| 316 | Bryan, Rodman & Haylin vs. Ownsley, (P) 40. |
| 674 | Bank of Mo. vs. Stubbfield & Stephens, (P) 49, 67, 71, 100. |
| 686 | Bayne vs. Bayne, (P) 70, 100. |
| 675 | Bank vs. Mills, (P) 70. |
| 684 | Bridewell, admr. vs. Bland & Hurt, (P) 72. |
| 672 | Burd & Tilden vs. Love, (P) 74, 95, 134, 145. |
| 596 | Beebe vs. Pemberton & Mattingly, (P) 83, 86, 96. |
| 773 | Broadwell vs. Givens & Clarkson, (P) 85, 88, 193, 148. |
| 779 | Bryan vs. Richardson, (P) 89. |
| 776 | Buckland & Weller, pet. for mill, (P) 77, 90. |
|  | Blair, J. H., clerk, acct., (P) 90, 229, 271, 321, 419, 484. |
| 795 | Buck vs. Cooksey, (P) 94. |
| 790 | Bank vs. Richardson, N., (P) 94. |
| 673 | Battzell vs. Miller, (P) 96, 148, 171, 193, 231, 390. |
| 791 | Bank vs. Reddish & Richardson, (P) 100, 111, 116, 167. |
| 816 | Buckley & Blackey vs. Knott, (P) 107. |
| 771 | Bank vs. Williams & Asbury, (P) 109. |
| 780 | Bank vs. Bland, (P) 109. |
| 781 | Bank vs. Rickard, (P) 110. |
| 832 | Bridewell vs. Coleman, (P) 133, 143, 165, 183. |
| 839 | Bates vs. Owsley, (P) 135, 165, 184, 194. |
| 859 | Burch vs. Robbins, (P) 141. |
| 822 | Bank vs. West, (P) 144, 149. |
| 848 | Bank vs. Forman, (P) 150. |
| 872 | Budd vs. Smith, (P) 172, 179. |
| 891 | Blain, Tompkins & Barret vs. Owsley, (P) 178, 240. |
|  | Blair, I. H., to sheriff, deed, (P) 182. |

| Case No. | Case and Page Numbers |
|---|---|
|  | Buckland & Weller to Sheriff, deed, (P) 182. |
| 880 | Bank vs. Ellis, (P) 186. |
| 881 | Bank vs. Burnett & Blair, (P) 187. |
| 882 | Bank vs. Stowen, (P) 187. |
| 971 | Bank vs. Dunbar & Rankin, (P) 191, 253. |
| 958 | Bank vs. Marks, (P) 197, 252. |
| 946 | Bank vs. Cardwell, Anderson & Blackwood, (P) 197, 248. |
| 956 | Bank vs. Henderson & Roberts, (P) 197, 252. |
| 945 | Blair, Tompkins, & Barret vs. Durkee, (P) 198, 269, 291, 295. |
| 1008 | Buford vs. Porter, (P) 203. |
| 907 | Brisco vs. Williams, (P) 206. |
| 985 | Baker vs. Munday, (P) 208. |
| 1011 | Bowler & Co. vs. Hughes, (P) 209. |
| 972 | Becket vs. Bowen, (P) 209. |
| 959 | Bank vs. Revely & Lafon, (P) 211, 252. |
| 950 | Bank vs. Morris & Lane, (P) 212, 250. |
| 953 | Bank vs. Hughes & Sublett, (P) 212, 250. |
| 957 | Bank vs. Haley & Johnson, (P) 212, 252. |
| 949 | Bank vs. Bozarth, (P) 212, 249. |
| 948 | Bank vs. Burchfield & Jones, (P) 212, 249, 423. |
| 954 | Bank vs. Colley, (P) 215, 251. |
| -51 | Bank vs. Givens & Dance, (P) 213, 248. (Corner torn) |
| 904 | Bayne vs. Bland, (P) 214, 242. |
| 952 | Bank vs. Dance, (P) 214, 249. |
| 947 | Bank vs. Holmes, (P) 214, 249, 701. |
| 943 | Bayne vs. Owsley & Sinclair, (P) 210, 226. |
| 942 | Bayne vs. Sinclair, Owsley, & Davis, (P) 220, 227. |
| 955 | Bank vs. Shumate, (P) 220, 251. |
| 970 | Bank vs. Northcraft, (P) 221, 265, 292. |
| 927 | Blakey & son vs. Porter, (P) 222. |
| 901 | Beckner vs. Blair, (P) 223, 243, 282, 305, 328. |
|  | Bright, Thos. J. to sheriff, deed, (P) 224. |
|  | Burford, Wm. to sheriff, deed, (P) 224. |
| 1024 | Buckner vs. Porter, (P) 235, 288. |
|  | Burnett, Geo. G. to fine, (P) 237, Omitted, (P) 244. |
| 1012 | Blakey, Ison vs. Hayden, (P) 244, 286. |
| 1068 | Bates vs. Frazier & Miller, (P) 274, 339. |
| 1079 | Bank vs. Bayne, Thos., (P) 276, 326. |
| 1037 | Bozarth vs. Curd, (P) 276. |
| 1081 | Bank vs. Hunsicker, (P) 278, 340. |
| 1082 | Bates vs. Martin & others, (P) 279, 345. |

| Case No. | Case and Page Numbers |
|---|---|
| 1060 | Bates vs. Ray, (P) 280, 591. |
| | Bayne, Tho. from Tate, sheriff, deed, (P) 311. |
| 1080 | Bank vs. Bradshaw, (P) 296, 312. |
| 1108 | Bates vs. Ray, (P) 308, 318, 347. |
| | Briscoe, deed of emancipation to colored man, Rueben, (P) 325. |
| 1134 | Bank vs. Redish, S. & Richardson, F. R., (P) 328, 336, 375, 406. |
| 1136 | Bank vs. Richardson, F. R. & P., (P) 328, 354, 384. |
| 1137 | Bank vs. Richard, I. A., (P) 328, 375, 385, 393, 407, 433, 482, 494, 497, 607, 608. |
| 1135 | Bank vs. Hotsenfiller, G. R. & Knott, L. W., (P) 334, 369, 594, 617, 644, 701. |
| 1143 | Bank vs. Lancaster, E. W., (P) 334, 404. |
| 1144 | Bank vs. Reveley, M. P. (P) 334, 364. |
| 1146 | Bank vs. Cardwell, Thos., (P) 335, 364. |
| 1145 | Bank vs. Barkley, Wm., (P) 335, 364. |
| 1141 | Bank vs. Lafon, John, (P) 335, 364. |
| 1147 | Bank vs. Croughton, Rob, (P) 336, 377, 404. |
| 1138 | Bank vs. Moore, W. & Givens, M., (P) 348, 385. |
| 1139 | Bank vs. Bayne, Thos., (P) 348, 354. |
| 1142 | Bank vs. Hamilton, A., (P) 349, 376. |
| 1140 | Bank vs. Hunsicker, A. (P) 353. |
| 1130 | Blair, J. H. vs. Wolf, John & Patrick, (P) 356, 360 (Torn may be other pages.) |
| 1176 | Bank vs. Amannerman, Saml., (P) 361, 383, 408. |
| | Bank vs. Asbury & Williams, (P) 364. |
| 1174 | Bates, Moses vs. Ray, (P) 365, 591, 612. |
| | Blair, J. H. from Tate, shff., deed, (P) 370. |
| 1180 | Bank vs. Haydon & Harper, (P) 376. |
| 1177 | Bank vs. Sublett, P. C., (P) 376. |
| 1175 | Bank vs. Long, Rueben, (P) 383. |
| 1179 | Bank vs. Howard, T. M., (P) 384. |
| | Bland, Chas. & Benj. from Tate, sheriff, deed, (P) 387. |
| 1208 | Baker & Brother vs. Benson, I. L., (P) 393, 446. |
| 1197 | Bibb, J. vs. Legg's admr., (P) 405. |
| 1206 | Bank vs. White, H. & I., (P) 406. |
| 1235 | Bates vs. Merrill, (P) 420. |
| 1237 | Beach vs. Reveley, (P) 42, 425, 472, 498, 505. |
| 1256 | Bacon & Hyde vs. Hughes, I. A., two case, (P) 426, 458, 469, 475. |
| | Bibb, I. B. vs. Legg, (P) 426, 464, 496, 540, 571, 605, 658, 679, 708. |
| 1270 | Brown, Saml. vs. Cooksey, (P) 440, 476, 479. |
| 617 | Conrad & Co. vs. Haner & Tate, (P) 4. |

150

| Case No. | Case and Page Numbers |
|---|---|
| 619 | Conrad & Co. vs. Gleim (?), (P) 4. |
| 604 | Croughton vs. Wright & Merrill, (P) 5, 29. |
| 645 | Clark vs. Revely, (P) 7, 49. |
| 570 | Cooksey & Colborn vs. Haner & Tate, (P) 28. |
| 602 | Ceil, Samuel vs. Wygate, Widow, (P) 39, 68, 120. |
|  | Clerk allowed acct., (P) 41, 77, 90, 229, 321. |
| 806 | Case vs. Wigginton, (P) 99. |
| 837 | Cooksey vs. Cordell, (P) 101, 164. |
| 769 | Crook vs. Dance, (P) 107, 110, 159. |
| 833 | Crockett & Gist vs. Vance, (P) 133, 149, 153, 156, 188, 194. |
|  | Coroner's bond approved. (P) 133, 304. |
| 826 | Conduitt vs. Turpin, (P) 148. |
| 852 | Colley vs. Munday, (P) 164, 184. |
| 869 | Camden vs. Wilson, Stuart, (P) 171, 195, 216, 232, 320. |
| 981 | Creath vs. Blair & Sutton, (P) 207. |
| 937 | Case vs. Wigginton, (P) 211, 242. |
| 903 | Clark, Eckzler vs. Owsley, A.B., (P) 212, 233. |
| 982 | Coleman vs. Overstreet, (P) 223. |
| 1015 | Cox vs. Hazelrigg & Stephens, (P) 232, 288. |
| 1021 | Colley vs. Garnett, (P) 244, 289, 309. |
| 1028 | Cotwell vs. Sublett & Cardwell, (P) 254. |
| 1066 | Crawford & Vance vs. Henderson, Hunt & Co., (P) 276, 344. |
| 1093 | Craig vs. Stuart, (P) 279. |
| 1051 | Crawford & Vance vs. Poage & Morris, (P) 280, 338. |
| 1050 | Crawford & Vance vs. Escue & Zimmerman, (P) 285, 357. |
| 1958 | Croughton vs. Triplett, (P) 301, 339. |
| 869 | Camden vs. Cordell, G, C., (P) 320. |
| 1133 | Clark & Earp vs. Mitchell, E. W., (P) 335, 367, 401, 439, 474. |
| 1169 | Conover, Geo. vs. Oyster, A., (P) 361, 386, 390, 403, 417, 420, 435. |
|  | Circuit attorney pro-tem (Wells, C.), appointed., (P) 364. |
|  | Coroner to deed, Smith R. and Duncan, Wm., admr. Easton, (P) 367. |
| 1223 | Creath, J. vs. Poage, L. (P) 406. |
| 1239 | Combs vs. Poage, G. E. & L., (P) 426, 440, 472, 495. |
| 1255 | Collins & Kellogg, vs. Hotsenssiller & Agge, (P) 442. |
| 1273 | Chouteau & Valley vs. Hughes, I. N. , (P) 443. |
| 1298 | Cason, E. vs. Durkee & Nelson, (P) 468. |

| Case No. | Case and Page Numbers |
|---|---|
| 1282 | Cambron, E. H. vs. Larne & Legg, admr. Legg, (P) 479. |
| 1349 | Cohover, N. vs. Oyster, A., (P) 508, 531, 544, 557, 550, 583. |
| | Carpeniter (sic), Thos. to Writ Ad. dam.(P) 524, 576, 653. |
| 1372 | Cumminns, J. J. vs. Harrison, Geo. P., (P) 539. |
| | Coroner Rankin ack. deed to Green, L. S., (P) 531. |
| 1373 | Cumminns, J. J. vs. Harrison, Geo. P., (P) 539. |
| | Croughton vs. Kinney, Geo. W., (P) 545. |
| | Chowning vs. Givens, Brann & Childers, (P) 546, 576. |
| | Cleaver, S. vs. Caldwell, Wm., (P) 549. |
| | Comstock vs. Comeggy, W., (P) 554. |
| | Caldwell, Jno. T. vs. Reddish & Winter, exr. of S. Reddish, (P) 562. |
| | Coroner Hawkins, board approved., (P) 581. |
| | Coleman vs. Thompson, Wm. & others, (P) 582. |
| | Cason, E. vs. Jones, John & others, (P) 588. |
| | Cardwell vs. Moose, (P) 593. |
| | Cotty, W. I. vs. Clary, S., (P) 595. |
| 1443 | Croughton, Robt. vs. Randolph, T. & Kearney, A. J. |
| 1472 | Creath vs. Morris & Price, exrs. Price, (P) 605, 611, 638. |
| | Corry, Wm. to emancipation lot of negroes, (P) 611. |
| 1483 | Cowgill vs. Sinclair, (P) 620, 656, 682, 709. |
| | Creath, Mary E. & others vs. Morris, Price & others, (P) 627, 647, 664. |
| 1506 | Croughton & Harper vs. Coryell, Forrest & Co., (P) 635, 639, 646, 663, 677, 708. |
| | Cannon, Nebold to emancipate slave, (P) 652. |
| | Cannon, Priscilla vs. Cannon, N. J., adm., (P) 676, 697. |
| | Collins, Wm. vs. Coryell, Jno. R., (P) 678. |
| | Cason, Jno. vs. Stevens, J. W., (P) 710, 711. |
| 1520 | Connable & Cunningham vs. Russell, (P) 642. |
| 1534 | Cannon, C. & others vs. McPherson & others, (P) 651, 671, 696. |
| | Cannon, Newbold to emancipate slave, (P) 652. |
| | Collins, Wm. vs. Coryyell, Jno. R., (P) 678. |
| | Cason, Jno. vs. Stevens, J. M., (P) 710, 711. |
| 676 | Davis & Hansen vs. Glinn & Reese, (P) 61. |
| 788 | Dryden vs. Colley & Huner, (P) 110. |

| Case No. | Case and Page Numbers |
|---|---|
| | Dryden, Green to sheriff, deed, (P) 147. |
| 890 | Deaver vs. Owsley, (P) 177. |
| | Durkee, H. J. to sheriff, deed, (P) 178. |
| 857 | Dolton vs. White, (P) 186, 254. |
| 967 | Dunlap vs. Dance, (P) 214, 257. |
| 979 | Day vs. Price, (P) 217. |
| 1017 | Daviess, admr. vs. Martin, (P) 239, 427. |
| 1031 | Durkee vs. Sublett, N. A. & others, (P) 245, 266, 301, 332, 378, 397, 428, 430, 455. |
| 1027 | Daggs vs. Owsley et al, (P) 259, 290. |
| 1097 | Duncan & Smith, adm. vs. Ray, (P) 308, 319, 373, 349, 373. |
| 1118 | Duncan & Smith, admr. vs. Hines & Tate, (P) 318. |
| | Devillis, John, senr. to sheriff, deed from Sublett, (P) 323. |
| | Devillis, John, senr. to sheriff, deed from Tate, (P) 324, 399. |
| | Daviess, Louisa A. to sheriff, deed from Tate, (P) 330. |
| 1132 | Daviess, Louis A. vs. Stith (?), I. H., (P) |
| | Dryden, J. D. S. from Sublett, Tate, sheriff, deed, (P) 366. |
| | Donley, George vs. Jones, Calvin C., (P) 367, 402. |
| 1228 | Daviss, I. vs. Glass & Ray, (P) 396, 402, 416, 438, 470, 492. |
| | Davis (sic), S., sheriff, deed from Tate, (P) 409. |
| 1253 | Durkee, C. vs. Hawkins, F. A., (P) 423, 473. |
| 1244 | Darrah & Pomeroy vs. Olds & others, (P) 435, 439, 461, 474, 496. 523, 525, 557, 589, 605, 633, 761. |
| 1313 | Durkee, L. vs. Shannon, admr., Frazier, (P) 452, 498, 545. |
| 1360 | Durkee, C. vs. Agee, P. C., (P) 504, 526, 531, 533. |
| 1376 | Durkee, C. vs. Baldwin, H., (P) 515, 520, 537, 572, 581. |
| 1381 | Dunn & others vs. Dunn & others (sic), (P) 516, 548, 579, 602, 648, 682, 686. |
| | Duncan, Owsley & others vs. Lillard, adm., Wooden vs. Hamer (?), (P) 525. |
| 1383 | Durrett, adm., Sutherland vs. Patterson, adm., Conley, (P) 546. |
| | Davis, Saml. vs. Singleton, Geo., (P) 544. |
| | Downing, Jas. vs. Brumbaugh, (P) 571. |
| | Delbridge vs. Board, J. M., (P) 580. |

| Case No. | Case and Page Numbers |
|---|---|
| | Delbridge vs. John B. P. Board (sic), (P) 280. |
| | Downing, Jas. vs. Braubaugh, Jno., (P) 585, 589. |
| | Dryden, J. D. S., deed from shff., Tate, (P) 590. |
| | Davis, Shadrach & others to Commissioners, (P) 591, 607. |
| | Dolly, H. vs. Horricker, Jno., (P) 595. |
| | Doan, King & Bigelow vs. Meyer, C. R., (P) 598. |
| | Daviss vs. Sullivan, (P) 678. |
| | Dunlap to emancipate a slave, (P) 631. |
| | Davis, Isaac vs. Clark, Thos., (P) 649, 680. 695. 707. |
| | Dick, Saml. vs. Coryell & others, (P) 657, 674. |
| | Dawson vs. Lowery, (P) 651, 675. |
| | Durkee, H. Jas. (sic) vs. Rider, Jas., (P) 681, 699. |
| | Durkee, H. Jas. (sic) vs. Thompson, G., (P) 681, 699. |
| | Dufriend vs. Gregory, (P) 707. |
| | Diffendaffer vs. Pisk, (P) 710. |
| 643 | Ellison vs. Glinn & Reese, (P) 3. |
| 612 | Ellison vs. Huner & tate, (P) 8, 16, 20, 26, 32, 62, 86, 268, 269, 287. |
| 629 | Earp, McMain & others vs. Revely & Stubblefied, (P) 10, 30, 47. |
| 606 | Easton vs. Reveley, (P) 13, 49, 52. |
| 677 | Ellmaker vs. Hunter & Tate, (P) 53, 130, 358. |
| 765 | Ewing vs. Alford, (P) 88. |
| 840 | Eaves vs. Blair, (P) 161. |
| | Easton, Joseph G. to sheriff, deed, (P) 146. |
| | Ellison, James to sheriff, deed, (P) 146, 218, 378. |
| 1010 | Ellison vs. Stowers, (P) 195. |
| 1014 | Elliott vs. Sublett et all, (P) 244, 262, 292, 309, 336, 366, 374, 391, 424, 425, 431, 441, 456. |
| 324 | Easton's admr. vs. Myers, John, (P) 354, 387. |
| | Easton's admr. to deed from Rankin, Coroner, (P) 367. |
| 1155 | Easton's admr. vs. Jefferies, (P) 373. |
| 1210 | Ellis, Wm., admr., Pemberton vs. Forman, I. W. & others, (P) 391, 436, 457, 472, 498, 501. |
| 1220 | Ellis, W., admr., Pemberton vs. Pemberton, J. & E., (P) 409, 422, 429, 431. |
| 1280 | English, Frosty to fine, (P) 410, 420. |

| Case No. | Case and Page Numbers |
|---|---|
| | Easton, Jos., sheriff, deed, from Tate, (P) 405. |
| 1219 | Ellis, Wm., admr., Pemberton vs. Pemberton, Eliza, (P) 410, 422, 429, 42. |
| 1268 | Ellis, admr., Pemberton vs. Wood's devise., (P) 418, 445, 666. |
| 1318 | Ellis, Wm. vs. Bradley, L., (P) 467. |
| | Ellis, Wm., deed from sheriff, Richardson, (P) 482. |
| 1357 | Ellis, admr., Pemberton vs. Richardson, F. R., (P) 505. |
| | Ellison vs. Homas, (P) 520, 546. |
| | Ellis, admr. vs. Board, J. M., (P) 574. |
| | Ellis, admr. vs. Dunbar, (P) 611. |
| 427 | Francis vs. Martin, (P) 1. |
| 430 | Fish vs. Marshall & Saller, (P) 10, 15, 41. |
| 630 | Fields, Forbes & Co. vs. Glenn & Rees, (P) 16. |
| 636 | Finley & Morris vs. Chandler, (P) 16, 37. |
| | Fuqua, Joseph, recognized, (P) 34. |
| | Fines to be certified, (P) 76, 189, 218, 271, 302, 321, 419, 704, 710. |
| 844 | Finley & Morris vs. Chandler, (P) 163. |
| 889 | Farr vs. Owsley, (P) 170, 246. |
| 888 | Fellows, W. H. vs. Stith, (P) 170, 313, 327, 537, 583. |
| 873 | Fielder vs. Threlkeld, (P) 174. |
| 908 | Fielder vs. Kenderick, (P) 191, 233. |
| 1009 | Fielder vs. Porter, (P) 203. |
| 917 | Forman vs. Cooksey, (P) 214, 247. |
| 965 | Forman, admr. vs. Green, (P) 219, 237, 261, 267, 2710, 480. |
| 938 | Futwell vs. Buford, (P) 219. |
| 1030 | Fortune vs. Sublett, (P) 245, 256, 300, 309, 353, 366. |
| 966 | Forman, admr. vs. Hughes & Roberts, (P) 26, 263. |
| 1048 | Fortune vs. Vertrees, (P) 303, 310, 341. |
| 1101 | Frazier vs. Quinn, (P) 319. |
| 1214 | Franklin, Jonah vs. Baker, Jno., (P) 396, 403, 418, 446, 451. |
| 1211 | Farr, Asa vs. Hughes, J. N., (P) 398, 407, 422, 425, 440, 475, 476. |
| | Fine on English, Frosty, (P) 410. |
| 1203 | Fretwell, Lothen vs. Fretwell's heirs, (P) 411, 416, 419, 439, 456. |
| 1257 | Filley vs. Huges, J. N., (P) 421, 432. |
| 1262 | Foree, Wm. G. vs. Harris, Wm. R., (P) 445. |
| 1307 | Fanleoner, Jos. vs. Indy, I. T., (P) 451, 506. |

| Case No. | Case and Page Numbers |
|---|---|
| 1339 | Faber, E. & F. vs. Stith, I. H., (P) 462. |
| 1365 | Frederick vs. Northcraft, (P) 492, 520, 576. |
| 1368 | Forman, J. W. vs. P. C. Sublett, (P) 510. |
| | Forrest, Geo. vs. Beckner & Cannon, (P) 549. |
| | Forrest, Chas. D. vs. Morrow, Joseph, (P) 588, |
| | Fuqua, D. H. vs. Robinson, Ben, (P) 609, 618, 634. |
| | Forrest, Chas. W. vs. Nunn (error) (sic) |
| 1493 | Filley vs. Hulett, Ben, (P) 621. |
| | Finley, E. Drake & others, (P) 651, 665, 667, 672. |
| 422 | Glinn, admr. of Rees vs. Francis & Redd, (P) 44, 93, 145, 169. |
| 641 | Goff & Peterson vs. Glinn & Rees, (P) 2. |
| 627 | Goodno vs. Jones, (P) 16. |
| 638 | Glenn & Rees vs. Hughes, (P) 32, 62. |
| 414 | Goldsbury vs. Lillard, (P) 33, 61, 75, 93. |
| 558 | Green vs. Weldon, (P) 37, 75, 127. |
| 559 | Glinn vs. Love, (P) 95, 135, 145. |
| 687 | Gardner vs. Smith, (P) 103. |
| 847 | Green vs. Madox, (P) 131. |
| 843 | Gist vs. Vance, (P) 159, 175, 188, 194. |
| | Green, Abner H., admitted to practice law, (P) 169. |
| | Green, I. S., jr. to deed, sheriff, Tate, (P) 187. |
| 1006 | Goldthwaite & Co. vs. Hughes, (P) 208. |
| 921 | Givens vs. Love, (P) 213, 263, 264, 282. |
| 926 | Glover vs. Cooksey, (P) 214, 253, 283. |
| 1020 | Griggs & Elliott vs. Humer & Tate, (P) 268, 293. |
| 1063 | Givens & Sullivan, (P) 282, 301, 320. |
| 1110 | Glover vs. Ray, (P) 308, 355, 591. |
| 1122 | Glover & Campbell vs. Frazier & Miller, (P) 332, 368. |
| 1112 | Glover, S. T. vs. Seaman, D., (P) 351. |
| 1172 | Green, James vs. Bibb, Jerome & others, (P) 373. |
| 1217 | Griggs & Elliott vs. Benson, J. D., (P) 395, 442. |
| 1215 | Glover, S. T. vs. Ray, (P) 408, 513, 591, 612. |
| | Glover, S. T., sheriff, deed from Tate, (P) 412. |
| | Green, I. S., sheriff, deed from Tate, (P) 412, 413. |
| 1265 | Garnett, R. S. vs. Stowes, Wm., (P) 438, 481, 500. |
| 1246 | Green, J. S. vs. Pugh, (P) 443. |

| Case No. | Case and Page Numbers |
|---|---|
| | Glover, S. T., deed from sheriff, Richardson, (P) 512. |
| 1410 | Green, J. S. vs. Gregory, W. S., (P) 521. |
| 1432 | Glover, Saml. vs. Jackson, Jacob, (P) 557. |
| 1458 | Gould & Maccrackin vs. Magee, C. R., (P) 598/ |
| 1599 | Glover, Green & Campbell vs. Myers, Jno. & others, (P) 715. |
| 642 | Hill & Jinney vs. Glinn & Rees, (P) 3. |
| 622 | Harwood vs. Davis, (P) 6, 30, 35. |
| 554 | Henrietta vs. Brady, (P) 8, 11. |
| 562 | Hallowell, Asbridge & Co. vs. Durkee, (P) 9. |
| 620 | Hubbs & Montillius vs. Shepherd, (P) 20, 245. |
| | Hughes, Henry F. to Recoginsance (?), (P) 23. |
| 569 | Huner, use of Morris vs. Tate & Thompson, (P) 24. |
| | Hughes, Henry F. to fine, (P) 25. |
| 640 | Hughes, assn. vs. Haley, (P) 31, 94, 164, 185. |
| | Huner ack. deed to Haley, (P) 41. |
| 571 | Heberton, Heiskell & Hoskins vs. Reveley, (P) 49. |
| 683 | Hatfield vs. Baker, (P) 51, 71, 94, 148, 170. |
| 671 | Hay vs. Owsley & White, (P) 52. |
| 680 | Haygood vs. Mills, (P) 54. |
| 784 | Hagood (sic) vs. Ewing, admr., (P) 83. |
| 801 | Heberton, Heiskell & Hoskins vs. Mitchell, (P) 99. |
| 763 | Haydon vs. Coffman, (P) 113, 166, 172, 184, 216, 232, 240, 248, 275. |
| | Hagood (sic), Wm. to sheriff, deed, (P) 128, 215. |
| 796 | Howerton vs. Ammerman, (P) 102, 108. |
| 849 | Harrell, Isaac vs. Harrell, Jno., (P) 131, 149, 157, 162, 175, 260, 281, 305, 324. |
| 834 | Harrell, Jno. vs. Harrell, Isaac, (P) 131, 162, 198, 217, 260, 282, 324. |
| 845 | Hayman vs. Richardson, (P) 135, 149, 175. |
| 841 | Hunnewell & Hill vs. Vance, (P) 139, 164, 165, 181, 196. |
| | Haner, Jacob to sheriff, deed, (P) 147. |
| 865 | Hagan vs. Northcraft, (P) 172, 201. |
| 863 | Hamilton vs. Asbury, (P) 178, 181. |
| 870 | Hamilton vs. Smith, admr., Hamilton, (P) 186, 216, 246, 284, 304, 315. |
| 918 | Heiskell, admr., Parke vs. Babbitt, (P) 205, 247, 267, 284, 307, 334, 361, 380, 401, 238, 514, 519, 553. |
| 978 | Henderson, Hant & Co. vs. Finley, (P) 208, 260. |

| Case No. | Case and Page Numbers |
|---|---|
| 930 | Henderson, Hant & Co. vs. Hayden, (P) 211, 241. |
| 929 | Henderson, Hant & Co. vs. Reddish, (P) 213, 240. |
| 934 | Hurt vs. Bland, (P) 219, 225, 245, 295, 307, 349, 363, 367, 379. |
| 932 | Henderson, Plant & Co. vs. Graves, (P) 221, 238. |
| 931 | Henderson, Plant & Co. vs. Lane, (P) 221, 238. |
| 986 | Hurt vs. Ramsey. (P) 224, 262, 293. |
| 1026 | Huner, admr. vs. Reese & Coleman, (P) 230, 289. |
| | Hamilton vs. Moore, (P) 244, 288, 308, 327, 348. |
| | Huner, admr., Coleman deed to Heiskel,(P) 256. |
| 1019 | Hawkins, admr., Harrell vs. Sinclair, P) 266. |
| | Hayman, Peter to sheriff, Tate, deed from Tate, (P) 267. |
| 1067 | Hayden, admr. vs. Emerson, (P) 285, 340. |
| | Henderson to sheriff's deed, (P) 289. |
| 1047 | Huner, admr. vs. Rees & Coleman, (P) 280, 337. |
| 1061 | Hawkins & Hamilton, (P) 295, 338. |
| 1062 | Hinton vs. Ramsey & Brown, (P) 296, 319. |
| 1059 | Hays vs. Porter, (P) 298, 342. |
| 1054 | Hunsicker, admr. vs. Owsley, Shank, jr., (P) 299, 311, 350, 358, 392, 399. |
| 1092 | Hudson vs. Brume, (P) 302, 326, 365. |
| 1100 | Hamilton, Elizth. vs. Johnson & Edwards, (P) 305, 317, 342, 354, 380, 400, 425, 453. |
| | Harper, E., admr. vs. Ridgeway, J. W., (P) 332, 354, 383, 402, 437. |
| 1185 | Hendrick, Jas. vs. Parson & Thayer, (P) 382. |
| | Honoker, Christian, naturalization, (P) 392. |
| | Hurt, Ossinum, sheriff deed from Tate, (P) 415. |
| 1216 | Hagood, William vs. White & Martin, (P) 415, 434, 471. |
| 1274 | Hanskeeker vs. Benson, J. S., (P) 423. |
| 1272 | Haydon vs. Haydon, (P) 428. |
| 1271 | Hagood, admr., Parsons vs. Ray, Wm. C., (P) 439, 471, 502, 528. |
| 1248 | Holtzlaw vs. Hayden, (P) 443. |
| 1311 | Haley, B. vs. Leeper, J., (P) 451, 472, 499. |
| 1283 | Harrison, G. P. vs. Adams, C., (P) 473, 505, 532, 534, 554, 558. |
| | Anderson, A. J., deed from Sheriff, Tate, (P) 478. |
| | Hudikafer vs. McKee, (P) 497. |

| Case No. | Case and Page Numbers |
|---|---|
| | Hagerman vs. Bibb on fifa. (sic), (P) 497. |
| 1369 | Hayman, P. vs. Steam Boat Ocean Wave, (P) 507, 519, 532. |
| 1397 | Hayman, P. vs. Haydon, (P) 520. |
| 1384 | Hay, Jos. vs. Lay, L.; Webber, E.; & Norris, (P) 547. |
| 1405 | Hagerman, B. F. vs. Richart, A. L., (P) 550, 570. |
| | Holliway, Benjn., (P) 558. |
| 1430 | Hutsessiller & Agee vs. Dance, (P) 562, 588, 600, 608. |
| 1419 | Hagerman vs. Jones, John C. M. H., (P) 572. |
| 1426 | Hinson, Geo. J. & Jane, admx. vs. Bowles & Young, (P) 575. |
| | Hawkins, coroner bond approved, (P) 581. |
| 1440 | Henderson, C. F. vs. Shepherd, J. E., (P) 598. |
| | Holliday to remission of fine, (P) 600. |
| 1475 | Hanall, Sherman & Co. vs. Owsley, E., (P) 609, 619, 636, 679, 694. |
| | Henderson & Fadoux vs. Smith, (P) 633, 639. |
| 1541 | Hagood, Wm. vs. Olds, W. E., (P) 653. |
| 1526 | Hagood, Wm. vs. White, (P) 654. |
| | Hall, Emanuel admitted as a citizen, (P) 662. |
| 1557 | Howard vs. brown, (P) 662, 710. |
| 1550 | Hamilton, Lewis vs. Hamilton, Jno. B., (P) 664, 670, 696, 698. |
| 1551 | Heiskill vs. Seamnan, (P) 685. |
| 1573 | Hulett, M. vs. Hampton, (P) 688, 717. |
| 1576 | Hawkins, F, A, vs. Boyd, J. & others, (P) 489. |
| 1598 | Haley vs. Stower, (P) 707. |
| 637 | John vs. Smith, (P) 8, 24, 27. |
| 588 | Jones vs. Mallory, (P) 20. |
| | Lillard, David M. to recognisance & fine, (P) 28. |
| 634 | Jefferies vs. Bland, (P) 30, 31, 34, 61. |
| 835 | Johnson & Co. vs. Owsley, (P) 163. |
| 968 | Jones vs. Gearhart, (P) 197, 255. |
| 964 | Janett & Furguson vs. Wilson & Stuart, (P) 227. |
| 1053 | Johnson vs. Gearhart, (P) 280, 338. |
| 1124 | Janis, Trabue, & Curd vs. White, Halsey, (P) 339, 366, 398, 474. |
| 1129 | Johnson, Mays vs. Stockton, Thos. B., (P) 356, 388. |
| 1196 | Jones, John vs. Jones & Bourne, (P) 396, 405, 433, 447. |
| | Jackson, Jacob vs. Parish, S. (?), (P) 397, 399. |

| Case No. | Case and Page Numbers |
|---|---|
| | Johnson, J. A., deed from sheriff, Richardson, (P) 477. |
| 1351 | Johnson, D. Vs. Hughes, D. B., (P) 507, 540, 542. |
| | Jewell vs. Jewell, (P) 620, 650, 679. |
| | Johnson vs. Meeker, (P) 624, 647, Woodyan, admr., (P) 675. (Note: This is exactly how this entry appears.) |
| 618 | Kimber vs. Huner & Tate, (P) 5. |
| 610 | King vs. Miller & Lockhart, (P) 20. |
| 611 | King vs. Bozarth, (P) 29, 48. |
| 811 | King vs. Witson, (P) 90. |
| 782 | Kelso vs. Forman, adm., (P) 106. |
| 836 | Kughler vs. Dwilbius, (P) 131. |
| 980 | Knott vs. Haydon, (P) 209. |
| 1069 | Keith vs. Poage, (P) 274, 340, 260. |
| 1090 | King vs. Legg, (P) 276, 342, 347. |
| | King, Samuel from sheriff - deed, (P) 277. |
| 1085 | Kenton vs. Reddish & Givens, (P) 285, 287, 293, 345. |
| 1205 | Kenedy, Julian & Co. vs. Parsons, (P) 416. |
| 1320 | Kenton, E. vs. Stowers & Givens, (P) 467. |
| 1346 | Kerfoot, E. vs. Kertfoot & others, (P) 480, 489. |
| 1414 | Kendrick vs. Kendrick & others, (P) 577, 585, 597, 607. |
| 1549 | Kingsland & Lyhtner vs. Dimmett, admr., (P) 665, 695, 701. |
| 1585 | Kerfoot, admr. Kerfoot vs. Stitte & others, (P) 709. |
| 1574 | Kendall vs. Holingshead, (P) 709. |
| 372 | Lanes vs. Holmes, adm. of Allen, (P) 2. |
| 146 | Lanes vs. Brown & others, (P) 5. |
| 623 | Lewis Co. vs. Tate & others, (P) 17, 29. |
| | Lillard, Davis M. to recoginisance & fine, (P) 28. |
| 146 | Lanes vs. Brown & others (sic), (P) 38. |
| 776 | Loyd vs. Bridewell, (P) 97. |
| 783 | Lewis Co. vs. Glinn, (P) 144. |
| 842 | Levick & Jenkins vs. Revely & others, (P) 140. |
| 960 | Lizenby vs. Rankin, (P) 192, 203, 259, 260, 294. |
| 913 | Laurue & Legg vs. Thompson, (P) 207. |
| 933 | Leight vs. Poage, (P) 211, 241. |
| 1077 | Lewis Co. vs. Ammerman & others, (P) 276. |
| 1070 | Lewis Co. vs. Ramsey & others, (P) 276. |
| 1073 | Lewis Co. vs. Tate & Hawkins, (P) 278, 343. |
| 1076 | Lewis Co. vs. Wash & others, (P) 286, 322. |

| Case No. | Case and Page Number |
|---|---|
| 1088 | Lewis Co. vs. Tate, Hunsicker & others, (P) 279, 326. |
| 1074 | Lewis Co. vs. Wash & others, (P) 286, 323. |
| 1078 | Lewis Co. vs. Rankin, James, (P) 287, 344. |
| 1075 | Lewis Co. vs. Rankin, John, (P) 287, 344. |
| 1087 | Levering & Palmer vs. Curd & Mitchell, (P) 296, 350, 375, 400. |
| 1071 | Lewis Co. vs. Clark & others, (P) 297. |
| 1072 | Lewis Co. vs. Woodson & others, (P) 298, 343. |
| 1052 | Leight vs. Hambaugh, (P) 298. |
| 1098 | Love vs. Givens, (P) 307, 347. |
| 1111 | Lillard, guardian vs. Frazier, (P) 311, 335, 363, 370, 379, 599, 625. |
| 1150 | Loudermilk, Jno. vs. Frazer (sic), T. S., (P) 352, 615. |
| 1162 | Ligon, Danl., petition for mill, (P) 357, 386, 390, 392, 421, 436, 443, 456, 497, 500. |
| | Love, Charles fined, (P) 423. |
| | Lindley, J. J., atty., enrolled, (P) 423. |
| 1258 | Lay & Webber, E. or Norris vs. Kiziah & Joyce (persons of color), (P) 439, 471, 509. |
| 1323 | Lynes, Jackson vs. Patee, G. W., (P) 447. |
| 1325 | Lynes, Jackson vs. Dixon, D. B., (P) 447. |
| 1336 | Louthan & Co. vs. Ammerman, Saml., (P) 448. |
| 1338 | Louthan & Co. vs. Forman, J. W., (P) 453. |
| 1286 | Lukens vs. Reeveley, M. P., (P) 466, 502. |
| 1316 | Lewis Co. vs. Davis & Marks, (P) 478. |
| 1347 | Larue & Legg, admr., Legg vs. Bibb, J. B., (P) 479. |
| | Lakenan, R. F., attorney, enrolled, (P) 486. |
| | Lillard, admr., Wooden vs. Huner, D., (P) 535. |
| 1391 | Lewis C. vs. Hughes, Sickels, Magee & Givens, (P) 529. |
| 1385 | Lattimer vs. Mays, admr., Lattimer, (P) 529. |
| 1414 | Lewis Co. vs. Ammerman, Kelsoe & others, (P) 572. |
| 1455 | Little, Geo. D. vs. Owsley, E., (P) 585, 598, 619, 642, 648, 661. |
| 1449 | Lewis Co. vs. Jos. Drake & others, (P) 599. |
| | Lamb, A. W., enrolled as attorney, (P) 635. |
| 1517 | Longmire, Jas. G. vs. Reese, L. & others, (P) 642, 663, 669, 680, 695. |
| 1528 | Lewis Co. vs. Buckland & Miller, (P) 649, 660. |
| 1529 | Lewis Co. vs. Blanchard & others, (P) 649, 680, 708. |
| 1530 | Lewis Co. vs. Knott, Reiley, Harris, (P) 649, 680, 708. |
| 1531 | Lewis Co. vs. Poage, Ellis & Miller, (P) 649. |

| Case No. | Case and Page Numbers |
|---|---|
| 1532 | Lewis C. vs. Mallory, C. P. & others, (P) 650. |
| 1533 | Lewis Co. Green & Ellis, (P) 650. |
| 548 | Miller vs. Smoot, (P) 6. |
| 445 | Murphy, Evans & Co. vs. London & Townsend, (P) 14, 44, 88, 144. |
| 649 | Magee & Hamilton, (P) 20, 39. |
| 569 | Morris vs. Tate & Thompson, (P) 24. |
| 542 | Morton vs. Williams, (P) 28. |
| 460 | Marks vs. Tooley, (P) 30. |
| 547 | Miller vs. Weston, (P) 32. |
| 439 | Marden vs. Wilcox, garnishee, (P) 34. |
| 530 | Magee & Love vs. Hamilton, guardian, (P) 40, 60, 74, 111. |
| 679 | Morton vs. White, (P) 53, 137. |
| | Munday & Tate, sheriff, deed, (P) 128. |
| 836 | McDaniel, use of Knighten vs. Devilbiss, (P) 131. |
| | Montgomery, J. J., acct. allowed, (P) 138, 229. |
| | Mallory to fine, (P) 139. |
| | Morton, Samuel to sheriff, deed, (P) 146. |
| | Mcaffee, John admitted to practice law, (P) 169. |
| 875 | Morton vs. White, (P) 181, 195, 204, 233. |
| 887 | Mitchell vs. Ball, (P) 184, 196. |
| 910 | McKinney vs. Hamilton, (P) 211, 255, 260. |
| 916 | Major vs. Foree, (P) 223, 245, 275, 308. |
| | Musgrove, sheriff, Clark Co., acct., (P) 229. |
| 1025 | Marion Co. vs. Dunn & Bradshaw (P) 231, 259, 290, 323, 352, 370, 387, 398, 422. |
| 989 | Marion Co. vs. Burch, (P) 235, 283, 306, 520. |
| | Mattingly, John to fine, (P) 237; remitted, (P) 244. |
| | Montillius to sheriff, deed, (P) 247. |
| 988 | Morton vs. White, (P) 256, 284. |
| 1038 | Musgrove vs. Durkee, (P) 256, 295. |
| 1033 | Merrell vs. Taylor, admr., Wright, (P) 264. |
| | McCann, John, naturalization, (P) 273. |
| 1094 | Maquire vs. Huner & Tate, (P) 280. |
| 1099 | Marion Co. vs. Harris & Anderson, (P) 281, 346. |
| 1096 | Martin vs. Mickley, (P) 308, 346. |
| 1103 | Morton vs. Staple, (P) 311, 349. |
| 1104 | Martin, Richd. vs. Johnson, Rush & others, (P) 313, 357, 382. |
| 1127 | Miller, John vs. White, Halsey, (P) 329, 376, 394, 441, 463, 493. |
| | Merrell, A. to deed from shff., Tate, (P) 329. |

| Case No. | Case and Page Numbers |
|---|---|
| 1126 | Miller, John vs. Smoot, Widdleton, (P) 329, 376, 394, 441, 463, 493. |
| | McReynolds, B. vs. Board, J. M., (P) 336, 372. |
| 1153 | McMurty & Bower vs. Cordell, Lewis C., (P) 353. |
| 1181 | Martin, R. C. & Honore vs. Johnson, J. C., (P) 375, 647. |
| 1186 | Miller, John vs. Stevens & others, (P) 383, 403, 443, 462. |
| 1170 | Martin, Richd. vs. Johnson & Rush, (P) 382, 403. |
| 1226 | Morrow, B. vs. Bunton & others, (P) 415, 436, 452. |
| 1261 | McKinney, vs. Turpin, C., (P) 426, 437, 452, 470, 500. |
| 1314 | Martin, Wm. B. vs. Martin, E., (P) 450, 474, 488, 530, 541, 563, 587, 601. |
| 1294 | Magee, A. vs. Ammerman, S. & others, (P) 452, 479, 506, 538, 560, 596. |
| 1287 | Mott & Schobee vs. Reeveley, (P) 466. |
| 1345 | McMain, Haven & West vs. Mitchell, E. W., (P) 475. |
| 1361 | McGander, J. H. vs. Cook, J., (P) 487. |
| 1367 | Magee, A. vs. Ammerman, S., Guard., (P) 507, 538, appeal case. (sic) |
| 1424 | Martin, R. C. vs. Harrison, (P) 570. |
| 1494 | Morgan & others vs. Reveley, M. P., (P) 594, 595. |
| 1460 | Morrow, B. vs. Hilbert J. H., (P) 595. |
| | Magee, A. vs. Stowers (garnishee), (P) 596. |
| | Magee, A. vs. Smith, D. C. (garnishee), (P) 596. |
| | McDaniels & Wills, deed emancaipation to Ness, (P) 605. |
| 1439 | McReynolds vs. Ellis, Seth, (P) 616. |
| 1481 | Manney & Weld vs. Durkee, H. I., (P) 619, 637. |
| 1510 | Martin & Co. vs. Covington, Harper & Co., (P) 641. |
| 1518 | Morrison, Jos. S. vs. Rees, L. & others, (P) 642, 663, 669, 680, 695. |
| 1494 | Morgan, Park & Co. v. Reveley, P. & others, (P) 494 (garnishee), 645, 677, 697. (Note: This case appears earlier.) |
| 1495 | Morgan, McClung & Co. vs. Reveley, M. P., (P) 495 (garnishee), 645, 677, 698. |
| | Missouri, State use town. 60, r. 7 vs. Adams, Chas. & others, (P) 652, 665, 696. |
| | Mitchell vs. Oyster, (P) 667, 674, 702, 704. |

| Case No. | Case and Page Numbers |
|---|---|
| 1553 | Morrison vs. Rees & others, (P) 669. |
| | McDaniel, Jno. vs. Bourie, A., (P) 670. |
| | M'Cabe, Edward, B., sign roll, (P) 670. |
| | Mitchell vs. Skinner, (P) 676, 697. |
| 1555 | Morris & Price vs. Poage, (P) 681 |
| | Mitchell vs. Hollingshead, (P) 700, Motion by Skinner. |
| 1558 | Mitchell, A. M. vs. Oyster, 702, 704. |
| 798 | Nebeker vs. Smith, (P) 98. |
| 792 | Norris vs. Ewing, (P) 127. |
| 866 | Nelson vs. White, (P) 173. |
| 915 | Newton vs. Martin, O'Ferrall & Thompson, (P) 203, 234. |
| 1125 | Norris, W. T. vs. Buckler, M. H., (P) 341, 351, 367, 401, 429. |
| 605 | Owlsey, A. B. vs. Pemberton, (P) 7, 20. |
| 562 | Owlsey, use of Hallowell, Ashbridge, & Co., vs. Durkee, (P) 9. |
| 666 | Osburn vs. Buckland & Webber, (P) 63, 73, 79, 81. |
| 831 | Owlsey, A. B. vs. Munday, (P) 164. |
| 1004 | Oyster vs. Leeper, (P) 199. |
| 1022 | Owlsey, J. B. vs. Ray, (P) 234, 259, 303. |
| 1036 | Oyster vs. Burch, (P) 235, 336, 498. |
| 1035 | Oyster vs. Richardson, (P) 245, 295. |
| | Oyster to deed from sheriff, Tate, (P) 330, 411. |
| | Oyster at (sic) Ammerman, Saml., (P) 377, 384. |
| 1229 | Owlsey, J. H. vs. Patton, J. S., (P) 416, 438, 470, 495. |
| 1238 | Owlsey vs. Hayman & Co., (P) 420. |
| 1266 | Olds, W. E. vs. Frazier, Jno. S., (P) 441, 469, 499, 527. |
| 1324 | Oyster, A., assee., West vs. Stowers, Wm., (P) 461. |
| 1365 | Owlsey, E. vs. Ramsey, S., (P) 468. |
| 1363 | Oyster, A. vs. Drake, J., (P) 507, 544, 562, 573. |
| 1388 | Oyster, A. vs. Shumate, Jas., (P) 520, 556, 584. |
| Trans. | Oyster, A. vs. Shumate & Ammerman, (P) 521, 525, 528, 533, 543. |
| 1408 | Owsley, Duncan & others, use Lillard, admr., Wooden vs. Huner, (P) 525. |
| | Oyster, A. vs. Johnson, John C., (P) 529. |
| 1395 | Oyster, A. vs. Olds, Thos. (P) 545. |
| 1418 | Oyster, A. vs. Olds, Wm. E., (P) 558, 607, 676, 697, 708. |

| Case No. | Case and Page Numbers |
|---|---|
| 1563 | Owsley, J. B. vs. Owsley, exr. Owsley, (P) 699, 703, 710. |
| 1591 | Oyster, A. vs. Lofty, W. & T., (P) 698. |
| 1592 | Oyster, A. vs. Lofty, W. & T., (P) 698. (sic) |
| 1597 | Owsley, Jno. vs. Owlsey, E., exr. of Owsley, (P) 699, 903, 710. |
| 1595 | Oyster, A. vs. Dillon, (P) 709. |
| 1577 | Owsley, Francis vs. Owlsey, E. & others, (P) 710. |
| 1572 | Oyster, vs. Revely & Mitchell, (P) 711. |
| 644 | Porter vs. Howerton, (P) 4. |
| 557 | Parker vs. Durkee & others, (P) 9. |
| 633 | Pritchard vs. Revely & Croughton, (P) 10, 23. |
| 583 | Perkins vs. Pemberton, (P) 14. |
| 627 | Prentice, use of Goodno vs. Jones, (P) 16. |
|  | Pemberton vs. Wolfe, (P) 83, 108, 144. |
| 764 | Poaque vs. Poaque, (P) 96, 102, 112. |
| 813 | Patterson, R. & C. vs. Huner & Tate, (P) 106. |
| 768 | Payne vs. Cooksey, (P) 144, 149. |
| 846 | Plant vs. Maddox, (P) 140. |
| 851 | Pye vs. Bradshaw, (P) 151. |
| 868 | Porter vs. Howerton, Burch, & Leeper, (P) 174. |
| 941 | Poage vs. Sullivan, (P) 190. |
| 944 | Palmer vs. Thomas, (P) 214, 264. |
| 1064 | Perrin vs. Givens & others, (P) 281, 339. |
| 1045 | Plant vs. Martin, (P) 297. |
| 1083 | Patten vs. Bradshaw, (P) 297, 312. |
| 1152 | Parish, Jos. vs. Jackson, Jacob, (P) 327, 334, 355. |
| 1164 | Parson, J. B. & Co. vs. Waltman, A. C., (P) 361, 375, 401. |
| 1171 | Patterson, R. & Co. vs. Benson, J. L., (P) 387. |
|  | Plant, M. W., sheriff deed from Tate, (P) 412. |
| 1335 | Pendleton, Riely & Co. vs. Reeveley, (P) 448. |
|  | Pittsford, Benj. to pet. for naturalization, (P) 453. |
| 1300 | Patterson, E. S., admr., Conley vs. Brown, S., (P) 483, 486, 501, 531, 541, 542, 555, 560, 561, 562. |
| 1374 | Pattee, Geo. W. vs. Dixon, D. B., (P) 520, 531, 536, 563. |
| 1396 | Phillips vs. Comegy, (P) 520, 543, 568. |
| 1473 | Pease & Co. vs. Burne, R. L., (P) 609, 613, 681. |
| 1544 | Price & Morrison vs. Poage, Levi, (P) 617. |
| 1547 | Porter, J. C. vs. Corysee, (P) 678. |
| 668 | Richardson, J. A. vs. Allen, (P) 3. |

| Case No. | Case and Page Numbers |
|---|---|
| | Quinn, admr. vs. Hurt & Wilson, (P) 204, 240, 292. |
| 614 | Rankin vs. Pemberton, (P) 7, 30. |
| 631 | Richardson, Plant & Co. vs. Pemberton, (P) 8, 21. |
| 514 | Richardson, W. P. & Co. vs. Williams, (P) 9, 14, 15, 51, 88, 144, 169. |
| 613 | Rees, guardian vs. Love, (P) 13. |
| 507 | Robbins vs. Burch, (P) 17, 48, 54. |
| | Richardson, Plant & Co. vs. Wolfe, (P) 20. |
| 578 | Richardson vs. Moore. (P) 22. |
| 551 | Ray vs. Smith, (P) 7, 24. |
| | Reese, George to fine, (P) 26. |
| 538 | Revely vs. Miller, (P) 29, 49, 56, 74. |
| | Reese, Addison for George Reese, (P) 34. |
| 665 | Rockhill, J. & Co. vs. Hamilton & others, (P) 72, 709. |
| 799 | Richardson, Plant & Co. vs. Richardson, F. R., (P) 82, 96, 121. |
| 786 | Richardson vs. Moore, (P) 85, 92. |
| 800 | Richardson, Plant & Co. vs. Force, (P) 98, 169, 182. |
| 777 | Reveley vs. Clayton, (P) 104. |
| 785 | Richardson vs. Weldon, (P) 111. |
| 805 | Reddish & Richardson vs. Chandler & Burford, (P) 121. |
| | Rankin, Jas., Coroner's bond approved., (P) 133. |
| 879 | Richardson & Reddish vs. Burford, (P) 180. |
| 936 | Robinson vs. Harrison, (P) 241. |
| 923 | Reddish vs. Stith, (P) 207. |
| 969 | Rees, A. vs. Smith, extrx., (P) 212, 225, 259, 268, 298, 299. |
| 920 | Richardson, Plant & Co. vs. Ray & others, (P) 217, 262, 278, 281, 306, 327. |
| 939 | Reddish vs. Sullivan, (P) 219, 245. |
| 922 | Richardson vs. Sublett, (P) 224, 238, 283. |
| 1023 | Roberts vs. Stower, (P) 237, 259, 289. |
| 1029 | Reeve vs. Webber, (P) 238, 268, 280, 310. |
| 1057 | Richardson vs. Ward, (P) 298, 300, 355. |
| | Reese, A., commissioned Judge, (P) 322. |
| | Reuben, colored man from Briscoe, deed of emancipation, (P) 325. |
| 1154 | Robinson, Wm. vs. Owlsey, Shanks & Bayne, (P) 353. |
| 1158 | Richart, A. L. vs. Baldwin, H., (P) 381, 393, 400, 417, 430. |
| 1322 | Reeves, A. R. vs. Revely, M. P., (P) 466. |

| Case No. | Case and Page Numbers |
|---|---|
| 1231 | Richardson, N. vs. Thompson, H., (P) 392, 407, 411. |
| 1224 | Redding, Sally D. & others vs. Wash & Nunn, (P) 396, 416, 430, 460, 496, 500, 541, 571, 599. |
| | Richardson, sheriff's bond approved., (P) 449, 581, 684. |
| 1301 | Reddish, S. vs. Sullivan, (P) 468, 488, 547. |
| | Ray, Wm. C., deed from late sheriff, Sublett, (P) 478. |
| | Richardson, J. A., acct. alld., (P) 484, 513, 552, 581, 602, 652, 684. |
| | Redd, John T., deed from Richardson, sheriff, (P) 510. |
| 1386 | Ralls, Jacob C. vs. Dixon, D. B., (P) 520, 559. |
| 1390 | Reveley vs. Weston & McKinney, (P) 523, 543, 571, 588. |
| | Rankin, coroner, ack. deed to Green, J. S., (P) 531. |
| 1370 | Roberts, H. vs. Ayres, Jeptha, (P) 551, 552, 561, 568, 579. |
| 1377 | Robinson vs. John, H. J., (P) 552, 575. |
| | Roberts, H. vs. Ayres, Editors' acct. allowed, (P) 568. |
| | Roberts, H. vs. Reddish, J. B., garnishee, Ayres, (P) 579. |
| 1491 | Reveley vs. Stonebreaker, (P) 620, 655. |
| | Roberts, admr., Richardson vs. Rush, admr., Staples, (P) 621. |
| 14-5(?) | Runnyan, Hillman & Co. vs. Harper, P. & E., (P) 624. |
| 1507 | Rockhill & Co. vs. Creighton, Harper, & Co., (P) 641. |
| 1567 | Rogers & Barney vs. Comegy, J. W., (P) 646, 671. |
| 599 | State vs. M'Lean, (P) 1. |
| 632 | Safford vs. Chandler, (P) 6, 14, 22, 60, 93, 116, 146, 170, 193, 288, 326, 358, 380, 386, 399, 439. |
| 624 | Souther vs. Lillard, (P) 6, 51, 56. |
| 531 | State vs. Harper, (P) 8. |
| 628 | Spraque & Co. vs. Huner & Tate, (P) 9, 23, 62, 86. |
| 635 | Skinner vs. Mills, (P) 28, 38, 56. |
| 651 | State vs. Bowles, (P) 18, 42. |
| 652 | State vs. Hughes, (P) 18, 43. |
| 653 | State vs. Rash, (P) 18, 42. |

| Case No. | Case and Page Numbers |
|---|---|
| 654 | State vs. Green, (P) 18, 27, 43. |
| 655 | State vs. Staples, (P) 19, 45. |
| 656 | State vs. Ellis, (P) 19, 44, 48. |
| 657 | State vs. Rodefer, (P) 19, 45. |
| 658 | State vs. Curd, (P) 18, 45. |
| 659 | State vs. Hall, (P) 18, 45. |
| 660 | State vs. Easley, (P) 19, 45. |
| 661 | State vs. Forge, (P) 18, 43. |
| 662 | State vs. Fraizer, (P) 18, 43. |
| 663 | State vs. Bozarth, (P) 18, 47. |
| 664 | State vs. Ayres, (P) 19, 46. |
| 639 | State vs. Lee, (P) 24, 31, 35. |
| 670 | Sheriff Sublett vs. Hiskell, (P) 29, 57. |
| 577 | Stanlinias & January vs. Cushman & Pritchett, (P) 32. |
| 407 | Shropshire & Owlsey vs. Bryan, Redman & Haylin, (P) 33. |
| 409 | Skinner vs. Lillard, Force & others, (P) 35. |
| 410 | Skinner vs. Force, Durkee 7 others, (P) 36. |
|  | Sheriff Sublett, deed to Barkley, (P) 39. |
|  | Sheriff allowed acct., (P) 41, 77, 129, 189, 229, 271. |
| 721 | State vs. Pearson, (P) 50, 118. |
| 703 | State vs. Garrett, (P) 50, 104. |
| 719 | State vs. Garner, (P) 50, 118, 157. |
| 720 | State vs. Lane, (P) 50, 122, 157. |
| 718 | State vs. Rees, (P) 50, 126. |
| 717 | State vs. Simpson, (P) 50, 118, 138, 167, 195. |
|  | Stiter, Price & Co. and Bryan, Redman & Haylin vs. Owlsey & Cooksey, (P) 55. |
| 743 | State vs. Davis, (P) 57, 126, 157. |
| 744 | State vs. T. Haydin, (P) 57, 124, 142. |
| 754 | State vs. Cummins, (P) 57, 81. |
| 757 | State vs. Wright, (P) 57, 126. |
| 690 | State vs. Coleman, (P) 57, 78, 130, 167. |
| 712 | State vs. Munday, (P) 57, 116, 156. |
| 713 | State vs. Huner, (P) 57, 119, 134. |
| 710 | State vs. Love, (P) 58, 127, 158. |
| 708 | State vs. Thompson, (P) 58, 117. |
| 702 | State vs. Allen, (P) 58, 100, 104, 158. |
| 706 | State vs. E. Nelson, (P) 58, 122, 132. |
| 762 | State vs. Geo. Reese, (P) 58, 75. |
| 731 | State vs. Wm. Hayden, (P) 58, 124, 157. |
| 745 | State vs. A. B. Owsley, (P) 58, 120, 136. |
| 746 | State vs. Fuqua, (P) 58, 123, 158. |
| 753 | State vs. Eversotte, (P) 58, 120, 160. |
| 705 | State vs. Hiram, (P) 59, 115, 159. |
| 758 | State vs. T. Rash, (P) 59, 68. |

| Case No. | Case and Page Numbers |
|---|---|
| 714 | State vs. Magee, (P) 59, 107, 109, 123, 136, 150, 156. |
| 709 | State vs. Dance, (P) 59, 122, 132, 134. |
| 760 | State vs. Lillard, (P) 59, 70. |
| 759 | State vs. Tompkins, (P) 59, 68. |
| 734 | State vs. Sublett, (P) 59, 119, 125, 152. |
| 716 | State vs. J. H. Owsley, (P) 59, 112, 160. |
| 715 | State vs. Hinkson, (P) 59, 115, 137, 138, 150, 156. |
| 761 | State vs. Henderson, (P) 60, 75. |
| 729 | State vs. Hudson, (P) 63, 124, 143. |
| 730 | State vs. G. D. Tolls, (P) 63, 124. |
| 747 | State vs. Wm. Hayden, (P) 63, 124, 159. |
| 723 | State vs. Wash, (P) 63, 123, 158. |
| 728 | State vs. Jas. Hamstead, (P) 63, 118. |
| 724 | State vs. Shackleford, (P) 63, 118, 152. |
| 725 | State vs. H. Nelson, (P) 63, 123, 160, 168. |
| 732 | State vs. S. Nelson, (P) 63, 119, 142. |
| 733 | State vs. John Hamstead, (P) 63, 121. |
| 726 | State vs. Tate, (P) 63, 105. |
| 727 | State vs. Botts, (P) 63, 124, 141. |
| 736 | State vs. Hagood, (P) 64, 81. |
| 735 | State vs. Musick, (P) 64, 119, 142. |
| 722 | State vs. Brisco, (P) 64, 122, 159, 168. |
| 737 | State vs. Becket, (P) 64, 119, 152, 192. |
| 738 | State vs. Burchfield, (P) 64, 125, 152. |
| 739 | State vs. N. D. Tolls, (P) 64, 125, 152. |
| 740 | State vs. West, (P) 64, 120, 161. |
| 741 | State vs. A. Bourne, (P) 64, 125, 160, 169. |
| 704 | State vs. John Hayden, (P) 64, 117, 130, 168. |
| 749 | State vs. Million, (P) 64, 120, 136. |
| 755 | State vs. Bowles, (P) 64, 113, 141. |
| 752 | State vs. E. Thompson, (P) 65, 125, 151. |
| 711 | State vs. Ball, (P) 65, 115, 158. |
| 701 | State vs. J. Hamilton, (P) 65, 97. |
| 756 | State vs. Wm. L. Smith, (P) 65, 126, 151. |
| 691 | State vs. Miller, (P) 65, 78. |
| 699 | State vs. Baker, (P) 65, 92. |
| 69-(?) | State vs. Wine, (P) 65, 80, 192. |
| 692 | State vs. Martin, (P) 65, 79. |
| 696 | State vs. Ramsey, (P) 65, 84, 92. |
| 694 | State vs. H. Thompson, (P) 65, 78, 143. |
| 697 | State vs. Young, (P) 65, 84, 130. |
| 689 | State vs. Austin, (P) 66, 79. |
| 698 | State vs. Williams, (P) 66, 85. |
| 748 | State vs. Colley, (P) 66, 113, 157, 171. |
| 695 | State vs. Herringe, (P) 66, 84. |
| 700 | State vs. White, (P) 66, 93. |

| Case No. | Case and Page Numbers |
|---|---|
| 742 | State vs. W. L. Smith, (P) 66, 117, 139. |
| 751 | State vs. Fuqua, (P) 66, 112. |
| 750 | State vs. H. Thompson, (P) 66, 78, 146, 151, 167. |
| 707 | State vs. Sublett, (P) 66, 116, 117, 138. Sheriff Sublett ack. deed to Ellison, Glover & Wright, Wright & McDaniel, and Mitchell & Williams, (P) 7. |
| | State vs. Hill, (P) 85. |
| 789 | Stewart vs. Huner, (P) 91, 175, 180. |
| 819 | State vs. Brown, (P) 94, 153. |
| 820 | State vs. Scarlet & Colbert, (P) 94, 153. |
| 580 | Shultmin & January vs. Love, (P) 95, 135, 146. |
| 821 | State vs. Cobb, (P) 103. |
| | Sheriff Sublett ack. deed to Tate, Munday, Hagood & Stith, (P) 128. |
| | Stith, Mary D. to deed ---- (?), (P) 129. |
| 760 | State vs. D. M. Lillard, (P) 132. |
| | Sheriff bond approved, (P) 132, 304. |
| 853 | State vs. Johnson & Warner, (P) 135, 154, 155, 176. |
| 854 | State vs. Warner, (P) 135, 154. |
| 855 | State vs. Johnson & Warner, (P) 135, 154, 155, 177. |
| 856 | State vs. Johnson, Wm., (P) 135, 153. |
| | State vs. Mallory, (P) 139, 185. |
| | Sheriff Sublett deed to Morton, Easton, Ellison, Dryden, Green & Huner, (P) 146, 147. |
| 823 | Sinclair vs. Pritchard, (P) 155, 162, 175, 192, 198, 210, 218, 226, 231. |
| 829 | Stith vs. Brady, (P) 163, 185. |
| 874 | Sublett vs. Allen, (P) 171, 179. |
| | Sheriff (late) Sublett deed to McMasters, (P) 171; Durke, H. J., (P) 178; Blair, (P) 183; Buckland, (P) 182. |
| 892 | State vs. Bigelow, (P) 172, 177, 178, 181, 188. |
| 862 | Stith vs. Richardson, (P) 173. |
| 894 | State vs. Quimby, (P) 176, 177, 181, 190, 193, 231, 235. |
| 896 | State vs. White, (P) 176, 208. |
| 895 | State vs. Escue, (P) 176, 191. |
| 877 | Smith vs. Richardson, (P) 179. |
| 897 | State vs. Ells, (P) 176, 192. |
| 878 | Sublett vs. Magee & Cummins, (P) 180. |
| 883 | Sappington vs. Ray & Brown, (P) 186, 217. |
| | Sheriff Tate ack. deed to Green, (P) 187. |
| | Smooot, Middleton to sheriff deed, (P) 201. |

| Case No. | Case and Page Numbers |
|---|---|
| 886 | Sublett & Campbell vs. Owsley & Gregory, (P) 182, 219. |
| 898 | Samuel Jamerson & Co. vs. Forman, admr., Pemberton, (P) 196. |
| 993 | State vs. Murphey, (P) 202, 206, 237. |
| 994 | State vs. Triplett, (P) 202, 204, 236, 277, 281, 284, 304. |
| 995 | State vs. Zimmerman, (P) 202. 230. |
| 992 | State vs. Hall, (P) 202, 230. |
| 1001 | State vs. Roberts, (P) 204. |
| 1003 | State vs. Coleman, (P) 205. |
| 1005 | State vs. Hamilton, (P) 205. |
| 987 | Smith, admr. vs. Becket, (P) 207. |
| 963 | Sowers vs. Colley, (P) 213, 257. |
| 961 | Sowers & Thompson vs. Colley, (P) 213, 234, 284, 306, 328, 361, 394, 421, 449, 508, 519, 553, 582. |
| 940 | Smith vs. Stowers, (P) 220. |
| 912 | Stowers vs. Martin, (P) 222, 262, 275. |
| 900 | Stevens vs. Turpin, (P) 222. |
| 909 | Smith vs. Bridewell, (P) 223. |
| 983 | Sinclair vs. Marks, (P) 226, 254. |
| 314 | Smith vs. Davis, (P) 226. |
| 1076 | Stillman & January vs. Smith, (P) 230. |
|  | Sheriff Tate, deed to Thompson, H., (P) 236; Hayman, (P) 267. |
| 1039 | State vs. Mitchell, White & others, (P) 238, 239, 290, 291, 301, 307, 322. |
| 1041 | State vs. Rodefer, (P) 239, 247, 278, 279, 291, 293, 299, 302, 310, 312, 321, 324, 332, 362. |
| 1040 | State vs. Green, (P) 239, 277. |
| 1034 | Sublett vs. Moore & others, (P) 244, 282, 325, 365, 397, 439, 456. |
| 1042 | State vs. Rodefer, (P) 246, 310, 333. |
|  | Sheriff Sublett, deed to Montillin, (P) 247; to Sublett, P., (P) 6, 263. |
| 991 | Smith vs. Bridewell, (P) 256. |
| 1016 | Stiltman & January vs. Smith, (P) 266, 287, 309. |
| 589 | Smith, E., extrix. vs. Richardson, (P) 269. |
| 1044 | Staples vs. Staples' heirs, (P) 270, 301, 314. |
| 1039 | State vs. Gay, (P) 272. |
| 1049 | Slaughter vs. Seebe, (P) 296, 313, 352. |
| 1091 | Skinner vs. Bourne, (P) 297. |
| 1055 | Skinner vs. Smith & Alford, (P) 300. |
| 609 | Taylor vs. Ray, (P) 6, 13, 26, 31, 38, 62, 142. |

| Case No. | Case and Page Numbers |
|---|---|
| 444 | Tucker vs. Owsley, (P) 15, 17, 108. |
| 650 | Triplett vs. Biggs, (P) 44, 73, 88. |
| 541 | Tucker vs. Owsley, (P) 46, 93, 127, 145, 188, 223, 232, 276. |
| 667 | Tucker vs. Owsley, (P) 67, 74, 111, 112, 127, 145, 187, 223, 232, 275. |
| 807 | Thompson vs. Green, (P) 105. |
| 775 | Trask vs. Huner, (P) 106. |
| | Tate & Munday to sheriff, deed, (P) 128. |
| 830 | Tate & Munday vs. Colley, (P) 131, 161, 174, 224, 248, 261, 270. |
| | Tate, C. B., sheriff, bond approved, (P) 133. |
| 864 | Triplett vs. Bozorth, (P) 143, 183. |
| 867 | Thompson vs. Colley, (P) 173, 204. |
| 902 | Turner vs. Bigwood, (P) 196. |
| 935 | Tompson vs. Givens & Reddish, (P) 197, 241. |
| 984 | Thompson, Hancy vs. Poage, (P) 201, 210. |
| 924 | Thompson, Hancy vs. Beckner, (P) 211, 340. |
| 962 | Thompson, Sowers & Co. vs. Colley, (P) 213, 257. |
| | Thompson, Harvey to sheriff, deed, (P) 236. |
| 1018 | Taylor vs. Given & Branch, (P) 245, 266, 290, 309, 331, 390. |
| 996 | Taylor, admr. vs. Merrill, (P) 263. |
| | Tate, C. B., to acct., (P) 271, 302, 321, 359, 419. |
| 1083 | Thompson & Co. vs. Bradshaw, (P) 297, 312. |
| 1095 | Thompson & Morton pet. for mill, (P) 302, 317. |
| 1109 | Trotter vs. Bryant, S. C., (P) 326. |
| | Taylor, John, deed from shf., Tate, (P) 330. |
| | Turner, Wm. H., deed from shf., Tate, (P) 330. |
| 1114 | Thompson, H. vs. Ray, M. & Brown, H. & I., (P) 352, 366, 401. |
| | Thompson, Harvey from Tate, shff., deed, (2), (P) 371. |
| 1149 | Tate, sheriff vs. Lewis Co., (P) 357, 372, 383, 411, 417. |
| | Turner, Wm. H. from Tate, sheriff, deed, (P) 387. |
| 1225 | Turpin, Chas. vs. Snodgrass, Jos., (P) 390. |
| 1209 | Taylor & Paulding vs. Benson & Blakely, (P) 393, 418, 440. |
| 1222 | Tevis, Scott & Tevis vs. Hughes, J. N., (P) 390, 401, 418, 522, 542, 556, 553. |
| | Thompson, S. C., attorney, enrolled, (P) 449. |
| 1326 | Tevis, Scott & Tevis vs. Hotsenssiller & Agee, (P) 450, 483, 507. |
| | Tompkins, Preston, notice to, (P) 492, 536. |

| Case No. | Case and Page Numbers |
|---|---|
| | Throckmorton, Thos., (P) 492. |
| 1392 | Trotter, Jos. S. vs. Poage, Levi, (P) 532. |
| | Tate, Site T., deed from sheriff, Sublett, (P) 535. |
| 1425 | Tate, C. B. vs. Hagood, admr., Prism, (P) 559, 592. |
| 1560 | Tillinghast vs. Coryell, (P) 643. |
| 1538 | Thompson, Jno. S. vs. Coryell, Jno. R., (P) 655. |
| 685 | VonPhul & McGill vs. Lillard, (P) 55, 82. |
| 999 | VanAllen vs. Eastman, (P) 234. |
| 1302 | VonPhul & McGill vs. Reevely, (P) 449, 450, 467, 488, 502, 537. |
| 1303 | VonPhul, H. vs. Turner, Wm. H., (P) 450, 504, 539, 557. |
| 501 | Wood & Abbott vs. Hance & Tate, (P) 10. |
| 351 | Wash vs. Allen & Cecil, (P) 12. |
| 630 | White vs. Owsley, (P) 13, 52. |
| | Weller, Jesse, pet. for naturalization, (P) 25, 272. |
| 539 | Wright vs. Austin, (P) 38, 48. |
| 592 | Walsh, J. & E. & Co. vs. Pemberton, (P) 54, 60, 144. |
| | Witnesses recognized, (P) 73, 116. |
| 774 | Woods, Christy & Co. vs. Long, (P) 70, 102, 106, 141, 183. |
| | Woodyard, H. M., permitted to practice law, (P) 81. |
| 802 | Woods, Christy & Co vs. Owsley, A. B., (P) 83, 156, 185, 216. |
| 812 | Warburton & King vs. Wilson, (P) 91. |
| 814 | Webster & son vs. Huner & Tate, (P) 91. |
| 794 | West vs. Merill, (P) 97. |
| 772 | Williams & Mitchell vs. Reveley, (P) 97, 102, 133, 134, 148, 183, 194, 235. |
| 803 | White vs. Huner & Tate, (P) 99. |
| 793 | Williams vs. Finley, (P) 128, 165, 170. |
| 850 | White & Co. vs. Henderson, Plant & Co., (P) 131, 133, 139, 140, 150. |
| | Ward vs. Richardson, (P) 137. |
| 824 | Withers & O'Shaughnessy vs. Crooker & Richart, (P) 162. |
| 876 | Wigginton vs. Durkee, (P) 181, 218, 225, 250, 255, 277, 288, 305, 308, 325, 378. |
| 884 | Wilson & Stuart vs. Owsley & Cooksey, (P) 186. |
| 885 | Wright vs. Wright, (P) 188. |
| 1105 | Wheeler & Meriwether vs. Hughes, (P) 209. |
| 977 | Womack vs. Maffett, (P) 211, 253. |

| Case No. | Case and Page Numbers |
|---|---|
| 1007 | Wurt, Musgrove & Wort vs. Camegy, (P) 227, 277. |
| 911 | Wigginton vs. Bates, (P) 22, 235, 274. |
| 925 | Wurt, Musgrove & Wort vs. Henderson, Plant, & Co., (P) 222, 242. |
| 589 | Wood & Oliver vs. Forman, adm. Pemberton, (P) 228, 440, 479, 510, 528, 558, 576, 666. |
| 485 | Williams, Ben P. & Co. vs. Hamilton, Magee et al, (P) 238. |
| 1032 | Wood vs. Moorehead & Singleton, (P) 266, 300, 317, 336, 363, 395, 425, 455, 465, 494, 522. |
|  | Wood & Oliver from sheriff, Sublett, deed, (P) 294. |
| 1056 | White vs. Eulton, (P) 296. |
| 1119 | Wright, W. T. vs. Taylor, admr., Wright, (P) 313. |
| 1148 | Wiley, Tho. vs. White, Halsey, (P) 335, 381. |
|  | Wright, W. T. from Tate, sheriff, deed, (P) 341, 410. |
| 1121 | Woods, Stacker & Co. vs. Johnson, Rush & others, (P) 343, 368. |
|  | Wells, Carty, appointed cir. atto. pro-tem, (P) 364, 494. |
| 1168 | Warburton, Doan & Co. vs. Stith, J. H., (P) 368. |
| 1193 | White, H. vs. Felix, W. G., (P) 382, 407, 418, 436, 473. |
| 1233 | Wurts, Musgrove & Wirts vs. Comegys, S. W. B., (P) 404. |
| 1207 | Warner, W. A. vs. Poage, L., (P) 406, 419, 427, 439, 453, 472, 494. |
| 1242 | Wurts, Musgrove & Wurts vs. T. S. Richardson, (P) 422. |
| 1234 | West & Vandeventer vs. C. Durkee, 438, 460, 493, 538, 600, 606, 635, 681. |
| 1290 | White, G. vs. Trotter, G. W., (P) 467. |
| 1321 | Wurts, Musgrove & Wurts vs. Reevely, (P) 469. |
| 1264 | Wood & Oliver, deed from Sublett, late sheriff, (P) 471. |
| 1355 | Wilson, W. vs. McMurty, J., (P) 485, 529. |
| 1358 | Waltman, admr. vs. Wright, (P) 487, 531. |
|  | Wurts, Musgrove & Wurts, deed from Richardson, shff., (P) 501. |
|  | Woodyard, H. M., 4 (sic) deeds from sheriff Richardson, (P) 511, 512, 513. |
| 1411 | White, Dixon & others vs. Trotter, (P) 522. |
|  | Wilson, Wm. C. vs. Wooden, Josh, (P) 572. |
| 1413 | Waltman vs. Doyle & Skinner, (P) 578. |

| Case No. | Case and Page Numbers |
|---|---|
| 1387 | Watts, Nelson Durkee, C. & others, (P) 571, 584. |
| 1448 | White, Halsey vs. Johnson Oferral, (P) 585, 614, 638, 666, 668, 681. |
| 1428 | Wilson, Wm. C. vs. Wooden, Joshua, (P) 594, 608, 636, 645. |
| 1435 | White, John vs. Spalding, V., (P) 602, 612, 644. |
| | Williams & McDaniel, deed emancipation to Wess (?), (P) 605. |
| 1498 | Walsh, J. & E. vs. Magee, C. R., (P) 606. |
| | Wagoner, Daniel, permitted to enroll as atty., (P) 610. |
| 1462 | White, H. vs. Cooksey, (P) 618. |
| 1523 | Withrow vs. Nelson, (P) 635, 640, 669, 678, 694. |
| | Williams vs. William, Chas., (P) 642. |
| 1539 | Woodyard, admr., Harper vs. Coryell, J. R., (P) 650. |
| 1522 | Walterman, A. C. vs. Hollingshead, (P) 657, 671, 699. |
| 1513 | Woodyard, admr., Hamilton vs. Hagood, admr., Smith, (P) 659. |
| | West, Richd. vs. Kate Kearney, (P) 653. |
| 1542 | Woodyard, admr., Hamilton vs. Becket & others, (P) 651, 665, 696. |
| | Woodyard, admr., Harper, E. vs. Coryell, (P) 679, 695. |
| 1570 | Wilson, Wm. vs. Baker, H., (P) 688, 698, 709. |
| 1571 | Williams, Ben & others vs. Williams, Chas. & others, (P) 689, 709, 712. |
| | Rawlings, S. A., enrolled as atty., (P) 693. |
| | Richart vs. Woodyard, (P) 716. |
| 551 | Yates vs. Smith, (P) 7, 24. |
| | Yore, John, pet. for naturalization, (P) 265. |
| 1540 | Yeatman, Pitman & Co. vs. Fore, O. L., (P) 632, 645, 675, 695. |
| | Young, A. & Co. vs. Croughton, R., (P) 649, 681, 708. |
| | Yates vs. Lafon, (P) 707. |
| | Young & Co. vs. Bartlett & others, (P) 708. |
| 505 | Sappington vs. Miller, (P) 306. |
| 1102 | Shannon vs. Martin & others, (P) 306, 341. |
| 1113 | Skinner vs. Marks, (P) 306. |
| | Sheriff (Tate) deed to Bayne & Anderson, K. P., (no page numbers stated) |
| 1107 | Sappington vs. Mitchell, Thos., (P) 312, 346. |
| 1116 | State vs. Cannon, N., (P) 319. |

| Case No. | Case and Page Numbers |
|---|---|
| 1115 | State vs. Bayne, Tho., (P) 320. |
| 1117 | State vs. Parsons, J. B., (P) 320, 323. |
| | Spoe. duces tecum (sic) to Agee, esq., (P) 321. |
| 1159 | State vs. Jackson, Jacob, (P) 322, 390. |
| 1161 | State vs. Bland, James, (P) 323. |
| | Sheriff late (Sublett) deed to Devilbies, John, sen., (P) 323, |
| | Sheriff (Tate) deed to Devilbies, John, sen., (P) 324, 399. |
| 1115 | State vs. Baynes, Thos., (P) 329. (sic) |
| 1116 | State vs. Cannon, N., (P) 329. (sic) |
| | Sheriff, Tate, to deed, Merrill, A., (P) 329. |
| | Sheriff, Tate, to deed, Taylor, Jno., (P) 330. |
| | Sheriff, Tate, to deed, Turner, Wm. H., (P) 330. |
| | Sheriff, Tate, to deed, Daviss, Louisa A., (P) 330. |
| | Sheriff, Tate, to deed, Oyster, A., (P) 330, 411. |
| | Sheriff, Tate, to deed, Skinner, W. P. & C. S., (P) 331. |
| 1159 | State vs. Jackson, Jacob, (P) 322, 331, 333, 360, 363, 364, 370, 372, 388, 390, 394, 417, 428, 433, 449, 453, 460. |
| 1163 | State vs. Conover, (P) 333. |
| | Sheriff, Tate, to deed, Wright, W. T., (P) 341, 410. |
| 1102 | Shannon, John vs. Martin, W. B.; Thompson, H.; O'Ferrall, John, (P) 347. |
| 1128 | Smith, E., extrix. vs. Richardson, P., (P) 348. |
| 1097 | Smith & Duncan, admr. vs. Ray, M. & I., (P) 349, 373. |
| 1755 | Smith & Duncan, admr. vs. Cannon & Jefferies, (P) 353, 373. |
| | Smith & Duncan, admr. vs. Myers, Jno., (P) 354, 387. |
| | Sheriff, Tate, to deed, McDaniel, John, (P) 354. |
| | Sheriff, Tate, to deed, Rush, Wm. M., (P) 355. |
| 1173 | Sullivan, Thos. vs. Sullivan, James, (P) 361, 391, 435. |
| 1199 | State vs. Parsons, J. B., (P) 362, 374, 419. |
| 1202 | State vs. Durkee, C., (P) 362, 365, 394. |
| 1200 | State vs. Bourne, H., (P) 362, 393, 432. |
| 1201 | State vs. Conduitt, P., (P) 363, 377, 394, 430, 453. |

| Case No. | Case and Page Numbers |
|---|---|
| | Sheriff, Sublett, to Dryden, J. D. S., deed, (P) 370. |
| | Sheriff, Tate, to Blair, J. H., deed, (P) 370. |
| | Sheriff, Tate, to Thompson, H., deed, (P) 371. |
| 1183 | Sowers, Peter J. vs. Bradshaw, Smith, (P) 375, 379, 409. |
| 1190 | Slaughter, R. V. vs. George Seeben, (P) 377, 379, 409. |
| | Sheriff, Tate, to deed, James Ellison, (P) 378. |
| | Sheriff, Sublett, to deed, Charles S. Skinner, (P) 378. |
| 1182 | Sowers, P. J. to Porter, James, (P) 385. |
| | Sheriff, Tate, to deed, Wm. H. Turner, (P) 387. |
| | Sheriff, Tate, to deed, Bland, Chas. & Benj., (P) 387. |
| | Scott, Tevis & Scott vs. Hughes, I. N., (P) 401, 418. |
| 1212 | Smith, Elizth. vs. Richardson, J. A. & F. R., (P) 408. |
| 1221 | Shanks, Jno. vs. Beckner, A., (P) 409. |
| | Sheriff, Tate, to deed, Glover, S. T., (P) 412. |
| | Sheriff, Tate, to deed, Plant, M. W., (P) 412. |
| | Sheriff, Tate, to Green, J. S., (P) 412, 413. |
| | Sheriff, Tate, to O. Hurt, (P) 413. |
| | Sheriff, Tate, to H. M. Woodyard, (P) 413, 414, 415. |
| 1204 | Sherwood, Jno. vs. Sutherland, A. N., (P) 415, 431, 473, 493. |
| 1195 | Stuart, A. H. vs. Ligon, (P) 416. |
| | Stith, sheriff bond, approved, (P) 420. |
| 1279 | State vs. Davis, Isaac, (P) 423, 426. |
| 1278 | State vs. Hamilton, J. B., (P) 424, 427. |
| 1259 | Smith, E. vs. Hayman & Co., pet. in det., (P) 425, 444. |
| 1275 | State vs. Baker, (P) 427, 460. |
| 1277 | State vs. Cordell, (P) 427, 459, 486. |
| 1276 | State vs. Jones, (P) 428, 461, 486. |
| 1247 | Smith, E. vs. Hayman & Co., asst., (P) 430. |
| 1269 | Sublett, asse., Stinnett vs. Hagood, admr., Parsons, est., (P) 433, 480. |
| 1267 | Smith, E. vs. Ammermman, (P) 435, 470, 488, 500, 508. |
| | Sheriff, Sublett, deed to, J. S. Green, (P) 434. |
| | Sheriff, Sublett, deed to, C. Rice, (P) 434. |

| Case No. | Case and Page Numbers |
|---|---|
| | Sheriff, Sublett, deed to, Isaac Briscoe, (P) 434. |
| | Sheriff, Sublett, deed to E. Finley, (P) 435. |
| 1260 | Stephens, I. vs. Turpin, (P) 437, 469, 499. |
| 1249 | Smith, E. vs. Ellison, Jas., (P) 444. |
| | Sheriff, Tate, deed to, E. Harper, (P) 445. |
| | Sheriff, Stith, deed to C. Durkee, (P) 445. |
| | Sheriff, acct. alld., (P) 445. |
| 1308 | Sickels, G. W. vs. Slaughter, R. V., (P) 449. |
| | Sunderland, Thomas, attorney, enrolled, (P) 449. |
| 1295 | Smith, D. C. vs. Ammerman, S. & others, (P) 451, 479, 510, 538, 586. |
| 1293 | Smith, Girard vs. Ammerman, S. & others, (P) 452, 472, 506, 521, 550, 560. |
| 1337 | Scott & Marsell vs. Reveley, M. P., (P) 454; garnishee, (P) 640, 645, 677. |
| | Sheriff, Richardson, deed to, J. A. Blair & Co., (P) 463. |
| 1340 | State vs. Tudor, A. B., (P) 463, 487, 522. |
| 1341 | State vs. Hughes, R. B., (P) 464, 487, 518. |
| 1343 | State vs. Smith, C. W., (P) 464, 487. |
| 1342 | State vs. Dasbach, H., (P) 464, 485, 521. |
| | Sheriff, Sublette, (late), to deed Wood & Oliver, (P) 471. |
| | Sheriff, Richardson to deed Johnson, J. A., (P) 477. |
| | Sheriff, Tate to deed Wurts, Musgrove, & Wurts, (P) 477. |
| | Sheriff, Tate, to deed, Henderson, A. J., (P) 478. |
| | Sheriff, Sublett to deed Ray, Wm. C., (P) 478. |
| 1285 | Sayre, E. K. vs. Thomas James, (P) 481, 489, 506, 533, 535. |
| 1312 | Stout, H. D., use, Kills vs. Stewart, A., (P) 481. |
| | Sheriff, Richardson to deed Ellis, Wm., (P) 482. |
| 1288 | Sayre, E. K. vs. Thomas Massey, (P) 483, 505, 534. |
| | Sheriff, Richardson, to deed Ellis & Richart, (P) 483. |
| | Sheriff, Richardson, acct. alld., (P) 484, 513, 552, 710. |
| 1354 | State vs. McMurty, Jas., (P) 488. |
| | Sterrett, A. D., notice to, 492, 536. |
| 1364 | State vs. Northcraft, (P) 492, 519. |
| 1371 | State vs. Kendall, S. B., (P) 495. 530. |

| Case No. | Case and Page Numbers |
|---|---|
|  | Spalding, J. vs. McKee, (P) 497. |
|  | Sheriff, Richardson, deed to, Wurts, Musgrove & Wurts, (P) 501. |
| 1366 | Smith, D. C., guard. vs. Ammerman, S., (P) 508, 510, 521  540; appeal case. |
|  | Sheriff, Richardson, deed to, Redd, John T., (P) 570. |
|  | Sheriff, Richardson, (4), deed to, Woodyeard, H. M. , (P) 511. |
| 1236 | Bates, M. D. vs. Johnson, J. C., (P) 444, 465, 647. |
| 1208 | Baker & Brothers vs. Benson, (P) 444. |
|  | Bayne, A. C., emancipate, slave, Bryant, (P) 448. |
| 1296 | Brown, S., admr. vs. Conley, S., (P) 451, 499, 537, 569. |
| 1297 | Brown, S., admr. vs. Baker, J. W., (P) 451, 499, 537, 569, 586. |
| 1328 | Bank vs. Tate, C. B., (P) 455, 476. |
|  | Blair, J. H., deed from sheriff, Richardson, (P) 463. |
| 1291 | Brown & Owens vs. Reveley, (P) 466. |
| 1284 | Bowman, G. B. vs. Hotsenssiller & Ellis, (P) 467. |
| 1333 | Bank vs. Dunbar, Blair & Ward, (P) 485, 494. |
| 1329 | Bank vs. Reddish & Caldwell, (P) 502. |
| 1330 | Bank vs. Olds, Hamilton & others, (P) 502. |
| 1359 | Bank vs. Martin, O'Ferrall, Woodyard, (P) 503. |
| 1334 | Bank vs. Nelson, N., (P) 503. |
| 1332 | Bank vs. Williams & Riddle, (P) 503. |
| 1353 | Bank vs. Richardson, J. A. F. R. & N., (P) 503, 544, 569, 648, 667. |
| 1352 | Booth, J. W. vs. Munday, (P) 507, 542, 571, 584. |
|  | Benson vs. Nelson, Jas., (P) 519, 521, 542, 569. |
|  | Bates, Henry to naturaliation, (P) 524. |
|  | Bank vs. Owlsey, A. B., (P) 545, 569. |
|  | Bank vs. Kelsoe, J. A., (P) 545. |
|  | Blair, J. G., clerk, acct. allowed, (P) 552, 581, 603, 624, 684, 667. |
|  | Broadwell, S. L. vs. Givens, Blair & others, (P) 555, 556, 594, 604, 647. |
|  | Boure, Whitfield, manumit, slaves, (P) 556. |
|  | Bland, Jas. W. vs. Oferral, Chas. & others, (P) 585, 618, 638. |
|  | Bullard, Geo. W. vs. Shaw, W. N., (P) 586, 589, 592, 593, 609, 612. |

| Case No. | Case and Page Numbers |
|---|---|
| | Boume, F. & D. vs. Cox, Jas. M., (P) 587, 597. |
| | Bank vs. Hotsenssillar, (P) 594, 644. |
| | Bowen vs. Durkee, (P) 604. |
| | Bank vs. Dureel, Ront & others, (P) 613. |
| 1484 | Bowles & Young vs. Hinson & others, (P) 613, 648. |
| | Bohen, W. & Jas. vs. Hollingshead, (P) 616, 640, 643. |
| 1471 | Beach & Eddy vs. Hughes, J. N., (P) 619. |
| | Bank vs. Magee, C. R. & others, 61, 96. |
| 1493 | Brewer, Jane vs. Durkee, Chauncey, (P) 621. |
| | Bohon, W. J. vs. Seaman & Nelson, (P) 624, 640. |
| | Beckner & others vs. Beckner & others, (P) 629, 658, 680, 674. |
| 1519 | Blair, J. G. vs. Lurdel, Peter, (P) 632, 638, 648, 664, 665, 694, 702. |
| 1509 | Brinton, R. B. & Co. vs. Croughton, Harper & Co., (P) 641. |
| | Boume, Rebecca vs. Boume, Wm. Estate, (P) 641. |
| | Bruford (?), Wm. to emancipate slave, (P) 646. |
| | Barker, Jno. L. vs. Singleton, Geo. C., (P) 648, 661. |
| | Bank vs. Stith, Roberts & Ellis, (P) 700. |
| | Bank vs. Durkee, L. & R., (P) 700. |
| | Bank vs. Woodyard, Gavn., & H. J. Durkee, (P) 701. |
| | Buckels vs. Owlsey, exr., Owlsey, (P) 703, 707. |
| | Sheriff, Richardson, deed, to H. M. Woodyard, (P) 512. |
| | Sheriff, Richardson, deed to Glover, S. T., (P) 512. |
| | Sheriff, Richardson, deed to Woodyard, H. M., (P) 513. |
| 1406 | State vs. Gill, Robert, (P) 527, 553. |
| 1407 | State vs. Jackson, Jacob, (P) 528, 554. |
| | Sheriff, Sublett, ack. deed to Tate, Lite, T., (P) 535. |
| 1404 | Sullivan, Thos. vs. Lillard, Ford & others, trustees, (P) 544, 570. |
| 1375 | Stimpson vs. Dazy, (P) 550, 551, 557, 577, 578. |
| 1429 | State vs. Herring, Robt., (P) 557. |
| | Sheriff, Tate, ack. deed to Hagood, admr., Parsons, (P) 563. |
| | Sheriff, Tate, ack. deed to Pattee, Geo. W., (P) 563. |

| Case No. | Case and Page Numbers |
|---|---|
| | Sheriff, Tate, ack. deed to Blair, Jos. H., (P) 564. |
| | Sheriff, Tate, ack. three deeds to Woodyard, H. M., (P) 564. |
| | Sheriff, Richardson, ack. deed to Wallace, John, (P) 565. |
| | Sheriff, Richardson, ack. deed to Hughes, J. C., (P) 566. |
| | Sheriff, Richardson, ack. deed to Woodyard, H. M., (P) 566. |
| | Sheriff, Richardson, ack. deed to Smith, Elizth., (P) 566. |
| | Sheriff, Richardson, ack. deed to Durkee, C., (P) 566. |
| | Sheriff, Richardson, ack. two deeds to Ellis, Wm., (P) 567. |
| | Sheriff, Richardson, ack. deed to Rousseau, Richd., (P) 567. |
| | Sheriff, Stith, by deputy, ack. deed to Woodyard, H. M., (P) 567. |
| 1421 | Shotter, admr., Fresh vs. Long, David, (P) 574, 593, 608, 637. |
| | Stimpson vs. Owsley, garnshe., Dazey, (P) 578. |
| 1452 | Sprague, A & W & Co. vs. Hayman, (P) 584, 610, 613, 636. |
| 1466 | State of Mo. vs. Charles Adams, (P) 589, 605. |
| 1465 | State of Mo. vs. Wainright, Danl. T., (P) 590, 608. |
| 1467 | State of Mo. vs. Kidwell, John, (P) 590, 609. |
| 1446 | State of Mo. vs. Dolly Vandepool & Smothers, (P) 590. |
| 1469 | State of Mo. vs. Roul, E. & Ross, Thos. D., (P) 590, 605, 632, 634. |
| 1468 | State of Mo. vs. Owen & Tumes, (P) 590, 606. |
| | Sheriff (late) Tate to shff. deed to J. D. S. Dryden, (P) 590. |
| | Sheriff (late) Tate, error in deed to Woodyard, (P) 600. |
| | Sheriff, Richardson, acknowledgement deed to George Forrest, (P) 601. |
| | Sheriff, Richardson, acknowledgement deed to Chancey Durkee, (P) 601. |
| | Smith, D. C. vs. Stowers, Thos., Wm. & others, (P) 604, 606, 612, 622. |
| | Salisbury & Co. vs. Cluff, (P) 606. |
| | Sheriff, Richardson, ack. deed to Pugh, M., (P) 610. |
| 1268 | State vs. Coryell, Jno. R., (P) 634. |

| Case No. | Case and Page Numbers |
|---|---|
| | Sheriff, Richardson, ack. deed to Sinclair, Susan, (P) 610. |
| | Sheriff, Sublett, ack. deed to Harrison, Cal, (P) 610, 614. |
| 1474 | Skinner, C. S. vs. Marshall, admr., Kennock, (P) 611. |
| 1487 | Shepherd vs. Clow, A. W., (P) 614. |
| | School lands, sale postponed, (P) 614. |
| | Sheriff, Richardson, ack. deed to Hume, Jas., (P) 614. |
| | Sheriff, Richardson, ack. deed to Woodyard, (P) 616. |
| 1488 | Seaman & Briggs vs. Bryan & others, (P) 617, 640, 674. |
| | Skinner vs. Trusslett, Geo. M., (P) 617. |
| | Sheriff, Richardson, ack. deed to, Lillard, (P) 617; Bright, (P) 622, two deeds; Nall, (P) 623; Redd, (P) 623; Haycraft, (P) 623; Durkee, (P) 623. |
| 1203 | State vs. Johnson, Josiah, (P) 626, 631, 633, 634, 652. |
| 1202 | State vs. Kirk, Elvin & Wm. C., (P) 626. |
| 1204 | Staples vs. Shanks, H. W., (P) 627, 657, 683. |
| 1561 | Sherwood vs. Haggerty, (P) 647, 670. |
| | Sheriff, Richardson, ack. deed to Anderson, Thos. L., (P) 652. |
| 1527 | Smith, R. vs. Thompson & Martin, (P) 654. |
| 1505 | Staples, Danl. & Robt. vs. Staples, George (minor), (P) 657. |
| 1569 | State of Mo. vs. Bowman, (P) 669, 685, 687. |
| 1584 | Seaman, D. vs. Nelson, Jas., (P) 673, 698, appeal. |
| 1548 | Seaman, D. vs. Byrne, Nelson, & others, (P) 674, 696, 697. |
| | Sheriff, Richardson, ack. deed to Wagner, (P) 674. |
| | Scott & Marshall vs. Reveley, T., garnishee, Reveley, M. P., (P) 677. |
| | State vs. Priscilla Cannon (negro), (P) 685. |
| | Sheriff, Richardson, ack. deed to Forrest, (P) 685. |
| | Sheriff, Richardson, ack. deed to Henderson, C. F., (P) 684. |
| | Sheriff, Richardson, to Durkee, L & R, (P) 687. |
| | State vs. A. Boume, (P) 693. |
| 1619 | State vs. Sesaw, (P) 699, 701. |
| | State vs. Clark, J. M., (P) 703. |

| Case No. | Case and Page Numbers |
|---|---|
| 1606 | State vs. Ewalt, Jno. (P) 703. |
| 1611 | State vs. Hinton, W., (P) 703, 704. |
| 1614 | State vs. Oyster, A., (P) 703, 705. |
| | Sheriff ack. deed to Magee, (P) 704. |
| 1607 | State vs. Nelson, Geo., (P) 704, 706, gaming house. |
| 1609 | State vs. Wadkins, E., (P) 704. |
| 1610 | State vs. Hinkerson, Jno., (P) 705. |
| 1608 | State vs. Nelson, Geo., (P) 705, 707. |
| 1612 | State vs. Muse, H., (P) 705. |
| 1613 | State vs. Pettit, G. K., (P) 705. |
| 1615 | State vs. Graves, Elias, (P) 705, 710. |
| 1618 | State vs. Dasback, H., (P) 705, selling liquor on Sunday. |
| | State vs. Walterman, A. C., (P) 705. |
| 1617 | State vs. Chaney, W., (P) 705. |
| 1618 | State vs. Dasbcak, (P) 706. (sic) |
| | State vs. Revely, M. P., (P) 706. |
| | Sheriff, Richardson, ack. deed to Bates, W. S., (P) 714. |
| | Sheriff, Richardson, ack. deed to Magee, Tho., (P) 716. |
| | Sheriff, Richardson, ack. deed to Lakeman, R. F., (P) 717. |
| | Sheriff, Richardson, ack. deed to Ellis, Wm., (P) 717. |
| | Sheriff, Richardson, ack. deed to Atchison, S., (P) 717. |
| | Sheriff, Richardson, ack. deed to Dawson, J. M., (P) 717. |
| | Sheriff, Richardson, ack. deed to Woodyard, H. M., (P) 717. |
| | Sheriff, Richardson, ack., deed to White, Jno., (P) 717. |
| | Sheriff, Richardson, ack. deed to Oyster, A., (P) 718. |

## Lincoln County, Missouri, Delinquent Tax List, 1843, Capitol Fire Documents, CFD 33, Folder 1599.

George Anson, Mathew Anderson, Alexander Anderson, Wm. H. Anderson, Anna Alexander, James Alexander, Alexander Alexander, Joseph B. Arthur, George Admire, James C. Admire, Wm. M. Admire, Thomas H. Admire, Joseph Abbott, Katherine Adkinson, Robert B. Allen, Presley Anderson, A. B. Bell, Constantine Bruce, A. S. Buchanan, Lewis Barker, James Blair (same for 1842), Bluford Behtel, Benjamin Berry, Harrison Bricoe, Harrison Blair, Layton Bradley, Augusta Bradley, A.B. Brown, James Baird, R. M. Barns, David Barley (crossed out), James

Bartlett, Jacob Brunk, David Brunk, William Bell, Armenius Briscoe, Samuel Briscoe, James M. Barker, Jonathan Baugh, J. A. Blackamore, Samuel Briscoe (sic), G. S. Burns (for 1842), Robert Bryan, John Barley, James Blanks (same for 1842), G. A. Bowen, Elisha Blailess, David Boid, Jeffery Beck, Samuel Blackmore, Chapman Bethel, John Bethel, Bledsoe Butler, John Blackaby, Elijah Buckhanan, Edwin Benet, J. H. Basket, James Bridge, Benjamin Blanton, John Colbert, Peleg (sic) Calvin, Preseley Coonrod, Samuel B. Craig, John Copenhauer, James Cochran (crossed out), O. N. Coffey, George Custer, William Crouch, John Carter, J. C. Cornwell, D. H. Capps (same for 1842), Thomas Capps (same for 1842), Wm. Cantrell (same for 1842), Hiram J. Cochran, Adam Coose, Frances B. Clare, Allen Clare, Felix Collard, A. B. Cruse, W. G. Collins, George H. Copper, A. C. Chandler, William Cook, Nancy Crouch, Nathan Coteney, James Calloway, James M. Calloway, James Carter (same for 1842), Wm. S. Cooper, James Creech, Joshua Creech, John A. Cupee, Thos. I. Conner, Wm. H. Crenshaw, Thos. Carr, John Crouch, Alvora Cottle, Adm., of Ira Cottle, jr., Isaac Collins, Jonathan B. Carr, Uriah Creech, Wm. T. Carter (same for 1842), John Cross, James H. Crouch, John Crocuh, Jacob Coffey, Whitson Cox, Benjamin Capps, Dabney Carr, Andrew Cunningham, Henry Cox, L. C. Carr, M. S. Degarme, James Day, Warren Dunivan, George Delger, George Dull (same for 1842), Nicholas Drumheller, Fielding Dawson, Robert Duff, Nicholas Dudley, J. S. Dumphy, Joseph Dyer, Seymore Davis, jr., Thos. Dutton, Stephen Darien, Samuel Davis, Robert Daniels, Thos. Earnest (same for 1842), Charles Dulaney, Elbert Earnest, J. M. Edmuns, Phoebe Estes Jacob Eddleman, Jane Earnest, John Earley, Aloysius Edlin, Larkin East, A. H. East, Wm. Elman, John Earley, Myes Evers, Wm. L. Elsberry, Thos. Ezzell, Job Flemming (same for 1842), Rufus Ellis, Josiah Fuller (same for 1842), Samuel Foster, Rachel Ford, John T. Ficklin, Jas. Ferguson, Beverly Foster, Elzet Foxwell, Wm. Frazier, Wm. P. Fisher, Elizabeth Fyfer, Benjamin Fisher, Samuel Farmer, Wm. Gordon, David E. Ferguson, James Foster (for 1842), Richard Gilleland, Thos. Grason, Matthias Gilleland, Jesse R. Gilleland, Christopher Gilpin, Dennis Galloway, James Green, John Goodrich, Hiram Gammon, McCoy Gruen, James H. Grant, Henry Generous (same for 1842), Benjamin Grant, Clifford Glavez, John M. Gwinn (same for 1842), George W. Gardner (same for 1842), George W. Graves (same for 1842), John Galloway, Joel Henry, James Gale, Malin Goodwin, Rufus Gibson, Elijah Galloway, J. M. Garner, George F. Gibbs, Margret Hall, Daniel Hall, William Hudson (crossed out), Thornton Hancock, George W. Huston, Richard H. Hill, Margaret L. M. Hagannan, William M. Harper (crossed out), B. F. Hesser, F. M. (?) Heisen, Wm. Hiler, Robert Harper, Samuel Huston, Calvin Huston, Beverly Harvey (same for 1842), Samuel Hall (same for 1842), Robert

Howell, Elizabeth Haff, Hugh Hall, Calvin Harral, John Henderson, Nathan Hall, snr., Nathaniel Hall, Joseph Ham, John Hill, Samuel Hall (sic), Charles Hall, Michael Herring, Andrew Hall, George W. Hardesty, Richard Harrell, Andrew Hill, Alexander Hill, Alexander Hill (agent for Thos. Hill, same for 1842), Malcom H. Hill, N. H. Hardin, Walker Hopkins, A. H. Hardin, Edward T. Hayslip, Lewis Hopwood, John Hitehouse, Martin Hammack, Mary Hammack (twice assessed, one paid), Wm. Jamison, Lemuel Holmes, Isaac Houston (same for 1842), James Hines, James Hobbs, John Hines, Jonathan Ingram, David Jamison, John Jonson, David A. Jamison, Robert Jaison, Absalum Jones, John Johnson (sic), Gilleam Jamison, John Jones, Ira kingsberry, Bryant Jeffery, George W. Jenkins, Duncan Jackson, Benjamin Kinion (crossed out), Matthew Knox, David Killer, Erasmus Knowleton, Wm. Knowleton (same for 1842), James Knox, Thos. Kennedy, John Keithlty, Chedister Lewis, Larkin Larence, Nelson Locker, Dvid Lafity, Elizabeth Lewis, Zadoc J. W. long, Hamilton Lay, W. W. Lewis C. M. Lacamp, Isaac Linn, Luther Linn, Richard Lawrence, Joseph Lennery, James Miller, Eliza Lucket (same for 1842), J. M. Luckett, Wm. S. Ligon, F. M. Lucket, Francis Mudd, Thos. N. Mudd (same for 1842), Jesse Morris, Lawrence Morris, William Morris, John Myers, Wm. Mitchel, John H. Martin (same for 1842), Anderson J. Martin, B. G. Martin, A. W. Mena, John Moroon, Austin Moore, Thos. McGowen, Rufus Moulder, William Mann, Alexander H. Martin (for 1842), William McCammel, John W. McKee, Thos. Maury, Wm. McMaham (same for 1842, 80 acres), Nathaniel Marvin, David Morris, Mary Myers, Robert McClanahan, Crawford McNear, A. B. Moss, T. K. Marsh, Thomas A. Miller, Ezekiel McDonald, Martin Myers, Hiram McDonald, John H. Morgan, John Morgan, Thos. P. Money, Cornelius Money, Wm. McKinney, R. M. Martin, Elijah Myers, Alexander Myers, Elijah Myers jr., T. Z. Martin, Alexander Martin, Peter Mavaratto, David Neil, Loyd L. McAtee, Andrew Newchruch, Thos. Nordike, Henry Owen, Hiram Neil, Squire Northcut, Cyrus Nichols, Thos. Norval, James Owen, William Owen, James Porter (same for 1842), John Paxton, Rachel Poor (same for 1842), Enoch Philips, John C. Pace, Mary Paxton, Joseph G. Powel, Jacob Pollard, Josep. C. Prewett, Thos. Pharris, W. M. Page, J. W. Payne, George Porter, J. W. Powel George Parsons, Adam Pine, Reuben Palmer, James Patterson, R. L. Patterson, Christian Profater, Thos. Poor, A. J. Poor, A. H. Poe, J. H. Parsons, Isaac Price, W. F. Price, Lucy Parsons, Avington Perkins, B. F. Philips, W. K. Roberts, John Parker, James Reasons, John Roberts (same for 1842), Deborah Renolds (sic), Woodson Reynolds, Washington Reynolds, David Reynolds, Thos. Ray, Michael Ramsower, John Ramsower (crossed out), John M. Reeds, J. W. Ransdale, Thos. A. Reid, Michael Reids, William Rossin, W. H. Roper, A. M. Ramsower, James H. Reid, Eli J. Rybolt, B. C. Ray, F.

W. Rose, Joseph Russel, Johnson Riley, Nancy Robertson (for 1842), Nancy Robertson, agent for Horatio Robertsons' heirs, William V. Ray, Benjamin R. Robertson, Lewis Riffle, Francis Riffle, agent for Saml. Denny, George Reid, Thos. Reid, Wm. C. Ricks, John Shrum, Z. Z. Sitton, John J. Steele, Elizabeth Sitton, E. G. Sitton, E. G. Sitton, agent for Wm. Triplett, H. W. Sperry (same for 1840 (sic)), Jesse Smith, Enoch Sevier, John Shannon, Isaac Springston, Isaac Springston, T. P. Stone, Peter Springston, Wiley Snider, Wm. Spradlin, John Shaw, Robert Shaw, Francis Sweeney, Thos. Shaw, W. A. Salley (crossed out), Napoleon Shaw, Samuel Smithers, Thos. Stublefield, Valerius Saunders, Elizabeth Smith, James Shaw, F. W. Sieper, Thomas Stone, Robertson Seymore, Leven O. Scot, J. H. Sidebottom, Henry Simmonds, David Stonisode, Cyrus Swan, George C. Smith, George Stonebreaker, George Shear, Caswell, Snead, David Shelton (for 1842), Thomas I. Stout, Thos. E. Smith, J. W. Settles, T. J. Sitton, J. W. Sitton, Matthew Sapp, Thos. Shumate (same for 1842) Malinda Sheburn (same for 1842), Thos. Sales, Leonard Sales, R. Suddarth, Lewis Suddarth Ira Suddarth, David Stonebreaker, George H. Smith, Wm. J. Thompson, Charles Thomasson, A. C. Thomas, Elizabeth Thomasson, Abner True, Lemuel O. Tucker, Wm. Tailor, Thomas Triplett, David C. Terry, Elizabeth Thomasson, Jonathan Tipton, Barnabas Thornhill, Simeon Thornhill (same for 1842), James F. Thomasson, Chancy Tuttle, John Turnbull, Henry Tipton, George Turnbull, James Tailor, Wm. J. Tally, Thos. Tiller, James Thornhill, John H. Triplett, T. J. Turner, James Taylor, James Taylor (sic), Archibald Taylor, J. S. Wilson, Isaac Uptegrove, senr., Armstead Uptegrove, Wm. Uptegrove, snr., Wm. Uptegrove, jnr., Bruffet Vincent, Alexander Vancar, James C. Verdier, Wesley Vandiver, William Vaughan, Nathaniel Williams, James A. Wren, Wm. Wade, Micajah Wheeler, William Whiteside, James Wilson, Shadrach Woodson, J. T. White, Jonathan Wood, Warring H. Walton, James Willis, Wm. Wade, Joseph Wright, Jesse Ward, Washington Wright, Wm. Washum, jnr. (same for 1842), Morgan Wright, jnr., Jackson Williams, Wm. Washum, senr. (same for 1842), John Wright, Charity Winters, Samuel Winters, Richard Wells, Robert Ware, Thos. E. Wells, John Wilkinson, Mathew Worthington, Thos. J. Wright, junr., Noah Willis, John Wilder, Garry Yale, Joseph Youngblood (for 1842), Carson D. Young, George W. Young.

Chariton County, Missouri, Delinquent State and Advalorum Tax, October Term, 1842, Capitol Fire Documents, CFD 33, Folder 1600.

Peter T. Abell, Wm. Carson & Co., B. English, Moorehead & Jacobs, Wm. R. Redding, Danl. Baughman, John Beatty, Weber & Parsons, Dutch Pedler (a footman), C. Usher (dram shop), F. Bade (foot pedler), R. Beazley & Co., Jas. C. Davis, Felix

Applegate, Wm. R. Allin, --- Conwell, I. R. Horsley, Claghorne & Co.

Johnson County, Missouri, Delinquent Tax List, 1843, Capitol Fire Documents, CFD 33, Folder 1602.
James Andrews, Solomon Abberson, Washington Bryant, James Bryant, Benj. F. Bailey, Daniel Buckner, Jesse Brewer, James Booker, Obed Bays, George W. Beck, John Bradshaw, Jeremiah Crowley, Isaac Bledsoe, James Bradshaw, Joseph Campbell, Wm. R. Crigger, Charles Childers, David Coffman, Henry Carle, William Crigger, Jessee Demasters, William Demasters, Foster Demasters, Augustine Demasters, Henderson Denning, Benj. S. Derrett, Benj. Dulany, Lewis Dunning, William Dillingham, Archibald Cunningham, Henry Danzey, John Daniel Enos Ellis, John Epperson, Thomas Emmerson, George Fitch, Johhnson Fitzgerald, John Fine, Henry Frazer, Martin P. Foster, James Finely, John Ferrin, Waston Forbus, Thomas Foster, Jonathan Fox, Stephen Gibson, Thomas Gennings, John B. Gibson, Margaret Gibbs, John B. Gibbons, William P. Hults, Alfred Henson, William H. Harris, William Hudson, Henry Hayslip, Richard Hullard, Dennis N. Hubbard, Dury Hurn, Andrew H. Harny, Wm. Johnson, Jesse Harrison, Joseph Hall, Richard Job, Daniel Kimbro, --- Kirkpatrick, Robert B. Lunford, David Lynch, Ira McCleland, William B. Moore, Justian Mills, Polly Mulkey, Elizabeth McCowan, Calvin Merrill, Charles Marcum, Joseph Morgan, John S. Mulkey, James Mulkey, William Ore, Thomas R. Odell, William Rutledge, Petere Star, Frederick Thurman, Wm. Todd, Clinton Thomas, Alfred Wooliver, Landy Westmoreland, William Wheeler, Bevil Whitworth, Findel Whitworth.

Jackson County, Missouri, Licenses, February Term, 1844, Capitol Fire Documents, CFD 33, Folder 1629.

| Name | Type | Issued | Expires |
|---|---|---|---|
| James McCountney | Inn & Tavern | Oct. 7, 1843 | Oct. 7, 1844 |
| A. Ritchtens | Grocery | Nov. 18, 1842 | May 18, 1844 |
| Wilsin Roberts | Grocery | Nov. 17, 1843 | May 17, 1844 |
| Lewis Vozle | Grocery | Nov. 17, 1843 | May 17, 1844 |
| M. L. Kutseo | Dram Shop | Nov. 17, 1843 | May 17, 1844 |
| R. H. McCountney | Merchant | Nov. 20, 1843 | May 20, 1844 |
| Wm. E. Shuster | Merchant | Nov. 6, 1843 | May 6, 1844 |
| E. A. Price | Merchant | Nov. 11, 1843 | May 11, 1844 |
| M. W. Burnben | Merchant | Dec. 1, 1843 | Jun. 1, 1844 |
| Saml. C. Owens | Merchant | Jan. 1 1844 | Jul. 1, 1844 |
| McCoy & Lee | Merchant | Jan. 1, 1844 | Jul. 1, 1844 |

Callaway County, Missouri, Delinquent Tax List, 1843, Capitol Fire Documents, CFD 33, Folder 1701.
William Armstrong, J. K. Allen, Benj. Anderson, S. T. Allen, P. G. Anderson, Wm. H. Allen, Wm. Acre, William Adams,

W. H. Adams, J. H. Adcock, Alfred Barrow, Joseph Bennett, Prestone Byers, J. A. Barnes, Abram Baker, William Bright, James Burks, Francis Banes, John Baysinger, R. H. Branch, Jefferson Branch, Michael Bumes, David Bowes, W. C. Bagby, Silas Barnes, David Drite, J. W. Barry, H. C. Berry, admin. for R. Berry, Felix Bryan, Alginion (?) Bryan, Geo. S. Boone, M. Blackburn & son, John Blunkall, R. M. Broughton, E. W. Baker (27 a, 89 a, 80 a), Robt, Burkee, Nathl. Bradford, Wm. A. Bethall, Abram Brake, John Burdit (40 a), Mathew Boswell (84-76/100 a), Mathew Bogan (40 a), James Caldwell, J. M. Combs, John Carrel (?), Jacob Crowson, Auston Corley, Edward Corley, Wm. Corley, J. Clingman, John Crags, B. D. Collins, W. Cannada, Alex. Causdan, M. Crawford, Madison Cruce, Thos. Cambell (sic), I. R. Crago, W. G. Collins, J. L. Clanton, Richard Curtis, Newman Clanton, David Craig, D. B. Davis, Thomas Davis, Ralph Dunn, Dangerfield Dunn, Francis Davis, Francis Driller, Peter Davis, Thomas Day, J. R. Daniel, Peter Day, D. L. Dunnigan, Beverly Drunkam, John Dougherty, Charles Dougherty, Jas. Deven, P. N. Doran, Hugh Dougherty, mathew Dougherty, W. Drake, J. M. Duckworth, John Dearing, D. M. Darn (40 a), Truman Day, James Dunsmore, Edward Davis, James Davis, T. L. Douglas, J. W. Duane, John Ellis, Saml. Edge, Peter Eisenhour, James Estes, Jacob Elder (39 a), Jas. Evans (40 a), John Evans, J. W. Edge, Cirus Easley, James Evans (sic), Abram Echart, James Elam, William Evans, Thos. Estes, James Fitzmaster, J. A. Freelly, James Foster, Perry Fleming B C. Fleming, J. C. Fleming, Nicholas Foy, N. A. Freeman, John Farnon, Thomas Free, George Foster, Nicholas Fry, Jas. Forguener, Thos. Fooche, Jas. W. Findley, D. L. Fabour, Y. J. Fox, Andrew Farrur, Macy Fowler, Asa Farrur, J. C. Gilmore, James Gibbs, George Gray, George Givens, R. D. Gray, Melinda Gray, E. A. Goodrich, J. W. Gray, Lucy Garrett, David Goodemon, Benj. Graham. Saml. Gibbs, R. F. Gregory, L. M. Glaver, H. T. Garham, Hezekianh Gatrell, George Hedges, W. M. Hatton, John Harvey, John Humphreys, Mathew Hall, Abner Hall, Samuel Hall, Chester Howard, William Huston, Skiles Halm, Henry Harper, James Hazebrigg, Samuel Hooker, L. L. Hukerson, John Hufington, Sampson Harison, Thos. Humphreys, Joshua Hufington, George Hufington, James Harvey Hardin Huchison, Samuel Hannah, Willis Hall, Lorenzo Hutts, May Hays, Peter Harris, George Harris, Samuel Hanley, M. G. Harrison, Stephen Hunt, John Jolley, T. G. Jones, Zachariah Jones, Henry Jones, George Johnson, John Kirkham, John Kelsey, Thos. Kimbrough, Fleming Kerley, A. J. Link, R. A. Litteral, Thos. Langley, Elis Lewis, Asa Lomar, John Langley Moses Langley, Andrew Langley, Anthony Limbar, Gorge (sic) W. Loyd Andrew Link, James Larson, Johnathan Langdon, James McKamey, George W. Lewis, Elizabeth Laren, Gabriel Lillard, Cornelius Langley, William Langley, J. W. Miller, Russell

Madin, George Morton, Francis McDonnald (40 a), John Mosby, James McKamy, Jas. McKamy (sic), John McIntire, Stephen Mosley, Jos. Mosley, N. B. McGuffin, Kenny King, A. Millikim, Mary Martin (56 a), Isaac Moore, William Miller, James Miller, Moses McClintock, James McCausland, Andrew McLaughlin, John McClaske, James Miller, Preseley Moore, D. B. McClure, James McKnight, Joel McConnel, A. Mattingly, James Miller, Isaac Maggart, Harvey McRoberts, Steph. Maddox, John Moore, David McKinney, Alford Newman (40 a), Thomas N--y, Garland Nichols, Miller Nunn, Azariah Nunn, A. B. Nantz, Barty Nichols, Berry Old, W. D. Oldham, Thos. H. Oliver, Linch Owen, E. M. Overfelt, Wiet Pace, Mary Ann Pace, J. H. Pawly, Henry Pulliam, John Price, Otho Rumbarger (82 a, 42 a, 42 a), Wm. Ross, Jos. Rittenhouse, Lewis Starks, George Sacrce, Ciphers Selby, Levi Smith, J. W. Smith, George Smith, David Scruggs, J. T. Smith, Benj. Sexton, Thos. Sloan, J. T. Smart, Thaden Southwood, A. N. Sanders, B. D. Suggett, W. W. Suggett, John Seal, Timothy Scruggs, Timothy Scruggs (sic), James Shobe, H. J. Spud, James Steel, G. S. Scott, Aaron Stephenson, Reuben Stewart (80 a), Thomas Stokes (80 a), Shelton Smith, M. Stockbarger, Robt. Scarbaraugh, William Scott, Elias Spicer, James Sanders, Elijah Steel (40 a), J. H. Tutt, G. G. Tutt, Andrew K. Tutt, D. H. Thompson (97 a), Jos. Thomas, William Thomas, Jos. Tuck, Richard Turner, James Terrel (40 a), M. H. Tindal, Saml. Tharp, W. M. Trimble, R. C. Tate, Zacahriah Tucker, R. C. Tate, C. W. Tate, J. H. Turner, John Tate, Wm. Thomas, William Underwood, J. H. Underwood, R. H. Vaugh, M. B. Vandam, E. H. Willet, Russell Ware, J. M. Wade, Thompson Walton, Benj. Wheeler, Alex Wright, Francis Watkins, William Washam, R. C. White, Richard Williams, Frederick White, Y. G. Walker, William Whitson, Paul Woods, Andrew Wiley, John Wadley, William Wallace, William Welch, W. P. Williams, Amos Wilcoxen, Robt. Williams, John Wardly (?), Araman (?) Wilcoxen, Oswell Williams, Harvey Wilcoxen, Stacy Woods, W. M. Walton, Jas. Woods, Jas. Woods (sic), Blagdon Wood, Archibald Williams, John Watson, T. R. Wrem, J. C. Young, Anthony Zumwalt, Frederick Zumwalt.

Portland Town Lots: John Purdett, Ambrose Brush, Daniel Gralbreath, Frances Driller, David Kirkham, Allen Nash.

Fulton Town Lots: J. Kennett, Joel McConnel.

<u>Jefferson County, Missouri, Runaway Slave Notice, December 19, 1844, Capitol Fire Documents, CFD 33, Folder 1702.</u>

A negro calling himself, John Kelty, about 40 years old, 5 feet, 7-1/2 inches tall, with large teeth and a large mouth and a dark complexion was apprehended as a runaway slave by Aaron Henry of this county. He was committed to jail on December 12, 1842 and advertised as the law directs. He was sold on April 15, 1844 to Thomas Moss for $264. Said

Aaron Henry charged $19.25 for catching the runaway. A bill of $156.75 was presented for keeping said slave in jail. M. Moss, sheriff, December 19, 1844. (Note: On the outside jacket of this document the negro's name is stated as Jack.)

Lafayette County, Missouri, Delinquent Tax List, 1844, January Term, 1845, Capitol Fire Documents, CFD 33, Folder 1703
Thomas I. Allen, Wm. Brown, Alexander K. Bishop, George W. Barrett, Samuel Bell, David Black, William Bell, James M. Brady, J. G. Berlin, Richard Boatman, Nancy Boatman, Joseph Browning, John Boykin, Vincent Browning, Robert H. Benson, Silas Backster, A. M. Chadwick, Harrison Crouch, John Cowan, Fleming Cox, Joh--- C. Dyer, John Dean, James L. Forsythe, James M. Fishback, John M. Fry, John Farris, Thos. Farris, John Grant, William Grant, Horace Goshen, Lewis Grant, Adam K. Reyburn, James L. Roberts, Samuel B. Shearer, Alvin Inow, Peter B. Stratton, George W. Stever, John Kerby, George B. Webb, Nathan A. Speer, Palmer Goselin, Presley Gilbert, John Hackney, Marshall Goshen, Joseph Good, Seonidus Giddings, George W. Herr, Isaac N. Hays, William R. Hays, Robert Hill, Jno. C. Helm, Christopher Jenks, Ann Mrrow (sic), William J. marshall, James C. Morehead, Maxwell Majors, Dandridge Morrow, Joshua Morehead, N. J. McAshan, Isaac Knight, Franklin Ores, Thomas Overton, Pleasant Powell, William Powell, Levi Perkins, Levi Perkins, agent for John Perkins, Henry Lison, Thomas Palmer, John T. Richardson, Thomas W. Reynolds, Chas. Williamson, William Sally, William Sanders, Samuel Tilford, George A. Thomas. R. W. Wilmot, H. Willey, Stephen White, B. G. Weaver.

Saline County, Missouri, Licenses, September Term, 1845, Capitol Fire Documents, CFD 33, Folder 1728.

| Name | Type |
| --- | --- |
| Jos. Huston | Grocery and Tavern |
| Jesse McMahan | Merchant |
| Jos. Hewit | Merchant |
| M'Daniel & Scott | Merchant |
| Strode & Donald | Merchant |
| Saml. J. Heron | Merchant |
| Wm. Hooke | Merchant |
| H. S. Mills | Merchant |
| McDnaiel & Turner | Merchant |
| N. Dickerson | Dram Shop and Merchant |
| J. A. J. Adderton | Merchant |
| Geo. Perrin | Merchant |
| Wm. R. McLeare | Tavern |

Ste. Genevieve County, Missouri, Aggregate Statement, 1845, Capitol Fire Documents, CFD 33, Folder 1728.
William Adams, Jesse B. Robbins, I. N. Littlejohn.

Johnson County, Missouri, Aggregate Statement, 1843, Capitol Fire Documents, CFD 33, Folder, 1601.
Isham Reece, Zachariah T. Davis, Thos. R. Wiatt.

Linn County, Missouri, Aggregate Statement, November, 1843, Capitol Fire Documents, CFD 33, Folder 1602.
Jeremiah Phillips, Enoch Kemper.

Lewis County, Missouri, Delinquent Tax List, 1842, December, 1843, Capitol Fire Documents, CFD 33, Folder 1606.
John Anderson, Geo. Arrowsmith, Stephen Ammison, Wm. B. Anderson, James Ayres, Samuel Allen, James Anderson, A. C. Bargo, James Bland, Daniel Broz, Washing. Broz, C. C. Blackston, Daniel Barger, William Beckett, William Brown, William Barnett, Lewis Busby, Thos. Baker, Wm. Bunton, Ephriam Blizzard, William Batton, Samuel Basder, Gilbert Brooks, James P. Charlton, Elizabeth Creasy, Alexander Cooper, W. P. Clow, John Camegy, William Cook, Dangerfield Coakley, John Curl, William A. Creacy, R. L. Cummins, Nimrod Curtis, W. H. Cummins, James H. Cannon, John Carson, John Collett, F. H. Duncan, Joseph Dodge, Harrison Davis, John Duncan, Maddison Downing, Isaac D. Davis, Frosty English, William Evans, Tho. B. Eads, Lewis Eads, G. Everzal, Alxandry (?) Ellis, Alford Eacers, H. C. Eskiel, J. W. Furman, John Fitzwater, Henry Floyd, Thos. Francis, Cabet Furquim, Wm. Fitzsimon, John Fu-Gate, R. C. Falkner, William Frank, James Fosset, James D. Glinn, John F. Glass, W. G. Foley, W. S. Gasway, Mourning Hart, Burton Grubb, John A. Gashart, M. E. Green, W. R. Harris, Thos. Hayden, H. Humphrey, John Humphrey, Collin Holmes, Isaac L. Hurrald, Eli House, Benjamin G. House, Patrick Henry, B. W. Higgings, Walter G. Hutson, Peter A. Hall, Robert Hering, J. C. Hatheway, C. Hagerman, Abraham Hide, John Hamilton, Philip Humble, Elrdige Haley, James Hutchison, J. L. Jenkins, David Jacob, Benjamin Jones, Rhueben Jeffers, R. Kemerman, Jeremiah Judson, Sanford Kendall, David Key, David Ledford, Randolph Keith, Rheubin Lane, John Lancaster, Geo. Lovel, Zacharias John Laning, James Lovel, Charles Reese, W. C. Ray, John M. Ray, Lewis Roderfer, Wellington Rogers, John Roberts, James Roberts, David Roderfer, sr., Benjamin Robinson, Andrew Reed, Silas Ramsey, Silvinus Rice, Geo. Sankes, Lewis Roberts, Martin Roberts, Samuel Serring, Alex Smith, Jacob Stephens, Oliver Stephens, William Smith, David Smith, Joshua Sankes, Geo. Shumbarger, John Smith, Grant Stowers, C---th Smith, John M. Strather, --- Shepherd, Joseph Stratton, Couty (?) Smithring, Joseph Stewart, Geo. Woodson, Wm.

Walker, Samuel Allen, Isaac Knott, William Allensworth. Geo. Arrowsmith, John Allingsworth, W. F. Asbury, Thos. Adams, R. L. Agee, Robt. G. Allen, Christopher Appleton, James Austin, Christopher Appleton, Jas. Anderson, Johnathan Adams, B. H. Allen, William Arron, Lewis Busby, James L. Bland, Andrew Beckner, Z---- Burchfield, Mary Beckner, L. Beckner, Thos. Bastrop, Mitchel Bribs, Benjamin Botts, Isaiah Bates, Thos. Bright, Nathaniel Brown, Geo. Barrett, jr., Edward Bare, Wm. Boman, Lewis S. Brown, Francis Brown, And. Blackston, David Bargo, John P. Botts, Christian Betts, Ephraim Blizard, John Brown, Edward Brookin, Geo. Bale, Smith Bradshaw, Geo. Bradshaw, Jarett Bare, Randolph Bullock, Andrew Broyed, David Balard, Thos. Balthrop, Loyed Creacy, John Creacy, Elizabeth Creacy, Jacob J. Cummins, James Caney, Joseph Cheasman, Nubold Cannon, jr., Rob. Cranfield, Alex. Cooper, James Cravens, Morris Curtus, John Carmagan, J. W. Carmagan, William Cook, Augustus Cobb, Dangefield Cooksey, Thos. Collins, Daniel Creacy, William Creacy, Stephen Cooper, Josiah Creacy, John N. Creacy, John Conner, James M. Coatman, Geo. C. Conover, R. J. Commons, John Carter, Jas. R. Crooks, Fleming Duncan, D. M. Davis, Geo. Drago, Joseph Dermeyer, P. H. Duncan, W. W. Daugherty, Isaac D. Davis, Sarah Davis, Alexr. Diffendoffer, Robt. Dunn, Robt. Dunn (sic), John Dolton, H. R. Eskin, Maddison Downing, John S. Davis, Jason B. Duncan, Jas. Dunn, William Ervins, Stephen Emmons, Geo. Eversal, V. P. Fink, Abraham Eliad, Frosty English, James Emmerson, John Frame, Thos. Fortune, Simon Fassett, John S. Frazier, John Fuget, Robt. B. Fulk, John C. Fakner, James H. Fassett, John F. Glass, Jacob Frandz, R. K. Flemming, W. H. Fulk, Abner Green, Chapman Green, W. S. Gresway, Wm. S.Gregory, Richard Gains, H. H. Graves, James Gray, Burton Grubb, James Green, John A. Gayhart, William Giles, William Green, William Guffoth, Martin E. Green, James D. Glinn, Wrick, Peter Grant, W. C. Glover, Alexr. Hansucker, Thos. Harris, Christian Hancock, Nichcol Homer, Thos. Hayden, Henry Humphrey, Samuel Hudson, W. P. Hughes, Mourning Hunt, John Humphrey, Edward Herald, Elizabeth Herald, Henry Hawkins, John Herald, Elijah Hayden, William H. Hamilton, Squire Hall, William Hayden, John Nayden, Collins C. Holems (sic), Eli House, John Hodman, Benjamin House, Patrick Henry, B. W. Higgins, Samuel Hazencraft, Jeptha Hewlet, W. D. Hudson, Peter A. Hall, S. Holmes, Robt. Hering, Marshal Humphrey, Derick Haines, Sarah Haines, Lewis Humprey, Harriett Harrison, James Hendricks, L. R. Hathway, Jeremiah Jefferies, David Jacob, James Johnson, Thomburg Jennings, Isreal Johnson, Fountain Jones, John H. Jackson, James A. Johnson, James Jones, Abbel Johnson, D. Q. Johnson, James Johnson, Thos. Johnson, Henry Jackson, R. H. Jennings, John C. Johnson, Benjamin James, R. Kinnerman, Mathew Kidwell, Kinferd Kindell, David Kirkham, Samuel Ledford, Reubin Lane, John Lancaster, John Loudermilk, John F. Lay, Zachia Loyd, David Legg, John Launing, George Lovel, R. A. Layton, James Lovel, Thos. Larew, Joseph Lacland, Sarena Lapman, William Legg, Charles Loove (sic), John Mills, Geo. Montash, W. M. Morris, Isaac Marshal, James McMillion, Hugh McMillion, Wm. McKmey, sr. (sic), W. L. Martin, David Marrow, Samuel McRoyel, Robt. Menefee, David McDaniel, Hillery M'heral, John Mobley, Thos. Musick, John McCann, Charles V. Maddox, Thomas McCann, H. H. Muitchell, Silvester McCubbin, Benjamin Morrow, Milton Million, John McDaniel, H. S. Morrow, Timothy Meredith, John E. Maddox, W. H. Mitchell, Gery Minor, Caleb Morgan, William May, Elijah May, W. T. Norris, Robert Noel, Napoleon Nelson, John N. Nunn, William Nunn, Edward Newton, Peter Overdier, Overdier & Correy, J. H. Owsley, Robert Owsley, William Osburn, Abraham Old, I. H. odle, W. E. Osburn, Levi Poque, William Plunket, Thomas F. Paine, Thomas Pullum, Joseph Parker, William Peake, Thomas Paine, Charles Pitcher, George Perkins, James Porter, Eliza R. Pemberton, Catharine Pulliam, John Pool, Charles Reese, Lewis Rodifer, Wellington Rogers, J. M. Rankin, James Roberts, M. P. Reveley, John Rodifer, Malon Roberts, John Roberts, David Rodifer, jr., William Ranes, Sarah B. Redding, Geo. Roff, David Rodifer, sr., Benjamin Robison, Andrew Read, Thos. H. Rigg, Silas Ramsey, Mary Ann Rodifer, John Sinclair, Joseph Souther, jr., N. C. Staples, Armstead Sinclair, B. W. Stith, A. L. St. John, Saml. Sewing, Moses Sevoyng (?), Jacob Stephen, Charles Shines, Wm. Smith, J. V. Sanks, Joshua Sanks, George Sanks, Warner Sanks, Bavil Smith, Charles Stephen, A. H. Smith, Elisha Smith, Alexr. Smith, Wm. Searcy, Milton M. Smith, George Shumeburg, John Smith, David Seamore, Thos. S. Sanford, J. S. Simon, W. L. Smith, J. L. Smith, Nathl. Sutton, M. E. St. Clair, Rachel Slaughter, Hubbard Smith, John Saxon, Joseph M. Trotter, Henry Tult, S. C. Thompson, P. R. Ferrel, Charles Tuly, Solomon Turpin, Wm. Tuly, G. M. Triplett, J. Triplett, Benj. Triplett, Ezra Tubbs, F. C. Turpin, W. A. Tuly, Dudley Tuly, C. C. Thayer, J. D. Thompson, Jacob Uld, J. H. Vanelere, W. S. White, Hedgemon Wine, Saml. Warden, Jno. White, Fredik. Wallace, Robt. Way, Elisha Wilson, Henry Wtterhold, Wesley West, George Woodson, Conrad Wilson, C. B. Wilcher, S. H. Williams, J. B. Wigginton, J. W. Williams, John Wash, sr., James Wigginton, Jery Worthington, J. B. White, Cornelius Washburn, Clement White, W. C. Wyly, S. W. Wright, Jas. Wisener, W. W. Walker, Jno. Walkin, Joseph White, J. C. Walls, A. C. Walls, Thos. Williams, Thos. Williams (sic), Louisa Wash, Jessee Witherow, Saml. Yale, Davd. Zimmerman.

St. Clair County, Missouri, Aggregate Tax Statement, 1843, Capitol Fire Documents, CFD 33, Folder 1612.
John Smarr, Charles P. Bullock.

St. Louis County, Missouri, House Bill No. 19, Act For The Relief Of Nathaniel Childs, St. Louis (City), Capitol Fire Dcouments, CFD 134, Folder 12,243.
Act presented to the General Assembly requesting that Nathaniel Childs, of the city of St. Louis, be exempt from the operation of section 10 of the "Act Regarding Divorces and Alimony," approved, November 23, 1855, Chap. 55. revised code of 1855. If this act for relief is passed it will be lawful for him to marry. Referred to committee in March, 1865. Rejected January 7, 1865.

Andrew County, Missouri, Rochester Cumberland Presbyterian Church, Helena, Mo.

### Register Of Elders

| Name | Ordained | Ceased To Act |
|---|---|---|
| Henry Blanket | Jun. 11, 1871 | |
| Wm. Hayter | | 1875 |
| S. . Irvin | | |
| George Lowes | Jun. 17, 1871 | 1875 |
| M. V. Piper | Jun. 17, 1871 | 1874 |
| W. P. Slade | | |
| John J. Signst | 1875 | |
| M. D. Mickles | Feb. --, 1892 | |
| J. F. Martin | Jun. --, 1892 | |
| Henry Maddox | Jun. 24, 1896 | |
| George Tethro | Jun. 24, 1896 | |
| Jas. D. Elder | Jun. 24, 1896 | |

### Register of Deacons

| Name | Ordained | Ceased To Act |
|---|---|---|
| W. M. Shanks | Jun. 17, 1876 | 1878 (died) |
| D. G. Caldwell | Feb. --, 1892 | 1898 (died) |
| Lura Wiloughby | Mar. --, 1894 | 1907 (died) |
| Mrs. M. F. Nuckols | Mar. --. 1894 | Jan. 8, 1932 |

### Register of Marriages

L. Buler and Sophia Slade, (MD) Oct. 2, 1870, (MG) A. Guthery.

James S. Blount and Flora Summers, (MD) Oct. 18, 1874, (MG) C. B. Powers.

### Register of Deaths

| Name | Died |
|---|---|
| Sarah McLathlue | Apr. 19, 1878 |

### Register of Adult Baptisms

| Name | Baptized | Minister's Name |
|---|---|---|
| Mrs. C. Frame | Mar. 20, 1871 | Layett Munker |
| Edward B. Willoby | Mar. 20, 1871 | Layett Munker |

| Name | Baptized | Minister's Name |
|---|---|---|
| Susan A. Shanks | Mar. 20, 1871 | Layett Munker |
| Susanah Shreve | Mar. 20, 1871 | Layett Munker |
| Elizabeth E. Peper | Mar. 20, 1871 | Layett Munker |
| Price Summers | Mar. 20, 1871 | Layett Munker |
| Laura Mitchel | Mar. 20, 1871 | Layett Munker |
| William Piper | Mar. 20, 1871 | Layett Munker |
| Mrs. Sallie Brown | Mar. 20, 1871 | Layett Munker |
| Elizabeth McGothlin | Mar. 20, 1871 | Layett Munker |
| Charles McGlothlin | Mar. 20, 1871 | Layett Munker |
| Martin V. Piper | Jun. --, 1871 | Layett Munker |
| Louisa Piper | Jun. --, 1871 | Layett Munker |
| Louisa Hayter | Feb. --, 1870 | A. W. Guthery |
| Psafine Yiles | Mar. 20, 1871 | Layett Munker |
| James Blount | Nov. --, 1872 | Layett Munker |
| Alice Metcalf | Nov. --, 1872 | Layett Munker |
| Mrs. Belton | Jul. --, 1872 | Layett Munker |
| Susan Osburn | May --, 1872 | Layett Munker |
| Wm. Cook | Jan. --, 1874 | T. M. Miller |
| Hannah E. Cook | Jan. --, 1874 | T. M. Miller |
| Maud Jayne | Jan. 29, 1893 | J. S. Wayman |
| Claud Caldwell | Jan. 30, 1893 | J. S. Wayman |
| Earl Bloomer | Oct. 29, 1899 | H. W. Fisher |
| Thos. N. Jaynes | Oct. 29, 1899 | H. W. Fisher |
| Ruby Bloomer | Oct. 29, 1899 | H. W. Fisher |

## Register of Communicants

| Name | Admitted | Dismissed |
|---|---|---|
| H. H. Blount | Sep. 5, 1870 | |
| Mrs. H--- Blount | Aug. 7, 1870 | |
| James S. Blount | Sep. --, 1871 | |
| Georganna Baker | Jan. 24, 1872 | 1874 |
| Mrs. Sarah Brown | Jan. 17, 1871 | |
| Mary Baker | Mar. 22, 1871 | 1874 |
| Miss Pasphene File | Aug. 7, 1870 | 1872 |
| Wm. Frame | Mar. 20, 1871 | 1884 (died) |
| Elizabeth Belton | Apr. --, 1872 | |
| Mrs. Joannah Gray | Sep. 18, 1870 | 1871 |
| Mrs. Sarah Pager | Mar. 20, ---- | |
| Mrs. Elvira P. Hicklen | | 1882 |
| Wm. Hayter | Aug. --, 1867 | 1879 |
| Louisa Hayter | May --, 1868 | |
| James H. Hill | Nov. --, 1867 | 1874 |
| Margaret Hill | Nov. --, 1867 | 1874 |
| Jane Hector | 1872 | |
| Henry Blotzer | Jan. 23, 1874 | 1874 |
| S. A. Irwin | Aug. --, 1868 | |
| Isabel J. E. Irwin | Aug. --, 1868 | |
| R. A. Irwin | Apr. 21, 1872 | |
| Wm. Cook | Mar. --, 1871 | 1873 |

| Name | Admitted | Dismissed |
|---|---|---|
| Joseph Irwin | Aug. --, 1868 | |
| Hannah Cook | Mar. --, 1871 | 1873 |
| Malinda Cook | Mar. --, 1871 | 1873 |
| George W. Louis | Aug. 7, 1870 | 1878 |
| Susannah Louis | Aug. 7, 1870 | |
| Lena Louis | Aug. 7, 1870 | 1878 |
| Elizabeth Millaken | May --, 1868 | |
| Elizabeth McGlothlon | Mar. --, 1871 | |
| Charles McGlothlon | Mar. --, 1871 | 1879 |
| Sarah McGlothlon | Feb. --, 1871 | Apr. --, 1878 |
| Laura Mitchell | Mar. --, 1871 | Jan. 20, 1873 |
| Alice Medcalf | Sep. --, 1871 | 1872 |
| Henry Mattox | Jan. 24, 1872 | |
| Henry Mattox | Jan. 24, 1872 | |
| Francis Patton | Feb. --, 1868 | |
| Clarissa Patton | Aug. --, 1868 | 1879 |
| Margaret Patton | Aug. --, 1868 | |
| Marten U. Piper | Mar. --, 1871 | 1878 |
| Elizabeth C. Piper | Mar. --, 1871 | 1878 |
| Wm. Piper | Mar. --, 1871 | 1882 |
| Rhoda Piper | Mar. --, 1871 | 1882 |
| Cyntha Ann Piper | Mar. --, 1871 | 1882 |
| Mrs. Louisa Piper | Jun. 17, 1871 | 1882 |
| Eliza Patton | Apr. 21, 1872 | 1876 |
| W. W. P. Slade | Sep. --, 1854 | |
| Isabel Slade | Aug. --, 1846 | |
| Elizabeth Slade | Mar. --, 1871 | |
| Achcy (?) Shrete | | 1881 |
| Lucy Simmons | Aug. --, 1868 | 1878 |
| Sophiah Slade | Aug. --, 1868 | |
| F. A. Simmons | Mar. 20, 1871 | |
| Anna Catharine Sharp | Aug. 7, 1870 | 1873 |
| Mrs. Mary Signist | Aug. 7, 1870 | |
| J. S. Sharp | Sep. 6, 1870 | 1873 |
| Frances E. Shrieves | Sep. 6, 1870 | |
| Catharine Signist | Sep. 6, 1870 | |
| Mary A. Shrieves | Sep. 6, 1870 | |
| Emma Sharp | Sep. 6, 1870 | 1873 |
| Rachel Scott | Sep. 6, 1870 | 1874 |
| Mary Slade | Mar. 1, 1871 | |
| M. M. Shanks | Feb. --, 1871 | Nov. --, 1876 |
| Susan A. Shanks | Feb. --, 1871 | |
| Price Summers | Feb. 20, 1871 | 1871 |
| Rebecca Sale | Feb. 20, 1871 | |
| Marshal Shanks | Feb. --, 1871 | |
| John P. Signist | Mar. 20, 1871 | 1873 |
| Armina Shrite | Sep. --, 1872 | |
| Lusinda Shreve | Apr. --, 1872 | |

| Name | Admitted | Dismissed |
|---|---|---|
| Jonathan Snowden | 1874 | |
| Henry B. Turner | Sep. 6, 1870 | 1873 |
| Amanada J. Turner | Sep. 6, 1870 | 1873 |
| Sarah Tumbleson | Sep. 6, 1870 | 1873 |
| Mrs. Tethro | Sep. 6, 1870 | |
| Edward B. Willougby | Mar. 20, 1870 | 1879 (d. 1881) |
| Armenta Woodward | Aug. 7, 1870 | |
| Ferneler (?) Woodward | Sep. 6, 1870 | |
| J. R. Williams | Mar. --, 1872 | |
| Jonathan Snowden | 1874 | |
| Henry B. Turner | Sep. 6, 1870 | 1873 |

INDEX

AAIR, 98
ABBAY, 23
ABBERSON, 187
ABBINGTON, 23
ABBOT, 147
ABBOTT, 60 65 147 173 183
ABELL, 186
ABERNATHY, 128 146 147
ABINGTON, 59
ABLE, 25 147
ABSTAN, 75
ACOCK, 128
ACRE, 101 187
ACRES, 75 81 86
ACRIFF, 68
ADAIR, 85 98 101 122
ADAMS, 17 50 55 65 68 72 75 76 86 95 97
    101 104 108 124 126 128 142 145 147
    158 163 181 187 188 191 192
ADCOCK, 98 188
ADDERTON, 190
ADDISON, 166
ADEN, 128
ADKINS, 34 75 105 146
ADKINSON, 183
ADMIRE, 64 183
ADRIAEN, 74
AEA, 85
AGAN, 108
AGEE, 101 146 153 159 172 176 192
AGGE, 151
AGNEW, 75 95
AIKIN, 68
AIMES, 108
AKIN, 26 75
ALBERTS, 125

ALDER, 43
ALDERSON, 2 75 101
ALDERSSON, 98
ALDRIDGE, 31
ALEXANDER, 14 28 62 64 65 68 72 73 75
    95 97 99 105 106 124 125 128 145 146
    183
ALFORD, 28 154 171
ALFRED, 37
ALKIN, 97
ALLBERT, 74
ALLCON, 128
ALLEN, 44 62 65 66 75 85 90 94 98 99 101
    104 108 122 124 125 128 147 160 165
    168 170 173 183 187 190-192
ALLENSWORTH, 192
ALLEY, 128
ALLIN, 73 186 187
ALLINGSWORTH, 192
ALLISON, 68 123
ALLNUTT, 90
ALLOWAY, 62
ALLRED, 71 72
ALSBURY, 72
AMANNERMAN, 150
AMBER, 145
AMENT, 75
AMINT, 75
AMMEL, 145
AMMERMAN, 147 157 160 161 163 164 178
    179
AMMERMMAN, 177
AMMERMON, 146 147
AMMISON, 191
AMOS, 126 147 148
ANDERS, 24

ANDERSIN, 22
ANDERSON, 2 22 25 26 32 35 36 50 58-60
  62 65 68 71 75 85 86 90 95 96 101 104
  123 126 128 146-149 158 162 175 182
  183 185 187 191 192
ANDREW, 119
ANDREWS, 75 128 187
ANGLIN, 128
ANSEL, 104
ANSLEY, 96
ANSON, 65 183
ANSPAUGH, 125
ANTHONY, 90
ANTILL, 75
ANTLE, 90
ANTON, 2
ANTRICTH, 124
ANTWERP, 25
APLEY, 111 112
APPERSON, 23
APPLEGATE, 187
APPLEGET, 68
APPLETON, 64 192
ARCHER, 68 147
ARCHIE, 60
ARGYLE, 90
ARMBRUSTER, 16
ARMISTEAD, 46
ARMSTRONG, 65 68 75 86 96 99 101 126
  128 187
ARNDUFF, 108
ARNETT, 75 79
ARNOLD, 19 59 68 86 90 104 122 128
ARNOT, 68
ARRON, 192
ARROWSMITH, 191 192
ARTERBURY, 72
ARTHUR, 85 105 183
ASBELL, 42
ASBRIDGE, 157
ASBURY, 86 146 148 150 157 192
ASH, 72 123
ASHBRIDGE, 164
ASHBY, 68 75 83 128 129
ASHCRAFT, 74 75 79 82 85 108
ASHECOM, 144
ASHER, 21 28 90

ASHERN, 145
ASHINHURST, 125
ASHINURST, 125
ASHLEMON, 86
ASKEW, 122
ASKIN, 146
ASLIN, 50
ATCHISON, 183
ATKINS, 141
ATKINSON, 3 73 75 98 101 124
ATTBURY, 73
ATTEBURY, 73
ATTERBERRY, 68 97
ATTERBURY, 72
ATWOOD, 147
AUGUSTINE, 145
AULDRIDGE, 75
AULL, 75
AUSBORNE, 99
AUSTIN, 22 95-97 101 104 129 169 173 192
AUTHOR, 60
AUXIER, 90
AVERIN, 60
AWBREY, 127 129
AYERS, 85 123
AYRES, 167 168 191
BABBIT, 123
BABBITT, 157
BABER, 108
BACKSTER, 190
BACON, 150
BADE, 186
BADEN, 110
BADGER, 95
BAENDER, 144
BAERGEN, 127
BAGBY, 101 126 188
BAGE, 17
BAGLEY, 72 90
BAGLY, 141
BAGWELL, 124
BAHANAN, 27
BAILEY, 16 37 38 60 76 101 104 108 114
  116 119 120 122 124 125 129 142 187
BAILIE, 14
BAILY, 60 72 96 99 101 124 125
BAIN, 141

BAINBRIDGE, 59
BAINS, 60
BAIRD, 65 108 183
BAKER, 2 3 9 19 20 68 72 73 76 84 86 90 97
    98 100 101 120 123 126 129 149 150
    155 157 169 175 177 179 188 191 195
BAKERY, 126
BALARD, 192
BALDRIDGE, 58 76
BALDWIN, 153 166
BALE, 192
BALEY, 37 64
BALIEU, 90
BALIN, 60
BALIS, 60 108
BALL, 60 116 162 169
BALLAGH, 108
BALLARD, 76 86 90 97 129
BALLS, 108
BALOW, 73
BALTHROP, 192
BALTOUSE, 145
BALWIN, 124
BANCE, 108
BANCROFF, 145
BANDY, 38 95
BANE, 60
BANES, 188
BANISTER, 71
BANK, 148-150 179
BANKS, 74 148
BANKSON, 95
BANTA, 38
BARBEE, 47 129
BARBER, 60 90 124
BARCLAY, 129
BARD, 60
BARDON, 97
BARE, 95 192
BARGER, 105 191
BARGIN, 76
BARGO, 191 192
BARK, 90
BARKER, 60 68 76 119 120 122 180 183
    184
BARKHURST, 129
BARKLEY, 150 168

BARLEY, 31 76 124 183 184
BARMONT, 90
BARNABY, 76
BARNARD, 22 23 76 86
BARNES, 43 62 68 71 86 90 124 129 141
    188
BARNET, 32 43 46 68 110
BARNETT, 68 76 86 90 113 129 191
BARNEY, 43 143 167
BARNS, 60 183
BARNWELL, 116
BARONS, 60
BARR, 86
BARRADA, 129
BARRAGER, 118
BARRET, 148 149
BARRETT, 34 68 75 129 190 192
BARRON, 16
BARROW, 17 90 101 188
BARRY, 4 104 145 188
BARSHOLD, 125
BART, 129
BARTEE, 144
BARTH, 108
BARTLETT, 65 101 175 184
BARTON, 68
BARTRAM, 76
BASDER, 191
BASE, 96
BASKET, 184
BASKETT, 62 144
BASKIN, 101
BASS, 99 108
BASSETT, 72 129 140
BAST, 28 33 37 38
BASTROP, 192
BATES, 15 23 148-150 174 179 183 192
BATTER, 145
BATTON, 191
BATTZELL, 148
BAUER, 38
BAUGH, 184
BAUGHMAN, 186
BAUMEISTER, 108
BAX, 111
BAXTER, 85 86 129
BAY, 129

BAYLEY, 32 37
BAYNE, 148-150 166 175 176 179
BAYNES, 176
BAYNHAM, 99
BAYS, 187
BAYSE, 76
BAYSINGER, 99 188
BAZILE, 129
BEACH, 150 180
BEACKNER, 192
BEALE, 129
BEALL, 71
BEAN, 68 129
BEAR, 71
BEARD, 95
BEASON, 43
BEATTY, 145 186
BEATY, 43 44 51 55 120 121
BEAUCHAMP, 85
BEAVIN, 101
BEAZLEY, 186
BECK, 60 75 184 187
BECKER, 20 108 145
BECKET, 90 149 169 171 175
BECKETT, 38 191
BECKMAN, 60
BECKNER, 149 156 172 177 180 192
BEDFORD, 90
BEDWELL, 76
BEEBE, 34 148
BEEHLER, 5 18
BEELER, 6
BEETS, 75 76
BEEVERS, 99
BEHAM, 108
BEHRLE, 75
BEHTEL, 183
BELAMY, 101
BELBRO, 65
BELCHER, 76
BELK, 90
BELL, 17 18 36 59 62 64 65 71 73 85 90 97 99 104 129 140 183 184 190
BELLMAR, 68 69
BELLOWS, 99
BELT, 62 123 129
BELTON, 195

BEMIS, 118
BENBROOK, 38
BENCHER, 59
BENET, 184
BENJAMIN, 124
BENNER, 145
BENNET, 62
BENNETT, 75 76 85 99 100 108 129 188
BENNIS, 85
BENNZETTE, 122
BENSON, 76 97 150 156 158 165 172 179 190
BENT, 108
BENTON, 59 98
BENTZ, 94
BERAL, 126
BERCHARD, 100
BERDIO, 141
BERGEN, 38
BERGER, 122
BERGSTRESSER, 140
BERHNER, 123
BERLIN, 128 190
BERM, 35
BERNARD, 101 108
BERNAY, 123
BERNES, 125
BERNETT, 126
BERNETTE, 126
BERNHART, 145
BERNIER, 62
BERRY, 16 43 44 76 85 90 97 101 104 124 125 129 183 188
BERRYHILL, 90
BERRYMAN, 75 129
BESBIT, 99
BEST, 76 77 90
BETHALL, 188
BETHEL, 184
BETHILL, 97
BETTER, 86
BETTIS, 60
BETTS, 192
BEURS, 85
BEVIS, 108
BEWLY, 106
BIBA, 43

BIBB, 124 150 156 159 161
BIBEY, 73
BIBY, 73
BICKERSTAFF, 76
BICKETTS, 76
BIGELOW, 154 170
BIGGERS, 22
BIGGS, 29 36 129 172
BIGLEY, 96
BIGS, 73
BIGWOOD, 172
BILDERBACK, 90
BILL, 86
BILLINGS, 25 26 30
BINEY, 144
BINEYNG, 144
BINGHAM, 85
BIRCHARD, 140
BIRD, 101 110 124
BIRKHEAD, 64
BIRNER, 128
BISHOP, 16 60 86 123 125 126 190
BITTICK, 15
BITTLE, 90
BIVENS, 90
BIXEN, 148
BLACK, 13 44 55 58 60 76 80 82-84 108 123 190
BLACKABY, 184
BLACKALY, 62
BLACKAMORE, 184
BLACKBIRN, 71
BLACKBURN, 76 97 188
BLACKENBURG, 101
BLACKEY, 148
BLACKMORE, 60 184
BLACKSTON, 77 191 192
BLACKSTONE, 75 90
BLACKWELL, 10 101 107 112 129
BLACKWOOD, 149
BLADEN, 85
BLAILESS, 184
BLAIN, 148
BLAINE, 144
BLAIR, 32 38 60 64 76 101 124 148-151 154 170 177-181 183
BLAKE, 13 129

BLAKELY, 76 90 172
BLAKEMAN, 22
BLAKEY, 76 149
BLANCHARD, 161
BLAND, 148-150 158 159 176 177 179 191 192
BLANK, 20
BLANKE, 144
BLANKENBAKER, 73
BLANKENSHIP, 43
BLANKET, 194
BLANKS, 60 184
BLANTON, 60 62 104 184
BLAYLOCK, 108
BLAZER, 76
BLEDSOE, 76 85 90 101 187
BLEIL, 122
BLESSING, 69
BLEVENS, 90
BLEVER, 73
BLEVINS, 76 90
BLIZARD, 192
BLIZZARD, 191
BLOCK, 2 15 60 75
BLOOMER, 195
BLOTZER, 195
BLOUNT, 101 105 194 195
BLOWERS, 107
BLUE, 23 26 35 37 43 55 73 89 108
BLUEBALD, 68
BLUMENTHAL, 12
BLUNALL, 104
BLUNDELL, 124
BLUNKALL, 188
BLUNT, 60
BLYTHE, 85 99 129
BOANENING, 64
BOARD, 104 153-155 163
BOARMAN, 24 25 33
BOATMAN, 190
BOATWRIGHT, 2
BOCHLMAN, 123
BODIN, 69
BODINE, 69
BOGAN, 95 188
BOGGS, 43 45 71 85 108 129
BOGGUSS, 101

BOGN, 95
BOHANNON, 90
BOHART, 90
BOHEN, 180
BOHLING, 15
BOHMER, 125
BOHON, 180
BOID, 184
BOIDSTAN, 90
BOIDSTON, 90
BOLDUC, 2 10
BOLEJACK, 76
BOLEN, 3
BOLING, 118 123
BOLINGER, 141
BOLVAR, 22
BOLWARE, 26
BOLY, 14
BOMAN, 192
BOMBARGER, 90
BOMER, 123 124
BONACKER, 20
BOND, 71 90 101 118
BONDINE, 69
BONE, 62
BONES, 15 76 79
BONN, 60
BONNE, 62
BONTZ, 148
BOOKER, 97 187
BOOKWOOD, 69
BOOM, 97
BOON, 47 55 62 69 111
BOONE, 64 101 104 122 188
BOOTH, 101 108 141 179
BOOTHE, 85
BOOZE, 104
BORDER, 144
BOREN, 76
BORGE, 2
BOSBINDEN, 62
BOSCHEN, 123
BOSWELL, 76 104 188
BOTTS, 73 142 145 169 192
BOUGHTON, 13 17 18
BOULEREAN, 73
BOULIN, 145

BOULWARE, 29 31 72 101
BOUME, 180 182
BOUND, 69 86
BOUNDS, 74 140
BOURE, 179
BOURIE, 164
BOURNE, 147 159 169 171 176
BOUSE, 76
BOUTON, 76
BOUYER, 129
BOWEN, 60 69 105 149 180 184
BOWER, 69 129 163
BOWES, 188
BOWLER, 149
BOWLES, 19 36 71 110-115 159 167 169 180
BOWLIN, 9 10 12 16 17 74 129 145
BOWLING, 27
BOWMAN, 143 179 182
BOWN, 34
BOYCE, 100
BOYD, 1 22 69 74 90 99 101 105 142 159
BOYER, 37 76 90
BOYKIN, 190
BOYNE, 9
BOZARTH, 69 149 160 168 172
BRACKENRIDGE, 31
BRADBERRY, 76
BRADEN, 85
BRADFORD, 50 97 122 188
BRADLEY, 44 62 64 71 76 85 86 99 120 124 142 155 183
BRADNEY, 143
BRADSHAW, 76 108 119 147 150 162 165 172 177 187 192
BRADY, 76 124 157 170 190
BRAFF, 60
BRAGDON, 141
BRAGG, 90 104 129
BRAILEY, 101
BRAINT, 108
BRAKE, 188
BRAMBER, 69
BRAN, 125
BRANAUGH, 129
BRANCH, 172 188
BRANDENBURG, 141

BRANDON, 76 99 110
BRANDT, 123
BRANHAM, 98 99 104
BRANN, 152
BRANNON, 73
BRANNUM, 121
BRANSON, 114
BRANSTETTER, 129
BRANT, 65
BRANTRAM, 97
BRANUM, 73
BRASFIELD, 76
BRASHEAR, 31 36 44 97
BRASHEARS, 21 27 31 36
BRASHER, 42
BRASHERS, 73
BRASKER, 42
BRATTON, 116
BRAUBAUGH, 154
BRAUGH, 126
BRAUGHER, 126
BRAWLEY, 90 129
BRAYTON, 146
BREADDY, 13
BREEDEN, 110
BREWER, 23 180 187
BREWINGTON, 129
BRIANT, 108
BRIBS, 192
BRICE, 35 108
BRICKEY, 17
BRICOE, 183
BRIDENSDOLPH, 144
BRIDEWELL, 148 160 171
BRIDGE, 184
BRIDGEFORD, 69
BRIDGEMAN, 90
BRIDGER, 108
BRIESTER, 18
BRIGGS, 35 73 86 182
BRIGHT, 101 143 149 182 188 192
BRIGMORE, 90
BRILES, 60 64 90
BRINDLEY, 12
BRINK, 46 52
BRINKER, 129
BRINTER, 90

BRINTON, 180
BRISCO, 149 169
BRISCOE, 35 43 62 64 72 76 85 150 178 184
BRISON, 19
BRISTOE, 124
BRITE, 97
BRITT, 64 123
BRITTAIN, 90
BRITTON, 69 76
BRIZENDINE, 28
BROADLEY, 101
BROADWELL, 101 148 179
BROCK, 76 124
BROCKMAN, 24 114
BROCKS, 99
BRODIS, 74
BRODY, 74
BROGAN, 142
BROKKING, 86
BRONK, 60
BROOK, 97 146
BROOKIN, 192
BROOKING, 86 129
BROOKS, 33 35 44 48 75 76 84 101 123 126 191
BRORAUGH, 121
BROTHERS, 23 37
BROUGHTON, 188
BROWER, 129
BROWN, 8 10 21 23 26 28-31 42-44 47 54 59 60 65-69 72 75 76 89 90 94 95 98 99 107 108 117 122 124-126 130 143 145 150 158-160 165 170 172 179 183 190-192 195
BROWNE, 130
BROWNING, 38 59 60 190
BROWNSING, 23
BROY, 86 146
BROYED, 192
BROZ, 191
BRUCE, 43 44 69 90 183
BRUFORD, 180
BRUMBAUGH, 153
BRUME, 158
BRUMFIELD, 76
BRUMLEY, 112

BRUMWELL, 130
BRUNK, 184
BRUSH, 189
BRUVRR, 144
BRVIN, 85
BRWONING, 69
BRYAN, 72 97 104 130 148 168 182 184 188
BRYANT, 22 69 71 76 86 95 97 108 124 172 179 187
BRYENT, 60
BRYSON, 122
BUBB, 127
BUCH, 95
BUCHANAN, 28 34 71 144 183
BUCHANNAN, 72 104
BUCHANNON, 25
BUCHANON, 27
BUCHER, 108
BUCK, 76 90 148
BUCKELS, 180
BUCKHANAN, 184
BUCKHANNAN, 32
BUCKHANNON, 22 27 86
BUCKLAND, 148 149 161 164 170
BUCKLER, 164
BUCKLEY, 148
BUCKMAN, 68 69 71
BUCKNER, 23 29 69 149 187
BUDD, 123 148
BUDISILL, 62
BUEHREN, 128
BUFORD, 27 28 32 33 35 149 155
BULER, 194
BULL, 34
BULLARD, 99 179
BULLEN, 69
BULLINGTON, 66
BULLOCK, 72 76 78 115 130 192 194
BULWARE, 95
BUMES, 188
BUMPASS, 110 111
BUNCH, 97 130
BUNHETT, 99
BUNNCOE, 76
BUNT, 96
BUNTEN, 90
BUNTON, 130 163 191

BUR, 35
BURCH, 94 96 130 148 162 164-166
BURCHFIELD, 149 169 192
BURD, 94 148
BURDEN, 130
BURDIT, 101 188
BURFORD, 74-76 149 166
BURGEN, 60
BURGESS, 4 13 18 19 59 74 90 117
BURK, 95
BURKE, 144
BURKEE, 188
BURKHART, 76
BURKHEAD, 60
BURKHOOD, 65
BURKLAON, 62
BURKS, 188
BURLOW, 85
BURNAM, 73
BURNBEN, 187
BURNE, 165
BURNET, 3 4
BURNETT, 90 99 101 149
BURNEY, 76
BURNS, 20 108 111 124 126 145 184
BURRAS, 74
BURRESS, 86
BURRIS, 76 78 80 82 85 146
BURROW, 76
BURRUS, 60
BURT, 101 104
BURTON, 72 74 76 140 141 144
BURY, 74
BUSBY, 191 192
BUSCHELL, 140
BUSCHOFF, 114
BUSH, 69 71 73 101 123 124
BUSHOLTS, 123
BUSSEY, 69
BUSTER, 8
BUSTICK, 145
BUTLER, 16 31 62 90 122 130 145 146 184
BUTRAM, 76
BUTT, 75
BUTTER, 108
BYAM, 126
BYANT, 22

206

BYARS, 21
BYBEE, 73 76 124
BYERS, 98 188
BYRD, 123 124
BYRNE, 182
BYRNS, 14 44
BYSTALF, 86
CADWALLADEN, 5
CADY, 105 107
CAFFEE, 123
CAFFERY, 7 8
CAGNEY, 2
CALAWAY, 72
CALDWELL, 22 26 34 38 101 122 152 179
    188 194 195
CALE, 118
CALHOON, 68
CALHOUN, 46 130
CALHOURN, 21
CALLAWAY, 60 101
CALLICOTTE, 97
CALLISON, 104
CALLOWAY, 60 74 76 77 184
CALLWAY, 95
CALVERT, 130
CALVIN, 97 110 184
CAMBELL, 59 188
CAMBRON, 152
CAMDEN, 151
CAMEGY, 174 191
CAMEL, 69
CAMERON, 29 34 77 96 130
CAMPBELL, 5 13 17 23 24 29 30 38 44 45
    60 69 76 77 84 90 101 126 130 143 145
    156 157 171 187 6126
CAMPLIN, 73
CAMRON, 24
CANADAY, 52 62
CANADY, 45
CANAGE, 69
CANAWAY, 23
CANEY, 192
CANNADA, 188
CANNON, 60 62 152 156 175 176 182 191
    192
CANON, 62
CANTERBERRY, 45

CANTERBURY, 29 32 44 54
CANTRELL, 85 184
CANTRILL, 60
CANTROL, 64
CAPE, 10
CAPP, 72 125 144
CAPPS, 184
CAPS, 60
CAPTEN, 100
CARDER, 69 73
CARDOM, 108
CARDSELL, 123
CARDWELL, 44 45 69 123 149-152
CARICO, 124
CARL, 90
CARLE, 187
CARLES, 96
CARMAGAN, 192
CARMICHAEL, 77
CARMON, 62
CARNELL, 77
CARNES, 90 91
CARNS, 90
CARPENITER, 152
CARPENTER, 41 77 90 95 122 123 125
CARR, 60 62 69 101 184
CARREGANE, 12
CARREL, 188
CARRICO, 68
CARRINGTON, 101 105
CARRIO, 68
CARROL, 77
CARROLL, 69 94
CARRY, 69
CARSIES, 28
CARSNER, 90
CARSON, 26 31 83 84 130 141 186 191
CARSTAPHEN, 21
CARSTARPHEN, 21 26 30 31 34
CARTER, 2 11 15 18 20 33 34 45 59 60 62
    69 71 72 74 77 82 85 87 95 98 105 108
    122 126 130 141 142 147 184 192
CARTHCART, 130
CARTON, 77
CARTWELL, 71
CARTWILL, 22 28
CARTWRIGHT, 69

CARTY, 5 60 174
CARUTHERS, 73 77 95
CARY, 77
CASE, 77 108 109 151
CASEY, 2 5 118-122 145
CASHION, 75
CASIDY, 46
CASON, 71 151 152
CASS, 62
CASSEL, 76
CASSELL, 77
CASSIDY, 15
CASSLAND, 123
CASSY, 117
CASWELL, 186
CATERS, 72
CATES, 90
CATHBIRT, 84
CATHEY, 77
CATLET, 90
CATON, 146
CATTRELL, 123
CAULK, 2 4 8 11 14
CAUSDAN, 188
CAUTHON, 67
CAUTHORN, 44 45 53
CAVANAH, 130
CAVE, 49 52
CAWTHORN, 69 73
CAYSON, 99
CAYWOOD, 124
CECIL, 173
CEICIL, 122
CEIL, 151
CEPHERS, 96
CEROLY, 85
CHABI, 96
CHACE, 97
CHADD, 90
CHADOWING, 77
CHADWICK, 190
CHAMBER, 87
CHAMBERLAIN, 60 141
CHAMBERLIN, 59
CHAMBERS, 83 95
CHAMBLIS, 76
CHAMPAIN, 111

CHANCELLOR, 125
CHANCEY, 123
CHANDLER, 12 13 60 72 140 155 166 167 184
CHANEY, 66 68 74 99 183
CHANY, 90
CHAPEL, 91
CHAPMAN, 19 28 69 94 140 141 143
CHARLES, 77 82 95 96 108
CHARLEY, 108
CHARLTON, 45 191
CHASTAIN, 125
CHASTEN, 65
CHATHAM, 85
CHAUNCEY, 126
CHAUTEAU, 130
CHAVEZ, 74
CHAWMING, 22
CHEAK, 62
CHEANEY, 100
CHEASMAN, 192
CHEATHAM, 100 101
CHESNUT, 96
CHESSER, 124
CHESTER, 123
CHEYENE, 109
CHICK, 101 104
CHILDERS, 77 79 101 152 187
CHILDS, 99 108 145 194
CHILE, 23
CHILES, 130
CHILTON, 77 130
CHINN, 69
CHITON, 24
CHITTICK, 90
CHITWOOD, 32
CHOUTEAU, 2
CHOWNING, 71 130 152
CHRISMAN, 77
CHRISTAIN, 142
CHRISTIAN, 77 142 146
CHRISTOPHER, 8
CHRISTY, 7 140 173
CHURCH, 87
CIBBAGE, 142
CINGCADE, 126
CISNEY, 123

CISSELL, 22 71
CLAGETT, 117
CLAGGETT, 60
CLAGHORNE, 187
CLANE, 60
CLANSEN, 123
CLANTON, 85 90 101 188
CLAPPER, 71
CLARE, 64 184
CLARK, 2 11 35 41 44 45 60 62 77 86 87 90 91 101 111 116 126 130 143 145 151 154 161 182
CLARKE, 64
CLARKSON, 85 143 148
CLARKSTON, 143
CLARY, 152
CLASLEY, 90
CLATTERBUCK, 99
CLAY, 59 69
CLAYBROOK, 72
CLAYBROOKE, 130
CLAYCOMB, 125
CLAYTON, 29 31 38 73 76 77 166
CLEAR, 65
CLEAVER, 23 27 35 38 152
CLEEK, 90
CLELAND, 130
CLEMENT, 73
CLENDENON, 46 48
CLEVE, 64
CLEVELAND, 100
CLICE, 59
CLINE, 95
CLINGMAN, 188
CLOUGH, 96
CLOW, 182 191
CLUFF, 181
CLYMER, 77
COAKLEY, 191
COAL, 71
COATES, 109 125
COATMAN, 192
COATNEY, 77
COATS, 60 72 73 90 97 101 130
COATSS, 97
COBB, 65 145 170 192
COBBS, 130

COBLE, 1
COCCHRAN, 64
COCHAM, 76
COCHRAN, 29 34 64 65 90 124 184
COCKERELL, 130
COCKRAN, 60 125
COCKRELL, 77
COCKRILL, 15 143
COFER, 115
COFFEE, 109
COFFERY, 7
COFFEY, 62 65 184
COFFMAN, 83 84 91 130 157 187
COFIN, 60
COGDALE, 90
COGGSHILE, 108 109
COHAGEN, 102
COHAN, 4
COHEN, 130
COHOVER, 152
COIL, 44
COKE, 64
COLBERN, 77
COLBERT, 15 64 170 184
COLBORN, 151
COLBURN, 17
COLDWELL, 69
COLE, 6 7 16 76 77 97 122 130
COLEMAN, 148 151 152 158 168 171
COLHOURNE, 27
COLLARD, 60 184
COLLETT, 191
COLLEY, 149 151 152 169 171 172
COLLIAN, 60
COLLIER, 87 101 130
COLLINS, 37 47 59 60 69 74 77 82 85 97 104 108 130 145 151 152 184 188 192
COLLOCH, 4
COLTON, 99
COLVIN, 87
COMBS, 26 30 34 69 76 90 91 98 123 124 151 188
COMEER, 119
COMEGGY, 152
COMEGY, 165 167
COMEGYS, 130 174
COMER, 96 101 118 119 122

COMMER, 119
COMMONS, 192
COMPTON, 60 130
COMSTOCK, 72 152
CONBOY, 108
CONCE, 60
CONDIFF, 74
CONDUITT, 151 176
CONGER, 99 100
CONLEY, 153 165 179
CONN, 32
CONNABLE, 152
CONNELL, 90
CONNELLY, 145
CONNER, 60 77 84 184 192
CONOVER, 151 176 192
CONRAD, 150 151
CONSOR, 108
CONSTABLE, 85
CONWAY, 77
CONWELL, 187
CONYERS, 69
COOK, 38 46 64 76 77 79 82 84 87 90 97 101 118 124 141 146 184 191 192 195 196
COOKE, 15
COOKSEY, 148 150 151 155 156 165 168 173 175 192
COOLEY, 10 77
COOLLEY, 130
COOMBS, 145
COOMME, 74
COON, 64
COONCE, 99 110
COONROD, 184
COONS, 98 101
COOPAGE, 69
COOPER, 8 46 59 62 69 77 101 110 123 125 130 145 184 191 192
COOSE, 184
COOTS, 76
COPELAND, 77 111
COPELIN, 90
COPENHAUER, 184
COPENHAVEN, 65
COPLAND, 111
COPLEN, 90

COPLEY, 77
COPLING, 112
COPPAGE, 122
COPPER, 184
CORA, 100
CORDELL, 151 163 177
CORDER, 130
CORDES, 7
CORKER, 95 96
CORLEW, 77
CORLEY, 59 96 146 188
CORNELIUS, 91
CORNES, 68
CORNET, 58
CORNETT, 77 79
CORNWALL, 65
CORNWELL, 125 184
CORREY, 193
CORRICO, 68
CORRINDER, 126
CORRY, 152
CORTNEY, 64
CORYELL, 152 154 173 175 181
CORYSEE, 165
CORYYELL, 152
COSTLEY, 39
COTENEY, 184
COTTER, 9
COTTINGHAM, 144
COTTLE, 60 64 127 184
COTTY, 152
COTWELL, 151
COUCH, 3 45 69
COUGHEROUR, 76
COULTER, 140 142
COULTON, 142
COURTNEY, 5 31
COUSE, 60
COVINGTON, 69 104 122 163
COWAN, 90 130 190
COWDEN, 115
COWGILL, 152
COWHERD, 71
COX, 25 32 34 60 62 69 71 73 74 77 85-87 90 95 104 115 131 151 180 184 190
COYLE, 2 51 104
COYLEY, 142

CRABTREE, 85 117 123
CRACH, 60
CRADDICK, 5
CRAFT, 18 124
CRAGO, 105 188
CRAGS, 188
CRAIG, 1 69 101 151 184 188
CRAIGE, 101
CRAIGHEAD, 101
CRANE, 108
CRANFIELD, 192
CRANK, 99
CRASTHWAIT, 31
CRAUCH, 64
CRAUSE, 140
CRAVENS, 131 192
CRAWFORD, 5 29 34 68 71 77 105-107 123 126 131 151 188
CRAYS, 77
CREACH, 60
CREACY, 191 192
CREAG, 104
CREASEY, 87
CREASMAN, 72
CREASON, 33 37
CREASY, 46 191
CREATH, 151 152
CREECH, 184
CREED, 45 71 73
CREEK, 77 83 95
CREEL, 146
CREERY, 11
CREIGHTON, 167
CRENSHAW, 62 85 123 184
CRESCO, 38
CRESSY, 122
CREUMES, 64
CREWS, 60 97 99 127 131 140
CREWSBAUER, 6
CREY, 90
CRIDER, 65 114
CRIGGER, 187
CRIGLER, 30 35 71
CRIGLEY, 73
CRIGLON, 131
CRIM, 69
CRIMM, 69

CRISMON, 113
CRISWELL, 99 105
CRISWLL, 99
CROA, 100
CROCKET, 22 23 28 44 48 90
CROCKETT, 28 71 146 151
CROCUH, 184
CROMWELL, 90
CROOK, 41 74 86 131 151
CROOKER, 147 173
CROOKS, 101 117 119-122 192
CROPPER, 60
CROSBY, 12 17
CROSE, 141
CROSS, 10 85 141-143 184
CROSSLAND, 77
CROSSWHITE, 45 46 98
CROSTHWAIT, 24 31 35 36
CROSWHITE, 74
CROUCH, 60 184 190
CROUGHTON, 150-152 165 175 180
CROW, 60 69 71 143
CROWLEY, 187
CROWSON, 98 188
CRUCE, 188
CRUCH, 60
CRUCHER, 69
CRUISE, 72 74
CRULL, 14
CRUMBELL, 95
CRUME, 64
CRUMP, 64 69 98 104
CRUNYA, 124
CRUSE, 184
CRUTCHER, 69
CRUTCHFIELD, 108
CRYLER, 30
CUBAGE, 142
CULBERT, 27
CULBERTSON, 21 24 25 28 30 31 33 37 110
CULLEP, 65
CULLEY, 122
CUMMINGS, 15 77 145
CUMMINNS, 152
CUMMINS, 76 86 131 168 170 191 192
CUMMISKEY, 2
CUMMISKY, 5 6

CUNNINGHAM, 59 62 69 72 77 125 144 146 152 184 187
CUNSLEY, 74
CUPEE, 184
CUPS, 60
CURD, 149 159 161 168
CURL, 90 131 191
CURRAN, 77 108
CURRY, 42 69 99
CURTIS, 90 109 110 122 188 191
CURTUS, 192
CUSHMAN, 168
CUSIC, 123
CUSICK, 76 77
CUSTER, 60 184
CUTTER, 109
DABEL, 145
DACE, 5
DACKS, 91
DACOMB, 120
DADEL, 123
DAGGETT, 109 131
DAGGS, 142 153
DALBY, 124
DALE, 71 78
DALL, 109
DALLAS, 104
DALLIS, 25 96
DALTON, 94
DALY, 75
DAME, 97
DAMERON, 131 141 143
DAMRELL, 71
DAMRON, 62
DAMSEL, 46 49
DANCE, 149 151 153 159 169
DANIEL, 1 2 24 32 35 45 62 71 91 95 105 187 188
DANIELS, 78 80 141 142 184
DANLEY, 144
DANSON, 123
DANZEY, 187
DARBY, 1 3 106
DARIEN, 184
DARLING, 120
DARN, 188
DARNELL, 59 87

DARNOLD, 59
DARRAH, 153
DARVEL, 35
DASBACH, 178
DASBACK, 183
DASHER, 126
DAUGHERTY, 91 146 192
DAULTON, 64
DAUSON, 124
DAVENPORT, 78 95 108 131
DAVID, 87 96
DAVIDSON, 7 46 53 91
DAVIESS, 153
DAVIS, 1 3 7 18 25 26 28-31 36-38 46 48 53 60 62 69 72-74 76-78 81 87 91 95-101 104 105 109 120 124 126 131 140 143 149 152-154 157 161 168 171 177 184 186 188 191 192
DAVISON, 77 78
DAVISS, 58 87 101 153 154 176
DAWKINS, 140 142
DAWSON, 38 41 60 69 72 84 91 101 131 154 183 184
DAY, 3 43 47 52 53 78 87 91 97 99 101 153 184 188
DAYTON, 71
DAZY, 180
DEAN, 91 95 141 190
DEANING, 69
DEARBOURN, 72
DEARING, 69 104 188
DEAVER, 74 153
DEBO, 101 145
DECROSS, 71
DEERING, 69
DEGARME, 184
DEHART, 68
DEHAVEN, 101
DEHSHOUT, 124
DEINS, 124
DEJARNATT, 64
DEJARNETT, 77
DEJAVERET, 46
DEJEVUET, 52
DEKART, 91
DELANEY, 46
DELBRIDGE, 153 154

DELERIER, 85
DELGER, 184
DEMAREE, 14
DEMASTERS, 78 131 187
DEMMITT, 27
DENEKE, 128
DENEY, 60
DENISON, 69
DENNING, 85 187
DENNIS, 46
DENNY, 186
DENOIER, 100
DENT, 1 74
DENTZ, 13
DEPEW, 105
DERBY, 78
DERMEYER, 192
DERRETT, 187
DESCOMBS, 119 122
DESHAIN, 91
DETCHEMENDY, 131
DETZEN, 123
DEVAL, 108
DEVEN, 188
DEVER, 69
DEVILBIES, 176
DEVILBISS, 162
DEVILLIS, 153
DEVOSS, 91
DEWITT, 124
DEYOUNG, 72
DIAN, 74
DICE, 77
DICK, 154
DICKERSON, 72 101 190
DICKEY, 77
DICKSON, 69 77 78 84 95 96
DIELLE, 10
DIERKS, 4
DIFFENDAFFER, 154
DIFFENDOFFER, 192
DIGGS, 62
DILION, 46
DILL, 108 141
DILLARD, 24 104 109
DILLEN, 91
DILLINGHAM, 187

DILLON, 15 108 124 165
DILY, 7
DIMERLICH, 109
DIMMETT, 160
DIMMINT, 33
DIMMITT, 32 38
DINGLE, 46 58
DINWIDDIE, 142
DIRSKILL, 101
DISHONG, 97
DITTMER, 7
DIVERS, 69
DIVINNEY, 109
DIXON, 91 100 108 131 161 165 167 174
DOAN, 46 47 52 55 58 154 174
DOANE, 87
DOBBINS, 60
DOBBS, 107 124 125
DOBSON, 10 87
DOCKING, 109
DODBACH, 128
DODD, 28 34 98 123
DODDS, 85 97
DODGE, 13 59 72 96 191
DODSON, 17 62 85 94 95
DOLAND, 77
DOLLARD, 73 96
DOLLINS, 46
DOLLY, 154
DOLTON, 153 192
DOMINICK, 108
DONALD, 190
DONALDSON, 71 123
DONEGAN, 8
DONELSON, 25
DONIPLANT, 60
DONLEY, 153
DONNAVAN, 2
DONNELL, 10 17 91 145
DONOVAN, 91 131
DOOLEY, 69 71 74 99
DORAN, 188
DORITY, 100
DORMAN, 106 107
DORRANCE, 14
DORREL, 91
DORRELL, 72

DORRIA, 18
DORSHIMER, 21
DOSIER, 99
DOSIRN, 60
DOSS, 123
DOTSON, 62 91
DOUB, 85
DOUCHIMER, 29
DOUGHERTY, 3 99 188
DOUGHTY, 19
DOUGLAS, 46 123 188
DOUGLASS, 60 101 110 144
DOWELL, 29 69
DOWLING, 15 144
DOWNEY, 96
DOWNING, 62 64 125 153 154 191 192
DOWNS, 65 66 68
DOWNSLL, 68
DOXEY, 131
DOYLE, 143 174
DRAGO, 192
DRAKE, 73 124 146 156 161 164 188
DRAPER, 64
DREYFUS, 35
DRIER, 4
DRILLER, 188 189
DRISDALE, 12
DRITE, 188
DRUMHELLER, 64 184
DRUNKAM, 188
DRY, 69 73
DRYDEN, 64 91 96 152-154 170 177 181
DUANE, 99 188
DUCKWORTH, 69 101 188
DUDLEY, 60 65 78 97 131 184
DUFF, 60 64 108 184
DUFRIEND, 154
DUGAN, 2
DULANEY, 69 74 77 184
DULANY, 60 62 74 85 187
DULEY, 97
DULIN, 101
DULL, 65 184
DUMPHY, 184
DUNAGAN, 102
DUNAWAY, 42 43
DUNBAR, 77 149 155 179

DUNCAN, 1 4 49 54 59 60 65 69 73 77 78 91 97 98 112 131 141 142 151 153 164 176 191 192
DUNCANSON, 102
DUNHAM, 59 102
DUNIVAN, 184
DUNKIN, 32
DUNLAP, 85 102 153 154
DUNN, 64 87 97 99 119 153 162 188 192
DUNNIGAN, 188
DUNNING, 187
DUNSMORE, 188
DUREEL, 180
DURHAM, 91 144
DURKE, 170
DURKEE, 149 151 153 154 157 162-165 168 173-176 178 180-182
DURLEE, 147
DURNELL, 66-68
DURRETT, 153
DUTTON, 60 184
DUVALL, 64 98
DVIS, 97
DWARF, 87
DWILBIUS, 160
DWYER, 145
DYAE, 102
DYE, 71 73 116
DYER, 60 65 68 104 123 184 190
DYSERT, 46
DYSON, 97
EACERS, 191
EADS, 31 105 191
EAGER, 120
EAGLESON, 118 120 121
EALES, 71
EALS, 37
EALY, 71
EARIXSON, 91
EARLEY, 91 184
EARLY, 60 91 146
EARNEST, 184
EARP, 19 151 154
EARSOM, 47
EASLEY, 77 78 80 168
EAST, 60
EASTMAN, 25 28 30 31 173

EASTON, 147 151 154 155 170
EASTWOOD, 1 125
EATHERTON, 140
EATON, 126
EAVES, 154
ECHARETT, 18
ECHART, 188
ECHLE, 123
ECKHART, 109
ECKOFF, 124
ECKZLER, 151
EDDE, 106
EDDLEMAN, 184
EDDY, 180
EDELEN, 65
EDGE, 99 188
EDINGER, 18
EDLEN, 65
EDMINSON, 84
EDMONDSON, 107 126
EDMUNDSON, 78
EDMUNS, 184
EDMUNSON, 78
EDNER, 13
EDWARD, 131
EDWARDS, 10 16 58 59 68 74 78 91 123 131 140 142 145 158
EHLERS, 20
EICHENBERGER, 144
EIDSON, 95
EISENHOUR, 188
EISLE, 78 109
ELAM, 60 102 188
ELDER, 68 115 116 188 194
ELDRIDGE, 124
ELER, 104
ELIAD, 192
ELISON, 91
ELKINS, 95
ELLER, 47
ELLESRIT, 91
ELLETT, 131
ELLINGTON, 122
ELLIOT, 60 62
ELLIOTE, 131
ELLIOTT, 21-23 27 31 36 78 91 118-121 140 156

ELLIS, 28 59 60 72 78 87 96 98 102 104 110 126 131 149 154 155 161-163 168 178-181 183 184 187 188 191
ELLISON, 69 91 131 154 170 177 178
ELLMAKER, 154
ELLS, 170
ELLSBURY, 62 63 69
ELLSTON, 46
ELMON, 60
ELMORE, 65
ELSBERRY, 184
ELSTON, 64
ELTON, 60
ELY, 21-24 26 27 31 32 35 36 146
EMBREE, 72 74
EMBREY, 122
EMERSON, 21 24 34 65 143 158
EMMERSON, 78 187 192
EMMONDS, 99
EMMONS, 5 99 109 192
EMS, 20 35
ENDRES, 108 109
ENEX, 42
ENGLAND, 69 123 124
ENGLE, 71
ENGLISH, 82 87 91 131 154 155 186 191 192
ENNET, 102
ENNETT, 99
ENNST, 128
ENO, 97
ENOCH, 72
ENOS, 78
ENRIGHT, 19
ENSLEY, 47
ENSON, 145
ENYART, 91
EPPERLT, 145
EPPERSON, 21 24 27 31-33 35-37 187
ERANSO, 142
ERNEST, 65
ERNOS, 100
ERP, 20
ERVING, 60
ERVINS, 192
ERWIN, 78 81 109 131 142
ESCUE, 151 170

ESHAM, 98
ESKIEL, 191
ESKIN, 192
ESLINGER, 109
ESS, 47
ESSA, 131
ESTEP, 2 4 7
ESTEPTS, 5
ESTES, 65 78 91 97 124 131 184 188
EUBANK, 72
EUBANKS, 47 56
EULTON, 174
EVANS, 5 13 47 54 58 60 69 72 74 78 79 83 91 99 100 102 120 140-142 162 188 191
EVERETT, 19 91
EVERHEART, 47 104
EVERINGHAM, 14
EVERS, 184
EVERSAL, 192
EVERSOTTE, 168
EVERZAL, 191
EVINS, 82
EWALT, 183
EWEING, 102
EWELL, 91
EWING, 78 84 91 154 157 164
EZZELL, 64 184
FABER, 102 156
FABOUR, 188
FADDERHASE, 59
FADOUX, 159
FAGAN, 22 23 28 71
FAGG, 124
FAIELDS, 47
FAIN, 125
FAIR, 102
FAKNER, 192
FALKNER, 87 191
FALLEN, 91
FANLEONER, 155
FANNING, 21 22
FANNON, 98
FANT, 102
FARISS, 102
FARLEY, 6
FARMER, 60 63 78-80 100 126 184
FARNANATS, 131

FARNON, 188
FARR, 109 122 124 155
FARRELL, 2 72 109
FARRIS, 91 131 190
FARRISS, 65
FARRUR, 188
FARTHING, 69 72
FARVALLY, 8
FASSETT, 192
FAUBION, 97
FAUCET, 74
FAULKNER, 99
FAUX, 109
FEALZE, 32
FEASTER, 125
FEELER, 113
FEELY, 78
FEENAN, 145
FELAND, 91
FELDMAN, 123 126
FELIX, 174
FELKORES, 104
FELLOWS, 155
FENDLEY, 65
FENNEL, 39
FENTON, 48 64 113
FEREE, 100
FEREL, 122
FERGUSON, 63 71 78 100 102 105-108 125 126 184
FERLEY, 5
FERREL, 69 74 78 193
FERRELL, 69 78
FERRIER, 97
FERRILL, 97
FERRIN, 97 187
FERRY, 63
FETZAR, 113
FEWSON, 78
FICKEN, 7
FICKLEN, 65
FICKLIN, 141 143 184
FIDLER, 91
FIELD, 22 24 51
FIELDER, 155
FIELDS, 45 68 86 91 155
FIFE, 32

FIGGINS, 23
FIGGON, 37
FIGHTENCAM, 18
FILE, 195
FILLEY, 155 156
FILSES, 86
FINCH, 91
FINCHER, 87
FINDLAY, 109
FINDLEY, 65 78 188
FINE, 19 78 127 131 187
FINELY, 187
FINEY, 78
FINGLE, 122
FINK, 109 192
FINKS, 22 47 73 94
FINLEY, 63 98 155-157 173 178
FINLY, 64
FINNELL, 131
FINNEY, 16 109
FINT, 143
FISH, 87 97 155
FISHBACK, 190
FISHER, 24 25 30 33 34 37 60 99 102 106 107 184 195
FISHPOOL, 95
FITCH, 187
FITZGERALD, 91 187
FITZHUGH, 67 68 102
FITZMASTER, 188
FITZSIMON, 191
FITZWATER, 121 122 191
FLANAGAN, 69 131
FLANERY, 47 91
FLANIGAN, 145
FLANNIGAN, 145
FLANZ, 145
FLEENOR, 95
FLEETWOOD, 78
FLEMING, 78 98 188
FLEMMING, 65 78 184 192
FLEMMNG, 78
FLENNER, 87
FLESHMAN, 99
FLETCHER, 35 39 60 77 91 102
FLING, 59
FLINN, 78

FLINT, 104
FLIPPEN, 123
FLOOD, 18 97
FLORY, 131
FLOUNEY, 78
FLOURNEY, 78
FLOURNOY, 131
FLOWEREE, 27 32 34
FLOWERRE, 33
FLOWERREE, 29
FLOYD, 11 48 59 67 77 81 191
FLY, 118
FOGEL, 108
FOLAND, 96
FOLEY, 63 191
FOLKS, 95
FOLLY, 4
FOLY, 63
FONDA, 78
FOOCHE, 188
FORBES, 155
FORBUS, 187
FORBUSH, 60 63
FORCE, 166 168
FORD, 31 38 47 60 69 72 99 109 180 184
FORE, 175
FOREE, 155 162
FOREMAN, 72
FORGE, 168
FORGUENER, 188
FORGUSON, 104
FORKINS, 60
FORKNER, 60
FORMAN, 32 37 38 69 148 154-156 160 161 171 174
FORREST, 68 152 156 181 182
FORSYTHE, 69 190
FORT, 47 59 102 124 131
FORTNEY, 41
FORTUNE, 155 192
FOSSET, 47 48 57 191
FOST, 49
FOSTER, 59 60 78 91 96 97 99 102 122 143 184 187 188
FOSTIN, 60
FOWKES, 69
FOWKS, 69

FOWLER, 71 74 78 91 132 141 188
FOWLKES, 69
FOX, 69 78 87 97 142 187 188
FOXTON, 132
FOXWELL, 64 184
FOXWORTHY, 104
FOY, 188
FRAIZER, 91 168
FRAKES, 91
FRAME, 192 194 195
FRAMPTON, 116
FRANCES, 142
FRANCIS, 26 155 156 191
FRANDZ, 192
FRANK, 191
FRANKLIN, 78 79 87 123 155
FRANSE, 78
FRAZER, 161 187
FRAZIER, 13 16 17 60 109 140 143 144 147 149 153 155 156 161 164 184 192
FREDERECY, 20
FREDERICK, 97 156
FREE, 188
FREELAND, 98 122
FREELLY, 188
FREEMAN, 42 45 78 82-84 91 102 122 123 125 141 188
FREEZE, 112
FRELDEN, 117
FRENCH, 104 132
FRESH, 181
FRESHOUR, 78
FRESSNA, 126
FRESTOE, 132
FRETWELL, 155
FREUND, 111
FRIGLEY, 87
FRISELL, 3
FRISSELL, 3
FRISTO, 109
FRISTOE, 78
FRITTA, 116
FRITZ, 109
FRIZZELL, 2
FROST, 1 4 5 78 80 81
FROSTY, 154 155
FROWBANK, 87

FRUIT, 22 58 73
FRY, 78 99 188 190
FRYENER, 87
FUCH, 74
FUDGE, 21 91
FUGATE, 69 91 191
FUGET, 47 192
FULK, 91 192
FULKERSON, 86 112
FULLER, 95 124 184
FULLERTON, 59
FULLINGTON, 142
FULTON, 65 78 79 132
FUNK, 132
FUQUA, 29 33 37 155 156 168 170
FUQUE, 22
FURGERSON, 100
FURGESON, 95
FURGISON, 99
FURGUSON, 69 78 159
FURMAN, 191
FURQUIM, 191
FUTWELL, 155
FYFER, 184
GABBERT, 69 91
GABLE, 108
GAINES, 72 102
GAINS, 49 50 119 192
GAINST, 73
GAITHER, 115
GALALAY, 5
GALAWAY, 64
GALBREATH, 48 97 124
GALBRETH, 74
GALE, 184
GALLAGHER, 145
GALLEHAD, 64
GALLEHER, 27 32
GALLENHAM, 145
GALLOP, 108
GALLOWAY, 60 63 184
GALOWAY, 63
GALPH, 48
GALVERN, 95
GALVIN, 5
GALWAY, 64
GAMACHE, 20 132

GAMBLE, 3 9 11 132
GAMMON, 60 184
GAMMONS, 96
GAN, 91
GANEWAY, 123
GANNET, 74
GANT, 48
GARBER, 109
GARDINER, 28
GARDNER, 91 110 123 132 156 184
GARHAM, 188
GARICK, 25
GARNER, 48 63 132 168 184
GARNET, 29 69
GARNETT, 34 72 151 156
GARRET, 74 91
GARRETT, 38 91 94 97 109 110 168 188
GARRISH, 31 34
GARRISON, 124
GARROT, 48
GARROTT, 104
GARRY, 123
GARTH, 122
GARTON, 91
GASAWAY, 79
GASH, 124
GASHART, 191
GASS, 48
GASSCOCK, 69
GASTON, 72
GASWAY, 191
GATES, 13 79 81 91
GATHER, 112
GATHRIGHT, 71 100
GATRELL, 188
GATSON, 71
GAULT, 87
GAUTIER, 4 7 12 14 15 19
GAY, 171
GAYDON, 39
GAYHART, 192
GEAMS, 60
GEARHART, 159
GEARS, 60
GEE, 56 58 97 98 141
GEER, 69
GELEANED, 60

GELKER, 6
GELMER, 68
GENEROUS, 184
GENNINGS, 187
GENTRY, 48 68 69 74 85 87 132
GEOGG, 53
GEORGE, 85 102
GERICK, 30
GERKE, 67
GERKEN, 6 123
GERKEY, 125
GERKIN, 6
GERNSAY, 23
GERRARD, 34
GERRISH, 31
GERRY, 74
GERTZER, 145
GESHORE, 91
GESS, 91
GETT, 1
GEVIS, 123
GEYER, 132
GIBBONS, 145 187
GIBBONY, 102
GIBBS, 102 184 187 188
GIBONEY, 132
GIBSON, 3 60 63 69 74 79 81 83 85 91 124 126 184 187
GIDDINGS, 190
GIDDIONS, 74
GIDEONS, 74
GIFFENS, 124
GILBERT, 36 69 74 87 97 102 122 190
GILBRETH, 79
GILES, 60 142 192
GILHAM, 79
GILKEY, 59 60
GILL, 91 97 180
GILLAM, 122
GILLASPY, 69
GILLEHAN, 60
GILLELAND, 132 184
GILLERLAID, 64
GILLESPIE, 26 37 109 120
GILLET, 91
GILLIAM, 18 132
GILLIS, 109

GILLMAN, 18
GILLUM, 65
GILMAN, 97
GILMER, 63 68
GILMORE, 60 79 91 100 102 188
GILPEN, 132
GILPIN, 57 184
GILSON, 87
GILSTRAP, 132
GIPSON, 42 97
GIRARD, 178
GISH, 11 125
GIST, 91 151 156
GIVEN, 85 132 172
GIVENS, 87 91 102 115 127 148 149 150 152 156 160 161 165 172 179
GIVINGS, 74
GLADDEN, 91
GLADNEY, 64
GLADWILL, 102
GLASBY, 3
GLASCOCK, 21 22 23 26 27 28 29 31 32 34 37 38 63 79 91 95 132
GLASGOW, 117
GLASS, 79 88 153 191 192
GLASSCOCK, 132
GLASSGOW, 98
GLAVER, 188
GLAVEZ, 184
GLAZEBROOK, 124
GLEIM, 151
GLEN, 79 91
GLENCY, 104
GLENDY, 104
GLENN, 21 60 69 72 155 156
GLIDEWELL, 116
GLINN, 146 152 154 156 157 160 191 192
GLOVER, 60 97 102 112 132 156 157 170 177 192
GLOWN, 60
GLOYD, 84
GLUNTZ, 109
GLUNZ, 109
GOAT, 123
GOATLY, 50
GOATTY, 48

GODWIN, 85
GOE, 69
GOETZ, 123 145
GOFF, 97 124 146 156
GOFORTH, 109
GOINGS, 69
GOLDING, 79
GOLDSBURY, 156
GOLDSMITH, 122
GOLDTHWAITE, 156
GOMLEN, 79
GONZA, 16
GOOCH, 9 69
GOOD, 91 190
GOODEMON, 188
GOODEN, 98
GOODLETT, 60
GOODMAN, 63 109
GOODNIGHT, 48 68 69
GOODNO, 156 165
GOODNOE, 88
GOODRICH, 60 69 184
GOODWIN, 71 109 184
GORDEN, 64 126
GORDON, 63 64 132 184
GORE, 21 22 25 27 33 69
GORIN, 132
GORRELL, 124 125
GORTON, 19 96
GOSELIN, 190
GOSHEN, 80 190
GOSHON, 60
GOSNEY, 69
GOSS, 69 123 124
GOTIER, 6
GOUGH, 74
GOULD, 157
GOVE, 112
GOWENS, 117
GOWING, 79
GRAFFENRATH, 123
GRAGG, 1
GRAHAM, 3 23 79 85 89 109 125 188
GRALBREATH, 189
GRALL, 109
GRAMMIS, 116

GRAN, 29
GRANT, 22 61 69 95 96 102 104 132 184 190 192
GRASHON, 124
GRASHONG, 124
GRASON, 65 184
GRAUS, 61
GRAVENS, 64
GRAVES, 59 63 69 142 143 158 183 184 192
GRAY, 29 39 48 63 73 79 99 100 141 188 192 195
GRAYHAM, 112
GRAYSON, 46 54 55
GREAR, 99
GREEN, 3 29 32 34 61 64 68 74 79 85 102 104 125 152 153 155-157 162 167 168 170-172 177 184 191 192
GREENING, 69 71
GREENWELL, 74
GREENWOOD, 85
GREER, 8 12 69 132
GREGARI, 20
GREGG, 79 109
GREGGORY, 91
GREGGS, 126
GREGORY, 95 97 99 104 125 154 157 171 188 192
GREOR, 102
GRESWAY, 192
GREY, 100 102 104 117 121 122
GRIDER, 132
GRIENER, 39
GRIFFIN, 33 48 78 97 132
GRIFFITH, 24 63 79 87 94 98 99 102 126
GRIGGS, 156
GRIGSBY, 109
GRIMES, 63 69 71 104
GRISHAM, 97
GRISM, 91
GRISWOLD, 59
GROOM, 91
GROSHONG, 125
GROSS, 69
GROVE, 72
GROVES, 69
GRUBB, 191 192

GRUBER, 145
GRUEN, 184
GRUGIN, 48 74
GRUNT, 79
GUERRAMT, 102
GUFFOTH, 192
GUIAN, 117
GUILFORD, 31
GUILIDEN, 61
GUILL, 95
GUINN, 91 95 125
GUION, 118
GULLETT, 132
GULLY, 12
GUNISON, 65
GUNN, 1 61 126 145
GUNNELS, 79
GURIN, 61
GUTHERY, 194 195
GUTHRIE, 99
GUTTIRE, 69
GUY, 102
GWIN, 72 85 124
GWINN, 61 132 184
GYER, 132
HACKLER, 79
HACKLEY, 69
HACKNEY, 190
HADEN, 22 33 36
HAFF, 185
HAGAN, 5 6 157
HAGANNAN, 184
HAGANS, 80
HAGAR, 143
HAGERMAN, 159 191
HAGERTY, 113
HAGGERTY, 182
HAGOOD, 157-159 169 170 173 175 177 180
HAHN, 109
HAIL, 80
HAILE, 12
HAINER, 22
HAINES, 24 69 71 79 80 88 95 192
HAINEZ, 88
HAINS, 125
HAISLIP, 65 79

HAJSE, 123
HALCOM, 65
HALCOMB, 61
HALDEBECK, 26
HALE, 14 61 99
HALEY, 49 143 144 149 157-159 191
HALL, 22 28 46 48 49 61 69 79 80 85 88 91
    92 95-97 99 132 159 168 171 184 185
    187 188 191 192
HALLIBURTON, 142
HALLOWELL, 157 164
HALLY, 64
HALM, 188
HALSEY, 159 162 174 175
HALTERMAN, 143
HAM, 61 79 99 102 185
HAMARD, 125
HAMBAUGH, 161
HAMBLIN, 97 104
HAMBY, 79
HAME, 61
HAMER, 153
HAMICK, 13
HAMILTON, 59 61 79 80 88 102 104 109 132
    140 142 148 150 157-159 162 166 169
    171 174 175 177 179 191 192
HAMMACK, 63 132 185
HAMMES, 140
HAMMET, 65
HAMMETT, 141 145
HAMMON, 61 145
HAMMOND, 18 61 65 102 132
HAMMONS, 61
HAMMONTREE, 79
HAMON, 63
HAMONY, 64
HAMPTON, 26 27 100 109 159
HAMRICK, 13
HAMSTEAD, 169
HANAGAN, 69
HANAH, 98
HANALL, 159
HANBROUGH, 79
HANCE, 173
HANCOCH, 65
HANCOCK, 59 91 132 146 184 192
HANCY, 172

HAND, 68 122
HANDCOCK, 59
HANDON, 22
HANER, 150 151 157
HANES, 57 92
HANEY, 72
HANLEY, 59 61 102 188
HANLON, 145
HANLY, 142
HANNA, 22 71 73
HANNAH, 102 188
HANNOR, 79
HANSBOROGUH, 36
HANSBOROUGH, 25 31
HANSBROUGH, 79 80
HANSE, 102
HANSEEKER, 158
HANSEN, 80 152
HANSFORD, 41
HANSON, 123
HANSUCKER, 192
HANT, 157 158
HARBERT, 79
HARD, 100
HARDEN, 102
HARDER, 16
HARDESTY, 64 68 185
HARDICK, 69
HARDIN, 8 49 88 92 185
HARDING, 59 104
HARDY, 21 22 24 25 30 31 35-37 92
HARE, 106 108 132 140
HARESTY, 68
HARGOOD, 71
HARIGER, 122
HARINGER, 74
HARISON, 48 49 54 56
HARKINS, 99 116
HARLAN, 141 142 145
HARLER, 100
HARLESS, 79 80
HARLEY, 145
HARLOW, 3 69
HARMAN, 48
HARMS, 123
HARNEGER, 74
HARNESS, 6 15

222

HARNEY, 126
HARNSER, 59
HARNY, 187
HARPER, 49 61 72 97 100 132 150 152 158 163 167 175 178 180 184 188
HARRAL, 185
HARRELL, 157 158 185
HARRELSON, 80
HARRINGTON, 91
HARRIS, 38 42 43 49 61 69 72 74 79 81 85 88 92 95 97 109 124 126 132 155 161 162 187 188 191 192
HARRISON, 10 16 44 74 79 80 88 102 104 115 116 132 152 158 163 166 182 187 188 192
HARRISS, 65 102
HARROW, 69
HART, 69 99 125 191
HARTELL, 125
HARTUNG, 128
HARVEY, 39 49 61 105 125 132 172 184 188
HARVY, 49 63
HARWOOD, 122 157
HARYMAN, 125
HARZRIDER, 126
HASKIN, 124
HASMON, 88
HASSELTON, 95
HASSET, 144
HASSETT, 144
HATCHER, 132
HATFIELD, 79 95 125 157
HATHAWAY, 120
HATHEWAY, 191
HATHWAY, 192
HATSBURGH, 145
HATTEN, 48 49 58
HATTON, 47 188
HAUGHTON, 61
HAUKINS, 74
HAUSTON, 31 64
HAVEN, 163
HAVENS, 20
HAVERSTICK, 11 16 17
HAWKINS, 22 28 31 32 35 37 64 69 74 79 85 118 145 152 153 158 159 192

HAWLEY, 91
HAY, 148 157 159
HAYCRAFT, 71 182
HAYDEN, 49 69 72 79 99 102 149 157 158 168 169 191 192
HAYDIN, 168
HAYDON, 88 150 157-160
HAYES, 7
HAYGOOD, 65 147 157
HAYLIN, 148 168
HAYMAN, 147 157-159 164 171 177 181
HAYNE, 125
HAYNES, 28 48 71 85 95 133 140
HAYS, 5 21-23 25 27 30-32 34 35 38 48 51 72 74 80 88 91 102 104 105 108 117 120 126 132 133 158 188 190
HAYSLER, 122
HAYSLIP, 185 187
HAYTER, 194 195
HAZE, 35
HAZEBRIGG, 188
HAZELRIGG, 151
HAZENCRAFT, 192
HAZLERIG, 100
HEADLER, 116
HEARST, 9 123
HEATH, 80 125 133
HEATHES, 142
HEATHESTONE, 74
HEATHMAN, 69 141
HEBERLE, 109
HEBERTON, 157
HECKEL, 46
HECKTER, 119
HECTOR, 195
HEDDING, 109
HEDGEPETH, 125
HEDGES, 74 102 109 188
HEDGSBETH, 91
HEDRICK, 145
HEEDSON, 124
HEELING, 99
HEER, 73
HEFINGTON, 61
HEILS, 15
HEIMSETH, 7
HEISEN, 184

HEISKELL, 157
HEISKILL, 159
HEIZER, 71
HELM, 122 190
HELMS, 69
HELNUCH, 123
HELSTAB, 16
HELTERBRAND, 17 133
HELTON, 110
HELTZALL, 109
HEMPELL, 18
HEMPHELL, 18
HEMPHILL, 39
HEMPSTEAD, 133
HENBRICHT, 123
HENDERSON, 6 61 74 77 80 84 91 92 97 99 102 133 149 151 157-159 169 173 174 178 182 185
HENDISON, 104
HENDRICK, 104 142 158
HENDRICKS, 77 79 192
HENDRON, 142
HENE, 99
HENLINE, 133
HENNDON, 74
HENNEGER, 69
HENNESY, 7
HENNIGER, 74
HENRIED, 16
HENRIETTA, 157
HENRY, 6 12 14 17 19 61 64 68 79 86 184 189-192
HENSELY, 104
HENSLEY, 13 17 79 92 102
HENSON, 39 72 187
HEPERON, 34
HEPLER, 49
HERALD, 192
HEREFORD, 109
HEREOLL, 61
HERGFORD, 95
HERING, 191 192
HERKETT, 122
HERNDON, 61 71
HERON, 190
HERR, 190

HERRICK, 51 55
HERRIGAN, 110
HERRIL, 79
HERRING, 91 102 180 185
HERRINGE, 169
HERRINGTON, 4
HERRON, 109
HERSMAN, 74
HERTZING, 145
HERVY, 63
HERYFORD, 95
HESS, 42 141
HESSER, 184
HETHERTON, 59
HEURMAN, 126
HEWETT, 71
HEWIT, 190
HEWITT, 61
HEWLET, 192
HEYLE, 109
HICALL, 26
HICHART, 74
HICKAM, 113
HICKERSON, 117 118
HICKESON, 65
HICKINSON, 117
HICKISTON, 104
HICKLEN, 195
HICKLIN, 27 31 75 77 78 80
HICKMAN, 71 91 92 111
HICKOX, 133
HICKS, 79 80 88 119
HICKUM, 79
HIDE, 91 191
HIGBY, 88
HIGGERSON, 8
HIGGINBOTHAM, 2 9 10
HIGGINGS, 191
HIGGINS, 2 9 68 192
HIGHLEY, 79
HIGHTON, 79
HIGHTOWER, 95
HILBERT, 163
HILDERBRAND, 7
HILDRETH, 35
HILEN, 61

HILER, 61 184
HILL, 8 15 43 61 64 69 79 80 85 91 96 97 102 104 133 157 170 184 185 190 195
HILLER, 96 99
HILLMAN, 167
HILTON, 21 64
HINCHER, 119
HINCLE, 80 81
HINDS, 95
HINES, 6 64 78 124 133 144 153 185
HINEY, 11
HINKERSON, 183
HINKLE, 117 118
HINKSON, 169
HINSHAW, 80 141
HINSON, 71 91 159 180
HINTON, 99 117 120-122 143 158 183
HIPHERY, 126
HIPSHEAR, 2
HIRAM, 168
HIRBY, 71
HIRSCH, 141
HIRTLIN, 99
HISCAL, 26
HISCATE, 73
HISER, 73 79
HISEY, 99
HISKELL, 168
HISOFELDER, 145
HITEHOUSE, 185
HITSON, 106
HITT, 133
HITTEBRIDLE, 109
HOARD, 100
HOBACK, 88
HOBBS, 49 61 79
HOCKADAY, 7 8 102
HOCKER, 69 80
HOCKINS, 72
HOCKSADAY, 104
HODGES, 124
HODMAN, 192
HODUSTON, 100
HOFFMAN, 89
HOGAN, 95
HOGERNSEN, 95
HOLCOMB, 61 80 133

HOLDEN, 133
HOLDER, 73
HOLEMAN, 102
HOLEMS, 192
HOLINGSHEAD, 160
HOLLAND, 92 125 126
HOLLENBECK, 133
HOLLEND, 102
HOLLIDAY, 69 72 159
HOLLINGSHEAD, 164 175 180
HOLLINGSWORTH, 69
HOLLIWAY, 159
HOLLOMAN, 133
HOLLOWAY, 69 72 73 79
HOLLYMAN, 125
HOLMAN, 92 133 144
HOLMES, 63 72 149 160 185 191 192
HOLOWAY, 65
HOLSCLAW, 127
HOLT, 25 99 104 118 122
HOLTMAN, 20
HOLTSZEN, 123
HOMAS, 155
HOMBY, 61
HOMELY, 61
HOMER, 192
HONEAY, 113
HONEY, 11
HONEYCUT, 123
HONLEY, 105
HONOKER, 158
HONORE, 163
HOOCHINS, 79
HOOD, 75 118
HOOK, 48 79 80 102
HOOKE, 190
HOOKER, 97 188
HOOPER, 78 80 95 105-107
HOOVER, 99 124
HOPKINS, 23 28 61 100 133 185
HOPPER, 81 85
HOPWOOD, 185
HORD, 73
HORINE, 8
HORN, 79 91 124 125
HORNBACK, 59
HORNBUCKLE, 100 102 109

HORNING, 109
HORNSBY, 80
HORR, 32
HORRICKER, 154
HORSLEY, 187
HORTON, 29 79 91
HOSKINS, 157
HOSS, 65
HOSTLER, 104
HOTSENFILLER, 150
HOTSENSSILLAR, 180
HOTSENSSILLER, 151 172 179
HOTZLAW, 158
HOUCHENS, 79
HOUCHIN, 49
HOUCK, 109
HOUDERSHELL, 64
HOUF, 102
HOUGH, 55 133
HOUNTZ, 145
HOUP, 57
HOUSE, 49 88 191 192
HOUSEMAN, 1
HOUSTON, 31 79 80 185
HOUX, 118
HOW, 49
HOWARD, 80 95 109 126 150 159 188
HOWDYSHELL, 63
HOWE, 69 99 105
HOWEL, 80
HOWELL, 61 69 73 133 185
HOWERTON, 157 165
HUBBARD, 49 59 61 63 73 74 85 117 141 142 187
HUBBLE, 79 91
HUBBS, 157
HUBET, 140
HUBRICHT, 123
HUCHISON, 188
HUCKABY, 106
HUDDLESTON, 92
HUDIKAFER, 158
HUDSON, 23 28 59 65 88 92 97 100 126 133 141 144 158 169 184 187 192
HUDSPETH, 92 133
HUEKSTOP, 65
HUFF, 42 91 102 122 125

HUFFAKER, 109
HUFFEFINGER, 124
HUFFINGTON, 100
HUFFMAN, 94 96
HUFFT, 78 79
HUFINGTON, 188
HUGES, 155
HUGHBANKS, 91
HUGHES, 59 61 79 80 91 92 102 104 133 148-151 155-157 160 161 167 173 177 178 180 181 192
HUGHLITT, 92
HUGHS, 65 114 125 133
HUGHSMITH, 61
HUKEL, 45 49
HUKERSON, 188
HULBARB, 59
HULEN, 61 140
HULETT, 156 159
HULL, 17 61 91 97 146
HULLARD, 187
HULTS, 35 187
HUMBLE, 191
HUME, 182
HUMER, 156
HUMES, 97
HUMMELL, 96
HUMPHREY, 92 95 191 192
HUMPHREYS, 100 102 188
HUMPHRIES, 65 100
HUMPREY, 192
HUNER, 152 154 157 158 160-162 164 165 167 168 170 172 173
HUNGATE, 48 49 52
HUNNEWELL, 157
HUNSICKER, 149 150 158 161
HUNSUCKER, 91
HUNT, 2 4 17 18 51 57 66 67 69 104 126 151 188 192
HUNTER, 61 74 85 91 97 102 109 133 154
HUNTON, 133
HUNTSBERRY, 30
HUNTSMAN, 65 141
HUNTSUCKER, 80 92
HURD, 71 133
HURDLE, 49
HURDLEN, 49

HURMAL, 60
HURN, 187
HURNDON, 79
HURRALD, 191
HURST, 14 95 96
HURT, 61 148 158 166 177
HUSK, 17
HUSKEY, 11 13
HUSON, 126
HUSSBETH, 145
HUSTAIN, 126
HUSTERBERY, 123
HUSTON, 59 61 71 98 133 184 188 190
HUTCHENS, 85
HUTCHERSON, 72 102
HUTCHESON, 113 115
HUTCHINS, 77
HUTCHINSON, 142
HUTCHISON, 69 113-115 133 191
HUTESON, 71
HUTHER, 145
HUTMACHER, 109
HUTSESSILLER, 159
HUTSON, 79 191
HUTT, 61 64
HUTTAN, 64
HUTTON, 61 147
HUTTS, 188
HUTZ, 102
HUTZER, 102
HYDE, 150
HYER, 133
HYMAN, 145
HYNSON, 4
HYTEN, 105
HYTON, 102
IDDINGS, 80
IDSON, 80
IGO, 92
IHRAIG, 105
INDY, 155
INGLE, 80
INGRAM, 65 123 124 185
INIS, 61
INLOW, 21 24 29 33 35 125
INOW, 190
INTLEMAN, 123

IRELAND, 68
IRVIN, 45 80 194
IRVINE, 55
IRWIN, 36 85 123 195 196
ISAAC, 88
ISGRIG, 6
ISHAM, 42
ISOM, 109
ISON, 80 149
ISONHOUR, 98
IVIE, 71
JABES, 123
JACK, 80
JACKMAN, 49 50
JACKS, 69 92
JACKSON, 22 50 61 64 69 70 72 79 80 83
    92 97 98 109 123 126 133 141 143 157
    159 161 165 176 180 185 192
JACOB, 159 191 192
JACOBS, 186
JACOBSON, 144
JAGLES, 123 125
JAMERSAND, 64
JAMERSON, 171
JAMES, 5 35 38 50 61 70 80-85 92 98 105
    123 133 147 178 192
JAMESON, 21 30 102 133
JAMISON, 3 37 50 63 65 98 133 185
JANE, 61
JANETT, 159
JANIS, 159
JANUARY, 168 170 171
JARMON, 50
JARVIS, 15 16 18
JAY, 109 124
JAYNE, 195
JAYNES, 195
JEAN, 142
JEANS, 102
JEEMES, 124
JEFFERIES, 24 154 159 176 192
JEFFERS, 92 104 191
JEFFERY, 185
JENKINS, 39 61 92 125 133 160 185 191
JENKS, 190
JENNING, 88
JENNINGS, 61 80 192

JENNURSON, 68
JENT, 95
JESSE, 50
JESSIN, 85
JETT, 37 74
JEWELL, 160
JILLET, 97
JIMERSON, 61 64
JINKINS, 92 123
JINNEY, 157
JINNINGS, 72 100
JINSON, 99 100
JOB, 78 187
JOBE, 79 80
JOBSON, 140
JOES, 80
JOHN, 61 133 159
JOHNS, 125
JOHNSON, 2 3 12 23 59 61 63 65 66 70-72
    80 85 88 92 95 97 102 115 116 122-126
    133 145 149 158-160 162-164 170 174
    175 178 179 182 187 188 192
JOHNSTON, 6 17 20 21 27 32-34 46 49 50
    105 109 133 134 143
JOINER, 65
JOLLEY, 188
JOLLY, 98
JONAS, 92
JONES, 3 8 10 21 22 24 32 35 44 50 61 65
    70 74 80 88 91 92 95 98 100 102 104
    105 112-115 118 123 124 134 145 149
    152 153 156 159 165 177 188 191 192
JONSON, 185
JOPLIN, 125
JOPLING, 134
JORDAN, 71 92
JORDEN, 70
JORDON, 70
JOSEPH, 21 88
JOURNEY, 95
JUDAH, 92
JUDGE, 68 122
JUDSON, 191
JUDY, 70
JUNOL, 126
JUNOLL, 126
JUSTICE, 109

JUSTIN, 85
JUSTUS, 110
KALD, 109
KALLAHAN, 59
KANAN, 92
KANATZER, 85
KANES, 92
KARGROVE, 92
KARNES, 92
KASSEBAUME, 17
KATIS, 61
KAVANAUGH, 134
KAVANUAGH, 145
KAYS, 91 124
KEALING, 145
KEARNES, 124
KEARNEY, 109 152 175
KEATH, 71
KECK, 109
KEE, 102
KEEF, 9
KEEFER, 92
KEEL, 109
KEEPER, 94
KEEPERS, 14
KEERAN, 80
KEES, 92
KEESAR, 19
KEETON, 50 80
KEISER, 41
KEITH, 160 191
KEITHLTY, 185
KELLER, 18 61
KELLING, 63
KELLOGG, 151
KELLY, 2 9 70 80 145
KELSEY, 109 188
KELSO, 160
KELSOE, 102 161 179
KELTY, 189
KEMERMAN, 191
KEMP, 98 102 122 134
KEMPER, 63 92 100 134 145 191
KEMPH, 63
KENAPPE, 143
KENDALL, 160 178 191
KENDERICK, 155

KENDRICK, 23 25 31 36 92 147 160
KENEDY, 160
KENNEDY, 104 125 185
KENNER, 92
KENNETT, 13 134 189
KENNEY, 91
KENNOCK, 182
KENOLEY, 96
KENPIN, 63
KENSINGER, 119 121 122
KENT, 142 143
KENTON, 160
KEONING, 85
KERBY, 123 190
KEREHEVAL, 31
KERFOOT, 160
KERLEY, 188
KERR, 125
KERRIGAN, 6
KERTFOOT, 160
KESINGER, 121
KESLER, 20
KESSEMAN, 125
KETHAM, 145
KEVANAUGH, 85
KEY, 102 109 191
KEYS, 91 92
KIBLER, 102
KIDD, 15
KIDNEY, 95
KIDWELL, 98 125 181 192
KIEFER, 123
KIEFFER, 50
KIETHLY, 95
KIGER, 102
KILGON, 140
KILGORE, 46 47-50 53 57 58 124
KILLAM, 61
KILLER, 95 185
KILLIAN, 61
KILLS, 178
KIMAR, 61
KIMBALL, 95
KIMBER, 160
KIMBERLAND, 80
KIMBLE, 65
KIMBRAUGH, 143

KIMBRO, 61 92 187
KIMBROUGH, 188
KIMDEN, 61
KIMON, 64
KIMSAY, 122
KIMSEY, 117 120 122
KINCADE, 51
KINCAID, 3 80 109
KINDELL, 192
KINEY, 72 92
KING, 25 31 47 63 64 72 73 80 92 95 98 100
    102 105-108 110 113 120 134 141 154
    160 173 189
KINGER, 109
KINGS, 98
KINGSBERRY, 185
KINGSBURY, 63
KINGSLAND, 160
KINGSTON, 59
KINION, 61 185
KINNADY, 59
KINNEMON, 88
KINNERMAN, 192
KINNEY, 152
KINNON, 102
KINON, 61
KIPLER, 18
KIPPER, 70
KIRCHOFF, 18
KIRK, 59 85 92 95 182
KIRKENDALL, 70
KIRKHAM, 188 189 192
KIRKLAND, 70 74
KIRKMAN, 92
KIRKPATRICK, 70 108 134 143 144 187
KIRKSTON, 91
KISAMORE, 92
KISER, 57
KISSLER, 92
KITCHEN, 98 140
KLABER, 109
KLAN, 19
KLEIN, 1
KLINE, 50
KLUGH, 72
KNAPP, 125
KNIGHT, 102 108 126 190

KNIGHTEN, 162
KNIGHTON, 80
KNOOTZ, 125
KNORPP, 16
KNOTT, 148 150 160 161 192
KNOWLES, 109
KNOWLETON, 185
KNOWLS, 125
KNOWLTON, 88
KNOX, 61 185
KOENIG, 18
KOHNER, 20
KOLMAN, 142
KORBER, 126
KOUNS, 102
KRAMME, 4
KRATHLEY, 61
KRATLOW, 109
KRAUS, 8
KRIESLER, 125
KRIET, 19
KRIGBAUM, 21 35
KRONES, 140
KUGHLER, 160
KUHN, 96
KULLMAN, 124
KULLOM, 59
KUMLE, 134
KUNSEY, 85
KUNTZ, 123
KUNTZE, 59
KUPPER, 80
KUTSEO, 13 187
KYDE, 48
KYLE, 13 61
LABEAUME, 24 30
LACAMP, 185
LACEFIELD, 92
LACKEY, 85
LACLAND, 193
LACY, 92 116
LADINGTIN, 92
LADY, 92
LAFERDY, 64
LAFITY, 185
LAFON, 149 150 175
LAIGHT, 109

LAIN, 74
LAIR, 134
LAKE, 70
LAKEMAN, 183
LAKENAN, 161
LAKIN, 44 51
LAMB, 32 47 73 161
LAMBERS, 145
LAMBERT, 61 95 96 122
LAMKIN, 19
LAMMON, 80
LAMPTON, 73
LANA, 85
LANAN, 134
LANCASTER, 88 150 191 193
LANCE, 85
LAND, 122 125
LANDE, 122
LANDERS, 80
LANDES, 134
LANDOTT, 17
LANDRETH, 108
LANE, 6 74 92 147 149 158 168 191 193
LANES, 160
LANFORT, 61
LANGDON, 188
LANGEMAN, 109
LANGFORD, 59
LANGLEY, 92 100 102 188
LANGTREE, 102
LANGWORTHY, 109
LANHAM, 13 92 134
LANING, 191
LANIUS, 3
LANKFORD, 61
LAPLANT, 100
LAPMAN, 193
LARAMORE, 102
LARCH, 104
LARD, 61
LAREN, 188
LARENCE, 185
LAREW, 193
LARKIN, 8
LARMER, 70
LARNE, 152
LARRENCE, 104

LARSON, 188
LARUE, 161
LASATER, 92
LASEY, 25
LASSCONTE, 80
LATTIMER, 161
LAUGHLIN, 61
LAUNING, 193
LAUNNON, 80
LAURENCE, 53 54 145
LAURUE, 160
LAURY, 63
LAUX, 88
LAW, 98
LAWLES, 92
LAWLESS, 143
LAWLEY, 145
LAWRENCE, 65 68 71 80 141 185
LAWS, 80
LAWSON, 79 102
LAY, 80 159 161 185 193
LAYTON, 61 88 193
LEA, 64
LEACH, 51 80
LEACHMAN, 71
LEADFORD, 88
LEAGEN, 63
LEAGUE, 126
LEAK, 28
LEAKE, 26 28 30 31 33 36 37 68 71
LEAPARD, 100
LEAR, 25 30
LECOMPTE, 134
LEDFORD, 21 31 35 191-193
LEE, 3 10 17 21 25 26 30 36 51 80 85 92 168 187
LEEK, 21
LEEPER, 54 98 104 158 164 165
LEGG, 150 152 160 161 193
LEHAY, 109
LEIBERT, 145
LEIBLI, 67
LEIGHT, 160 161
LELL, 73
LEMON, 125 126
LEMONS, 11
LEMORY, 63

LENEAR, 61
LENEY, 22
LENNERY, 185
LEOB, 83
LEON, 109
LEONARD, 33
LEROY, 100
LESLIE, 123
LESTER, 145
LETCHER, 102
LETRAMTRE, 85
LETTER, 31
LETTR, 24
LEVAUGH, 51 58
LEVERING, 29 161
LEVI, 165
LEVICK, 143 160
LEVIN, 61 92
LEVINGSTON, 134
LEVIT, 102
LEWELLEN, 68
LEWELLWEN, 134
LEWICKI, 13
LEWIS, 1 14 63-65 71 74 80 85 88 98 109 120 122 134 143 159 160-162 185 188
LEWISON, 92
LIEWELLEN, 68
LIGGIN, 63
LIGHT, 20 124
LIGHTNER, 74 80
LIGON, 161 177
LILES, 64
LILFORD, 64
LILLARD, 153 156 159-161 164 167-170 173 180 182 188
LILLIE, 142
LILLY, 63
LIMBAR, 188
LINBERRY, 74
LINCH, 92
LINDLAY, 73
LINDLEY, 161
LINDNER, 116
LINDSAY, 124
LINDSEY, 64 122 134
LINERBER, 59
LINGLE, 126

LINGLIE, 126
LINGO, 140
LINK, 134 188
LINN, 61 95 185
LINNEY, 22
LINTON, 70
LINVILLE, 92
LIONBERGER, 134
LIPE, 95
LIPES, 95
LIPSCOMB, 85
LISCOMB, 109
LISLE, 92
LISON, 190
LITE, 180
LITER, 35
LITERELL, 51
LITRELL, 51 52
LITTERAL, 74 188
LITTLE, 34 74 80 98 104 161
LITTLEE, 126
LITTLEJOHN, 191
LITTLETON, 114
LITTRELL, 117 118
LIVINGSTON, 13 134
LIZENBY, 160
LMARR, 29
LOAPEN, 104
LOCKER, 65 185
LOCKHART, 66 160
LOCKRIDGE, 48 51 55
LOFF, 68
LOFLAN, 23
LOFLAND, 23 27 37
LOFTTAN, 31
LOFTY, 165
LOGAN, 59 61 65 95 102 123
LOGEN, 123
LOGSTON, 109
LOMAS, 61
LOMAX, 65
LONDON, 88 109 162
LONDSEY, 123
LONG, 1 2 4-8 12 14 15 38 63 64 70 71 80 95 100 102 134 150 173 181 185
LONGACRE, 80
LONGLEY, 100

LONGMIRE, 161
LOOMIS, 85
LOOP, 113
LOOVE, 193
LORTON, 44 50 51
LOTHEN, 155
LOTHROP, 92
LOUDERMILK, 161 193
LOUIS, 61 109 196
LOULAND, 92
LOUTHAN, 161
LOVE, 72 104 146 148 156 161 162 166 168 170
LOVEL, 61 191 193
LOVELACE, 65 114 134
LOVELADY, 126
LOVELESS, 102 125
LOVERRING, 29
LOVIL, 65
LOVING, 61
LOW, 24 30
LOWDERMILK, 88
LOWE, 88
LOWEN, 147
LOWER, 78 92 107
LOWERY, 74 80 154
LOWES, 194
LOWRY, 123 140
LOYD, 98 122 160 188 193
LRYMAN, 126
LUBBERT, 111
LUCAS, 80 92 96 134
LUCK, 74
LUCKET, 59 185
LUCKETT, 63
LUDWICK, 80
LUKE, 71
LUKENS, 161
LUNDY, 80
LUNFORD, 187
LUPER, 50
LUPTON, 71
LURDEL, 180
LURSON, 109
LUSK, 134
LUTHER, 92
LUTTLE, 74

LUZOEDER, 100
LYAGER, 34
LYCOOK, 119
LYHTNER, 160
LYLE, 21 26 27 36
LYLES, 59
LYNCE, 5
LYNCH, 21 23 33 36 55 61 78 80 85 134 187
LYNES, 161
LYNN, 80 145
LYON, 80 100
LYONS, 52 71
M'CABE, 164
M'CANNE, 140
M'CARTY, 14
M'CULHY, 140
M'DANIEL, 190
M'GAW, 34
M'GOWEN, 34
M'GOWN, 35
M'HERAL, 193
M'LEAN, 167
M'MURTY, 34
MABE, 58
MABERRY, 65
MACCRACKIN, 157
MACE, 35
MACKAY, 1 7 12 14 15 19
MACKINSON, 125
MACKINTON, 59
MACKMAHAN, 64
MACKSEY, 6 7
MADDEN, 5
MADDOX, 15 18 37 102 165 189 193 194
MADGETT, 92
MADIN, 189
MADISON, 110
MADOX, 74 156
MAFFETT, 173
MAFFTY, 92
MAGAFFIN, 8 10
MAGAN, 85
MAGARD, 102
MAGEAN, 10
MAGEDE, 161
MAGEE, 110 157 161-163 169 170 174 175 180 183

MAGGART, 189
MAGGE, 146
MAGINNIS, 65
MAGOFFIN, 9 10 12
MAGRUDER, 22 71
MAGUFFIN, 8
MAGUIRE, 109 162
MAHAN, 36 45 47 52
MAHAR, 101
MAHONEY, 109
MAIDEN, 61
MAIGE, 63
MAIMES, 98
MAIZE, 117 118 120 121
MAJOR, 70 100 101 135 146 162
MAJORS, 81 109 190
MAKISSON, 126
MALIN, 63
MALLERY, 144
MALLET, 135
MALLORY, 70 159 162 170
MALLOT, 107
MALLOTT, 107
MALLOY, 145
MALONE, 81 88 102 141
MALOY, 96
MALREY, 51
MALSEY, 52
MANEGHE, 112
MANES, 2 12
MANESS, 3 4
MANGFED, 101
MANION, 4 72
MANLAY, 65
MANN, 92 142 185
MANNEN, 15
MANNEY, 163
MANNING, 61 71 140 143 144
MANSFIELD, 51 53 92
MANSHIP, 135
MANUEL, 74
MANWARRING, 11
MAPLE, 143
MAPPIN, 70
MARCH, 88 92
MARCUM, 187
MARDEN, 162

MARDERS, 71 72
MARELL, 72
MARGESON, 120
MARKAM, 61
MARKER, 92
MARKESACK, 92
MARKLE, 23 32 35
MARKLES, 32
MARKS, 92 147 149 161 162 171 175
MARR, 70 71
MARRETT, 65
MARROW, 193
MARRS, 89 145
MARS, 92
MARSDEN, 13
MARSELL, 178
MARSH, 185
MARSHAL, 59 193
MARSHALL, 43 61 135 140 155 182
MARSUSAN, 32
MARTEN, 123
MARTIN, 12 23 28 46 52 57 59 61 63-65 70 72 74 81 86 92 98 100 102-105 120 123-125 143 145 147 149 153 155 158 162-165 169 171 175 176 179 182 185 189 193 194
MARVIN, 185
MASON, 59 70 73 100 122 135 141
MASSEY, 59 61 81 135 178
MAST, 92
MASTERS, 84
MASTERSON, 5
MASTIN, 52 53 109
MATEER, 73
MATHENY, 104
MATHERS, 59
MATHERY, 53
MATHEW, 58 81 125
MATHEWS, 3 4 11 13 63 64 88 98 145
MATHIA, 81
MATHIEU, 141 142
MATHIS, 144
MATNY, 109
MATSON, 24 30
MATTHEWS, 12 39 59 72 85 135
MATTINGLY, 148 162 189
MATTINGSBY, 109

MATTOX, 70 196
MAULSBY, 135
MAUNCE, 71
MAUPIN, 12 70 74 100
MAURY, 185
MAUSEL, 18
MAUTZ, 61
MAUZY, 64
MAVARATTO, 185
MAXCY, 70
MAXFIELD, 72
MAXWELL, 80 81 92 135
MAY, 92 98 135 193
MAYER, 146
MAYFIELD, 4
MAYHALL, 23 27 37
MAYO, 142
MAYS, 53 63 74 86 117 159 161
MAZE, 117
MAZINGOE, 103
MCAFFEE, 162
MCALEXANDER, 79 81
MCANINCH, 81
MCANULTY, 3
MCARLIN, 100
MCASHAN, 190
MCASLIN, 100
MCATEE, 185
MCBRIDE, 70
MCCABE, 1 142
MCCAIN, 92
MCCALL, 98 104 117 123 124
MCCAMMEL, 185
MCCAMMON, 61
MCCAMPBELL, 102
MCCAMS, 70
MCCAN, 120
MCCANN, 70 118 122 162 193
MCCANNE, 142
MCCARNS, 70
MCCARTY, 51 52 70 85 92 102 109 145
MCCARVEN, 98
MCCARY, 92
MCCATCHEN, 92
MCCAUSLAND, 189
MCCAY, 21 63
MCCHORD, 70

MCCLAIN, 16 81 126
MCCLAINE, 88
MCCLANAHAN, 102 185
MCCLAREN, 125
MCCLARY, 134
MCCLASKE, 189
MCCLEELAND, 98
MCCLELAN, 80
MCCLELAND, 81 187
MCCLELLAN, 134
MCCLELLAND, 98
MCCLINTIC, 104
MCCLINTOCK, 189
MCCLUNG, 81 163
MCCLURE, 47 71 102 189
MCCLUREHAN, 102
MCCOLLINS, 122
MCCOLOUGH, 81
MCCOLUCK, 96
MCCOLUGH, 95
MCCOMAS, 109
MCCONNEL, 102 189
MCCOOL, 7 81
MCCORD, 81
MCCORKLE, 92
MCCORMACK, 16 39 40 44 63 104
MCCORMAK, 124
MCCORMICK, 44 45 51 104 134
MCCOUNTNEY, 187
MCCOWAN, 187
MCCOY, 63 109
MCCRACKEN, 66 102
MCCRAW, 81 85
MCCRAWL, 81
MCCRAY, 92
MCCREARY, 3 30
MCCRESEY, 134
MCCRKLE, 92
MCCUBBIN, 104 193
MCCUEN, 112
MCCULLOCH, 102
MCCULLOCK, 59
MCCULLOUGH, 134
MCCULUM, 61
MCCUNE, 15 24 146
MCCUTCHEN, 98

MCDANIEL, 7 20 50 67 80 81 85 92 104 134
   162 164 170 175 176 190 193
MCDANIELS, 163
MCDONALD, 10 46 48 50 51 52 63 81 86 92
   100 185
MCDONEAL, 59
MCDONNALD, 189
MCDONNELL, 109
MCDONOLD, 64 134
MCDOWAL, 92
MCDOWEL, 63
MCDOWELL, 85 88 142
MCELHINEY, 134
MCELROY, 21-23 25 28 33
MCELURATH, 126
MCELVAIN, 81 117
MCFADDEN, 51 70 109
MCFARLAN, 65 134
MCFARLAND, 61 65 70 96 102 122-124 134
MCFARLING, 73
MCFERREN, 78
MCFERRIN, 80-82
MCGANDER, 163
MCGARRY, 100
MCGARVER, 61
MCGARY, 100
MCGAW, 59
MCGEE, 25 30 47 52 70 102 109
MCGEERTSON, 25
MCGILL, 74 173
MCGINAS, 23
MCGINIS, 63 95
MCGINNIS, 23 24 30 65 94 95 134
MCGLANTHLIN, 88
MCGLOTHLER, 85
MCGLOTHLIN, 195
MCGLOTHLON, 196
MCGONNIGAL, 134
MCGOTHLIN, 195
MCGOWAN, 64 102
MCGOWEN, 37 61 185
MCGOWN, 59 71
MCGRATH, 146
MCGREA, 24
MCGREGOR, 111 115
MCGRUDER, 74

MCGRUE, 70
MCGUFFIN, 189
MCGUIRE, 64 81 85
MCGURK, 109
MCHENRY, 135
MCHOURN, 92
MCILHANEY, 85
MCINDEAR, 104
MCINTIRE, 102 189
MCINTOSH, 64 102
MCINTUSH, 53
MCINTYRE, 53 104
MCKAMEY, 100 188
MCKAMY, 189
MCKARNEY, 70
MCKAY, 4 7 12 14 29 32 61
MCKEE, 40 59 81 96 135 158 179 185
MCKEEN, 3
MCKENNEY, 70 104
MCKEY, 70
MCKILL, 78
MCKINE, 98
MCKINEY, 63
MCKINNEY, 81 98 102 104 141 162 163 167 185 189
MCKINZE, 59
MCKLANE, 117
MCKMEY, 193
MCKNIGHT, 79 81 189
MCKUTCHIN, 109
MCLABISH, 71
MCLANE, 42
MCLATHLUE, 194
MCLAUGHLIN, 102 189
MCLEAN, 142
MCLEARE, 190
MCLINTON, 104
MCLOUD, 61
MCLROY, 36
MCMAGHAN, 85
MCMAHAM, 185
MCMAHAN, 98 190
MCMAIN, 154 163
MCMANAMA, 70
MCMASTERS, 170
MCMERTY, 123
MCMILLEN, 41

MCMILLION, 193
MCMINN, 135
MCMULLIN, 10 16 51 80
MCMURDOUGH, 125
MCMURTY, 27-33 35 38 70 104 163 174 178
MCNAMES, 92
MCNEAL, 72 96
MCNEAR, 185
MCNEEL, 74 92
MCNIGHT, 59
MCNINN, 112
MCNUTT, 17 65 71
MCPHERSON, 27 34 38 74 88 92 152
MCQUEEN, 115
MCQUERRY, 106
MCQUINN, 92
MCQUIRE, 92
MCRAY, 92
MCRENOLDS, 73
MCREYNOLDS, 81 163
MCROBARAS, 98
MCROBERTS, 52 59 189
MCROYEL, 193
MCSPADDEN, 84
MCSWAIN, 51 52
MCSWEENEY, 144
MCTEE, 63
MCVAY, 144
MEAD, 146
MEADOR, 81
MEADOW, 80
MEADOWS, 92 98 106 107
MEALS, 72
MEANECA, 13
MEANS, 81 92 125
MED, 81
MEDCALF, 196
MEDFORD, 82
MEEK, 81
MEEKER, 145 160
MEEKS, 95
MEGRANN, 6
MEIER, 40
MEINKEN, 96
MEISNER, 95
MELCHINDEC, 104
MELCHUR, 8

MELEASE, 109
MELEY, 135
MELLON, 52
MELONE, 81
MELTON, 68
MENA, 185
MENAFEE, 135
MENECKE, 110
MENEFEE, 34 193
MENIFEE, 27 28
MENNIFEE, 32
MEREDITH, 22 32 38 104 193
MERILL, 173
MERIWETHER, 64 115 116 173
MEROY, 32
MERRAWINE, 51
MERRELL, 162
MERRILL, 150 151 172 176 187
MERRIMAN, 61
MERRITT, 29
MERRYWEATHER, 112
MERTENS, 124
MESLER, 123
MESSICK, 85
METCALF, 44 51 110 195
METEER, 104
METEERS, 36
METTS, 13
MEUZEBRAFF, 6
MEYER, 109 123 145 154
MEYERS, 145
MICHAEL, 92
MICHAELS, 140
MICHALES, 126
MICHARD, 16
MICKLES, 194
MICKLEY, 162
MIDDLETON, 51 71 123 170
MIDLER, 95
MIKHAL, 145
MILAKIN, 49
MILBURN, 135
MILES, 68 85 115
MILHOUSE, 72
MILIKIN, 58 72
MILLAKEN, 196
MILLANS, 123

MILLER, 14 33 44 51 52 59 61 65 67 70 72
    73 81 85 92 95 98 100 103-105 109-111
    115 122 125 126 135 142 143 145 148
    149 156 160-163 166 169 175 185 188
    189 195
MILLIAMS, 100
MILLIGAN, 74
MILLIKIM, 189
MILLION, 70 73 169
MILLIUS, 124
MILLON, 73
MILLS, 27 29 36 70 81 118 135 146 148 157
    167 187 190 193
MILLSAP, 81
MILLSAPP, 61
MILLSAPS, 109
MINER, 52
MING, 100
MINNIS, 146
MINOR, 61 70 135 193
MINTER, 125
MIRES, 81
MISCAL, 81
MITCHEL, 92 185 195
MITCHELL, 32 61 65 81 95 98 106 107 111
    125 135 140 151 157 161-165 170 171
    173 175 193 196
MITHCELL, 47
MIZE, 109 110
MIZELL, 115
MOAD, 117
MOBERLY, 72 85 92 142
MOBLEY, 95 193
MODREL, 92
MOEYMOLD, 123
MOFFETT, 71 81
MOLINARI, 141
MONCRIEF, 95
MONEY, 185
MONROE, 125 135
MONTASH, 193
MONTGALL, 109
MONTGOMERY, 30 81 92 95 135 162
MONTILLIN, 171
MONTILLIUS, 157 162
MONTRAY, 92
MOODY, 85 96 97

MOON, 8 9 10 11 98 135
MOOR, 51 81 100
MOORE, 8 59 61 63 65 70 89 92 95 100 102 103 109 117-119 121 122 127 146 150 158 166 171 185 187 189
MOOREHEAD, 174 186
MOORES, 100
MOORHEAD, 52 68
MOOSE, 152
MOPING, 65
MOPPINS, 110
MORE, 61 63 72 103 126 127
MOREHEAD, 24 190
MORELAND, 74 92 126
MORGAN, 59 63 92 100 109 124 135 140 144 163 185 187 193
MORGART, 120
MORIARTY, 109
MORIS, 64
MORISS, 80
MORLAND, 60
MORLEY, 135
MOROON, 185
MORRIS, 47 53 80 81 92 95 96 98 109 127 142 148 149 151 152 155 157 162 164 185 193
MORRISON, 59 61 70 163-165
MORRISS, 65 80 81 85
MORROW, 92 135 146 156 163 190 193
MORSEY, 145
MORTEN, 109
MORTON, 71 109 125 162 170 172 189
MOSBY, 104 189
MOSELEY, 70 98
MOSELY, 103
MOSER, 43
MOSES, 150
MOSLEY, 45 70 73 189
MOSS, 12 21 23 24 61 65 103 135 185 189 190
MOTHERSHEAD, 2 12
MOTT, 163
MOULDER, 61 185
MOURTS, 64
MOXLEY, 104
MOYER, 23
MRROW, 190

MUDD, 61 64 65 68 88 185
MUDGET, 135
MUIR, 103
MUITCHELL, 193
MUKES, 70
MULDROE, 52 53
MULDRON, 25 32
MULDROW, 53
MULKEY, 40 81 92 187
MULLINS, 85 95
MUNDAY, 149 151 162 164 168 170 172 179
MUNFORD, 61
MUNHOSS, 92
MUNKER, 195
MUNROE, 61
MUPIN, 70
MURATA, 63
MURFA, 104
MURFEY, 104
MURPHEY, 92 171
MURPHY, 1 5 15 18 59 61 65 68 81 95 100 120 122 135 140-143 162
MURRAY, 119 120 122 135
MURREY, 61
MURRY, 63 66 81
MUSE, 183
MUSGROVE, 162 174 178 179
MUSICK, 51 81 169 193
MYERS, 52 53 63 65 104 154 157 176 185
MYRE, 95
NAILOR, 81
NAKIN, 114
NALL, 182
NALLY, 64
NANCE, 104 110
NARRIS, 109
NASH, 17 92 101 189
NAYDEN, 192
NEAL, 23 29 33 35 98 103 120 124 125 135
NEBEKER, 164
NEBERGALL, 141
NEBO, 145
NEBOLD, 152
NEELE, 63
NEELY, 8
NEFF, 67 95
NEIL, 92 98 122 185

NEILL, 101
NELSON, 63 70 74 81 95 96 103 106-108 111 151 164 168 169 175 179 180 182 183 193
NESBIT, 70 103
NESBITT, 71
NETHERTON, 135
NEUELL, 124
NEVINS, 103 105
NEW, 63 145
NEWBILL, 125 135
NEWBOLD, 152
NEWCHURCH, 61 185
NEWELL, 125
NEWKIRK, 53
NEWLAND, 23 34 61 99
NEWLIN, 86
NEWMAN, 81 126 141 189
NEWSOM, 70 103
NEWSON, 103
NEWTON, 34 35 82 85 103 164 193
NICHOL, 70
NICHOLAS, 85
NICHOLES, 81
NICHOLS, 19 61 65 98 103 119 120 122 143 185 189
NICHOLSON, 103 123
NICKELSON, 118
NICKLES, 100
NICKLIN, 63
NIECE, 125
NILACK, 96
NILLSON, 95
NIPP, 95
NISE, 70
NIVENS, 92
NIX, 81
NIXON, 126
NOEL, 72 73 193
NOLAN, 19
NOLAND, 80 85 92
NOLEN, 81
NOLLEY, 103
NOLLINGHAM, 96
NOLTON, 61
NONAN, 7
NOONAN, 70

NORDIKE, 185
NORMAN, 71 109 135
NORRIS, 53 92 122 159 161 164 193
NORTHCRAFT, 149 156 157 178
NORTHCUT, 185
NORTHCUTT, 24 25 29 30 34 63
NORTON, 34 35 53 55 61 75 81
NORVAL, 185
NORVEL, 48 53
NOVEL, 63
NOYCE, 23
NUCUM, 23
NULL, 7 14 15 17 61
NUNALLY, 81
NUNN, 65 145 156 167 193
NUTT, 85 136
O'BRIEN, 56
O'BRYAN, 14
O'CONNER, 42
O'MARRA, 5
O'SHAUGHNESSY, 173
O'TOOLE, 85 92
OARDY, 37
OBANION, 63
OBANNON, 93 136
OBERCHON, 15
OBRIAN, 81
ODELL, 187
ODLE, 193
ODNALD, 53
OFERRAL, 175 179
OFERRALL, 164 176 179
OFFETT, 23 53
OFFUT, 27
OFFUTT, 27 33 98
OGAN, 127
OGDEN, 73 126
OGDON, 53 54
OGLE, 11 12 17 18 135
OGLEVIE, 61
OLD, 189 193
OLDAM, 73
OLDEN, 109
OLDHAM, 74 81 92 103 135 189
OLDJAM, 81
OLDS, 100 153 159 164 179
OLIVE, 64

OLIVER, 81 98 100 103 104 126 174 178 189
OLYER, 90
ONEAL, 81 144
ONICH, 136
ORE, 187
ORENBERY, 123
ORES, 190
ORKINS, 117
ORME, 98
ORR, 70 71 75 81 118-122 124
OSBORN, 112
OSBORNE, 141
OSBOURN, 17
OSBURN, 42 43 125 164 193 195
OSBURNE, 17
OSGOOD, 110
OSLIN, 44 53 54 56 57
OSSINUM, 158
OSTER, 147
OSTRANDER, 79
OSWALD, 141
OUNSBY, 74
OUSLEY, 81 148
OVERALL, 64
OVERDIER, 193
OVERFELT, 73 103 189
OVERFETT, 103
OVERSHINER, 126
OVERSTREET, 136 151
OVERTON, 103 190
OWEN, 79 92 104 127 143 144 181 185 189
OWENS, 6 61 81 92 126 179 187
OWIGS, 61
OWINGS, 53 54 144
OWLSEY, 92 164-166 168 179 180
OWNSLEY, 148
OWSLEY, 136 146 148 149 151 153 155 157-159 161 164 165 168 169 171-173 181 193
OXIER, 101
OXLEY, 81
OYSTER, 151 152 163-165 176 183
PACE, 63 101 103 105 189
PADAS, 85
PADDOCK, 61
PADELFORD, 13

PAELEY, 93
PAESY, 46
PAGE, 64 70 136 185
PAGER, 195
PAINE, 95 103 193
PAINTER, 71 143
PAKMEN, 63
PALLETT, 14
PALMER, 11 17 63 70 82 93 103 109 161 165 185 190
PALSGROVE, 95
PALSON, 32
PARIS, 71 136
PARISH, 65 66 70 159 165
PARISS, 29
PARK, 61 163
PARKASAN, 41
PARKE, 20 65 157
PARKER, 2 12 27 29 32 33 37 61 71 81 82 93 96 100 165 185 193
PARKS, 70 74 95 125 136
PARKWOOD, 74
PARMER, 61
PARRES, 68
PARRIS, 28 68
PARSLEY, 123
PARSON, 63 158 165
PARSONS, 63 64 66 68 70 82 147 158 160 176 177 185 186
PARTON, 66
PATCHEN, 93
PATE, 54 58
PATEE, 23 161
PATEL, 110
PATERSON, 25 63
PATRICK, 70 81
PATTEE, 165 180
PATTEN, 93 165
PATTERSON, 31 46 59 64 70 73 93 106 125 136 153 165 185
PATTISON, 18
PATTON, 81 85 96 98 103 144 164 196
PAUK, 61
PAUL, 82 122 140
PAULDING, 172
PAULSON, 125
PAVILION, 24

PAVILLION, 30
PAWLY, 189
PAXTON, 66 82 185
PAYNE, 22 28 33 58 81 82 96 110 165 185
PAYNTER, 71
PAYNTON, 146
PAYTON, 81
PEAKE, 24 29 147 193
PEAL, 125
PEARIELEL, 28
PEARSON, 44 54 56 93 136 168
PEASE, 165
PECHER, 145
PECK, 68 82
PEDLER, 186
PEEK, 59 73
PEELER, 127
PEERCY, 70
PEERS, 109
PEERY, 54
PEETER, 140
PEEVY, 49
PELKINGTON, 142
PEMBERTON, 76 82 99 103 125 148 154 155 164-166 171 173 174 193
PENCE, 9
PENDLETON, 73 165
PENICK, 93
PENINGTON, 59
PENN, 23 28 68 71 74 104
PENNELL, 136
PENNINGTON, 96
PENNY, 61 66
PENROD, 16
PENTZE, 110
PEPER, 195
PEPERS, 95
PEPPER, 2
PEPPERS, 6
PERDEW, 35
PERKINS, 10 47 52 55 61 64 74 101 165 185 190 193
PERMAUD, 16
PERPATER, 63
PERRIN, 73 165 190
PERRY, 5 6 42 43 54 96 101
PERSILLE, 82

PERSINGER, 93 136
PETE, 93
PETERS, 136
PETERSON, 15 40 146 156
PETHAFF, 145
PETROSS, 103
PETTEET, 60
PETTERS, 93
PETTIGREW, 82
PETTIS, 81
PETTIT, 82 183
PETTY, 54 98 103
PETTYGREW, 81
PETTYMAN, 75
PEVIS, 61
PEW, 127
PEYTON, 82 103 104
PFINESTER, 16
PFNISTER, 16
PHAGE, 74
PHARRIS, 185
PHARRISS, 40
PHEGLEY, 123 127
PHELPS, 30 71 98 109 136
PHEOBUS, 63
PHILABAR, 85
PHILBERT, 93
PHILIP, 85
PHILIPS, 16 58 59 82 95 185
PHILLIPS, 20 73 95 96 103 125 126 136 145 165 191
PHIPPS, 41 42 82 141
PICA, 98
PICKER, 145
PICKETT, 73
PICKETTS, 82
PICKLE, 70
PICKREL, 93
PIEFFER, 70
PIERCALL, 68
PIERCE, 11 21 22 25 27-31 34 36 103 123
PIERCEALE, 37
PIERCEALL, 33
PIEREALL, 26 28
PIERRE, 1
PIKE, 93
PILCHER, 82

241

PILE, 79 146
PINE, 185
PINK, 6
PINSON, 10
PIPER, 110 194-196
PIPKIN, 5 11 12 136
PISK, 154
PITCHER, 95 136 193
PITMAN, 95 127 175
PITTS, 107
PITZER, 6 14
PLANT, 158 165 166 173 174 177
PLATT, 125
PLEAGE, 104
PLEASANTS, 82
PLESANT, 59
PLUMER, 63
PLUMMER, 96
PLUNKET, 193
POAG, 70
POAGE, 70 71 81 147 151 160 161 164 165 172-174
POAGUE, 82
POAQUE, 165
POE, 63 85 92 185
POGUE, 126
POICE, 93
POINDEXTER, 36 99 103
POINTER, 85
POLAND, 95
POLLARD, 61 64 74 185
POLLY, 104
POLSON, 24 142 144
POMEROY, 153
POOL, 70 97 193
POOLE, 109
POOR, 114 185
POPE, 144
POQUE, 193
PORTER, 10 20 54 61 63 73 76 77 81 82 93 103 109 136 149 155 158 165 177 185 193
PORTIS, 93
POSON, 125
POTET, 93
POTHIFF, 145
POTHOFF, 98

POTTER, 59 64 81 82 104 140
POTTS, 54 81 82 136
POUELL, 125
POULTON, 93
POUND, 5
POUNDS, 3
POWEL, 54 73 93 185
POWELL, 61 73 80 82 98 100 123 190
POWER, 70
POWERS, 70 110 117 119-122 194
PRATT, 98
PRATTE, 10 75
PRENTICE, 165
PRESSLY, 61
PRESTON, 61 82 84 145 172
PRETTYMAN, 82
PREWETT, 185
PREWITT, 64 71
PRICE, 8 9 59 63 70 71 73 74 81 82 85 93 99 103 104 109 110 124 136 152 153 164 165 168 185 187 189
PRICHARD, 95
PRICHETT, 74
PRIEST, 28 29 32-34 70 136
PRIESTER, 145
PRIGMON, 136
PRIGMORE, 76 79 82 113
PRINGLE, 59
PRISM, 173
PRITCHARD, 165 170
PRITCHET, 59
PRITCHETT, 9 78 136 168
PRITCHITT, 61
PROCTOR, 124
PROFATER, 185
PROFFITT, 136
PROPST, 15
PRUEKET, 95
PRUETT, 66 67 79
PRYOR, 89 95
PUCKETT, 136
PUELLIN, 20
PUFFER, 144
PUGH, 103 146 156 181
PULIAM, 100
PULIS, 33 35 103
PULLAM, 81 193

PULLEN, 28
PULLIAM, 82 100 101 189 193
PULLIN, 10
PULLUM, 193
PULUS, 52 55
PURCALL, 68
PURCELL, 136
PURCHELL, 74
PURDETT, 189
PURDOM, 33-35 110
PURDY, 136 145
PURINTON, 143
PURKET, 82
PURKINS, 82
PURNELL, 124
PURRINGTON, 59
PURSIVILLE, 82
PURVIS, 104
PYE, 165
PYEATT, 5
PYLE, 42 82
PYLES, 82
QUALE, 140
QUARLES, 146
QUARLY, 71
QUARRELS, 122
QUAYLE, 144
QUESENBERRY, 136
QUICK, 98
QUIGLEY, 74
QUILEY, 145
QUIMBY, 170
QUINBY, 124
QUINN, 155 166
QUIREY, 73
QUISENBERRY, 82 136
RABIDOUX, 93
RADFORD, 140
RAGAN, 14 42 82 85 110
RAGLAN, 122
RAGLAND, 74
RAGSDALE, 71 74 93
RAINOW, 29
RAINS, 136 143
RAINWATER, 124
RALEKIN, 103
RALLS, 21-38 82 167

RALPH, 93 136
RALSTON, 126
RAMBAM, 125
RAMELSBURG, 145
RAMEY, 70
RAMSAY, 110 136
RAMSEY, 82 100 158 160 164 169 191 193
RAMSONN, 61
RAMSOWER, 185
RAMSY, 101
RAND, 125
RANDALL, 61
RANDLE, 140
RANDOLPH, 95 103 105 152
RANES, 193
RANEY, 64 70
RANGLE, 93
RANKIN, 11 13 17 98 136 149 152 154 160
   161 166 167
RANNEBARGER, 98
RANNEY, 98
RANNY, 136
RANSDALE, 185
RANSDALL, 70
RANSLEY, 20
RAPP, 20
RASETEL, 93
RASH, 18 167 168
RATCLIFF, 83
RATLIFF, 89 141 144
RAVELL, 110
RAWLEY, 100
RAWLINGS, 98 145 175
RAWLINS, 82 124
RAWLS, 93
RAWSON, 103
RAY, 64 70 73 93 126 136 145 146 150 153
   156 158 164 166 167 170-172 176 178
   185 186 191
RAYBURN, 82
REA, 74 95 96
READ, 44 55 64 82 103 104 193
READER, 82
READY, 71
REAGAN, 143
REAMS, 93
REANDO, 8

REASON, 66
REASONS, 185
REAUX, 85
REBARD, 136
RECISAR, 20
RECOR, 93
RECTOR, 82 93
RED, 126
REDBAUGH, 145
REDD, 156 167 179 182
REDDING, 147 167 186 193
REDDISH, 148 152 158 160 166 167 172 179
REDDY, 145
REDERICK, 93
REDFIELD, 82 136
REDFORD, 136
REDISH, 37 150
REDMAN, 168
REECE, 191
REED, 32 49 55 66 74 82 85 95 101 103 116 123-125 136 191
REEDS, 66 185
REELFIELD, 95
REES, 146 155-158 163 164 166 168
REESE, 137 152 154 158 161 166 168 191 193
REEVE, 166
REEVELEY, 161 163 165
REEVELY, 173 174
REEVES, 100 123 166
REGAN, 110
REGENT, 59
REID, 12 63 64 73 74 185 186
REIDS, 185
REIFSEL, 123
REILEY, 61 161
REINBERG, 96
REINICK, 85
REISER, 20
RELFE, 137
REMKY, 125
RENARD, 16
RENFRO, 99
RENOE, 103 105
RENOLDS, 185
RENSCH, 110

RENSOME, 100
REPPY, 9
REQUA, 95 137
RESCH, 18 20
RESER, 106
RESS, 82
REVELEY, 150 154 157 163 166 167 173 178 179 182
REVELY, 149 151 154 160 165 166 183
REYBURN, 190
REYNAL, 59
REYNOLDS, 11 43 44 49 50 54 55 56 59 66 82 83 93 100 103 113 127 141 144 185 190
RHEA, 16
RHOADES, 137
RHODES, 28 32 38 103 110
RIANS, 95
RIBER, 59
RICE, 21 23-25 27 30 31 38 70 72 77 80 82 83 103 117 140-142 144 177 191
RICHARD, 150
RICHARDS, 64
RICHARDSON, 11 93 96 109 116 125 137 146 148 150 155 157 160 164-167 170 171 173 174 176-183 190
RICHART, 147 159 166 173 175 178
RICHE, 104
RICHTER, 6 14 66
RICK, 1
RICKARD, 148
RICKETTS, 137
RICKEY, 61
RICKMAN, 43
RICKS, 63 186
RICO, 142
RIDDLE, 12 61 82 124 179
RIDER, 59 80 82 154
RIDGBY, 73
RIDGEWAY, 43 93 99 140 158
RIDGWAY, 55 93
RIEHL, 122
RIELY, 165
RIFFLE, 186
RIGES, 111
RIGG, 193
RIGGS, 43 61 127

244

RIGHT, 64
RILARD, 61
RILEY, 12 68 70 103 104 110 114 137 186
RINDS, 61
RINHE, 2
RINNICK, 85
RINNY, 21
RIORDAN, 110
RISSLE, 63
RITCHER, 14 93
RITCHTENS, 187
RITTENHOUSE, 189
RITTER, 16 115
RLLS, 22
ROADS, 82
ROBB, 29 30 34 93 142
ROBBERSON, 112
ROBBINS, 148 166 191
ROBERDS, 103
ROBERSON, 63 137
ROBERT, 8 93 109
ROBERTS, 8 16 22 55 73 74 82 93 95 122 127 143 144 149 155 166 167 171 180 185 187 190 191 193
ROBERTSON, 9 63 82 93 140 186
ROBIN, 82
ROBINET, 93
ROBINSON, 12 29 47 61 63 93 96 103 104 109 137 145 147 156 166 167 191
ROBION, 137
ROBISON, 70 193
ROCE, 24
ROCHILD, 93
ROCKHILL, 166 167
RODEFER, 168 171
RODERFER, 191
RODES, 93
RODGERS, 26
RODIFER, 193
RODMAN, 148
ROE, 74
ROFF, 193
ROGERS, 1 3 5 7 14 21 26 59 63 70 73 93 103 115 122 137 167 191
ROHRER, 96 137
ROLAND, 61
ROLANDOE, 36

ROLEN, 82
ROLHJE, 4
ROLL, 103
ROLLAND, 82
ROMESBURG, 141 144
RONT, 180
ROPER, 61 185
ROSE, 64 186
ROSENBAUM, 96
ROSER, 118
ROSS, 29 34 62 65 67 93 124 137 181 189
ROSSER, 110
ROSSIN, 185
ROTERMUND, 7
ROTH, 68
ROTHIWELL, 140
ROTHROCK, 137
ROTHWELL, 16 104
ROTT, 68
ROUL, 181
ROULAND, 37
ROUNDTREE, 93
ROUNSBERGER, 18
ROUSE, 72
ROUSEY, 93
ROUSSEAU, 181
ROUTH, 42
ROWDEN, 111
ROWDON, 82 84
ROWE, 13
ROWLAND, 82 137
ROY, 120
ROZIER, 75
RUBEY, 137
RUBISON, 68
RUBY, 82
RUCKER, 70 100 109 127 137 140
RUDY, 101
RUFORD, 95
RUGGLES, 137
RULE, 95 96
RUMBARGER, 189
RUMMONS, 59
RUNDICIL, 70
RUNKLE, 55 70
RUNNER, 118
RUNNYAN, 167

RUPP, 143
RUSH, 62 163 167 174 176
RUSSEL, 54 55 82 93 107 146 186
RUSSELL, 70 99 106 117 121 122 152
RUSSMAN, 96
RUSSO, 113
RUTHERFORD, 143
RUTLEDGE, 93 144 187
RUTZER, 141 142
RYAN, 41 42 95 99 145
RYBOLT, 62 185
RYE, 63
SACKET, 146
SACRCE, 189
SADLER, 70
SAFFORD, 167
SAGE, 62 82 100 103
SAGER, 109 110
SAILING, 56
SAILOR, 55 56
SAINTCLAIR, 40 193
SAINTJOHN, 193
SALE, 5 137 142 196
SALES, 93 103 137 186
SALING, 70
SALISBURY, 181
SALLEE, 62 103
SALLER, 155
SALLEY, 186
SALLY, 70 99 123 124 190
SALLYNG, 70
SALMON, 122
SALSBERRY, 124
SALSBERY, 123
SALSY, 137
SAMMONS, 65
SAMONS, 62 65
SAMPLE, 95
SAMPSON, 93 103
SAMUEL, 72 142 143 151
SAMUELS, 85
SANDERS, 63 66 70 73 104 137 189 190
SANDES, 70
SANDFORD, 65 66 124
SANDISON, 144
SANDS, 62 126
SANFORD, 21 65 137 193

SANIZER, 70
SANKES, 191
SANKS, 193
SANNE, 6
SANNER, 73
SAPP, 63 186
SAPPINGTON, 137 170 175
SARGENT, 11
SARTONIONS, 96
SASEY, 37 38
SASSEN, 126
SATTERBEE, 141
SAUL, 24 25 30
SAUNDERS, 23 75 83 98 101
SAUTTER, 110
SAVAGE, 83
SAWYER, 73
SAWYERS, 85 105
SAXON, 193
SAYE, 137
SAYERS, 137
SAYRE, 140 178
SAYRES, 70
SCARBARAUGH, 189
SCARLET, 170
SCEIT, 20
SCHAEFFER, 145
SCHAFFER, 145
SCHEL, 145
SCHELL, 110
SCHLIE, 145
SCHNACK, 142
SCHOBEE, 163
SCHOEPH, 110
SCHOLL, 104
SCHOOLER, 55 56
SCHUETTE, 128
SCHUTS, 59
SCHUYLER, 124
SCHWABE, 144
SCOBEE, 23 66 70 72
SCOBY, 73
SCOIELD, 95
SCOT, 95 104 186
SCOTT, 15 19 33 64 66 70 72 83 93 98 100
    103 104 111 120 125 126 137 140 145
    172 177 178 182 189 190 196

SCOTTY, 110
SCRIVENER, 126
SCROGHAM, 106
SCRUGGS, 189
SCUDE, 62
SEABOURN, 12
SEABY, 73
SEAGRASS, 62
SEAL, 2 189
SEALE, 98
SEAMAN, 143 156 180 182
SEAMNAN, 159
SEAMORE, 193
SEAR, 17
SEARCY, 72 193
SEARGEANT, 32
SEARINGER, 75
SEARS, 81-83 85 140
SEASE, 83
SEATON, 63
SECRE, 103
SEE, 83 124
SEEBE, 171
SEEBEN, 177
SEEBER, 147
SEELY, 31 34
SEGAR, 140
SEGER, 140
SELBY, 99 103 189
SELLARDS, 93
SELLERS, 83 93 124
SELLY, 27
SEMPLE, 145
SEMSON, 117
SERGEANT, 24
SEROTER, 31
SERRING, 191
SERVANT, 15
SESAW, 182
SETTLE, 23 80 83 140
SETTLES, 63 186
SEVIER, 186
SEVOYNG, 193
SEWING, 193
SEXTON, 189
SEY, 109
SEYMORE, 186

SHACKLEFORD, 66 169
SHACLEFORD, 100
SHADRACH, 154
SHAFFER, 74
SHANK, 158
SHANKS, 70 93 166 177 182 194-196
SHANLEAVER, 93
SHANNON, 37 62 98 137 153 175 176 186
SHANON, 64
SHAPLEIGH, 9
SHARACK, 145
SHARF, 145
SHARKEY, 110
SHARP, 59 62 70 72 73 83 93 117 120-122
    124 196
SHATLOCK, 72
SHAVER, 111
SHAW, 62 66 95 106 142 179 186
SHAYLOR, 82
SHAYS, 93
SHEAR, 186
SHEARER, 190
SHEATES, 103 104
SHEBURN, 186
SHECKLE, 37
SHEEN, 93
SHEETS, 99 103
SHELBY, 103
SHELEY, 100
SHELL, 109
SHELLY, 83
SHELTON, 13 62 82 83 93 137 186
SHEPARD, 23
SHEPHARD, 49
SHEPHERD, 2 3 53 55 56 93 137 157 159
    182 191
SHEPPARD, 3 85
SHERER, 126
SHERMAN, 59 62 70 73 145 159
SHERWOOD, 93 177 182
SHEUSTER, 83
SHIELDS, 21 24 56 137
SHINES, 193
SHINKLE, 116
SHIPLEY, 65 83
SHIPLY, 83
SHIPP, 62 141 144

SHIREZ, 59
SHIRKY, 62
SHIRLEY, 82
SHITTON, 62
SHIVELY, 82
SHOBE, 98 189
SHOCK, 55 125
SHOEMAKER, 137
SHOHONG, 36
SHOHONY, 31 37
SHONER, 124
SHOOT, 70 73
SHOPHER, 73
SHORE, 127
SHORT, 68 127
SHORTRIDGE, 70 73
SHOTEAU, 23
SHOTT, 70
SHOTTER, 181
SHOTWELL, 110
SHRADER, 137
SHRAUR, 75
SHRETE, 196
SHREVE, 195 196
SHRIEVES, 196
SHRITE, 196
SHROPSHIRE, 168
SHRTRIDGE, 103
SHRUM, 62 65 66 126 186
SHUBIN, 96
SHUCK, 38 63 68
SHULL, 123 124
SHULTMIN, 170
SHULTS, 93
SHULTZ, 93
SHUMATE, 147 149 164 186
SHUMATER, 83
SHUMBARGER, 191
SHUMEBURG, 193
SHUMNELL, 126
SHUPE, 83
SHUSTER, 83 187
SHUTEMAN, 103
SHUTS, 62
SHUTTS, 28
SICKEL, 96
SICKELS, 161 178

SICKLES, 75
SIDEBOTTOM, 186
SIDNER, 75
SIEPER, 186
SIFERD, 7
SIGHST, 194
SIGNIST, 196
SIKES, 85
SIKIN, 70
SILKEY, 59
SILVER, 93
SILVERS, 93
SIMMONDS, 186
SIMMONS, 85 105 107 137 196
SIMMS, 70 72 110
SIMON, 193
SIMONDS, 62
SIMPCOE, 103
SIMPSON, 41 42 59 70 72 78 82 83 98 101 109 110 168
SIMS, 23 47 48 55 56 58 83 93 137
SINCLAIR, 73 83 103 149 152 158 170 171 182 193
SINGLETON, 93 144 153 174 180
SINKER, 59
SIPE, 93
SIPES, 86
SIPP, 19
SISK, 35 104
SISSON, 59
SITE, 173
SITTEN, 66
SITTON, 63-65 98 186
SKAGGS, 124 137
SKEEL, 17
SKIDMORE, 137
SKINER, 63
SKINNER, 7 55 56 93 141 164 167 168 171 174-177 182
SKIVIN, 142
SKYLES, 112
SLACK, 137
SLADE, 194 196
SLATER, 62 63 110
SLAUGHTER, 101 171 177 178 193
SLAVENS, 62
SLAYBAUGH, 93

SLEASE, 83
SLOAN, 83 84 148 189
SLOANE, 83
SLOOSON, 35
SLOSS, 31 35
SLOSSON, 22 32-35
SLY, 141
SMALL, 28 35
SMALLEY, 72
SMARR, 194
SMART, 101 103 125 137 143 144 189
SMATHAN, 62
SMEDLEY, 16
SMELSER, 83
SMELSON, 37 38
SMIH, 93
SMILEY, 55 65 117
SMIRL, 14
SMITH, 3 5 8 10-13 16 18 23 24 27 28 33-35
    37 40-42 47 50 51 53 55 56 59 62-64 70
    73 75 82 83 85 86 93 95 96 98 99 103
    104 106 109 110 117 119 122-124 126
    138 140-143 145 147 148 151 153 156
    157 159 163 164 166 169-171 175-179
    181 186 189 191 193
SMITHEE, 70
SMITHERS, 62
SMITHEY, 98
SMITHRING, 191
SMOOOT, 170
SMOOT, 95 105 162 163
SMOTHERS, 181
SNAHEL, 124
SNEAD, 64 83 186
SNEDICOR, 103
SNEL, 93
SNELL, 70 74 103 104 138
SNELLING, 93
SNIDER, 2 72 83 93 137 186
SNIDOW, 73
SNIVELY, 138
SNODGRASS, 95 96 112 119 122 172
SNOWDEN, 138 197
SNYDER, 95
SOCTON, 140
SODA, 109
SOLLERS, 93

SON, 96
SORENSE, 83
SOSEY, 25 28 30
SOUENSCHEIN, 110
SOUTHER, 167 193
SOUTHERLAND, 126
SOUTHLAND, 93
SOUTHWOOD, 189
SOWERS, 171 172 177
SOX, 21 29 55
SOYSTER, 126
SPAIN, 82
SPAINHOUR, 77 83
SPALDING, 175 179
SPARKS, 70 73 75 83 98 140 144
SPARROW, 66
SPEAR, 104
SPEARS, 62
SPED, 98
SPEED, 70 85
SPEER, 190
SPEERY, 54
SPENCE, 110
SPENCER, 55 56 70 85 93 104 109 110
SPERRY, 55 66 186
SPETTS, 20
SPICER, 103 189
SPIERS, 62
SPRADLIN, 186
SPRADLING, 66
SPRAGUE, 181
SPRAQUE, 167
SPRINGER, 4
SPRINGSTON, 186
SPROWL, 70
SPUD, 98 189
SQUIRES, 63
STAATS, 141
STACEY, 78
STACKER, 174
STACY, 82
STADTLER, 111
STAFFORD, 145
STAGMILLER, 110
STAILY, 83
STALCUP, 70
STALEY, 83

STALLARD, 59 63
STALLCUP, 85
STALLS, 93
STANDFORD, 73
STANFORD, 21
STANIFORD, 82
STANLEY, 100 127 138
STANLINIAS, 168
STAPLE, 162
STAPLES, 9 167 168 171 182 193
STAR, 187
STARK, 95 103 138 141 142 145
STARKS, 99 189
STATELER, 83
STEEL, 70 103 104 138 189
STEELE, 63 186
STEEPLES, 83
STEEPLETON, 83
STEEVETT, 72
STEGMILLER, 109
STEIN, 145
STEINBACK, 96
STEINBERG, 18
STENGER, 93
STEP, 45 46
STEPHEN, 193
STEPHENS, 59 63 65 66 70 73 74 82 83 93 99 110 111 123 148 151 178 191
STEPHENSON, 83 93 189
STERHLI, 18
STERLING, 77 83
STERRETT, 178
STERRIT, 73
STEURHMAN, 126
STEVENS, 25 93 110 143 152 163 171
STEVENSON, 72 122 142
STEVER, 103 190
STEWARD, 23 25 83 99
STEWART, 56 64 66 70 83 98 110 124 125 145 170 178 189 191
STICE, 70
STICKELMAN, 63
STILJUS, 123
STILL, 43 55
STILLES, 125
STILLMAN, 171
STILTMAN, 171

STIMPSON, 180 181
STIN, 110
STINE, 83 109
STINEBOUGH, 63
STINNETT, 177
STINSON, 83 96
STITER, 168
STITH, 153 155 156 166 170 174 177 178 180 181 193
STITTE, 160
STOCKBARGER, 189
STOCKTON, 40 110 113 138 140 159
STOKER, 14
STOKES, 67 100 114 189
STOM, 64 65
STOMMELL, 145
STONE, 35 48 55 59 65 77 83 99 100 103 122 127 138 186
STONEBRAKER, 63
STONEBREAKER, 167 186
STONISIDE, 186
STOOKEY, 98
STOOTEE, 4
STOPLET, 99
STORK, 83
STORY, 83 84 126
STOTTS, 110
STOUT, 63 72 178 186
STOVER, 19 70
STOW, 15
STOWEN, 149
STOWER, 159 166
STOWERS, 29 154 160 163 164 171 181 191
STOWES, 156
STRAER, 26
STRAIN, 70
STRAP, 16
STRATHER, 191
STRATTON, 125 126 190 191
STRAUBE, 55
STRAYER, 75
STREAKLIN, 83
STRIBLING, 70
STRICKLAND, 55 56 93 138
STRICKLEN, 98
STRICKLIN, 50

STRIFFIN, 83
STRODE, 29 190
STRONG, 40 79 83
STROUP, 17
STRSELECRKI, 13
STUART, 73 86 93 110 151 159 173 177
STUBBFIELD, 148
STUBBLEFIED, 154
STUBBLEFIELD, 66
STUPPLEBAN, 93
STYLES, 75
SUBLETT, 149-151 153-156 166-171 173 174 176-178 180 182
SUBLETTE, 178
SUDDARTH, 63 186
SUDDETH, 66
SUENAY, 125
SUERINGEN, 124
SUGETT, 100
SUGGETT, 98 100 103 105 189
SUGNOR, 93
SUITER, 125
SULIVAN, 81
SULLENS, 14 83
SULLIVAN, 59 145 154 156 165-167 176 180
SULSENHISER, 138
SUM, 93
SUMMERS, 93 96 123 125 126 194-196
SUN, 93
SUNDERLAND, 178
SURATT, 125
SURBER, 55
SURGAIN, 65
SUTHERLAND, 126 153 177
SUTLIFF, 143 144
SUTTLES, 65
SUTTON, 125 148 151 193
SWAGG, 59
SWAIN, 75 109
SWAN, 34 103 186
SWANEY, 13
SWANN, 75
SWARTZ, 96
SWATTS, 73
SWEARINGEN, 98
SWEENEY, 141 186
SWEENY, 110

SWEET, 16 110
SWETMAN, 142
SWICEGOOD, 67
SWIFT, 83 123 124
SWINDELL, 73
SWINDLE, 55 74
SWINEY, 74
SWINFORD, 59
SWINGAIN, 65
SWINNEY, 73 74 93 96
SWINNY, 72 73
SWITZER, 140
SWOET, 66
TABOR, 83 89 138
TACKETT, 83
TACKITT, 83
TAILER, 124
TAILLOR, 83
TAILOR, 64 65 83 125 186
TALBERT, 138
TALBOT, 84 103
TALBOTT, 3 83
TALIAFERRO, 35
TALIFERIO, 66
TALIFERRO, 66
TALLEY, 96 103 109
TALLY, 56 83 186
TALMAN, 141
TAMLEY, 86
TAMLY, 86
TANDY, 86
TANNER, 70 93
TAPLEY, 29 35 38
TARANCE, 66
TARKINGTON, 83 84
TARRENT, 83
TARTER, 101
TATE, 70 84 98 103 109 138 146 147 150 151 153-158 160-162 164 165 167 169- 181 189
TATLON, 138
TATMAN, 103
TATUM, 100 103
TAYLOR, 20 22 27 31 35 36 43 57 59 63 65 79 80 83 84 86 89 93 95 98 99 106-108 110 162 171 172 174 176 186
TAYOR, 96

TEAGUE, 65 83 93
TEDFORD, 144 145
TELFIRD, 65
TEMPLE, 83
TEMPLETON, 83 124
TENISON, 44 51 52
TEODORSKI, 13
TERFELER, 6
TERREL, 189
TERRELL, 103
TERRILL, 115 138 140 142 144
TERRY, 103 127 140 142 186
TETHRO, 194 197
TEVIS, 172 177
THACKER, 104
THACKSTON, 100
THAKEN, 123
THARP, 83 86 103 189
THATCHER, 103
THAYER, 158 193
THEEL, 1
THEEN, 73
THEOBALD, 110
THERLKELD, 71
THERMAN, 58
THEWING, 1
THIET, 19
THIRTY, 140
THOES, 109
THOMAS, 2 13 14 20 22 30 40 59 62 63 65-67 70-72 74 77 83 86 93 95 98 100 103 109 117 120 122 124 125 138 165 187 189 190
THOMASON, 75
THOMASSON, 62 186
THOMPSON, 7 30 56 59 65 71-75 93 95 99 105 109-111 138 141 142 152 154 157 160 162 164 167-173 176 177 182 186 189 193
THOMSON, 63 143
THORHHILL, 62
THORNBAUGH, 93
THORNHILL, 62 103 186
THORNTON, 84 95
THORP, 93
THORTON, 94 110
THRAILKELL, 75

THRALKILL, 103
THRASHER, 122
THREAYNER, 5
THRELKELD, 155
THRESHER, 117
THROCKMORTON, 56 173
THROGMORTON, 103
THURMAN, 41 93 94 103 187
THURMOND, 62
THURSTON, 124
TIBBS, 96
TIBS, 103 104
TIDWELL, 83
TIERNEY, 141
TIGG, 124
TILDEN, 148
TILFORD, 190
TILLER, 63 186
TILLERSON, 141
TILLERY, 138
TILLETT, 71
TILLINGHAST, 173
TILMAN, 95 119
TILTON, 109
TINDAL, 189
TINDEL, 100
TINDELL, 126
TINKER, 93
TINNINGS, 62
TINSEY, 103
TINSLEY, 56 93
TIPPETT, 138
TIPTON, 63 64 93 98 125 186
TITHROW, 93
TOBIN, 93 110
TODD, 18 40 56 83 187
TOLIVER, 106
TOLLER, 86
TOLLIVER, 105
TOLLS, 147 169
TOLSON, 123
TOMLIN, 85 146
TOMLINSON, 99
TOMPKINS, 89 148 149 169 172
TOMPSON, 66 83 126 172
TOOLEY, 2 162
TOOMBS, 141

TORANNCE, 93
TORRANCE, 22
TOWNS, 124
TOWNSEND, 96 122 125 162
TOWNSLER, 122
TOY, 15
TRABUE, 159
TRACY, 21 22 29 31 32 34 37 95 138
TRAIL, 62 63
TRAMMEL, 126
TRASK, 172
TRAUST, 97
TRAVIS, 115
TRAYNOR, 5
TRENT, 124
TRIBBEE, 71
TRIGG, 99 138
TRIMBLE, 93 103 127 189
TRIPLET, 63 65
TRIPLETT, 63 151 171 172 186 193
TRIPLITT, 23
TRISSEMITER, 119
TRITCH, 143
TROTTER, 172-174 193
TROUT, 71
TRUAX, 125
TRUE, 186
TRUEMAN, 103
TRUETT, 57 99
TRUITT, 33 109 110
TRULOVE, 66
TRUMBO, 71
TRUSSLETT, 182
TUBBS, 193
TUCK, 189
TUCKER, 10 11 16 65 74 75 78 79 83 98 100 103 104 125 138 172 186 189
TUDOR, 178
TUEL, 138
TUGGLE, 62 70 83
TUGLER, 65
TULL, 83
TULT, 193
TULY, 193
TUMBLESON, 197
TUMES, 181
TUNER, 72 93

TUNSTALL, 138
TURENNE, 145
TURK, 122
TURLEY, 8 34 57 99 103 138
TURMAN, 101
TURNBALL, 64
TURNBULL, 186
TURNER, 2 20 21 23 49 56-58 62 72 74 95 99 100 103 109 122 125 138 141 144 145 148 172 173 176 177 186 189 190 197
TURNHAM, 138
TURPIN, 151 163 171 172 177 193
TURVIS, 72
TUTT, 98 100 189
TUTTLE, 64 96 99 120 122 138 148 186
TWYMAN, 71
TYDINGS, 74
TYLOR, 106
UCHER, 20
ULD, 193
ULRICH, 20
UMPHREY, 89
UNDERWOOD, 23 72 84 93 94 98 103 189
UPTEGROVE, 186
UPTIGROVE, 66
UPTON, 72 89
URIE, 83 84
USHER, 186
UTTERBACK, 72
VAIL, 96
VALLE, 4 10 19 138
VANALLEN, 173
VANARSDALL, 71
VANAUSDALE, 138
VANBIBBER, 103 146
VANCAR, 186
VANCE, 57 63 124 151 156 157
VANCLEAVE, 98
VANCOURT, 1 9
VANDAM, 189
VANDEPOOL, 181
VANDERGRIFF, 30
VANDEVANTER, 72
VANDEVENTER, 174
VANDEVER, 124
VANDIVER, 186

VANDOVER, 62
VANELERE, 193
VANGUNDY, 94
VANLEFERELLE, 86
VANMETER, 94
VANNOY, 84
VANPOOL, 126
VANSARSAALL, 75
VANSCHOIKE, 75
VANSLIKE, 78 83 84
VANTON, 96
VANTRICHT, 99
VANTUYL, 40
VANWINKLE, 84
VARBLE, 94
VARDEMAN, 24 25 30 38
VARDIMAN, 48
VARNDINBURG, 116
VASQUES, 13 19
VAUGH, 71 189
VAUGHAN, 104 105 112 145 186
VAUGHN, 57 62 71 73 84 94
VEACH, 71
VEASMAN, 111
VENABLE, 57
VERDIER, 65 186
VERDIN, 62
VERMILION, 68
VERMILLION, 35 36
VERSSERMAN, 145
VERT, 94
VERTREES, 155
VESSOR, 94
VEST, 57 99
VESTAL, 84 94
VICTOR, 66
VIER, 99
VINCAN, 101
VINCENT, 66 126 138 141 186
VINSON, 73
VINYARD, 8 12 17
VIOLETTE, 72
VIRDEN, 2
VIVION, 71 99 139
VOGEL, 108 110
VOLKMAN, 145
VONPHUL, 173

VOORHIES, 94
VOWEL, 79
VOZLE, 187
WADE, 4 62 84 96 117 119-121 145 186 189
WADERY, 103
WADKINS, 58 59 89 183
WADLEY, 189
WADLY, 101
WAGGONER, 63 100
WAGNER, 110 182
WAGONER, 175
WAID, 74
WAINE, 62
WAINRIGHT, 181
WAINSCOT, 101
WAIR, 84
WALACE, 123
WALDEN, 71
WALDENBLADE, 65
WALDRIDGE, 120
WALIS, 94
WALKER, 16 30 62 66 84 86 94-96 98 109
    116 139 189 192 193
WALKIN, 193
WALL, 3 84 96
WALLACE, 42 62 100 122 123 125 145 147
    181 189 193
WALLER, 32 71 73
WALLERS, 34 123
WALLICE, 63
WALLIS, 84
WALLKINS, 96
WALLS, 71 122 125 193
WALRAND, 84
WALSH, 7 109 173 175
WALTEN, 146
WALTER, 74 84
WALTERMAN, 175 183
WALTERS, 71 84
WALTHAL, 124
WALTICE, 110
WALTMAN, 165 174
WALTON, 62 72 103 139 186 189
WALTRIP, 96
WAMACK, 64
WAMBLE, 62
WANSLY, 101

WANTLAND, 122
WARBURTON, 173 174
WARD, 43 59 84 95 99 101 109 166 173 179 186
WARDEN, 84 193
WARDLY, 189
WARE, 4 62 103 142 186 189
WARFIELD, 109
WARFORD, 141
WARNER, 139 145 170 174
WARREN, 14 62 71 84 103 109 124 125 139
WARRINGTON, 109
WARSON, 84
WASH, 122 139 160 161 167 169 173 193
WASHAM, 62 189
WASHBURN, 193
WASHEN, 64
WASHINGTON, 25
WASHUM, 186
WASKEY, 110
WASSON, 139
WASTE, 96
WATERS, 1 3 28
WATKINS, 21 28 31 37 84 94 103 118 119 121 122 189
WATSON, 24 26 32 36 86 94 103 139 189
WATTE, 64
WATTS, 53 57 63 64 75 79 84 114 175
WAUGH, 65
WAY, 193
WAYLAND, 143
WAYMAN, 195
WAYMIRE, 94
WAYN, 58
WAYNE, 42 57 58
WAYNER, 101
WEAR, 110
WEATHERFORD, 123
WEATHERS, 84
WEAVER, 17 29 34 58 104 124 125 139 190
WEB, 94
WEBB, 12 71 73 84 109 119 122 124 190
WEBBER, 96 159 161 164 166
WEBER, 7 186
WEBSTER, 122 173
WEED, 84

WEEDER, 116
WEEKS, 122
WEEMS, 104
WEHMEYER, 95
WEIDEMAN, 109 110
WEIDMAN, 109
WEIL, 111
WEIMAN, 125
WEIR, 84
WEISBERG, 144
WEISNER, 123
WELBALS, 6
WELBERN, 35
WELBOURN, 37
WELCH, 49 58 62 71 76 78 79 116 189
WELD, 163
WELDON, 126 156 166
WELDY, 41
WELHOFF, 125
WELL, 62
WELLBORN, 139
WELLER, 148 149 173
WELLMAN, 26 139
WELLS, 6 64 65 98 99 103 109 139 151 174 186
WELSH, 5 145
WELTON, 98
WENDALL, 125
WEPKE, 145
WERRY, 109
WESLEY, 145
WESS, 175
WEST, 57 62 71 84 89 99 103 125 139 148 163 164 169 173-175 193
WESTFALL, 84 96
WESTMORELAND, 84 187
WESTON, 139 162 167
WESTOVER, 84
WETHERFORD, 73
WETHERS, 73
WEVER, 73
WEYAND, 95
WEYER, 114
WHALEY, 98 126
WHARTON, 124
WHEATON, 139

WHEDBEE, 139
WHEELER, 4 62 66 84 89 116 124 145 173 186 187 189
WHELER, 65
WHELON, 59
WHERRY, 54
WHIDBEE, 122
WHIPPLE, 139
WHITAKER, 116
WHITE, 2 11 58 66 71 72 74 75 84 86 96 100 101 103 109 110 123-126 139 143 144 150 153 157-159 162 164 169-171 173-175 183 186 189 190 193
WHITEHEAD, 62 84 94
WHITEMAN, 84 86 120
WHITENACK, 117
WHITENBURG, 74
WHITESIDE, 64 186
WHITESIDES, 65 120
WHITFIELD, 179
WHITHAM, 14
WHITING, 8
WHITLEDGE, 139
WHITLESEY, 84
WHITMAN, 141
WHITMIER, 20
WHITSETT, 94 117 120 121
WHITSIDE, 118
WHITSIDES, 119
WHITSLER, 94
WHITSON, 189
WHITTAKER, 103 118
WHITTEN, 124
WHITTINGTON, 124
WHITWORTH, 1 5 75 120 187
WIATT, 191
WIBBER, 145
WICKHAM, 119
WICKLIFFE, 124
WICKS, 98
WIDEMAN, 4
WIEDELICH, 109
WIELAND, 110
WIESE, 123
WIFLEY, 103
WIGGINTON, 71 151 173 174 193
WILBERN, 25

WILBORN, 84
WILBOURN, 84
WILBUN, 65
WILBURN, 52 94 104 105
WILCHER, 193
WILCOCK, 30
WILCOX, 25 145 162
WILCOXEN, 189
WILCOXSON, 103
WILDER, 186
WILDERSON, 42 43
WILES, 71
WILET, 2
WILEY, 9 103 127 139 144 174 189
WILFLEY, 73
WILFREY, 51
WILHELM, 94
WILHITE, 1
WILKERSON, 64 71 72 94 103 105
WILKINSON, 64 139 186
WILKS, 41
WILL, 94
WILLAMS, 9
WILLARD, 7 126 139
WILLE, 18 20
WILLET, 84 189
WILLETT, 84
WILLEY, 3 190
WILLIAM, 86
WILLIAMS, 3 4 10 11 13 17-19 32 36 44 49 51 57-59 62 65-67 71-73 75 84 86 89 93-96 98 100 101 103 105 122-124 139 142-144 148-150 162 166 169 170 173-175 179 186 189 193 197
WILLIAMSON, 72 75 84 103 120 122-124 126 190
WILLING, 17 139
WILLINGHAM, 45 47 50 53 57 58
WILLINGS, 103
WILLIS, 71 73 94 186
WILLJACK, 19
WILLMAN, 65
WILLMOTT, 84
WILLOBY, 194
WILLOCK, 139
WILLOUGBY, 197
WILLS, 71 123 163

WILLSON, 65 73 95 96
WILMOT, 58 190
WILMOTT, 84
WILOUGHBY, 194
WILSON, 1 4 7 8 15 22 25 27 29 31 32 34-36
    48 51 57-59 62 64 66 71 72 81 84 85 91
    94 100 103-105 110-112 122 125 139
    140 141 143 145 151 159 166 173 175
    186 193
WILTON, 89
WIMSELL, 68
WINE, 169 193
WINEHOPE, 117
WINFREY, 146
WING, 62
WINGATE, 125
WINGLES, 19
WINKLER, 94
WINN, 33 37 98
WINSON, 114
WINSOR, 98
WINSTON, 84 139
WINTER, 152
WINTERS, 186
WINTON, 41
WINUL, 98
WIRT, 74 144
WIRTS, 174
WIRY, 111
WISDOM, 58 125
WISE, 7 16 64 103 125
WISELEY, 100
WISEMAN, 117 122
WISENER, 193
WISSNER, 20
WITHEROW, 193
WITHERS, 38 71 173
WITHINGTON, 64
WITHROW, 62 175
WITLEY, 94
WITSAN, 64
WITSON, 160
WITT, 62
WODIEZA, 20
WOLERY, 103
WOLF, 74 110 117 121 150
WOLFE, 37 41 165 166

WOLFF, 118 119 121 122
WOLFSKILL, 139
WOLTZ, 103
WOMACK, 64 94 139 173
WOMBLE, 62
WOMBLES, 62
WOOD, 7 9 53 66 71 74 75 84 100 105 139
    143 155 173 174 178 186 189
WOODALL, 96
WOODEN, 153 161 164 174 175
WOODFOLK, 62
WOODFORD, 110
WOODING, 57
WOODS, 32 35 46 49 52 57 58 71 95 99 173
    174 189
WOODSON, 58 62 71 72 89 109 139 161
    186 191 193
WOODSWORTH, 105
WOODWARD, 197
WOODYAN, 160
WOODYARD, 173-175 177 179-183
WOODYEARD, 179
WOOLARD, 84
WOOLDRIDGE, 42
WOOLF, 120
WOOLFOLK, 122
WOOLIVER, 187
WOOLSEY, 139
WOOTEN, 84
WOOTON, 94
WORCESTER, 94
WORD, 59
WORKMAN, 139
WORLAND, 75
WORT, 174
WORTHINGTON, 186 193
WORTHLEY, 139
WOUNDERLY, 94
WRAY, 59 95 139
WREM, 189
WREN, 66 186
WRENN, 98
WRICK, 192
WRIGHT, 5 6 8 21 24 27 29-31 33 35-37 49
    59 62 64 68 71 72 83 84 94-96 98 99 110
    122 125 126 139 151 162 168 170 173
    174 176 186 189 193

WRINKLE, 105 107 108
WTTERHOLD, 193
WUERTZ, 105
WUNCH, 125
WURT, 174
WURTS, 174 178 179
WURZ, 110
WYGATE, 151
WYLIE, 25 31 34 35
WYLY, 193
WYMAN, 11
YAGER, 42 139
YAKEE, 71
YALE, 43 62 186 193
YANCY, 101
YANKEY, 85
YANTIS, 103
YATES, 68 94 104 105 175
YEATMAN, 175
YEATS, 140
YEIDA, 17
YELDELL, 105
YERWILL, 144
YILES, 195

YOCHAM, 86
YOCUM, 84 85 86
YORE, 175
YORK, 85
YOSTI, 140
YOUNG, 7 14 15 19 32 35 58 62 68 71 72 84 86 94 101 103 104 123 125 140 159 169 175 180 186 189
YOUNGBLOOD, 186
YOUNGER, 42 94
YOUNT, 100
YOWELL, 71-73
ZAGAR, 68
ZARNES, 120
ZARRAGAR, 118
ZFRAZIER, 143
ZIEGLER, 94
ZIGLER, 75
ZIMMER, 114
ZIMMERMAN, 35 62 64 151 171 193
ZINK, 145
ZUMATT, 64
ZUMWALT, 100 189

Other Heritage Books by Sherida K. Eddlemon:

Missouri Genealogical Records and Abstracts:
Volume 1: 1766-1839
Volume 2: 1752-1839
Volume 3: 1787-1839
Volume 4: 1741-1839
Volume 5: 1755-1839
Volume 6: 1621-1839
Volume 7: 1535-1839

Missouri Genealogical Gleanings 1840 and Beyond, Volumes 1-9

1890 Genealogical Census Reconstruction: Mississippi, Volumes 1 and 2

1890 Genealogical Census Reconstruction: Missouri, Volumes 1-3

1890 Genealogical Census Reconstruction: Ohio, Volume 1
(with Patricia P. Nelson)

1890 Genealogical Census Reconstruction: Tennessee, Volume 1

A Genealogical Collection of Kentucky Birth and Death Records

Callaway County, Missouri, Marriage Records: 1821 to 1871

Cumberland Presbyterian Church, Volume One: 1836 and Beyond

Dickson County, Tennessee Marriage Records, 1817-1879

Genealogical Abstracts from Missouri Church Records and
Other Religious Sources, Volume 1

Genealogical Abstracts from Tennessee Newspapers, 1791-1808

Genealogical Abstracts from Tennessee Newspapers, 1803-1812

Genealogical Abstracts from Tennessee Newspapers, 1821-1828

Tennessee Genealogical Records and Abstracts, Volume 1: 1787-1839

Genealogical Gleanings from New York Fraternal Organizations
Volumes 1 and 2

Index to the Arkansas General Land Office, 1820-1907
Volumes 1-10

Kentucky Genealogical Records and Abstracts, Volume 1: 1781-1839

Kentucky Genealogical Records and Abstracts, Volume 2: 1796-1839

Lewis County, Missouri Index to Circuit Court Records, Volume 1, 1833-1841

Missouri Birth and Death Records, Volumes 1-4

Morgan County, Missouri Marriage Records, 1833-1893

Our Ancestors of Albany County, New York, Volumes 1 and 2

*Our Ancestors of Cuyahoga County, Ohio, Volume 1*
(with Patricia P. Nelson)

*Ralls County, Missouri Settlement Records, 1832-1853*

*Records of Randolph County, Missouri, 1833-1964*

*Ten Thousand Missouri Taxpayers*

*The "Show-Me" Guide to Missouri: Sources for Genealogical and Historical Research*

*CD: Dickson County, Tennessee Marriage Records, 1817-1879*

*CD: Index to the Arkansas General Land Office, 1820-1907 Volumes 1-10*

*CD: Missouri, Volume 3*

*CD: Tennessee Genealogical Records*

*CD: Tennessee Genealogical Records, Volumes 1-3*